Stephen Kershaw wrote his PhD under Richard Buxton, arguably the world's leading scholar on Greek myth. He has taught Classics in numerous establishments, including Oxford University Department for Continuing Education and Warwick University. He runs the European Studies Classical Tour for Rhodes College and the University of the South, and has been a guest lecturer for Swan Hellenic for over 20 years. His *Brief Guide to the Greek Myths* was published by Constable & Robinson in 2007.

Highlights from the series:

A BRIEF HISTORY OF

CLASSICAL CIVILIZATION

Stephen Kershaw

RUNNING PRESS
PHILADELPHIA · LONDON

ROBINSON

Constable & Robinson Ltd
3 The Lanchesters
162 Fulham Palace Road
London W6 9ER
www.constablerobinson.com

First published in the UK by Robinson,
an imprint of Constable & Robinson Ltd, 2010

A copy of the British Library Cataloguing in
Publication data is available from the British Library

UK ISBN 978-1-84529-886-9

1 3 5 7 9 10 8 6 4 2

First published in the United States in 2010 by Running Press Book Publishers

US Library of Congress Control Number: 2009943289
US ISBN 978-0-7624-3986-7

Running Press Book Publishers
2300 Chestnut Street
Philadelphia, PA 19103-4371

Visit us on the web!
www.runningpress.com

Printed and bound in the EU

To Lal, Mum, and Hebe for their unconditional love

CONTENTS

ACKNOWLEDGEMENTS

My heartfelt thanks go out to the teachers, tutors, students, colleagues and institutions that have helped to shape this book from conception to completion: Salterhebble C.P. School and Heath Grammar School, Halifax; Bristol University; Richard Buxton, John Gould, Niall Rudd, John Betts, Earl McQueen and Richard Jenkyns; Cherwell College, Oxford; Andy Thompson and Rob Butler; St Edward's, Wychwood and Oxford High Schools; Linda Lyne; Oxford University Department for Continuing Education; Maggie Herdman; Warwick University; Rhodes College and the University of the South; Sally Dormer and Graziella Seferiades; Swan Hellenic Cruises; and Leo Hollis at Constable & Robinson.

The Roman World
(late 2nd century CE)

Eboracum (York)

BRITANNIA

Verulamium • Camulodunum
Londinium

GERMANIA INFERIOR

BELGICA

GERMANIA SUPERIOR

Trier

Rhenus (Rhine)

Danuvius (Danube)

RAETIA

NORI

LUGDUNENSIS

Liger (Loire)

AQUITANIA

Lugdunum

Alpes

Mediolanum

Aquileia

Garumna (Garonne)

NARBONENSIS

ALPES COTTIAE

Mantua

Arausio
Tolosa • Nemausus • Arelate • Genua
Narbo Martius

ALPES MARITIMAE

Padus (Po)

Mutina

UMBRIA

Ariminum

HISPANIA CITERIOR

Iberus (Ebro)

Numantia

Emporiae • *Rhodanus (Rhône)* Massilia

Tarraco

Tiberis

LUSITANIA

Tagus

CORSICA

Roma
Ostia •

APULI

Saguntum

Baetis Corduba

Balearic Is

SARDINIA

Cumae
Neapolis
Herculaneum
Pompeii

Gades
• Munda
BAETICA

Carthago Nova

SICILIA

MAURITANIA TINGITANIA

Caesarea

MAURITANIA CAESARIENSIS

Cirta

Carthago
Bulla Regia

Rhegium
Agrigentum

Syracuse

Zama • Hadrumentum

NUMIDIA Thapsus

AFRICA

Leptis Magna

Key:

BELGICA Provinces

0		250		500		750 miles

0	250	500	750	1000 km

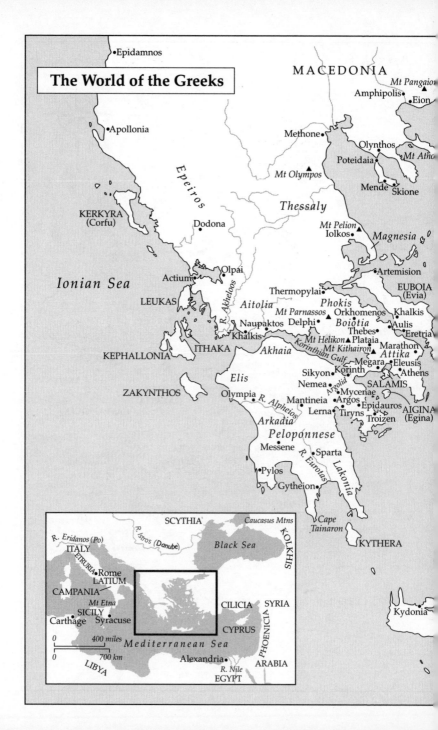

INTRODUCTION

From Grecian urns to Julius Caesar, Roman orgies to Cloud Cuckoo-land, Classical civilization has left an enormous footprint on our cultural environment, both shaping and enriching the lives of millions over millennia, often in ways that are now completely taken for granted. Greece has given us democracy, philosophy, tragedy, comedy, oligarchs, oratory and ostracism; the Roman legacy not only includes unsurpassed engineering skills, the foundations of our legal system, and the fundamental concept that all free people have inalienable rights as well as duties, but, paradoxically for a people that often saw itself in highly militaristic terms, the benefits of peace. It was the *Pax Romana*, 'Roman Peace', which, despite being constructed out of centuries of warfare, allowed Roman civilization to spread across Western Europe and ultimately to shape medieval, Renaissance and modern culture. Many of the underlying ideas of this vibrant tradition came from Greece, but they were transmitted in Latin.

Nowadays 'Reception Studies', tracing the influence of the Greek and Roman world in the culture of later generations, is one of the most dynamic aspects of Classical scholarship. It can tap into an immense wealth of material ranging from Harry Potter to fashion trends, ballet and contemporary dance, art, theatre, television and film, opera and musical genres encompassing classical, jazz, rock and the avant-garde. Much of our literary tradition comes directly from the Greeks and Romans; the world's biggest sporting event is the Olympic Games; and the controversy surrounding the *Elgin Marbles*, with the Greek government demanding 'the reunification of a mutilated monument belonging to the world's cultural heritage', and the British Museum countering that the sculptures are integral to a world museum telling the story of human cultural achievement, is very much a live issue; we work like Trojans; when in Rome we do as the Romans do; and it's all Greek to me.

There is no possibility that a book such as this can provide comprehensive coverage of all the history and culture of a time frame that stretches from the epic heroes of Greek mythology to the fall of the Roman Empire. Instead, it focuses on a number of key aspects of Greek and Roman civilization, particularly, but not exclusively, from the 'classical' eras of Greek and Roman history, many of which feature on the syllabi of GCSE, A level, and undergraduate courses, but which will also be of interest to any general reader with no intention of ever sitting an exam. The literary and artistic achievements of these often astonishingly sophisticated people will fall under the spotlight, but so too will their everyday lives, along with some of the most important events and processes that shaped the world in which they lived. On the way, we will confront the fascinating issues of their hopes, fears, aspirations, humour, beliefs, morals, values, tastes, politics and strategies for everyday survival.

The book moves in a roughly chronological sequence, although each chapter is organized thematically. We pick up the story in the Bronze Age and focus on the Minoans of Crete, who formed what is arguably Europe's first civilization, the Mycenaeans (whose culture was rooted largely in mainland Greece), and Troy, which is central to any understanding of later Greek culture. As we start to emerge from the prehistoric world of myth and archaeology we arrive in the Iron Age and encounter the unsurpassed epic poetry of Homer's *Iliad* and *Odyssey,* the standard by which all later literary works were judged (and found wanting). An outline of Greek history, from the mid-seventh to the end of the fifth century BCE follows, tracing the development of the world's first democracy, the challenges it faced from 'barbarian' invaders, the ascendancy of Athens, and its terrible Peloponnesian War with Sparta. Within that historical context we move to the domestic level, to survey the ways in which the Greeks interacted with one another socially, and with their gods, which included not only oracles but athletics. A slight sidestep then takes us into Sparta, whose oligarchic constitution and distinctive social organization illustrates a very different model of how a Greek state might be organized, and provided later inspiration for the English Public School system and the Hitler Youth. The words 'Greek' and 'Tragedy' now form an inseparable pair, and after a survey of the context in which the plays were performed, we will look at some remarkable dramas by the 'big three' tragedians, Aeschylus, Sophocles and Euripides. Our survey of the art and architecture of Ancient Greece takes in the distinctive Red- and Black-Figure vases, temples and their decoration, and concludes with an overview of free-standing sculpture down to the start of the Hellenistic era. Comedy was another of Greece's crucial contributions to the repertoire of world culture, and we make our transition to the world of Rome via the rumbustious Aristophanes, through the more sedate Menander, to Rome's two star dramatists, Plautus and Terence, whose work drew heavily on their Greek predecessors.

Benjamin Disraeli said of his wife that 'she is an excellent creature, but she never can remember which came first, the Greeks or the Romans'.[1] Essentially the Greeks do, but there is a degree of overlap, in which the Romans ultimately conquered Greece, leading in some Romans' eyes to a reciprocal cultural conquest of Rome by Greece. Once in the Roman world, we will take a historical survey of one of the defining eras of world history, that of the transition from the Roman Republic into the Roman Empire, meeting many of Rome's greatest celebrities on the way. Under its first Emperor Augustus, Rome produced some of antiquity's finest and most influential literature, none more so than Virgil's *Aeneid*. As we turn from legend to the everyday lives of the Roman people in both the Republican and Imperial eras, we will examine their social hierarchies, day-to-day habits, relationship with their gods, and recreational activities. They were some of the greatest builders ever to have walked the planet, and remains left after a cataclysmic eruption of Mount Vesuvius in 79 CE provide us with an intimate and moving insight into the Roman urban environment. Despite its truly astonishing success, the Roman Empire could not sustain itself forever, and the final chapter takes us through the complex, though strangely low-key, events that led to the final demise of Rome at the hands of barbarians in the fifth century CE.

Sometimes the evidence at our disposal is incredibly clear, but at other times totally lacking, aptly described as not the missing pieces of a puzzle, but the only remaining pieces of a puzzle that is itself missing. Yet a centuries-long tradition of scholarship, allied to the more recent science of archaeology, still enables us to construct a vivid picture of what Edgar Allan Poe described as 'the glory that was Greece and the grandeur that was Rome'.[2]

A Note on Spellings

The question of Greek, and sometimes Latin, names transliterated into English is always a difficult problem, and has to be a personal decision. Until quite recently the convention was to Latinize Greek names, so that not only does Klytaimnestra (the straight transliteration from the Greek) become Clytemnestra, Alexandros become Alexander, and Menelaos become Menelaus, but names frequently get changed into their Roman (not always exact) equivalents, so that Odysseus becomes Ulysses, Hera becomes Juno, and Zeus becomes Jupiter or Jove. Other names have developed quite familiar anglicized versions such as Pompey (he was Pompeius), Achilles (Akhilleus), Terence (Terentius), or Darius (Dareios or Daryush). Many academic works now tend to be quite scrupulous about sticking as close to the original as possible, but in the interests of 'user-friendliness' I have taken the imperfect and inconsistent, but nevertheless very common, decision to use the original spellings of the lesser-known proper names, and keep the Latinate forms of the main players.

I

THE MINOANS OF CRETE: THE FIRST EUROPEANS

How silent the libations of distress,
And soft the brush of wrinkled feet on stone . . .

C. A. Trypanis, *Cnossus*

Mythology, Discovery and Chronology

As Odysseus says in Homer's *Odyssey*:

> Out in the dark blue sea there lies a land called Crete, a rich and
> lovely land, washed by the waves on every side, densely peopled and
> boasting ninety cities . . . One of the ninety towns is a great city
> called Knossos, and there, for nine years, King Minos ruled.[1]

The mythical tradition makes Minos the first to establish rule over
the sea, yet he is also redolent with bull imagery, most notably in the
tale of his wife's erotic interest in one particularly fine animal that
was consummated with the complicity of the architect Daedalus. It
was the same engineer who subsequently constructed a highly
complex underground structure called the Labyrinth to confine the
fruit of this union: the Minotaur. Illustrations of the Labyrinth
appeared on coins of Knossos; the first century CE Roman author
Pliny the Elder gave a fanciful description of it;[2] and, in 1632,
William Lithgow, who wrote *The Totall Discourse, Of the Rare
Aduentures, and painefull Peregrinations of long nineteene Yeares
Trauayles*, claimed that he was shown the entrance itself.

In 1878, a Cretan antiquarian, coincidentally named Minos Kalokairinos, discovered the remains of some large storage jars at Knossos, about 5 km from the sea in the middle of Crete's northern coast, and initiated an international race to find the ancient city and turn myth into reality. The victor in that race was Arthur Evans, keeper of the Ashmolean Museum in Oxford, who purchased the site from the 'native Mohametans, to whose almost inexhaustible powers of obstruction I can pay the highest tribute',[3] and secured the agreement of the Greek authorities. Work commenced on 23 March 1900.

Evans had hoped to find an early system of writing; he uncovered an entire civilization as ancient as, albeit distinct from, that of Egypt. He called this culture 'Minoan', even though we don't know how the people referred to themselves, and it is likely that *Keftiu* (Egyptian), *Kaptaru* (Akkadian) and *Caphtor* (Hebrew) could all refer to them. As a good archaeologist should, Evans not only excavated voraciously, but published energetically, notably the four larger-than-life and deeply passionate volumes of *The Palace of Minos at Knossos*.[4] Less laudable were what Evans called his 'reconstitutions' of the buildings that he created on the basis of fresco fragments – 'You can't tell the original from the restoration' is a typical criticism – but, however irksome to the purists, the 'reconstitutions' are very much part of the modern 'Minoan experience', as enjoyed by the million-plus people who visit Knossos every year.

Fixing the precise dates of Minoan chronology is tricky. Scholars use the styles and sequences of pottery to establish 'relative chronology' (the order in which things happened), and try to plug this in to fixed dates derived from Egypt, combined with radio-carbon dating and tree-ring calibration, to determine 'absolute chronology' (precisely when things happened). Minoan relative chronology comes in two types: Early Minoan (abbreviated to EM), Middle Minoan (MM) and Late Minoan (LM), each divided into I, II, and III; some of these phases are divided into A and B, and the Late Minoan is further subdivided by numbers: for example, Late Minoan III A 1 (LM III A1). A looser designation of Prepalatial, Protopalatial (Old Palace), Neopalatial (New Palace) and Post-palatial periods gives quite a straightforward overview of cultural and architectural development. Scholars pretty much agree on the order of events, but not on the absolute chronology, thereby leaving both expert and non-expert alike facing a confusing picture in which, for instance, the Late Minoan period can start as early as 1600 BCE (the 'conventional' chronology) or as late as 1700 BCE (the 'high' chronology).

The 'Palace' of Minos at Knossos

The centrepiece of the Minoan civilization is the enormous, multi-storeyed, richly decorated complex at Knossos. Displaying very high-quality architecture, and containing archives and storage facilities, it overcame earthquakes, fires, repairs, rebuildings and reorganizations, to remain in use for a very long time – at least the equivalent of that from Shakespeare's day to ours. Initially it seemed a confused, confusing and labyrinthine ensemble, and Evans, believing that 'the Palace traditionally built for Minos by his great craftsman Daedalus has proved to be no baseless fabric of the imagination',[5] called it 'the Palace of Minos'. But this was premature, since there is nothing to prove that it was a king's palace, let alone Minos' palace.

The modern theories lean more towards seeing a harmonious design, sensitively integrated into the surrounding environment: a venue for public and private religious, political, ceremonial, commercial, manufacturing, artistic, social and other activities. One helpful analogy is that of a medieval monastery, overseeing a large agricultural economy and funding arts and crafts with the surplus, and it is from the phases of destruction and rebuilding of this complex that we derive the dates of the rise and fall of Minoan society.

Distinctive features of Prepalatial Cretan society (c.3650/3500 or 3000/2900 to 1900 BCE) include group burials in circular *'tholos'* tombs, a mottled reddish-brown pottery known as Vasiliki ware, and the appearance of 'peak sanctuaries' – either holy caves or buildings, or a bit of both. Prepalatial Minoans manufactured stone vases, used seals both to label agricultural produce and as talismans, and made tools and weapons from copper. Archaeobotanical studies indicate the intense cultivation of the olive and the consumption of almonds, grapes, pears, cereals, legumes, broad beans and lentils, the last two of which can also be used as animal fodder and/or manure. Chemical analysis of cooking vessels shows that the

Cretans were enjoying vegetable stews with lots of olive oil, eating foods that contain marine animal oil, consuming meat, leafy vegetables and fruit, and washing it down with resinated wine.

Further organic residue analysis of vases provides evidence for the production of aromatics. A key ingredient here was oil of iris, which nowadays is one of the most expensive commodities in the perfume industry. A papyrus from Egypt dating to c.2200 BCE reads:

> One sails to Byblos today, what shall we do concerning 's-trees' for our mummies? One used to bury the priests with deliveries of them, one used to embalm the great with oil; as far as Keftiu they are unable to come and gold is lacking.[6]

The reference to Keftiu is possibly a moan about disruption of trade with Crete, maybe in an exotic commodity like perfumed oil, and it has been suggested that trade in such products might have generated some of the wealth that built the first palaces.

The Protopalatial (Old Palace) Period
The development of the 'Old Palaces' at Knossos, Mallia and Phaistos certainly inaugurated a new phase in Crete's history (from MM I B to MM II or III A, c.1900 BCE onwards), although nowadays there is much debate as to how, when and why these complexes developed: some scholars prefer a 'Steady State' theory of gradual development; others lean towards more of a 'Big Bang'.

The Old Palace at Knossos became a focal point for a major settlement, controlling territory in excess of 1,000 square kilometres. It was designed around an open Central Court, which was aligned towards Mount Iouchtas, and contained extensive food storage facilities. A distinctive West Court, situated outside the palace, seems to have been the venue for harvest festivals, ritual dancing or the redistribution of grain, although the interpretation of three distinctive large round pits, known as *koulouras*, is problematical: they lack moisture-proofing or roofs, which rules out grain storage on a long-term basis, and various theories link them to harvest ceremonies, planters for trees, or even rubbish pits. Further storerooms on the east side housed huge storage jars (*pithoi*), which were made in sections that were joined together while the clay was damp, and then decorated with relief patterns that often imitate the ropes used to manoeuvre them. In the mythological tale of 'Pandora's box', Pandora released the evils into the world from a *pithos*, not a box.

Religion, administration, trade, arts and crafts all seem to have taken place in the Old Palace. There was weaving on an industrial scale, and the exquisite wheel-made Kamares-ware pottery, the dark surfaces of which were attractively decorated with red, orange and white stripes and flowers, was exported to the eastern Mediterranean and Egypt. The Old Palace bureaucrats used pictorial signs known as 'Cretan Hieroglyphics' and a syllabary (where syllables are represented by a unique symbol) called 'Linear A': 'linear' because the signs, all left-justified, were written in horizontal lines from left to right. Numerals and ideographic signs for things such as 'dog', 'wine', etc., are clear enough, but sadly we do not know what language(s) these scripts represent. The content seems to be accounts, receipts or labels, dedicatory inscriptions, and graffiti, while sealings – not to be confused with seal-stones – were used to show that the string closing a container had not been tampered with.

We might not know their language, but we do know about their drinking habits. One tripod cooking pot contained wine flavoured with pine resin and toasted oak: retsina. The resin acts as a preservative, while the oak gives a taste similar to some single malt Scotch whiskies or 'oaky' chardonnays. It is possible that they enjoyed a beer or two as well, since an acid found in beer-brewing vats in Egypt has also been found in Minoan cooking vessels.

The Old Palace at Knossos was destroyed *c.*1700 BCE (late MM II B or early MM III A) in a fire that may have been caused by a seismic event, human agency, or a combination of the two. Some remarkable finds that fit this scenario were made at Anemospilia on Mount Iouchtas, a structure of which the contents suggest that it was a shrine. It was destroyed so quickly that whatever was going on there was frozen in time. A male, some forty-seven years old, lies face up, wearing a ring of iron (rare) and silver, and an agate seal-stone; a female, approximately twenty-eight years old, is sprawled face-down; and an eighteen year-old male lies on his side next to what may be an altar, in a posture suggesting he had been tied up. A bronze lance-head is placed across his body. Could this be a priest and priestess making a human sacrifice, trying to ward off some impending catastrophe? If it is, it would be highly unusual, and consequently it has been rejected by many scholars, but embraced by the media.

Ironically, this devastation initiated the acme of Minoan wealth and influence. A new palace was constructed at Knossos, keeping the essential functions of the complex, but developing stupendous art and architecture that suggests that the wealth and quality of life of the Minoans was on a par with that of pharaonic Egypt. Minoan-style frescoes from this period at Tel Kabri in Israel and Tel el-Dab'a in Egypt indicate vigorous overseas trade, while domestic peace and security gave rise to a building boom.

As this era of wealth progressed, Crete became much more unified, possibly with Knossos as the 'capital' and Linear A as the script of choice for administrative purposes. Also from this era, perhaps, is the iconic Phaistos Disc, stamped on both sides with pictographic symbols arranged in a spiral with groups of signs divided by lines. Decipherment is practically impossible, and a significant swathe of opinion now regards the disc as a forgery.

At Knossos, access to the New Palace was controlled by the imposing west facade and by entrance porticoes on the south-west and north. The West Court continued to be used, with the Theatral Area, approached by the Royal Road, probably used for public events. Shrines and storerooms on the west side of the palace were approached via the Corridor of the Procession, where a fresco depicted around 350 life-size figures bearing gifts or offerings. The western half of the north end of the building was the administration area.

Throughout the palace complex, fabulous figured frescoes show us the physical appearance, dress, ships, plants and animals of the Minoans. The rough surface of the walls was covered with a layer of mud mixed with straw, and then two or three layers of lime plaster (stucco). A preliminary sketch was incised or painted (the yellow ochre cartoon can sometimes still be seen underneath the finished painting), with straight lines being created by stretching a string across the damp plaster to make a slight impression, which again is occasionally visible. The final painting began when the stucco was still damp (*buon fresco*), and individual details such as ornaments were added, either on to the dry stucco (*fresco secco*), or on to the still-wet painted parts. A basic palette of colours was used: red (obtained from ferrous earths and haematite); yellow (yellow ochre); black (carbon); blue (glaucophane; 'Egyptian blue', i.e. silicon, copper oxide and calcium oxide; perhaps azurite); white (the natural colour of the lime plaster); and mixtures to achieve greys, browns and pinks. Low relief was sometimes used to make subjects stand out. Eyes were usually depicted frontally, with heads in profile, and artists followed a conventional colour-coding practice: red for men's skin and bronze; white for women's flesh; yellow for gold; and blue for silver, and sometimes to represent the green of plants or the grey of monkey fur and shaven heads.

The most iconic and controversial of all the Minoan frescoes is the 'Priest-King' or 'Lily Prince', who is made up of several discrete relief fragments on a red background: a crown of lilies and peacock feathers; a torso with a lock of hair, a lily necklace, and a clenched right hand held diagonally across the body, which is adorned with floral motifs; part of a left arm; a kilt and codpiece, plus the upper left leg; and a fragment of a right thigh. Evans assembled these into a male figure leading a sacred bull. But challenges now abound: are all the fragments from one figure? Was the flesh red or white? The musculature is definitively male, but the lily crown is associated with Minoan sphinxes and priestesses, not with men. Should the pose be more commanding/confrontational? The evidence is too fragmentary even to determine the figure's gender – Evans' Priest-King might have been a Priestess-Queen, or something completely different. Still, this definitive image is now the logo for the Minoan Lines shipping company.

The heart of the palace complex lay between the west facade and the Central Court. The pillar crypts, incised with double-axe (*labrys*) marks, stand adjacent to the Vat Room, which contained objects thought to be part of the foundation deposit of the original palace. The Tripartite Shrine and the Throne Room complex were located in this area, with the latter sporting a splendid fresco of griffins flanking a smallish seat, on whose occupant they may confer power and protection. Evans believed that this was the throne room of the 'Minos' (a title rather than a name, similar to 'pharaoh'), but the interpretation and dating of the space is tricky. Opposite the throne is a sunken chamber (*adyton*) accessed by a stairway. This might be a lustral basin. In the building called Xeste 3 at Akrotiri on

Santorini there is a similar structure, featuring a painting of a girl with a bleeding foot, a bare-breasted adult woman, a (possibly) pre-pubescent girl in a translucent veil, and 'horns of consecration' covered with red (blood?) streaks, in a landscape teeming with crocuses (possibly used to alleviate period pains and/or as a dye for the yellow cloth worn by females). Another fresco shows girls taking crocuses to a seated woman/goddess. One 'flower gatherer' wears eye and lip make-up, and has most of her hair shaved off in a pre-adult manner, except for a single lock at the back, and wisps over her forehead. The imagery has been interpreted as relating to a girl's first menstruation.

One of the most famous Minoan artefacts is the faience (glazed earthenware) 'Snake Goddess'. She is bare-breasted, wears a flounced skirt, holds snakes in her hands, and has a feline creature on her head, perhaps indicating fertility and dominance over nature. Minoan religion was heavily focused on nature and regenerative forces, and the goddess who dominates the Minoan pantheon is frequently depicted descending from the sky or joining worshippers in fertility cults based on trees or rocks. The prominence of females in Minoan art leads some to assert that Minoan Crete was run by women, and others, such as 'Sir Galahad' to express outrage at the very thought of it:

> Women, women, nothing but women, just like on the Riviera, overdressed, permed, in high heels, a naked young man or two around . . . no sign of venerable old men. There's no place for them in a female realm . . . men are in subordinate positions, pages, cup-bearers, flautists, field-workers, or sailors . . . not one king, priest or hero. What was at first taken automatically to be a male ruler, on a half flaked fresco, turned out to be a woman too. Women are queens, priestesses, goddesses – never serving girls.[7]

Nevertheless the snake goddess, and the large number of representations of the double axe (*labrys*), which the archaeology suggests may have been used by Minoan priestesses, could well indicate that women held an influential position in some aspects of Minoan society.

The 'Grandstand' fresco, which depicts bare-breasted, flouncy-skirted Minoan ladies sitting either side of a tripartite pillared shrine, in the midst of a crowd of male faces, might provide a clue to the type of event that took place in the Central Court. However, another suggestion (alongside frequent attempts to bring the mythical tale of Theseus and the Minotaur into the equation) is that it was a 'bull-ring'. Another fresco shows a white-skinned figure, whose hair is knotted at the nape of the neck, wearing a variegated kilt with a codpiece, calf-length boots and lots of jewellery, grabbing a mighty onrushing bull by the horns; in the centre a person with burnt-sienna coloured skin, a quite plain yellow kilt, and no jewellery, performs a back-flip over the bull's back, which would bring the figure to earth facing away from the beast; behind the bull, facing it, with outstretched hands, stands a second white figure who resembles the first. Evans interpreted the activity as a girl acrobat trying to gain purchase for a somersault over the animal's back, similar to what the person in the yellow kilt is performing, while the second female is about to catch the flying figure when he lands. But, if the white figures are girls, why are they wearing male clothes? Is this a rite of initiation in which young males emerge from a 'feminine guise' into adulthood by exhibiting their superiority over the bull? Are stunts like these feasible? Did they occur at all? If so, where? The answers are elusive, although there are enough representations in other media to indicate that this type of activity did take place, and the horns of some excavated bull skulls have been sawn down, presumably for 'health and safety' reasons.

The north end of the palace is divided by a passage coming up from the North Pillar Hall, which could have supported dining halls on the upper floor, and the north entrance of the palace was adorned with a large bull fresco. On the east side of the palace an impressive Grand Staircase led down from the Central Court to the so-called Queen's megaron (a hall surrounded by windows, a fore-hall and a light-well, decorated with an exquisite dolphin fresco), and the Hall of the Double Axes. These rooms could have served as offices, meeting chambers, reception rooms or sleeping areas, or a combination of these. There were also highly advanced water systems, piping water to a lavatory and draining it away – Minoan domestic hygiene was excellent (they also shared their medical expertise with the Egyptians).

Minoan artistic skills extended to producing seals from gold, ivory, steatite and quartz, sometimes in the shape of animals with flat under-surfaces, sometimes lentoid (lens-shaped) or amygdaloid (almond-shaped) with slightly convex sides, or flattened cylinders. The confident, fluidly rendered designs range from linear patterns, swirls and spirals to pastoral and hunting scenes, birds, fish, plants and animals. Highly impressive pottery appears, most notably the dark-on-light 'Plant Style' or 'Floral Style', the shining example of which is the exquisite 'Jug of the Reeds' from Phaistos, and the stylized 'Marine Style', with its engaging octopuses, fish, shells and seaweed. Attractive small-scale sculpture in terracotta, representing deities or worshippers, and in bronze, exemplified by statuettes such as the British Museum's man giving the 'Minoan salute', and its engagingly energetic depiction of a man leaping over a bull, confirm a high level of artistic sensibility.

The Downfall

Ultimately the Neopalatial period ended in widespread destruction by fire at the end of LM I B (c.1425 BCE 'conventional' or c.1550 BCE 'high' chronology), although the palace at Knossos itself does not show evidence of being too badly hit.

One intriguing find from this time is a series of buildings in which the bones of at least four children, with butchery marks, were found in a cooking pot along with some edible snails and at least one sheep. Did this signify human sacrifice and propitiatory ritual cannibalism, with the Knossians attempting to avert some imminent disaster? The jury is still out, but we can say with confidence that new people had by then arrived on Crete, and that they were making some radically different lifestyle-choices.

A great deal has also been made of the possibility that a volcanic eruption on the island of Thera (Santorini), 100 km to the north of Crete, caused the downfall of the Minoans. No one has since witnessed such a cataclysm. The Therans were in the process of rebuilding their property, damaged by a powerful earthquake that had hit the island, when the eruption began with four explosive steam blasts, which between them left an ash deposit 10–15 cm thick. This possibly prompted a mass exodus from the island – no bodies have yet been discovered in the archaeological remains, and there is hardly any precious material left behind. Perhaps the main eruption took place some weeks later, generating an eruption column some 30–40 km high in less than twenty-four hours. This deposited around 6 m of debris, which buried and preserved much of the settlement at Akrotiri, filling the lower parts of the buildings, but leaving the uncovered areas exposed to the incredibly violent events that were to come. What goes up must come down and, as the eruption column collapsed, it created a 'base surge', where clouds of hot gas expanded outwards horizontally at very high velocity. This destroyed all the protruding parts of the buildings, and made dune-like deposits of pumice between 8 m and 12 m deep. Four enormous explosions then generated pyroclastic flows – fast-moving currents of hot gas and rock – which laid down deposits up to 55 m deep in places. Finally, further massive gas-rich and much more fluid pyroclastic flows deposited ash, pumice and small lithics to a depth of 40–50 m. The general consensus is that the entire event lasted just three or four days, emitting 30–40 cubic kilometres of material.

That much is widely agreed. Yet the big issues of the date and effects of the eruption are much more controversial. In the late 1960s Spyridon Marinatos excavated Akrotiri on Thera, which had a rather Minoan-looking culture, and posited that the eruption not only destroyed the Minoan civilization, but was also the origin of the Atlantis myth.[8] The eruption might well have been considerably more devastating than the 1883 Krakatau eruption, whose consequent tsunamis took 35,000 lives, so the suggestion that tsunamis, air-borne debris, fire and temporary climate change might wipe out an entire civilization was attractive. However, subsequent studies, involving pottery analysis, Carbon-14 dating, dendro-chronology (the study of the 'bar-code' created by the annual growth rings in trees), the acid detected in cores taken from the polar ice-caps, mapping the air-fall debris, and finds of pumice at Tel el Dab'a in Egypt, have been inconclusive, especially in regard to dating – an interval of between 90 and about 175 years between the eruption and the demise of the Minoans seems likely.

So if the Thera eruption did not destroy the Minoan civilization, what did? Architecture in the Cretan countryside shows that they started to place greater emphasis on security and storage. Was this the result of internal tensions? All of a sudden, Minoan exports went into decline and, in Egypt, as we enter the LM II pottery phase, the tomb paintings of Amenemhab, Kenemun and Anen, which purport to portray Keftiu, actually show figures that are not authentic Minoans. The Keftiu on the tomb of Useramon, dating from 1451 BCE, have their codpieces painted over with Mycenaean-looking kilts in the tomb of Rekhmire a generation later, perhaps indicating a new style of clothing on Crete. Something had gone wrong.

New funerary customs, very like those of mainland Greece, now appear: burial with bronze weaponry and boar-tusk helmets in 'Warrior Graves', or with large numbers of bronze vessels; pit graves; tombs with long, narrow, rock-cut entrance passages (*dromoi*) leading to rectangular burial chambers; *tholos* tombs of distinctly mainland style; and so on. And if all this suggests that new people were on the island, the appearance of clay tablets written in Linear B script, which expresses the Greek language, confirms who these military-minded, bureaucratically motivated people were. They were the Mycenaeans.

2

MYCENAE: 'RICH IN GOLD'

Where are the birth-places of the heroes?
  The few you see hardly break the plain,
I passed you by, Mycenae, and knew you,
  dead, more desolate than a goat-field,
  talked of by goat-herds. 'It stood here' (said
  the old man) 'covered in gold, the giants built it . . . '
                                        Alpheios of Mytilene[1]

The Mycenaean Age (c.1600–1100 BCE) played a critical role in the development of Greek mythology. Generally, the mythical significance/insignificance of a place tends to correspond to that which it had at that time. For instance, in Homer, Mycenae (Mykenai), with its stock epithet 'rich in gold', was extremely important.

The fact that Greek mythology and Mycenaean archaeology have to compensate for our lack of Mycenaean history makes life difficult. Yet it was with information of this sort that Mycenaean culture was first unearthed and named by Heinrich Schliemann (1822–90) in the 1870s. His archaeological and personal credibility is often questioned: he romanticized, exaggerated and distorted details of his personal life, looked almost exclusively for evidence to support his belief that Homer was 'true', and often missed or even destroyed crucial material. Yet his discoveries were astounding. He dug up the relics of a dynamically enterprising people who readily assimilated ideas from the likes of the Egyptians, Hittites and Minoans, ran with them, integrated them with their own society based on the Greek mainland, and created a scintillating and original new civilization.

Mycenae itself stands on a rocky outcrop overlooking the fine agricultural land of the Argive plain, has a good water supply, and, though it is a little distance from the sea (visible from the citadel), with the city of Tiryns in between, has access to good landing places for ships. An extensive network of paved roads and strong bridges also facilitated communication with other areas. Yet the common question, 'Where did the Mycenaeans come from?' admits of no simple answer. It used to be asserted that the peace of Early Bronze Age Greece was shattered in around 2200 BCE by invaders, possibly from Anatolia, who destroyed the indigenous settlements and replaced them with their own, but 'invasion theories' carry little weight nowadays. A picture of gradual arrival, settlement, amalgamation, dispute and conflict might be less sexy than alien invaders or hordes of marauding barbarians, but it is probably more accurate.

During the Middle Bronze Age their civilization was pretty unimpressive. Skeletons reveal a mixed racial stock, strong and muscular, but suffering from childhood malnutrition, bad teeth, arthritis and malaria. The men were 1.60–1.70 m tall and lived to around 30–45 years old; women 1.48–1.56 m with an average lifespan of 25–40 years. But then, as we enter the Late Bronze Age, *c*.1600 BCE, we see greater prosperity, allied to contact with Egypt, Syria, Macedonia, the Black Sea, Italy and even Spain. The Mycenaean Age proper had begun (see Table 2.1, overleaf).

We can establish a reasonably well-defined relative chronology based on the stylistic development of Mycenaean pottery: thus 'Late Helladic (LH) III B' denotes the pottery in use at the height of Mycenaean prosperity in the thirteenth century BCE. The absolute chronology has been fixed by cross-referencing this material to Egyptian finds, the dates of which are generally accurate to within a few years. The Carbon-14 and dendrochronology dating methods contribute further to this process, but also have a tendency to challenge and confuse it. Some scholars like to divide the chronology of the Mycenaean Late Bronze Age into:

- Formative period: LH I and LH II A (*c*.1575/50–1450 BCE)
- Palace period: LH II B to III B2 (*c*.1450–1200 BCE)
- Post-Palatial period, covering LH III C and 'sub Mycenaean' (*c*.1200–1050/1000 BCE).

Table 2.1 Mycenaean Chronology

Date	Period	Mainland Greece
BCE		
3000	EARLY BRONZE AGE	Early Helladic
2000	MIDDLE BRONZE AGE	Middle Helladic
1600		Late Helladic I
16th century		
1500	Early/	Late Helladic II
15th century	Formative	
1450		Late Helladic II B
1400		Late Helladic I
14th century	Palatial	
1300	LATE BRONZE AGE	Late Helladic III B
13th century		
1200	Late/	
12th century	Post-Palatial	Late Helladic III C
1100		
11th century		
1050		The End

These people were great bureaucrats. Thousands of inscribed clay tablets have been found, fired hard in conflagrations that occurred during the Mycenaean occupation of Knossos, and also at Mycenae itself, Tiryns, Thebes, Pylos and Khania. About half the signs on the tablets are similar to the earlier Linear A, suggesting verbal communication between Minoans and Mycenaeans, and the script became known as Linear B. It was deciphered by a British architect, Michael Ventris, (assisted by John Chadwick and others), who, on 1 July 1952, announced on BBC radio that the tablets were written in a difficult and archaic form of Greek. His theory was supported by the discovery in 1953 of a tablet that had ideograms of three-legged cauldrons of which the accompanying signs read *ti-ri-po-de* (tripods). So many tablets have now been discovered that even the handwriting of individual scribes can be identified.

Linear B is not literature; it was used to keep lists on long thin bars known as 'leaf tablets', the contents of which might be transcribed and collated on to larger, rectangular 'page tablets'. The tablets show personal touches such as doodles, sketches and spelling mistakes, and the script is composed of nearly 100 different signs (see Table 2.2, overleaf), which can be summarized as:

1. Decimal-based numerals (1, 10, 100, 1,000, 10,000);
2. Pictograms, ideograms or logograms that indicate what is being counted. Sometimes they look like what they stand for, but they can be quite abstract: the head of a goat, sheep or pig, with a single line descending vertically with two short cross strokes, indicates a male creature; two vertical lines indicate a female.
3. Syllabic signs that spell words. These can represent the vowels *a, e, i, o* and *u*; a consonant + a vowel (*pa, pe, pi, po, pu*); or a consonant + semivowel + vowel (*nwa, dwo,* etc.). Difficulties arise because, for example, *pa* can also sound as *pha*, or *ba*; *ka* as *kha*, or *ya*; *ra* as *la*, as in ancient Egyptian; extra vowels find their way into clusters of consonants; and final consonants are missed out. So *ko-no-so* = Knoso(s); *a-re-ku-tu-ru-wo* = the man's name Alektryono(n); *pe-ma* = (s)pe(r)ma (seed); *ti-ri-po* = tripo(s) (tripod).

Table 2.2 Some Linear B Transcriptions

Linear B	Transcription	English	Linear B	Transcription	English
e-ra3-wo	elaiwon	olive oil	ko-wo	korwos	boy
qa-si-re-u	guasileus	chief	me-ri	meli	honey
i-je-re-ja	hiereia	priestess	pa-ka-na	phasgana	swords
i-qo	hikkwoi	horses	to-pe-za	torpezda	table
ka-ko	khalkos	bronze	tu-ka-te	thugater	daughter
ko-wa	korwa	girl	tu-ro2	turoi	cheeses

It is an inflected language in the same way as classical Greek, and there are two distinct dialects: one used by the scribes, thought to be upper-class speech; the other being closer to the speech-patterns of the lower classes. Personal names come through, too: Thyestes, Alexandra, Theodora, Glaukos (Grey-eyed), Ekhinos (Sea-urchin), Poimen (Shepherd), Khalkeus (Smith). At Pylos we find Orestes, Achilles, Tros, Theseus, and Hector, which proves that Homer was using genuine Bronze Age monikers, albeit those of workaday Mycenaeans, not mighty heroes.

Shaft Graves and Tholos Tombs
The decipherment of Linear B sent twentieth-century scholars into paroxysms of delight, but this pales into insignificance at the joy

experienced by their late-nineteenth-century counterparts at the finds in the 'shaft graves' contained in Grave Circle A at Mycenae that were made by Heinrich Schliemann.[2] The older Grave Circle B was subsequently excavated in 1951. Both the Linear B tablets and the shaft graves prove that the presentation of the Bronze Age in the Homeric epics is often anachronistic: Homer's heroes were cremated; Mycenaeans were buried. Initially this was in rectangular grave pits lined with stone slabs known as a 'cist graves', but from c.1620 BCE onwards, elaborate shaft graves were dug. These comprised a rectangular shaft sunk up to 2.5 m into the rock. A layer of stones was scattered on the floor, and then a chamber, roofed over with squared timbers with copper sheet ends, was created at the base of the shaft. This was frequently large enough for several bodies plus their grave goods. The shaft was filled with earth, and the grave marked with a *stele* (stone slab) up to 2m high. The graves were regularly reused.

There were 26 graves enclosed by the circular stone wall of Grave Circle B, including 14 royal shaft graves. Of the 35 individuals found, 22 have been studied by osteoarchaeologists and forensic scientists: 16 were adult males aged 23–55 years, with large hands and feet, and an average height of 1.71 m; 4 were female averaging 1.59 m tall; and 2 were children aged 2–5 years. They were of mixed racial stock, led active lives, and were quite a lot bigger than the Minoans. For example, the male Zeta 59 was tall, broad-shouldered and thick-boned, with an arthritic spine, a large head, a long horsey face, and depressions in his skull inflicted by a right-handed opponent – clearly he was involved in fighting. There is little sign of dental or infectious diet-related disease, although one male suffered from gallstones. Surprisingly, given that their pottery depicts marine life, they ate almost no marine foods. The electrum (a mixture of gold and silver) death mask belonging to Gamma 55 disappointingly showed very little resemblance to the face whose skull it was reconstructed from, indicating that the masks were not accurate likenesses.

Grave Circle B contained many items of gold jewellery, which has a 'bling'-like quality, even though much of it is artistically second-rate. The high-quality items include a gold sword hilt and some finely ornamented sword blades; a gold cup; and an utterly exquisite rock-crystal bowl with an exceptionally delicate duck's-head handle – a real masterpiece.

However, the finds from Grave Circle B are as nothing compared to what Schliemann had already found in Grave Circle A, a group of shaft graves used by a dynasty coming to power *c.*1600–1500 BCE. The two Grave Circles overlap chronologically, with Circle A being used for a generation longer.

Grave Circle A, as we have it, was the product of a rebuilding programme during the thirteenth century BCE. It comprises a roughly circular, hollow parapet of limestone slabs with a formal entrance, enclosing some ordinary graves and six large shaft graves, deeper and larger than those in Circle B, and cut into the bedrock. A seventh, similar grave, stood outside the circle. The six family tombs each have several occupants, usually laid with their heads to the east and feet to the west in a chamber roofed with twigs and branches and covered with a layer of clay and slate slabs.

Each grave was marked by a west-facing sandstone *stele* that was either plain or sculpted, generally with battle or hunting scenes, one of which depicts a charioteer hurtling in the direction of an individual holding a sword, thought by some to represent funeral games. The remains of eight men, nine women and two children were discovered. The males are 25–45 years of age, and stand 1.65–1.83 m tall – just half a centimetre shorter than the average modern Greek. They have a similar muscularity to the occupants of Grave Circle B, ate a mixture of meat and plants, got about 20 per cent of their protein from marine foods, and between them exhibit osteoporosis, arthritis of the spine, and a well-healed fractured vertebra.

There are those who think that Schliemann may have 'sexed up' some of the graves with finds from elsewhere in order to intensify interest in himself and his work, although the case against him is by no means conclusive. In a telegram dated 28 November 1876 to King George of Greece, he confidently asserted:

> I have discovered the tombs which the tradition proclaimed by Pausanias indicates as the graves of Agamemnon, Cassandra, Eurymedon and their companions, all slain at a banquet by Clytemnestra (Agamemnon's wife) and her lover Aegisthus.[3]

If they were authentic, Schliemann's finds were stunning. Five of the males had burial masks made of hammered gold sheets. One had a splendid gold breastplate decorated with spirals, and a gold mask showing an aquiline face with a beard and a moustache, which has become known as the 'mask of Agamemnon', even though it was another occupant of the same grave that Schliemann believed to be the great king. That extraordinarily well-preserved body became known as the 'shaft grave mummy' (even though it had not been mummified), and in a telegram to a Greek newspaper, Schliemann said: 'This corpse very much resembles the image which my imagination formed long ago of wide-ruling Agamemnon',[4] later abbreviated to the apocryphal but catchy, 'Today I gazed upon the face of Agamemnon.'

Other grave goods included elaborate necklaces, earrings, rosettes, ornaments originally attached to the funeral shrouds, a large woman's crown decorated in the repoussé technique of hammering gold (and silver) from the inside, and some plain gold sheets covering the bodies of the children who were buried with the three women in Grave III. There were ceremonial swords with hilts decorated with gold plate or discs, whilst others had ivory or marble pommels, and a dagger, the blade of which is inlaid with gold, silver and black enamel (an alloy of silver and sulphur frequently referred to as *niello*), shows warriors hunting lions on one side, and a lion hunting antelope on the other.

Also for ceremonial use was a *rhyton* (= conical ritual drinking vessel) in the form of a lion's head made of sheet gold; a Minoan-influenced one with a silver bull's head with gilded horns; a stag-shaped *rhyton* imported from the Hittite civilization; and the silver 'siege rhyton', decorated with repoussé scenes of soldiers assaulting a city. Mycenaean metallurgy also encompassed the techniques of granulation (using tiny droplets of gold to decorate objects) and cloisonné (soldering a pattern of fine wire on to a base plate and setting it with inlays of stone or glass) to produce objects of astonishing delicacy.

Drinking cups of gold and silver included the so-called Cup of Nestor, which resembles in some ways, if not in size, the description of the *depas amphikypellon* used by Nestor in the *Iliad*:

It was set with golden nails, the eared handles upon it
were four, and on either side there were fashioned two doves
of gold, feeding, and there were double bases beneath it.

Another man with great effort could lift it full from the table,
but Nestor, aged as he was, lifted it without strain.[5]

Imported luxury items also included amber from northern Europe;
ostrich eggs from North Africa; ivory from Egypt or Syria; Cretan
stone vases; and lapis lazuli from Afghanistan.

In about 1490 BCE (LH II A) the Mycenaean elite stopped using
shaft graves and opted for more imposing *tholos* tombs (popularly
known as 'beehive' tombs). Nine of these have been excavated
outside the citadel of Mycenae, but none have the engineering and
aesthetic sophistication of the 'Treasury of Atreus',[6] built around
1410 BCE. This is approached by a 39 m long *dromos* (entrance
passage; pl. *dromoi*) that is lined with imposing polygonal stone
walls. This leads to a doorway ornamented with half columns of
Egyptian porphyry and decorated with carved zigzags, spirals and
rosettes. The lintel is an enormous block of stone estimated to
weigh more than 100 tonnes, but the structural stresses above it
were displaced on to the mighty door jambs by a corbelled[7]
relieving triangle. The triangle was concealed by a facade of red and
green bands of spirals and lozenges between two smaller carved
pillars. Having crossed the threshold, you enter a circular chamber
14.3 m across and 13 m high, whose slightly pointed dome is built
of beautifully dressed ashlar blocks that decrease in size up to a
central keystone that locks the whole structure in place. Layers of
clay were applied over the dome to waterproof it, and the whole
edifice was covered with earth. The body itself was probably
interred in the side-chamber, which opens off the main one.

Neither the body nor any treasure survives, although extrapo-
lation from other sites suggests an inhumation accompanied by
grave goods appropriate to sex and status: jewellery, mirrors,
weapons, gold cups and so on. After the funeral, the tomb entrance
was closed. Drinking cups (*kylikes*) are regularly found smashed on
the floor of the *dromoi*, along with the bones of sacrificial animals,
and of horses (sometimes in pairs) that may have pulled the chariot
carrying the deceased to the tomb. The Treasury of Atreus was
undoubtedly intended to be seen as the awe-inspiring architectural
masterpiece that it is. It was presumably built during the lifetime
of its occupant, and while it is likely that the *dromoi* of humbler
chamber tombs were filled in after the burial, the grandiose entrance

of this very labour-intensive project does not look like it was meant to be hidden.

There are also several cemeteries around Mycenae, which comprise groups of chamber tombs housing members of the 'middle class'. The tombs are hewn from the natural rock, and contained relics of many generations, accompanied by good quality vases, clay figurines, and possibly objects of sentimental value, like one traveller's(?) Egyptian seal. The silent masses are not buried in shaft graves, *tholoi* or chamber tombs, and their grave goods tend to be very mundane: personal things such as tools, spindle whorls, razors and terracotta models or figurines, many of which are female in one of three shapes named after the letter of the Greek alphabet that their poses resemble – phi, psi and tau (Φ, Ψ and Τ). Children were regularly buried with feeding bottles.

The Citadel and Settlement of Mycenae

The Mycenae citadel was a grandiose complex of buildings surrounded by some of the most impressive fortifications ever constructed. In making an approach to the ruler, you would pass through a *propylon* (entrance portico), a 7 m square canopied porch with a column on each side, which opened into a small open courtyard. Walking from there up the gradually sloping West Passage, you encountered the Great West Portal, in front of which was a balcony with stupendous views out across the Argive plain. From the Portal a passageway gave access to the Main Court, 11.5 × 15 m, covered in painted stucco to simulate large marble tiles.

The layout of the *megaron* (King's Hall) accessed from the Main Court resembles that of a Classical-era temple. First you would enter a two-columned porch (*aithousa*), which housed two small altars and a libation bowl. Moving through huge wooden double doors mounted on bronze pivots, you would find yourself in a vestibule (*prodomos*) with a floor made of painted stucco, bordered with 1 m slabs of gypsum. Another impressive doorway finally led you into the *domos*, or Great Hall, an imposing space, 12.96 × 11.50 m, floored like the vestibule, and walled with frescoes depicting a battle involving horses, chariots, warriors and their womenfolk. Facing you was the central round hearth (3.7 m across), decorated with flames and spirals painted round its sides. Four stuccoed wooden columns around the hearth supported an upper storey, and it is assumed that the throne itself was to your right. It is an appropriate setting for a mighty ruler.

The palace also had designated areas for religious worship, accommodation, workshops for craftsmen, and facilities for storing agricultural produce. The surrounding town covered some 32 ha, and the quality of the buildings suggests affluent owners. For instance, the House of the Oil Merchant contained seven store-rooms filled with oil storage and transport jars, as well as nearly forty Linear B tablets; and the House of the Sphinxes contained thousands of pieces of ivory, including a plaque decorated with its eponymous sphinxes.

All the signals that the citadel of Mycenae broadcasts seem militaristic, yet it may have been fear, rather than aggression, that lurked behind these fortifications, since it was quite late in their history that the Mycenaeans started to build truly mighty fortresses. Pottery excavated in the foundations of the walls shows that the main fortifications of Mycenae began only around 1350-40 BCE, but then, around 1250 BCE, the citadel was nearly doubled in size as the walls were extended to enclose a series of religious buildings, along with Grave Circle A, which was also refurbished on a more monumental scale. The Great Ramp leading up to the citadel was added at this time, along with a new postern gate and a tower.

The great symbol of Mycenaean civilization, the Lion Gate, belongs to this phase. It is flanked on the left by the natural rock of the hill (with a facade of 'conglomerate'[8] blocks), and on the right by a rectangular bastion of massive conglomerate masonry, which constricts the passageway and exposes the unshielded side of any attacker to missile fire from above. The threshold, sides and lintel of the gate each weigh more than 20 tonnes, while the wall above uses corbelling to form a relieving triangle over the lintel. The triangular space is filled by a sculpted panel of grey limestone, carved in relief with two leonine creatures facing one another, with their front legs on two altars that flank a central Minoan-looking column with an architrave above it. Dowel-holes for attaching the animals' heads suggest that they were *gardant* (facing outward). Animals placed like this are often regarded as *apotropaic* (to ward off evil), symbolizing protection, strength and stability. However, questions as to what inspired the subject-matter, where the Mycenaeans acquired the slab itself, what it actually looked like (painted? stone, wood, or metal heads?), what kind of animals (lions, as the second-century CE traveller Pausanias said? lionesses? griffins?), and what its meaning was, are fraught with controversy. None of the scholarly answers, however brilliantly argued, can be anything other than pure speculation.

The final phase of fortification, which began around 1200 BCE, extended the walls to protect access to a secret underground cistern, fed via an aqueduct from a nearby spring, and added sally-ports to allow authorized personnel to enter or exit the citadel discreetly. There are also ten or so 'blockhouses' in the Mycenae area, which could be signal stations, sometimes (fancifully) interpreted as the beacons of Aeschylus' *Agamemnon*.[9]

Who or what the Mycenaeans were afraid of is not entirely clear. Siege engines were not widely used, so any defensive purposes would have been adequately served by smaller walls. Part of their function must have been simply a display of invincibility. Mycenae's walls, on average, are 7.5 m thick and more than 8 m high, although they are not as massive as those at nearby Tiryns, which were the first to be described as 'cyclopean'. The myth related that Proitos, the founder of Tiryns, had his citadel built by the Cyclopes, who also built the citadel at Mycenae in the next generation,[10] and later Greeks believed that such massive well-shaped blocks could only be the work of mythical monsters. In reality, the Mycenaeans constructed them of an inner and outer skin with a rubble filling, using hammers and a pendulum saw, which was one of the most technologically advanced devices of its day. The average cyclopean block could have been drawn on a sledge by fourteen oxen, before being rolled down from above or raised into position from below with the aid of earth ramps, but the Linear B tablets tell us nothing about the timescale, the labour force, or its working schedules.

Society, Economy and Religion

Mycenaean society was highly structured, based on a hierarchy of meticulous administrators who were at least as important as the aristocrats (although there may have been some overlap). What is odd, though, is the almost total anonymity of the kings. At the top was the *wa-na-ka* (wanax), the 'king', who sometimes presided over religious rituals; second in power and status was the *ra-wa-ke-ta* (lawagetas), 'the leader of the people'; and each local area had its *qa-si-re-u* (basileus), 'chieftain'. Priests and priestesses (*i-je-ro-wo-ko*) also had high status, as did the aristocratic *e-qe-ta* (hequetai), the 'followers' of the *wanax* (king). An extensive bureaucracy of scribes and officials ran the palace and local areas, and beneath them came the free citizens, who had their own organization and spokesmen, and owned land. At the bottom of the pile were the slaves (*do-we-ro* (male) or *do-we-ra* (female), giving us *dowelos*, which in Classical Greek was *doulos* = 'slave').

Mycenae's epithet 'Rich in Gold' begs the question: where did it come from? Not from Mycenae: it came from Nubia, Egypt, Macedonia or the island of Thasos, and was probably paid for by a healthy agricultural economy that in turn sustained the activities of craftsmen, soldiers, sailors and rulers, who are characterized by an Odysseus-like resourcefulness.

Barley and wheat were the staple crops. Workers' rations were distributed by the *kotyle* (= cup of 0.6 litres): three per day of barley; half as much of wheat (which has a higher nutritional value). Emmer wheat can be roasted and mixed with nuts to make portable snacks; barley is good in soups and stews, or as the basis for beer; and some slave women were given figs as well as grain. Forensic archaeological analysis of the interiors of their cooking vessels gives fascinating results: at Thebes they were eating pork, cereals, pulses and honey; at Midea the archaeologists who found cereal and oil on a 'griddle tray' wondered whether or not this was to prevent pancakes from sticking; and evidence from the House of the Sphinxes and the Granary at Mycenae suggested porridge made of bitter vetch (which requires pre-boiling to remove its toxicity), lentils, grass peas, wheat, barley and broad beans. Mycenaeans cooked using olive or safflower oil, used a wide variety of native herbs, and also ate almonds, pears, cherries, plums, wild strawberries, carob, walnuts, chestnuts and pistachios.

Olives and vines were particularly important: you can grow them on relatively poor ground despite limited rainfall; cereals can be cultivated between olive trees, allowing the maximization of manpower. All three crops are hoed, harvested and tended at different times of the year; and they are storable as oil, fruits or wine. Olive oil was exported, and provided an essential ingredient for the manufacture of perfumed oil and ointment. The Linear B tablets give us the other ingredients:

Axotas gave to Thyestes [*tu-we-a*] the perfume maker the following ingredients to make perfume: coriander [*ko-ri-a2-da-na*] seeds 576 litres; cypress [*ku-pa-ro2*] seeds 576 litres 157 16 units; fruit 240 litres; wine 576 litres; honey 58 litres; wool 6 kilograms; wine 58 litres.[11]

References to flax workers also suggest the production of linseed oil and linen, and the textile industry was a key element in the economy of the Mycenaean kingdoms, with about 200 women recorded as making cloth at Pylos.

Substantial herds of oxen are implied by the Linear B tablets, and rather charmingly plough oxen were called things such as Dapple, Dusky, Noisy and Whitefoot. However, sheep and goats comprised the majority of the livestock (75 per cent of the animal bones from Mycenae are from sheep and goats, and a series of tablets from Knossos lists nearly 100,000 sheep), supplemented by small herds of pigs. These animals produced milk and cheese, wool and cloth, meat and leather.

Hunting and fishing were also part of the picture. Bronze fish-hooks, lead weights and fish bones have all been found. Mycenaean aristocrats loved to hunt with hounds (*kunagetai* = 'hunter', literally 'dog-leader'), and a fantastically lively fresco from Tiryns depicts hunters accompanied by spotted hounds, wearing red collars and surrounding a boar, which is being speared. Hare, duck, goose, partridge, fox, deer and even turtles were hunted for food and/or fur, while lions were hunted for sport. Horse bones are relatively infrequent, although the tablets do list horses in the context of military equipment, with white horses being particularly popular. Horse rearing may have been a major generator of wealth, especially in what Homer calls 'horse-pasturing' Argos.

Mycenaeans exploited sources of copper, silver and lead, and became key players in the Mediterranean metals trade. Lead was used as weights for fishing nets; to keep the hems of women's clothing in place; and also used for mending pottery, showing that ceramics had quite a high value. Copper and bronze were used for jugs, braziers, cauldrons, frying pans, lamps, tweezers, pins, saws, drill bits, pruning knives, horses' bits, octopus spears, scale pans and so on. The Linear B tablets from Pylos mention nearly 300 bronze smiths, so clearly this was a major facet of the economy.

The wreck of a merchant ship, Ulu Burun, which sank near Kas off the Turkish coast in *c*.1315 BCE revealed even more: 354 copper ingots (more than ten tonnes in weight), one tonne of tin ingots, terebinth resin found in Canaanite jars, turquoise and cobalt-blue glass ingots, and large quantities of Cypriot pottery. There were also some ebony logs, ostrich eggs, seals and a scarab from Egypt bearing the name of Nefertiti, elephant and hippopotamus ivory, faience and tin vessels, a gold cup and a gold and bronze Egyptian statuette. Various bronze tools, cylinder seals, oil lamps, wooden writing boards and fishing tackle probably belonged to the crew, and two Mycenaean swords, two seals, spearheads, and amber and glass beads suggest that two high-ranking Mycenaeans were aboard.

This extraordinary range of items from Egypt, the Aegean, Cyprus, Syro-Palestine, Mesopotamia and the Baltic points to a trade in both luxury goods and essential raw materials, in exchange for which the Mycenaeans offered olive oil, aromatic oils, 'chariot kraters' decorated with scenes of horses, chariots, bulls and other animals, textiles, slaves and possibly the services of mercenary soldiers. They capitalized on the fall of Knossos in *c*.1425 BCE, and by the thirteenthth century BCE they had gained control of the eastern trade routes, and forged well-developed political links with Egypt and the Levant: an inscription found in Kom el Hatan may document an official diplomatic mission by emissaries of the pharaoh Amenhotep III (1390–1352 BCE), which visited, among other places, Phaistos, Mycenae, Thebes or Kato Zakro, Nauplion, Kythera, Troy and Knossos. Faience plaques with the cartouche of the same pharaoh were found at Mycenae.

Trying to discover what the Mycenaeans believed in, who their gods were, and how they worshipped them is fraught with difficulty. We know that they held processions, gathered at shrines, performed rituals, danced, made offerings and sacrifices, and perhaps induced religious hysteria with alcohol and opium, but we have no religious texts, myths or hymns to give us access to the beliefs themselves, and archaeologists have not for certain identified any true Mycenaean temple.

One name for a goddess (or goddesses) that appears quite often is Potnia, although usually qualified by epithets that make it hard to tell whether we are dealing with different goddesses or different facets of the same goddess. On one tablet she is called *a-ta-na po-*

ti-ni-ja (Athana Potnia), 'Mistress Athena', which appears in Homer, but in later Greek the fertility goddesses Demeter and Persephone were called 'the Potniai', and it may be that the Mycenaean Potnia was an Earth Mother goddess. The tablet also gives us the names of three other familiar Greek deities: *e-nu-wa-ri-jo* is Enualios, an alternative name for Ares; *pa-ja-wo* resembles Paieon, an alternative name for Apollo; and *po-se-da(o)*, Poseidon. Dionysos has also been tentatively identified, which would represent a serious challenge to the received wisdom that the Dionysos cult only began in Greece after the end of the Dark Age.

On the citadel of Mycenae is a Cult Centre, which is made up of several shrines on three levels. The Room with the Fresco is accessed via an ante-room, which contains a bath for ritual washing, an oval hearth, a bench-shaped altar with traces of ash, and a substantial altar painted with Minoan-style 'horns of consecration' and a socket that may have held a double axe. A fresco behind it shows a female worshipper/priestess/goddess with bunches of wheat and a griffin, while above them are two larger robed females facing each other (warrior goddesses?), one carrying a large sword and the other holding a spear/staff in salutation. Between them, two small male figures (worshippers?) appear to float in the air. Other rooms in the complex contained platforms, tables or altars (it is hard to tell these apart), bench altars, bowls, 'idols' and beads of glass paste, carnelian, amber, rock crystal and lapis lazuli. There was also a 'processional way'. But this is all we know: the finds are the only clues as to what happened in the rooms.

The Linear B tablets, however, refer to ceremonies such as the Spreading of the Couch, which is a common spring fertility ritual throughout the Near East, and to *di-pi-si-je-wi-jo*, probably the Festival for the Dead (*dipsioi* = the 'Thirsty Ones', a euphemism for the dead), rather like the Classical Athenian All Souls Day, which concluded the Anthesteria festival, where the new wine was broached. The Spreading of the Couch was the second part of the Anthesteria, and the first part, the Opening of the Jars, may have an equivalent in the tablet entry, 'new wine': this major Classical Athenian festival may go back at least to 1200 BCE.

Gold, wool, perfumed oil, barley, figs, flour, wine, olive oil and honey were acceptable offerings to the Mycenaean divinities, and so were cows, pigs, goats, sheep and wild boar. A painted stone *larnax* from Aghia Triada, dating from the period of Mycenaean rule in Crete, depicts men carrying two animals and what seems to be a model boat towards a standing figure in front of a small building with a 'horned' decoration on its roof and a tree beside it; women bring buckets; there are double axes with birds perching on them, and a basket of fruit or bread; musicians perform; two women ride in a horse-drawn chariot; others in elaborate headdresses are drawn in a chariot by winged griffins; a spotted ox is trussed up on an altar, with blood pouring out of its throat, while two goats await a similar fate. That much is clear, but the meaning and context is elusive.

The nature of the religious experience has been inferred from the 'Great Goddess' ring, which depicts a female (goddess? priestess?) seated under a tree, giving or receiving a bunch of poppy heads. Also present are two small females, a woman in a flounced skirt holding a bunch of lilies and other flowers, an upright double axe (which in Minoan Crete symbolized the Great Goddess), a weird figure-of-eight shield with a head, legs, arms and a sword, the Sun and Moon, and six animal heads. Quite what is going on in this possibly opium-fuelled scenario is utterly baffling.

More controversial still is a recent suggestion that human sacrifice may have occurred on occasion. A large tablet from Pylos, belonging to the last days before its destruction, could be listing offerings that included people:

> At Pylos, he consecrates (or sacrifices) at Sphagianes and he brings gifts and leads the *po-re-na* (= sacrificial victims?): to Potnia one Gold cup, one woman; . . .
> To Iphimedeia one Gold dish, to Dia one Gold dish, one woman;
> To Hermes Areias one Gold cup, one man . . .
> To Zeus one Gold dish, one man; to Hera one Gold dish, one woman.[12]

The interpretation depends partly on reading the otherwise unknown word *po-re-na* as 'sacrificial victims', since the deities are offered a gold vessel and a man or woman (women to goddesses; men to gods). This could merely be a reference to offering slaves to the deity as servants, or indeed simply to figurines, but those who want to see something more bloodthirsty cite the use of 'leads' rather than 'carries' as evidence for a genuine human sacrifice, perpetrated in a last desperate attempt to ward off the destruction of Pylos.

War, Peace, Art, Food, Alcohol and Drugs

If the Mycenaeans have acquired a reputation as great warriors, it is partly on the basis of their military hardware. One of the most interesting finds is the 'Dendra panoply', the earliest surviving complete suit of metal armour from Europe. This comprises a full corselet whose hammered bronze breast and back plates were hinged together on one side and custom-made to fit the wearer – a fairly narrow-shouldered man about 1.68 m tall. Three-part shoulder pieces were fitted to the body; a high collar protected his neck; and a skirt of three overlapping bronze plates covered his lower body. The suit was leather-lined and held together with rawhide thongs. It affords a high level of protection and flexibility to a warrior wielding a sword or a thrusting spear, and vividly brings to life both the Linear B ideograms of body armour and Homer's description of Hector as 'covered with bronze all over'.

The armour was accompanied by a pair of greaves, a wrist protector, and a Homeric-looking boar's tusk helmet with metal ear guards attached to a padded leather cap:

> and on the outer side the white teeth
> of a tusk-shining boar were close sewn one after another
> with craftsmanship and skill.[13]

Although an oddity for Homer, this seems to have been the helmet of choice for the Mycenaean warrior elite: the boar's tusk segments work like the ceramic plates in modern bullet-proof vests, but an adult wild boar is an exceedingly dangerous animal, and you need around fifty pairs of tusks to make one helmet. Hunting a helmet's-worth of boars indicates considerable martial prowess. The defensive armoury was completed by either a big rectangular 'tower shield' of raw ox hide stitched on to a wicker framework, so-called after the one that Aias wields in the *Iliad*,[14] which is as big as a wall, or a large 'figure of eight' type. So when Homer's Agamemnon wields two spears and a round shield, he is using (anachronistically) gear from the eighth century BCE.

When on the offensive, a Mycenaean fighter might use a 70 cm or more long rapier-like sword for cut-and-thrust fighting, until, in the second half of the fourteenth century BCE, a shorter blade with a double cutting edge used for slashing was introduced. Short daggers, sometimes superbly ornamented, were also used. Bronze-pointed heavy thrusting spears were essential items, too, and there is ample evidence for the use of the bow, with arrows tipped with flint, obsidian and bronze. Hundreds of two-horse chariots, whose cars had four-spoked wheels and a hide-covered wicker-framed body, are itemized on the Linear B tablets, along with the availability of spare parts. This is somewhat surprising, given that they are very unsuited to the Greek terrain: they were possibly deployed more as prestige transport for kings or nobles than as shock-troops on the battlefield. All this weaponry was extremely costly, so only a small number of warriors could have been heavily armed. Nevertheless, Mycenaean warriors may have hired them-selves out as mercenaries to foreign powers such as Egypt.

Naval forces were also deployed: at Pylos more than 600 rowers are listed on a group of tablets, which may record preparations for a naval operation big enough to man between 12 and 20 ships, although nowhere near the 90 that Nestor of Pylos led to Troy in Homer.

One glib comparison often made between the Minoans and the Mycenaeans is that the Minoans were a group of artistically gifted peaceniks, whereas the Mycenaeans were a bunch of warmongering philistines. This is simply not true. It is clear, for instance, that there was plenty of music to provide a soundtrack to Mycenaean life, played on seven-stringed lyres, or on the more professional four- or seven-stringed *phorminx,* which may have been the instrument of choice of bards to accompany their songs. The main wind instrument was the *aulos,* made from two tubes of cane, metal, wood, ivory or bone, each with either a single saxophone-type reed or a double reed like an oboe. For percussion, a *sistrum* gave tambourine-style effects.

There was a large-scale Mycenaean textile industry manu-facturing clothing from sheep and goat wool, linen, and also some silk. Fabrics, which were treated with oil to give them a slight lustre, were patterned and colourful, with dyes being extracted from animal, vegetable and mineral sources: saffron or onion skins create yellow; indigo makes blue; the murex shellfish gives purple, etc. The basic form of Mycenaean dress was a long tunic, belted at the waist, sometimes covered by a knitted shawl, but the most elaborate female outfit worked a look which channelled Minoan fashions. Coming on trend in *c.*1550 BCE, it comprised an underskirt that doesn't always show, a tiered wraparound skirt tied with a cord belt at the waist, and a tight short-sleeved bodice or bolero made of several pieces of material, decorated with intricately woven braid, and fastened under the bosom. It was drawn back to expose the breasts, but sewn together below to give a bit of uplift. Necklaces, bracelets, earrings, hairpins and ankle bracelets completed the ensemble. Males sometimes wore simple short-sleeved tunics, or pleated kilts, often with chequered braid on the fringe round the hem, and with a linen loincloth as underwear. Men of status are sometimes depicted wearing a long patterned or flounced ankle-length tunic. People might go barefoot, or wear leather boots.

Hairstyle seems to have been influenced by age, occupation and/or social status, as well as personal taste. Young boys and girls are depicted shaven-headed, with a ponytail and a characteristic lock of hair above the forehead. Around puberty, their hair might be allowed to grow short and curly with the forelock and ponytail, or be kept partly shaven with several uncut locks. On reaching puberty they were allowed to have a single lock, and grow their hair. Homer described the Greeks at Troy as long-haired, but mature Mycenaean males exhibit a variety of hair lengths, and appear both clean-shaven or with beards and optional moustaches.

All human life is present on the frescoes that adorned the walls of Mycenaean buildings: processional scenes; 'trophy paintings' to impress visitors or to symbolize victory in battle; pictures of bull leaping; horses and grooms with chariots; friezes of dogs and stag hunting; riddling sphinxes; and enigmatic cult scenes. However, the Mycenaeans seem to have been less interested in large-scale sculpture (the *stelai* from the Grave Circles, and the Lion Gate being notable exceptions), and there is relatively little sculpture in the round (although a stuccoed and painted female head, which has a strange rosette motif on the chin and each cheek is quite striking). Some fairly good-quality ivory work appears on the handles of weapons and mirrors, combs and cylindrical boxes, and as inlays on furniture, and there is also an exquisitely carved group depicting two women and a small child. On an even smaller scale, beads and seal-stones were made from gold, rock crystal, carnelian, agate, sardonyx, steatite and amethyst, or imported amber and lapis lazuli. Faience production techniques (firing a coloured glaze on to the surface of an unvitrified soft core) were probably picked up from Egypt, and true glass (often described 'glass paste') was moulded by Mycenaean artisans into beads and inlays.

Mycenaean ceramic ware was wheel-made and became so standardized that changes in fashion are easily discerned by the expert eye, allowing the establishment of an accurately dated sequence of developing shapes and motifs. There were *kraters* (mixing bowls) for preparing wine, jugs for pouring it, and extremely elegant cups with shallow delicate-handled bowls on top of high slender stems for drinking it. Storage containers ranged from *pithoi*, often more than 1.5 m high, to narrow-necked amphorae or 'stirrup-jars' – closed vases with a false mouth, and a separate spout beside it for pouring. This pottery was 'painted' with an iron-rich clay slip that turned into a glossy red or black during the firing. The decoration tended to be built up in parallel horizontal zones, and recurrent motifs, many of which show Minoan influence, including double axes, leaves, spirals, stylized flowers and shells, and vertical lines and zigzags. By c.1450 BCE the distinctly Mycenaean 'Palace Style' appeared, which recycled motifs from the Cretan Floral and Marine styles, but became so stylized that by the thirteenth century BCE the origin of the motifs was often unrecognizable. The 'octopus test' to distinguish between the vibrant octopi of the Marine Style and their practically abstract Palace Style counterparts is a good, if crude, way of identifying these styles. Pictorial decoration was not common and the most famous example is the Warrior Vase from the citadel at Mycenae, showing eleven almost Disneyesque warriors marching off to war.

The Mycenaeans were not averse to getting intoxicated, and the importation of resinated wine in Canaanite jars suggests a penchant for exotic Eastern flavours. Wine with herbs such as laurel, lavender and sage was popular, and a tripod cooking pot from Chania contained resinated wine with rue, a narcotic and stimulant: heady stuff indeed. Very weird to modern taste is a mixed fermented beverage made of wine, barley beer and honey mead that may have been regularly used in cult practice, and one of the oddest occurrences of this mixture is from a vessel probably used for feeding babies.

The terebinth resin that was sometimes added to wine might also have been used in medicines. Certainly plants like Cretan dittany, coriander, saffron, cumin, figs and myrtle were all used medicinally, and a Linear B tablet from Pylos that includes the word *pa-ma-ko* (Greek, *pharmaka* = 'drugs') has a reference to *e-pi-ka*, (Greek, *ibiskos* = 'tree mallow'/'hibiscus'), whose root is commonly used as a remedy for gastrointestinal disturbances and oral inflammations. Pins with bronze stems and crystal heads in the shape of poppy capsules have been found in both Grave Circles at Mycenae, and the production of opium latex by incising unripe poppy heads was definitely known around 1300 BCE. Raw opium is a powerful narcotic, analgesic and sedative, and may have been applied directly to wounds, or pieces of wool soaked in a solution of opium and saffron could have been used as suppositories to alleviate internal pain.

Rise and Fall

As Mycenaeans' power was moving on an upward trajectory, they were presented with an opportunity to take over the central position that Crete had enjoyed for so long, and they grabbed it. The majority of the Minoan Palaces were suddenly destroyed, along with Cretan naval supremacy, around 1425 BCE. The reason for this is unclear, although the Mycenaeans often get the blame. Yet the destruction on Crete appears to be much more comprehensive than would be needed to facilitate a political takeover: earthquake, insurrection, civil war, socio-economic collapse or some combination of these seems more likely.[15]

Although the Mycenaeans did not possess an 'Empire' in any meaningful sense, they did ultimately dominate the entire southern Aegean: from here on, Mycenaean pottery, not Minoan, is found in Egypt, Syria and Cyprus, and from *c.*1400 BCE onwards their fifty-oared ships were ferrying settlers to Crete, Rhodes and the Aegean coast of Anatolia. However, despite the Mycenaean presence on Crete, indigenous religious traditions there seem to have carried on much as they had before, and indeed a bull-leaping fresco at Mycenae, probably dating from a time when there were Minoan frescoes still available to copy on Crete, shows that the cultural influence was not entirely one-way.

The Palace of Minos at Knossos remained in use for at least two or three generations, and maybe for a lot longer, until it was again destroyed by fire in c.1370 BCE, c.1190 BCE or even later. There has been scholarly dispute about this, with a ferocity inversely proportional to its conclusiveness, for more than seventy-five years. One current focus of the debate concerns whether Knossos remained the principal centre of the island after c.1370, or whether Chania (ancient Kydonia) in western Crete took over. The Post-Palatial period, c.1370/?1190–c.1000 BCE, takes us to the end of the Bronze Age and the beginning of the transition to the Classical period. Throughout the Aegean many sites were abandoned or destroyed in the LM III B pottery phase (c.1190), with the Linear B documents recording the very last year of the economic administration. There were troubles on the mainland at this time, but what form they took in Crete is uncertain, although refugees from the mainland are a likely factor.

A highly distinctive painting from this era is 'La Parisienne', an elegant Minoan/Mycenaean lady with large eyes, curly hair, red lips and a retroussé nose, who has a knot binding her hair at the nape of her neck, which many scholars regard as 'sacred', possibly an apotropaic device and/or a symbol of a Minoan goddess. Her less elite counterparts who 'inhabited' the cemetery at Armenoi on Crete in the LM III period give us an indication of how precarious her life might have been: 34 per cent of the children died before reaching the age of 2, and 57 per cent before they were age 5; she could expect to live to about 28 years old, with 20–25 being the most dangerous (childbearing) time. Average female height was around 1.55 m, and dental health was very problematic, involving cavities (which indicate a diet rich in carbohydrates), disruption in the formation of the enamel caused by nutritional deficiencies or infectious disease, gum infections and plaque, although a woman in Tomb 132 did practise dental hygiene to eradicate the latter. Such women also had a range of diseases to contend with, including osteomyelitis (inflamation of the bone marrow), brucellosis (transmitted to humans through bacteria in goats' milk), TB (contracted through infected cows' milk), osteoporosis, scurvy, rickets and anaemia caused by iron deficiency. Cancer was a potential risk, too. However, they probably led an active lifestyle and had a good knowledge of orthopaedic techniques, so were able to take care of injuries such as bone fractures.

The woman in Tomb 132's male counterpart could expect to live three years longer on average. There is no indication of her actual partner's cause of death, but he was aged between 35 and 50, stood 1.68 m tall, and suffered from osteoarthritis in a way that suggests he put continual stress on his back and neck. His teeth were a real mess, too: he had lost twenty-three of them, and the nine that were left were absolutely riddled with cavities and showed extreme variations in their patterns of wear, indicating that he might have been using them as tools, very possibly during a lifetime spent as a weaver.

Henry Miller pertinently wrote that Mycenae 'wears an impenetrable air: it is grim, lovely, seductive and repellent. What happened here is beyond all conjecture.'[16] And so it is. Quite how and why the Mycenaean civilization disintegrated in the twelfth century BCE is still a mystery. The enormous efforts devoted to Mycenae's walls in the thirteenth century BCE were replicated at Tiryns and Athens, and Linear B tablets from the Pylos refer to 800 men being sent to the coast, perhaps to guard against seaborne aggressors. Yet much of this was to no avail. By about 1200 BCE the key political and economic centres, such as Mycenae, Tiryns, Pylos, Thebes, Orkhomenos and Gla (although probably not Athens), had suffered destruction by fire and the sea-routes were disrupted. Archaeological chronology can have a tendency to make things look more sudden than they were: 'only fifty years' is a long time to people who routinely died aged twenty-eight, and many of the changes were gradual and cumulative. Nevertheless, many sites never recovered even a glimmer of their former significance, and there is nothing to show who or what was responsible.

One of the most commonly regurgitated theories is that of the Dorian Invasion. Yet although Greek myth talks of 'the Return of the Heraklids', in which the Dorians and the descendants of Herakles made themselves masters of the Peloponnese eighty years after the Trojan War, the ancient historical sources give no impression of any single migration of large numbers of people, and the very concept of the 'return' of the Heraklids implies that they were not alien intruders. Furthermore, the argument that the Doric dialect was introduced to Greece by incomers after the fall of the palaces is currently countered in terms of the East Greek dialects (Attic-Ionic, Aeolic and Arcado-Cypriot) being related to that of the Palace rulers, with Doric and North West Greek being the dialect of the lower classes. An invasion significant enough to overwhelm the Mycenaeans would also have left clear-cut archaeological evidence from a very specific date and with a geographically traceable itinerary. None of this exists. In fact, the archaeology shows that Mycenaeans continued to live in the ruins of their palaces, and the whole concept of a 'Dorian Invasion' is now widely regarded as untenable.

So was it an 'archaeologically invisible' enemy, who only left evidence of destruction? There was a dramatic depopulation at the end of the Mycenaean period, which might suggest a diaspora rather than an influx of newcomers. The 'Sea Peoples' – seaborne warriors of very vague identity – caused havoc in the eastern Mediterranean in the late thirteenth and early twelfth centuries BCE, until Ramses III of Egypt crushed them in 1191 BCE. Pylos had worries about a threat from the sea, even though Pylos itself is a good way from the eastern Mediterranean and there is no evidence to implicate the Sea Peoples in sacking it. The Mycenaeans, however, do not seem to have felt the same unease.

Might the troubles have been internal? Greek mythology is replete with tales of domestic turmoil, notably the murder of Agamemnon at Mycenae, and the near takeover of Odysseus' realm by Penelope's suitors. But myth is not history, and again the archaeology is silent or inconclusive. It would undoubtedly be easier for, say, an oppressed substratum of society to bring down a fortress such as Mycenae or Tiryns from within rather than from without, and this would leave fewer traces, but the theory is as speculative as it is attractive, and the destructions may have resulted from different causes in different places.

Climate change is a modern preoccupation that is sometimes brought into the discussion, but pollen evidence shows no sign of extreme climatic changes, and the tablets of Pylos present a picture of prosperous arable and pastoral activity. Another environmental theory blames overexploitation of land by the palace bureaucracies, thus leaving the kingdoms trying to support a much bigger population than the land could sustain, and hence very vulnerable to even a short period of drought. But the Linear B tablets show sign of neither drought nor famine.

There is evidence for a mighty earthquake at the end of the thirteenth century, but the 'apocalypse' theory of an enormous seismic event taking out Mycenae, Tiryns and Pylos all at the same instant is unconvincing: Pylos is really too far from Mycenae for them both to have been destroyed like this, and, when the Minoans on Crete suffered similar tragedies, they bounced back, built more luxurious palaces, and went from strength to strength. A variant seismic theory goes for an 'earthquake storm', such as has affected Turkey in recent decades, with one earthquake triggering another along the tectonic lines and destroying the palaces piecemeal; other speculation focuses on water, since seismic movements can frequently block-up springs, which to a citadel such as Mycenae would have been as catastrophic as the demolition of its walls. These are all interesting, but unproven. The temptation to look for the single 'smoking gun' is always great, but the reality is probably far less dramatic: Mycenaean civilization went out with a whimper, not a bang.

Around 1100 BCE, this great Bronze Age people finally merged into what is conventionally called the Dark Age. Yet it was not entirely gloomy: the Greeks progressed from the Bronze Age to the Iron Age; and though the art of writing, now redundant with the demise of the bureaucracy, disappeared from the Greek world, and without writing there is no history, there was still poetry. The Irish have a saying that a writer is a failed talker, and within that illiterate context emerged the finest poetic works that Greece produced: the poems of Homer.

3

TROY: THE GREAT ADVERSARY?

[A] divine race of heroes of whom part were destroyed by evil war
and dread battle, some beneath the gates of seven-gated Thebes . . .
others at Troy whither they were borne on ships over the great
gulf of the sea.

Hesiod, *Works and Days* 161f.

The Mythology of Troy's Foundation

At the heart of Homer's poetry lies Troy, the mighty city that
Achilles fights against in the *Iliad* and Odysseus returns from in
the *Odyssey*. The mythical Trojans traced their ancestry back to
Dardanos, who founded Dardania (or Dardanos) in the foothills of
Mount Ida. His grandson Tros eventually inherited the kingdom
and called the region *Troia* or *Tro(i)as* ('the Troad') – the part of
present-day Turkey close to the Dardanelles (also named after
Dardanos). Of Tros' three sons, Ganymede was taken by the gods
to be Zeus' wine-pourer;[1] Assaracus was the grandfather of
Anchises, who had an affair with Aphrodite, who gave birth to
Aeneas; and Ilos went to Phrygia, which is close to the Troad, and
took part in some games where, in addition to his prize for winning
the wrestling, he received a dappled cow and instructions to found
a city in the place where the animal lay down. The beast reclined at
the Hill of Ate (Delusion) in Phrygia, and here Ilos built his city. He
called it *Ilion*, which is the normal designation (earlier *Wilion*), not
'Troy', although its inhabitants are *Troes* (Trojans).

Ilos was the father of the Trojan king Laomedon. In mythology,
the walls of Ilion were erected for Laomedon by Poseidon and

Apollo, along with the mortal Aiakos, whose involvement was crucial, since with only immortal builders the walls would have been impregnable. In Laomedon's reign, Ilion was captured by Herakles, after which Podarkes, later called Priam, ascended the throne. By his wife Hekabe (Hecuba) he had a prodigious series of sons (nineteen of his fifty sons were by her) and beautiful daughters, including Hector, Paris and Cassandra. Priam reigned during the Trojan War.

The Quest for Homer's Troy

That is all mythology, but, for the Greeks, the Trojan War was an historical event the end of which was dated to 1334/3 BCE (Douris), c.1250 BCE (Herodotus), 5 June 1209 BCE (the Parian Marble), or 1184 BCE (Eratosthenes), and Homer's Troy came to be identified with the ruins of a citadel in the Troad, located 6 km east of the Aegean coast and 4.5 km south of the Dardanelles. This entire area had been settled by Aeolian Greeks from about 800 BCE onwards. However, the fact that the Classical Greeks and Romans *called* it Ilion did not necessarily mean that it *was* the site of Homer's Troy. In any case, in the sixth century CE the site was abandoned and, when the region finally came under Turkish rule, the smallish hill on which the citadel had stood came to be known as Hisarlık = 'furnished with a citadel'.

The Homeric memories persisted: the Anglo-Saxon pilgrim Sæwulf had the 'very ancient and famous city of Troy' pointed out to him; peripatetic Renaissance antiquary Cyriac of Ancona walked the Trojan plain in 1444 CE, and when he set sail for Imbros and saw Samothrace peeping over the top just as Homer says, he remembered the passage in the *Iliad* where Poseidon watches the fighting from the 'top of the highest summit of timbered Samothrace'. For him, this proved that Homer had told the truth. When Constantinople fell to the Turks in 1453 CE, followed by much of Greece, Mehmet II the Conqueror visited the site and reputedly said: 'It is to me that Allah has given to avenge this city and its people: I have overcome their enemies.'

The first real scholarly attempts to pin down the exact location of the events of the *Iliad* began in the eighteenth century: Robert Wood's *Essay . . . on the Original Genius of Homer* (1769) established the premise that the location of Troy and the historicity of the

Trojan War could be determined by field research; in a lecture to the Royal Society of Edinburgh in 1791, Jean Baptiste Lechevalier argued that the Trojan War was historical fact; Jacob Bryant retorted by denying that the war had taken place and asserting that Troy had never existed. Those opinions pretty much encompass the scholarly positions of today.

Byron was a true believer:

> I've stood upon Achilles' tomb,
> And heard Troy doubted; time will doubt of Rome.[2]

In his diary for 11 January 1821 Byron wrote:

> We *do* care about the authenticity of the tale of Troy . . . I venerate the grand original as *the truth of history* . . . and of place; otherwise it would have given me no delight.[3]

It also mattered to Frank Calvert (1828–1908), who began to excavate at Hisarlık in 1863. The British Museum considered sending him £100 for preliminary work, but dithered and lost the opportunity. The man who stole the glory was Heinrich Schliemann, who obtained permission to excavate, and exploited his personal fortune to do so. His first campaign at Hisarlık began in April 1870, and his hunch that Priam's Troy was to be found there seemed to be corroborated by his finds of impressive masonry and, thanks to the alleged help of his beautiful Greek wife Sophia, fabulous jewellery:

> In the name of divine Homer, I baptise (this sacred locality) with that name of immortal renown, which fills the heart of everyone with joy and enthusiasm: I give it the name of TROY and ILIUM.[4]

These finds made him an international celebrity.

Schliemann initially thought he had discovered five prehistoric forts/settlements and, contrary to what is now standard archaeological practice, he numbered them I to V, from the bottom (oldest) up. Above these prehistoric settlements, he identified two more, one Greek, one Roman, from the historical period. In 1882 Schliemann was joined by the great excavator Wilhelm Dörpfeld, who was able to discern nine major levels. These were dubbed 'Troy I' (the oldest) through to 'Troy IX'. Dörpfeld continued to work for two seasons after Schliemann's death, supported financially by Sophia.

American archaeologists from the University of Cincinnati resumed excavations between 1932 and 1938, under the direction of Carl Blegen. He maintained the essence of Dörpfeld's nine layers, but refined them into more than forty different strata (e.g. Troy IIId, VIh, etc.). The main building material – dried mud bricks – had a limited life, and needed constant renovation. Old structures were levelled and new ones were built on top of them, so a man-made mound arose, expanding both vertically and horizontally. Blegen was both an excellent archaeologist and a committed 'Homerist':

> It can no longer be doubted . . . that there really was an actual historical Trojan War, in which a coalition of Achaeans, or Mycenaeans, under a king whose overlordship was recognized, fought against the people of Troy and their allies.[5]

The most recent excavations have been carried out since 1988 by an international team, initially directed by Manfred Korfmann from the University of Tübingen, and, after his death in 2005, by Ernst Pernicka. The 'Troia Projekt' is a multidisciplinary venture financed by state and private funding, but its excavations have generated considerable controversy and criticism, particularly as Korfmann believed that Homeric tradition reflected a specific historical event.

From Foundation to Destruction: Myth and Archaeology

Troy's oldest three levels comprise what Korfmann christened the 'Trojan Maritime Culture' (2920–2200 BCE[6]), which spread into both the Aegean and the Sea of Marmara, and whose commercial and cultural influence can be discerned as far as Malta, Bulgaria, Asia Minor and Afghanistan. Troy I (2920–2350 BCE[7]) was less than 100 m across, fortified by a wall approximately 2.5 m thick (renovated several times), containing the foundations of spacious 'long-houses', with some fine herringbone masonry (in which alternating stone courses are set in opposing diagonals), and one outstanding structure of the 'megaron' type: one long rectangular room, with a hearth at the centre, and a forecourt created by extending the long side walls. Troy I's economic life was built on animal husbandry, agriculture, trade, fishing, hunting and weaving. The cemetery has not been located, but infant burials were found beneath house floors. The settlement was ultimately destroyed by fire.

Troy II (*c.*2550–2250[8]), which contained seven different levels (Troy IIa to IIg), began its existence about the same time as Babylon. The citadel is 125 m in diameter, surrounded by a 6 m high stone wall surmounted by a mud brick superstructure, and accessed via two monumental main gates, one of which was approached by a ramp paved with limestone slabs. Inside was a complex of courtyards and large buildings, dominated by the Great Megaron, a columned rectangular building with a central hearth that was entered via an open portico, which gives the impression that the citadel was the preserve of a powerful and wealthy elite. Outside the citadel lay a lower city of about 90,000 square metres, possibly surrounded by a wooden palisade the foundations of which are preserved as a negative impression cut into bedrock near one of the gates.

The economy was similar to Troy I's, although with further-flung trading partners. The development of the potter's wheel led to the manufacture of new ceramic forms, including tall drinking vessels with big double handles and round bases like the *depas amphikypellon* of Homer,[9] and we see the first use of bronze. An abundance of sheep and goat bones, spindle whorls and traces of a loom indicate wool production, which the Trojans may have grown rich on, because more than twenty 'treasures', including what Schliemann called 'The Treasure of Priam', were unearthed in Troy II. These comprise weapons, ornaments of gold and electrum, various silver, copper and bronze finds, and the iconic 'Jewels of Helen' that were worn in a famous photograph by Sophia Schliemann: earrings, a golden diadem and other jewels from the hoard that Schliemann claimed to have found on 31 May 1873, which are now mainly displayed in the Pushkin Musem in Moscow. There are those who doubt whether the Treasure of Priam is authentic, and certainly Schliemann's claim that Sophia was at his side when he made the discovery is bogus: we know that she was in Greece at the time. However, the general consensus is that the hoard is probably genuine.

The reason why so much treasure was deliberately buried seems to be fear. Troy II was destroyed in a fire that left a 2 m-deep layer of ashen remains. Schliemann calculated: treasure + impressive monuments + conflagration = Homer's Troy. Yet this proved to be a premature conclusion. Firstly, we do not know what, or who, caused the destruction, although in around 2300 BCE various parts of Anatolia were undergoing traumatic events. But if alien 'sackers of cities' (as Odysseus is called) perpetrated this violence, we need to explain why the inventory of finds of Troy III (2250–2200 BCE[10]) generally resembles those of Troy II, indicating cultural continuity. Did the people who sacked the city just move on? Did they mingle with the original inhabitants and assimilate their culture? Were they from the same region and culture? The fortification wall of Troy II was probably reused, and the structures on the citadel grew smaller and more numerous during Troy III, which implies that many people lived within the walls and that the citadel was no longer the preserve of an elite ruling class. Does this indicate that the destruction was linked to local regime change? If Troy's destruction was due to a natural disaster from which the population fled, later to return, why was the treasure not retrieved? We can but speculate.

Secondly, Troy II is about 1,000 years too old to be Priam's Troy. At this period there were no 'Greeks' in Greece[11] to launch an assault from Mycenae as described in the *Iliad*. Schliemann probably (and reluctantly) came to accept this just before he died. Dörpfeld persuaded him that there was a better candidate in a more recent level, which would fit the chronology and the archaeology much better.

Troy III also ended in fiery destruction, and it could be that some of the 'treasures' belonged to this period, but this level seldom enters the running to be Priam's Troy, and neither do Troy IV and V (*c*.2200–1740/30 BCE[12]). The settlement became something of an isolated, insignificant backwater in a period that saw the emergence of new forces in the Near East, notably the Hittites. Its living conditions were irregular and quite crowded, and it was eventually destroyed in another serious fire. However, this marked the start of a new era; the most celebrated phase of its history was about to happen.

Troy VI (1740/30–1300 BCE[13]) really represents the zenith of Troy. A new fortress, with a cultural layer of 5–6 m deep and eight sub-phases (Troy VIa-h[14]), now surrounds a much larger settlement. The fortification walls, constructed by expert masons, have a slight glacis on the exterior, vertical interior faces, and are made from beautifully laid limestone ashlar blocks (without mortar) that form one solid mass, like in an Egyptian pyramid. The walls are divided into sections by distinctive vertical offsets, the function of which is enigmatic, and they are mighty: more than 4 m thick, up to 9 m high in places, originally surmounted by a mud-brick superstructure, and with impressive projecting towers, particularly near the major gates. Tower VIg also enclosed a 10 m deep artesian well or cistern. The gates themselves were well fortified, and at the main gate in the south a drain runs down the centre of the road under the pavement.

Inside the walls, independent buildings were constructed on rings of concentric terraces going up towards the city centre. No identifiable palace survives, but the foundations of houses reveal large, rectangular structures: some are of the *megaron* type; the 'Pillar House' (27 × 12.5 m) had two large pillars in its main room, presumably supporting a second storey; House VI F preserves evidence for half-timbering, and traces of an interior stairway suggest it had two storeys; and House VI M has an L-shaped plan with an open court occupying the space between its two wings. Extensive storage provision on the ground floor of many of the houses implies that the residential areas were on the upper floor.

Archaeological campaigns at Hisarlık have also focused on the area beyond Troy's citadel wall, with interesting results. A cemetery revealed more than 180 cremation urns dating to Troy VIh, most of which contained the remains of more than one individual, sometimes adults and children together. The grave goods were generally poor, which might indicate lowly social status or reflect a massive burial programme for large numbers of victims of the earthquake that shattered Troy VIh, to stop the bodies becoming a source of disease. On the other hand, this might have been the normal mode of burial.

Geomagnetic imaging has shown that Troy VI was surrounded by quite an extensive settlement, leading Korfmann to estimate a population of between 4,000 and 10,000. A wide U-shaped ditch cut into the bedrock was found about 450 m outside the citadel, and parts of a second ditch 150 m beyond that, which Korfmann interpreted as defences against chariot attacks. This is pure guesswork, however, and others argue that they might be part of a water drainage and reservoir system. There is certainly a water cave dating back to the third millennium, with underground tunnels extending some 160 m in length, which served Troy VI. Korfmann identified this with the 'subterranean passageway' of the god KASAL.KUR, who was invoked to witness a treaty sworn between the Hittite king Muwattalli II and King Alaksandu of Wilusa (c.1280 BCE). Korfmann's critics dismissed the proposed fortification system and suggest he has overestimated the site's significance and extent. Many think he has been too imaginative in his reconstruction, aiming for spectacular 'results'. However, arguing that the original fortress of Troy VI would be the royal citadel, with a lower settlement attached, is eminently reasonable.

Troy's economic power came from intensive trade with Central Anatolia (the Hittites), and with the Mycenaean cities of continental Greece, the Aegean islands and Cyprus, besides sustenance through agriculture, animal husbandry and weaving. Artefacts made of gold, electrum, bronze and lead, although relatively scanty, are good quality; the textile industry was thriving; ivory now appears in quantity; intensive use of horses occurs for the first time, giving echoes of Homer's description of the Trojans as 'tamers of horses' to those who want to hear them; and standing stones (*menhirs*) in front of Tower VIi have tempted some to postulate a cult involving pillars and columns (or *baetyls*) on the Minoan model.

The pottery remains are fascinating: ninety of the ninety-eight different shapes identified are new, indicating a definite break in the cultural tradition. A highly distinctive, lustrous wheel-made pottery called 'Grey Minyan Ware' now appears. It gets its name from its resemblance to the Grey Minyan pottery of Middle Helladic (MH) Greece, but the two should not be confused: Troy's 'Grey Minyan' is a local ware; the shape ranges of the two types are very different; and MH Grey Minyan pre-dates Troy VI. Nevertheless, the interchange of pottery between Troy and the Mycenaeans provides crucial information for establishing chronology: pottery from the southern Aegean begins to appear in Troy VIb; Mycenaean Late Helladic I (LH I) pottery begins in Troy VId; and in Mycenaean terms, the destruction of Troy VI happened during the LH IIIB period – just after c.1300 BCE.

So Troy VI coincides with Mycenaean culture in a way that Troy II does not. Could this be the city that Agamemnon sacked? Dörpfeld persuaded Schliemann that it was, and this settlement has become known as 'the Homeric city', although we must be aware that this convention prejudges the issue: conclusive evidence as to whether or not the Mycenaeans attacked Troy at all, let alone in a single operation, is lacking in the evidence so far. The walls were destroyed at the end of Troy VIh by what many authorities think was a massive earthquake, but there are no convincing signs of a general conflagration,[15] and, although aspects of Troy VI certainly match Homer's descriptions, so can the Hittite acropolis of Hattusa, and the citadels of Mycenae and Tiryns. Neither are these architectural features confined to the Late Bronze Age: Homer's description might dovetail with Troy VI, but it is still a poetic vision of what the city *might* have looked like.

Another fundamental question is: 'Who were the Trojans anyway?' In Greek literature from Homer to the fifth century BCE we see no ethnic or cultural opposition between Greeks and Trojans. Both sides worship the same gods and speak Greek, and it is only after the Persian invasions of Greece that Troy started to acquire an incredibly negative image and the Trojans came to personify generic barbarism. Historically speaking, Homer was wrong: Troy was only ever a relatively minor player in a world dominated by the superpowers of Assyria, Babylonia, Egypt and the Hittites. As the Hittites expanded their influence in *c.*1400 BCE, they imposed vassal status on several western kingdoms, and letters and treaties show that they had contact with Troy.

Schliemann took the swastika motifs that he found on artefacts from Troy as proof that the Trojans belonged to the Aryan race. The rather chilling overtones of this observation have to be taken in context: 'Aryan', derived from Sanskrit *arya* (= noble), was used in the nineteenth century as a synonym for what we now call 'Indo-European', and during the Early Bronze Age quite a lot of Indo-European speaking newcomers arrived in Anatolia, including the Hittites and the Luwians.

Because Troy VI shows a major break with the preceding culture, it has been suggested that the Luwians took it over. The earliest written document from Troy is a seal written in Luwian hieroglyphics found in level VIIb1, but this does not prove that the

Trojans spoke Luwian: it was the language of the Hittite political elite, and just because the seal was found at Troy does not prove that it came from there – seals are portable. The kingdom of Troy may have been created by a dynasty of Luwian ethnic origin ruling a multi-ethnic population, but, if Luwian was Troy's official language, Homer's identikit Greeks and Trojans start to look like a literary construct: in reality their languages were probably mutually unintelligible.

The term 'Luwiya' was ultimately replaced in the Hittite texts by 'Arzawa', and these Arzawa lands became Hittite vassal states. The records of the Hittite king Tudhalija I, who ruled during the Troy VI phase (although not during Troy VIh, the destruction level), mention hostilities with places that could have Homeric relevance: the land of Wilusiya and the land of Taruisa. Wilusiya features in the Hittite archives as a western Anatolian Arzawan kingdom. Could it be (W)ilion, the Ilios of Homer? 'Taruisa' might be pronounced Taruwisa, Tarwisa, Truisa or Troisa. Could this be Troia, Troy? Not if the normal rules of Greek phonology apply, but the juxtaposition of Wilusiya and Taruisa is certainly enticing, although possibly coincidental, and some academics see it as evidence that Troy was the capital of the Arzawan kingdom called Wilusiya in the Troad.

The last level that has a bearing on the Homer debate is Troy VII (1300–950 BCE[16]). The finds from sub-level Troy VIIa are almost indistinguishable from those of Troy VIh, implying that Troy VIIa's inhabitants survived the earthquake that levelled Troy VIh. Remains of houses outside the walls also show that a lower city still extended beyond the citadel just as it had in Troy VI. The fortifications themselves were reconstructed, protecting water supplies consisting of a well in a paved courtyard and the refurbished cistern/well in Tower VIg.

Some of Troy VI's houses were reused, but many were simply built over by far more densely packed, irregularly planned, one-storey, multi-roomed structures. The floors of many houses contain pits for large storage *pithoi*, and the excavators have argued that this indicates a population preparing itself to face some external threat. But this could be as much down to a radical decrease in floor space of the average Trojan dwelling as evidence for a Homeric siege, and the encroachment of common dwellings into the citadel might equally indicate that the ruling elite had been ousted in a revolution.

The Mycenaean palaces on the Greek mainland cease to function around this time, and contemporary Hittite texts also indicate local uprisings in the area.

The date of Troy VIIa's destruction lies between 1250 and 1180 BCE, with the latter being the more likely on the basis of LH IIIC Mycenaean sherds in its ruins. For those who seek to make the Trojan War of Greek myth into an historical event, Troy VIIa is a good bet as it perished in a general conflagration. In addition, all the postulated preparations for siege had failed; there are a few spearheads and arrowheads embedded in the walls, plus some mutilated skeletons that were not found in burial contexts. Finally, Troy VIIa imported far less Mycenaean pottery. Might this mean that the assailants were Mycenaeans? Possibly, but the quantity of Mycenaean ceramic imports was diminishing elsewhere, which may signify a more general decline in Mycenaean trade: this hypothetical slump is as likely as a hypothetical siege as an explanation for the dearth of Mycenaean imports.

Furthermore, if the dating of the LH IIIC sherds is correct, then Troy VIIa's destruction was practically coeval with that of the Mycenaean palaces, when the Mycenaeans would have had problems assembling a coalition of the sort described by Homer. Unless, that is, the Mycenaean destructions occurred in the absence of large numbers of potential defenders who were away besieging Troy. But many other cities apart from Troy fell in Anatolia, possibly at the hands of the so-called Sea Peoples. It has been mooted that displaced Mycenaeans might have been among the Sea Peoples, but there is no proof of this. And, at the end of the day, Troy VIIa is a patched-up, earthquake-damaged city in economic decline: it does not look like a home for heroes.

The contemporary Hittite documents, however, do provide further exquisite teases for the 'Homerists'. One comes from King Muwattalli II (1296–1272 BCE = Troy VIIa):

> I, My Majesty, will not abandon you . . . and I will kill the enemy on your behalf. If your brother or someone of your family withdraws political support from you, Alaksandu . . . and they seek the kingship of the land of Wilusa, I, My Majesty, will absolutely not discard you, Alaksandu.[17]

Could Alaksandu = Alexandros, the alternative name of Paris? Another document from Muwattalli II mentions a bandit called Piyamaradu (= Priam?) and Wilusa on the same tablet. It tells how Gassus, the Hittite commander, arrived with his Hittite troops:

> [And whe]n [they . . .] set out again(?) to the country of Wilusa in order to attack (it), [I, howe]ver, became ill. I am seriously ill, illness holds me [pro]strated.
> [*A paragraph divider occurs here*]
> When [Piyam]aradu had humiliated me, he set Atpa [agai]nst me(?)[18]

However, it is not clear that the Hittite troops were in the area to liberate Wilusa from Piyamaradu, and the paragraph divider may indicate that his activities had nothing whatsoever to do with Wilusa. Even if the mythical tradition has preserved the name of a genuine ruler of Troy, it does not confirm the historicity of the *Iliad.*

Another aspect of this debate concerns the fact that Homer's Greeks are called *Akhaioi* ('Achaeans'). Some Hittite texts refer to a place called *Ahhiyawa* (with an earlier form *Ahhiya*), which is phonetically close (although not necessarily identical) to 'Achaea/Akhaia'. Hattusili III (1265–1240 BCE), and Tudhalija IV (1240–1215 BCE) called the kings of Ahhiyawa 'Great Kings', as they did the rulers of Babylon, Syria and Egypt. We know from the 'Tawagalawa Letter' to the King of Ahhiyawa that Hattusili III was involved in a dispute with Ahhiyawa concerning Wilusa around 1250 BCE. Piyamaradu had turned to insurgency, operating out of Millawanda (Miletus?), which was under the indirect control of the King of Ahhiyawa. Hattusili wanted the King of Ahhiyawa to hand over Piyamaradu, and notes that the people he was harassing had already appealed to Tawagalawa ('Eteokles'?), the King of Ahhiyawa's brother.

> Tell Piyamaradu that in the matter of Wilusa over which we were at enmity, he has changed my mind and we have made friends . . . for war is wrong for us [*Later he says*] Now we [i.e. Hattusili and the King of Ahhiyawa] have reached agreement on the matter of Wilusa over which we fought. [19]

This might suggest that the Hittites fought with Ahhiyawan (Mycenaean) aggressors over Troy, but alternatively this could just have been a diplomatic crisis, or the fighting might have been about the control of Wilusa without the city being directly involved in the fighting. Whatever the case, this falls woefully short of anything resembling a conflict on a Homeric scale, and the theory remains unproved.

There probably was a war at Troy; whether or not it was *the* Trojan War is an open question. The archaeological evidence does not tell us that the attackers were Mycenaeans, and may well imply that they were not. The fact that 'Coarse Ware' pottery (*Buckelkeramik*), which is closely related to pottery that appears in more-or-less contemporary contexts at sites in Greece, appears immediately after the destruction of Troy VIIa, may identify the sackers of Troy VIIa as coming from the Danube region. However, the trouble with this theory is that the quantities of *Buckelkeramik* are relatively small, and otherwise there is cultural continuity between Troy VIIa and VIIb1.

Frustratingly, literary evidence is almost entirely non-existent. The first evidence for writing that we have comes from Troy VIIb1: a lentoid bronze seal in Luwian hieroglyphics, with the name of a male scribe on one side and the name of a female on the other. Such seals were used by kings and bureaucrats throughout the Hittite empire and its vassal states, and it has now become the logo of the Troia Projekt.

The cause of the end of Troy VIIb1 is another unsolved mystery. There is no sign of any general destruction preceding Troy VIIb2, although this settlement, in its turn, was probably destroyed in a conflagration after a century or less of occupation, *c*.950 BCE.

A hiatus followed. Aeolian Greeks occupied the site in the late eighth century BCE, roughly when Homer's epics were being committed to writing. The preceding oral tradition is less interested in recording historical fact than in presenting a version of the past that legitimizes the present. In that context, the tale of the Trojan War justified Greek military movements into Asia Minor – it was a 'Just War', and therefore became a crucial tale for Greek colonists moving into the region. If the Trojan War was an historical event (and Herodotus makes the telling point that Priam would never have risked the devastation of his kingdom, family or people for the sake of a female foreigner), and if Hisarlık was the site of this conflict, then the bards who sang about it between c.950 and 750 BCE could only have known an unimposing heap of rubble there. Homer clearly knew the Trojan topography pretty well, except that the Bronze Age coastline had altered significantly by his time, and his understanding of the Mycenaean world is sketchy.

So if we want to argue for the historicity of the Trojan War, we must prove when and where it happened, and that Mycenaeans were the aggressors. There are many places where Mycenaeans might have made pirate raids, and various scholars want the Trojan War to be a conflation of these activities. Others separate Troy from Hisarlık altogether, and locate it, for instance, in northern Greece, Egypt, Karatepe in south-east Turkey, or even in Britain, just outside Cambridge. Essentially, belief or disbelief in the historicity of the Trojan War seems like a leap of faith.

The great classicist Moses Finley concluded that 'we are confronted with this paradox that the more we know, the worse off we are', and argued that 'Homer's Trojan War must be evicted from the history of the Greek Bronze Age'.[20] Peter Jones made the apt analogy of someone reading a James Bond novel 3,000 years from now, finding that Dunhill, Martini, White's and Boodles all actually existed, and concluding that *You Only Live Twice* was history.[21] The *Iliad* portrays what Homer *thought* the heroic world should look like, and in the end Troy's magic is nothing to do with 'history', but all about a great poet's imagination. At the conclusion of Euripides' tragedy *Trojan Women*, the women call out to Troy:

Soon you will fall and lie
With the earth you loved, and none shall name you! . . .
All has vanished, and Troy is nothing![22]

Not so. Troy has not vanished; Troy is not nothing.

4

THE WORLD OF GREEK MYTH AND EPIC: HOMER'S *ILIAD* AND *ODYSSEY*

Nothing the peoples of Europe have produced is worth the first known poem that appeared among them. Perhaps they will yet discover the epic genius, when they learn that there is no refuge from fate, learn not to admire force, not to hate the enemy, nor to scorn the unfortunate.

Simone Weil, *L'Iliade ou la Poème de la Force*, 37[1]

Homer's *Iliad: The Wrath of Achilles*

The Greeks placed the epic poem at the head of their hierarchy of genres, with Homer as its premier exponent. And rightly so: Homer's *Iliad* and the *Odyssey* represent our first meaningful examples of European poetry, and they justifiably enjoy unparalleled respect. However, we don't know precisely who 'Homer' was, where he (or she) came from, whether he wrote both poems, or indeed whether each poem was written by just one author, although it is likely that the *Iliad* was committed to writing maybe around 750 BCE and the *Odyssey* some 25 years later.

Nor can we tell whether Homer physically wrote the poems or dictated them to scribes, or whether they were memorized by 'rhapsodes' (public reciters) and transcribed later. It is generally agreed, however, that, the Greek alphabet, adapted from the Phoenician alphabet during the eighth century BCE, was developed at just the right time. Prior to that, the poems had been passed on by illiterate oral bards, operating in a tradition that goes back generations.

There is sound evidence that some people could indeed memorize Homer's poems in their entirety, and it is likely that they went through countless different versions before they crystallized into the form in which we know them. An oral poet beginning a recitation is rather like a jazz musician at a jam session: everyone knows the piece, where it starts and finishes, and what the underlying structure is, but, having performed it many times before, they can give it endless new twists and turns. They each have their own distinctive phrases, and finding an entertaining and creative route through the piece is essential – *oime*, 'path/song-way', is the Greek for a poet's song. To assist this process, Homer uses highly formulaic language: phrases, lines or even whole passages recur constantly; events such as warriors arming, scenes of arrival or departure, and descriptions of fighting are related using the same words; and objects and people have stock epithets – 'swift-footed Achilles', 'the wine-dark sea', 'lovely-ankled nymphs', and so on.

The 15,693 lines of the *Iliad* are divided into 24 'books' of dactylic hexameter poetry. In what is quite a simple story, we experience just over seven weeks of incredibly intense action set during the Trojan War. It is important to be aware that the author of the *Iliad* does not narrate the entire Trojan War, nor mention the Wooden Horse. Rather, he begins in the final year of the war, in which a coalition of Greeks – called Achaeans (men of Achaea), Argives (men of Argos) or Danaans (descendants of Danaos) – is besieging Troy under the leadership of Agamemnon. Their objective is to recover Helen, the wife of Agamemnon's brother Menelaus, who had been abducted by the Trojan prince Paris. Agamemnon has been allocated a captive Trojan girl called Chryseis as a concubine, but, when her father Chryses comes to ransom her, Agamemnon simply insults him. Chryses prays to Apollo, and the god inflicts a plague on the Achaean army. When the soothsayer Calchas explains the reasons for Apollo's actions, Agamemnon grudgingly agrees to return the girl, which ends the plague. When Agamemnon demands a replacement, Achilles, who is unarguably the finest Greek warrior, albeit with less standing than Agamemnon, opposes him. Agamemnon responds by seizing Briseis, Achilles' prize-girl.

Homer's heroes are intensely competitive and the ensuing dispute is all about who gets public rewards: the best fighters or the leaders (regardless of whether they are right or wrong). The key issue at stake here is *time* ('honour'), which is equated with a person's social value. Hence its importance to the heroes. Their ultimate goal is to win eternal fame (*kleos*), so what matters above all else is the opinion of their peers.

In Homer's world many attributes confer *time*, such as wealth, the number of your subjects, or even the quality of the advice you give. Later in the narrative Sarpedon explains the heroic value-system as focused on a reciprocal relationship with society:

> Glaukos, why is it you and I are honoured before others
> with pride of place, the choice meats and the filled wine cups
> in Lykia, and all men look on us as if we were immortals,
> and we are appointed a great piece of land by the banks of
>   Xanthos,
> good land, orchard and vineyard, and ploughland for the planting
>   of wheat?
> Therefore it is our duty in the forefront of the Lykians
> to take our stand, and bear our part of the blazing of battle.[2]

Achilles is not a team player, but a helpful model for understanding his cultural values is that of a team game: individual stardom often conflicts with the interests of the team; everyone knows who the opposition are, and tries to defeat them; when games are played in public, they become vehicles for conspicuous displays of success; and winning is the only thing that counts. Achilles feels devalued, so he retires to his tent under a pall of heroic anger, accompanied by his close friend Patroclus. His sea-goddess mother Thetis appeals to Zeus to allow the Achaeans to be defeated in his absence, just to prove the point.

The *Iliad*'s very first word, 'wrath' (*menis*), has told us what the poem is about – the wrath of Achilles – and it immediately begins to explore this theme. Odysseus doesn't really care about the rights and wrongs of the quarrel, but he does know that by alienating the finest fighter, Agamemnon has done something that could well lead to failure; if the Greeks return empty-handed from a ten-year war they will lose *time*: and it will all be Agamemnon's fault.

So, having set up the situation, Homer then interrupts the narrative and outlines a vast 'Catalogue of Ships' on the Achaean side, plus details the Trojans and their allies. The armies are mighty, and, as they now engage in combat, Paris chickens out of a duel with Menelaus that would have resolved the conflict instantly. His brother Hector, Troy's finest warrior, who judges behaviour partly in terms of stereotypes of how men *should* behave and partly in terms of *consequences*, feels ashamed by this:

> Surely now the flowing-haired Achaeans laugh at us,
> thinking you are our bravest champion, only because your
> looks are handsome, but there is no strength in your heart, no
>   courage.[3]

Awesome feats of heroism take place elsewhere on the battlefield, however, as when the Greek hero Diomedes wounds the goddess Aphrodite and the war god Ares, but events are inconclusive. If a common complaint about the *Iliad* is that it is a poem told by a man, for men and about men, it should be pointed out that there is a sensitive awareness of the domestic perspective, too. Before Hector's impending return to the fray in Book 6, we meet his wife Andromache and their baby son. Unlike Paris, Hector will not skulk away from the battle – the sanction of public opinion from both women and men is too strong, and there is simply too much at stake. Hector tells Andromache that he cannot bear the thought of her being dragged into captivity by some bronze-armoured Achaean, and their exchange leads to an incredibly powerful moment that is clearly not concerned with male dominance. As he holds out his arms to their son, the baby sees Hector's helmet and screams with fright. But this makes his parents laugh, and Hector takes off his helmet and puts it on the ground.

>   Then taking
> up his dear son he tossed him about in his arms, and kissed him,
> and lifted his voice in prayer to Zeus and the other immortals . . .
> So speaking he set his child again in the arms of his beloved
> wife, who took him back again to her fragrant bosom
> smiling in her tears; and her husband saw, and took pity upon her,
> and stroked her with his hand.[4]

Hector is constantly described as 'manslaughtering', but he is not mindlessly violent. He and the other heroes would rather not fight at all. But fight Hector does, notably with 'Great' Aias (Ajax) of the terrible sevenfold-ox-hide shield. Both warriors survive with honour.

The Greeks then decide to build a wall to protect their encampment, and as the Trojans start to get the upper hand they become confident enough to bivouac (set up camp) on the plain with the intention of storming the Greek position the next day. There is such pessimism in the Greek high command that Agamemnon publicly acknowledges that the quarrel with Achilles was his own fault. He dispatches an embassy to Achilles, offering to give back Briseis in pristine condition, along with many other valuable compensatory gifts. It is interesting that the offer includes a number of cities, the existence of which is corroborated by Linear B tablets, but which actually formed part of Nestor's kingdom at Pylos, not Achilles' own. Nevertheless, Achilles' old tutor, Phoinix (Phoenix), stresses the importance of accepting the gifts:

> But if without gifts you go into the fighting where men perish,
> Your honour [*time*] will no longer be as great, though you drive
> back the battle.[5]

Without concrete evidence of compensation, the Greeks would simply assume that Achilles had given in. And in any case Achilles rejects the ambassador's offer out of hand.

These events are followed by a night-time scouting expedition by Odysseus and Diomedes (an unheroic oddity that scholars generally agree was not written by Homer). Dawn then rises from her bed at the start of Book 11 to herald a day of intense fighting that takes up eight books.

The Achaeans initially gain the initiative, but as many of their key fighters – Agamemnon, Diomedes, Odysseus, Eurypylus, Machaon – are rendered *hors de combat*, the Trojans storm right into their camp. The Greeks recover momentarily, memorably when Zeus is seduced by his wife Hera, who anoints herself with ambrosial oil, arranges her hair, puts on an exquisite robe with a hundred-tasselled belt, adds gorgeous earrings, completes the outfit with embossed sexy sandals, and then borrows a girdle from Aphrodite with depictions of beguilement, loveliness and passion for sex and whispered endearments. Zeus cannot resist. Somewhat insensitively he tells her that none of his lengthy back-catalogue of lovers has aroused him like this. They make love, and he immediately falls asleep, allowing a brief, but temporary Greek ascendancy before he wakes up seething; Apollo smashes the Greek defences, and Hector's onslaught leaves the Greeks fighting to save their ships. Nestor's exhortation shows that the common soldiers have public opinion as their sanction, too:

> Dear friends, be men; let shame be in your hearts and discipline
> in the sight of other men, and each of you remember
> his children and his wife, his property and his parents.[6]

The Greek reverses are precisely what Achilles wanted, but Patroclus has become increasingly uneasy. He talks Achilles into allowing him to borrow his armour and lead out his Myrmidons, although Achilles adds one caveat:

> But obey to the end this word I put upon your attention
> so that you can win, for me, great honour [time] and glory [kudos]
> in the sight of all the Danaans . . .
> When you have driven them from the ships, come back.[7]

Achilles is still primarily concerned with his own status, which would be diminished if Patroclus went any further. To regard him as motivated by personal vendetta, lacking social responsibility, or just plain childish, misses the fundamental reason for his wrath: his time, the value/worth/honour that is his entire raison d'être, has been undermined.

The battle-weary Trojans think that the new arrival is Achilles himself, and Patroclus saves the ships and slaughters, among dozens of others, Zeus' special favourite Sarpedon. But he forgets Achilles' instructions, and pushes his success too far. Apollo disorients him, Euphorbus strikes him in the back with a spear, and Hector finishes him off before stripping Achilles' armour from Patroclus' body. The Greeks manage to retrieve the corpse itself, but they end up in headlong retreat.

At the news of Patroclus' death Achilles descends into intense grief, remorse and rage, and when Thetis tells him that he will die almost immediately if he takes revenge on Hector, he accepts the price:

> I must die soon, then; since I was not to stand by my companion
> when he was killed. And now, far away from the land of his
>   fathers,
> he has perished, and lacked my fighting strength to defend him.[8]

The *Iliad* has framed the fundamental question: 'What is a man's life worth?'; and Achilles knows the answer: he values his life at the price of revenge on the person who killed his dearest friend. He imposes his own death sentence, not to win everlasting *kleos* or to champion the Greek cause, but because he feels responsible for Patroclus' death.

Achilles' fearsome war cry is enough to make the Trojans turn back. In the meantime, Thetis gets Hephaistos to forge him some superb new armour, including a magnificent shield depicting various scenes of war and peace.

Achilles' anger towards Agamemnon now mutates into a much more savage hatred for Hector, and with that in mind he calls off the feud with Agamemnon, and announces his willingness to re-enter the war. Agamemnon responds favourably, justifies his conduct on the basis that Zeus, Destiny, Erinys and Delusion were responsible, and offers gifts in abundance. Satisfied, Achilles then sets out to kill Hector, in the clear knowledge that this will accelerate his own death – a fact prophesied to him by his own horse, Xanthos. Meanwhile, Hector has latched on to the hope of achieving a decisive Trojan victory and has rejected some sound advice to retreat back to Troy. Zeus allows the gods to participate in the battle, and Achilles' onslaught is so ferocious that Poseidon has to save Aeneas, and Apollo rescues Hector.

The carnage is so extreme that the river god, Scamander, tries to drown Achilles because he has clogged up his channels with corpses. Hephaistos intervenes and the other gods engage: Athene defeats Ares and Aphrodite; Poseidon wins a war of words with Apollo; and Hera makes Artemis burst out crying. All the Trojans except Hector are driven inside their city. As he stands alone to face Achilles, with his parents and fellow Trojans looking on, the sanction of public opinion provides such a powerful motivation that Hector *has* to fulfil his obligations. He regards the recent Trojan defeat as his own fault:

> I feel shame before the Trojans and the Trojan women with trailing
> robes, that someone who, is less of a man than I will say of me:
> 'Hector believed in his own strength and ruined his people.'
> Thus they will speak; and, as for me, it would be much better
> at that time, to go against Achilles, and slay him, and come back,
> or else be killed by him in glory in front of the city.[9]

Isolated at the key moment, Hector's nerve fails him. He makes a dash for safety. Achilles gives chase for three circuits of the walls and, as one of his defining epithets is 'swift-footed', Hector cannot outrun him. As Achilles bears down on him, Homer mixes horror and violence with beauty and tranquillity in a brilliant simile:

> And as a star moves among stars in the night's darkening,
> Hesper, who is the fairest star who stands in the sky, such
> was the shining from the pointed spear Achilleus was shaking
> in his right hand with evil intention toward brilliant Hector.[10]

Hector knows that his chances are minimal. He is no match for Achilles. He goes down fighting.

Achilles strips Hector's body (he was wearing Achilles' original armour, taken from Patroclus), and drags it behind his chariot back to the Greek camp. All this should have resolved Achilles' anger, but it does nothing of the sort, and so, rather than glorifying the achievements of the victors, Homer takes us to two funerals, which frame one of the most extraordinary personal confrontations in Greek literature.

Patroclus receives magnificent obsequies, complete with sacrifices of animals and Trojan prisoners, plus a series of spectacular athletic competitions that are contested with intense commitment. There are those who argue that a homosexual relationship between Achilles and Patroclus lies at the heart of the *Iliad*. Achilles cannot keep his 'manslaughtering hands' off Patroclus' corpse, but sex has nothing to do with it: this is military male-bonding, not homoerotic passion, and they both sleep with women.

Homer's focus then shifts from the public to the private. Achilles will not hand over Hector's body, and he is trying to mutilate it by dragging it behind his chariot. But Apollo prevents any damage to the corpse, and ultimately, assisted by Hermes, Hector's father Priam makes his way into Achilles' tent to negotiate the ransom of the body. There is no standard protocol for such an encounter. Priam, who is weak, old and vulnerable, puts his request to his frighteningly violent enemy:

> Honour then the gods, Achilles, and take pity upon me
> Remembering your father, yet I am more pitiful;
> I have gone through what no other mortal on earth has gone
>   through;
> I put my lips to the hands of the man who has killed my children.[11]

Achilles sees reflections of his own father Peleus in Priam, and the two men weep together for their lost loved ones. Achilles finally takes the old king by the hand, and speaks to him:

> Surely you have had much evil to endure in your spirit.
> How could you dare to come alone to the ships of the Achaeans
> and before my eyes, when I am the one who has killed in such
>   numbers
> such brave sons of yours? The heart in you is iron. Come, then,
> and sit down upon this chair, and you and I will even let
> our sorrows lie still in the heart for all our grieving.'[12]

Killing Hector did not bring 'closure' to Achilles, which is why this moment where he and Priam look at each other with respect is so astonishing: it becomes clear that there is more to life than revenge, and more to manhood than slaughtering other men. Achilles grants Priam his request.

Homer then takes us to Hector's funeral, and the lamentations not only from his wife Andromache and his mother Hecabe, but also, rather surprisingly, from Helen, who praises his honour and gentleness (The *Iliad* has well been described as 'the tragedy of Hector'[13]).

Homer opened the poem by asking the Muse to help him sing of the wrath of Achilles, and he has found the perfect conclusion. The wrath and the *Iliad* are ended.

The Odyssey

The tale of the fall of Troy is not unique to Homer's poems. Greek epics of lesser status dealt with that theme, and the definitive version is to be found in Virgil's *Aeneid*. The *Odyssey*'s 24 books (12,110 lines) tell the story of the homecoming of one of the Achaeans' greatest warriors: Odysseus. He has been away from his home on Ithaca for twenty years in total: ten fighting the Trojan War; seven with the nymph Calypso; and three having the adventures that he recounts in Books 9–12, one of which was with Circe.

For roughly the last three years, 108 bachelors from Ithaca and the nearby islands had been paying court to Odysseus' wife Penelope. In Homer's world, 'excellence' depends on birth, wealth, power and position. Males must be manly and brave – Christian virtues such as humility, meekness or unselfishness are signs of weakness – and females have to be chaste and loyal, although beauty may count for more. The suitors come from such a background, but they are behaving outrageously, even if Penelope is well worth pursuing. She is (presumably) a widow, physically attractive, accomplished, intelligent and (best of all) the queen of a significant realm. However, she is clinging to the hope that Odysseus will return and, to keep the suitors at bay, she formulates a ploy of weaving a shroud for Odysseus' father Laertes' future funeral. They must wait until it is finished.

> Thereafter, in the daytime she would weave at her great loom,
> But in the night she would have torches set by, and undo it.[14]

Meanwhile, the suitors simply make themselves at home in Odysseus' palace, at his expense, and ultimately discover Penelope's trick.

In these circumstances, the *Odyssey* begins with an invocation to the Muse, which makes it clear that Odysseus is not a drifter 'off to see the world': his focus is his *nostos* ('homecoming'), and he is strongly motivated by love for his wife, his son Telemachus and his kingdom. The opening lines also give huge importance to Odysseus' often difficult relationship with his comrades, and emphasise that his failure to get them home is not his fault. He will ultimately resume his rightful place as the head of a family and the leader of a state, which is why his accountability to his followers is heavily stressed at the outset. So there are two levels of action: one about the problems of an individual (the story of one man's return to his home and family), and the other about the function of a society (the tale of the return of a king who justly eliminates potential usurpers, and re-establishes his rule).

The narrative structure of the *Odyssey* is not linear, and a divine level is also introduced when Athene addresses a Council of the Olympian Gods, at which Zeus agrees that Odysseus should be allowed to head for home. However, before we can hear about this, Homer narrates the 'Telemachy'.

Athene tells Telemachus to go and look for his father. Telemachus is not a mature adult, and although he is outraged by the behaviour of Penelope's suitors, and wants to assume power in the household, he simply cannot handle the situation, in which the suitors are transgressing every precept of *xenia* ('hospitality') in an orgy of song, dance, food and booze. One of the poem's primary concerns is how to receive and treat *xenoi*, 'stranger-guests', and Telemachus immediately shows us the correct way:

> Thinking it a shame that a stranger should be kept standing at the gates, he went straight up to his visitor, shook hands, relieved him of his bronze spear and gave him cordial greetings.
>
> 'Welcome, sir, to our hospitality!' he said. 'You can tell us what has brought you when you have had some food.'[16]

The suitors, on the other hand, are behaving as though they were (very bad) hosts rather than guests, and when Telemachus asks them to leave they refuse point blank; they really deserve what is coming to them.

Telemachus and Athene (now disguised as Mentor, a friend of Odysseus who looked after his household while he was away) now make their way to Pylos, where they are sumptuously entertained by Nestor, who got back from Troy long ago. Telemachus makes a positive impression on the garrulous old man, and his son Peisistratus joins Telemachus on a visit to Menelaus and Helen at Sparta. From Menelaus we receive important information about Odysseus' talent for disguise and self-control, and also a report that he is alive, 'weeping big tears in the palace of the nymph Calypso'.[17]

As a perfect host, Menelaus offers gifts of horses and a chariot to Telemachus, which he politely declines, in words that say much about Ithaca and its place in the tale:

> In Ithaca are no broad horselands or meadows. Goat-pasture it is, and more lovely than horse-pasture. None of the islands that lie out to sea is good for horse-riding or full of meadows, least of all Ithaca.[18]

Perversely, the fact that Ithaca is a remote, infertile fastness makes Telemachus love it even more. The island will end up in safe hands, but at that moment in time the suitors have discovered Telemachus' absence and are preparing to ambush him. We thus know precisely what Odysseus is coming home to.

In Book 5 we finally meet Odysseus in person. Zeus dispatches Hermes to tell Calypso (her name derives from the Greek *kalypto*, 'I conceal/cover') to let Odysseus go. For seven years she has kept him on her island of Ogygia, offering him immortality if will stay, but that is not what he wants. He wants to go home. So he sets sail on a raft, only to be wrecked in a storm sent by Poseidon. The goddess 'Ino called Leukothea' comes to his rescue in the form of a gannet, and Athene helps, too. Mentally and physically battered, Odysseus finally swims ashore on the island of Scherie.

His initial thoughts on Scherie are illuminating:

> What are the people whose land I have come to this time,
> and are they violent and savage, and without justice,
> or hospitable to strangers, with godly mind?[19]

The positive qualities here are obvious: hospitality and justice; the negative traits are violence and savagery (which indicate a lack of civilized society). It is noticeable that the sanction is fear of the gods, indicating a very different moral compass from that of the *Iliad*.

The grisly, naked Odysseus now meets the gorgeous Nausikaa, princess of the Phaeacians, who respect strangers, live in an enchanted place far from civilization, and are expert seafarers. Using his considerable social skills, and benefitting from a bath, Odysseus wins over Nausikaa, and she takes him home to meet her parents,

Alkinoos and Arete. They live in an amazing palace, constantly supplied with fruit and vegetables by a miraculous garden. But there is to be no fairy-tale romance, just a touching parting. Odysseus prays that he will see the day of his homecoming, but tells Nausikaa:

> So even when I am there I will pray to you, as to a goddess,
> all the days of my life. For, maiden, my life was your gift.[20]

Despite pressure from Arete, Odysseus does not yet divulge his identity, although he shows what kind of man he is when, during the ensuing feasting and athletic contests, he wins a discus contest by a massive margin. The bard Demodokos sings songs that make him weep: one about a quarrel between Odysseus and Achilles (Odysseus is already a celebrity), and another about the Trojan Horse (again cementing Odysseus' heroic status). Odysseus' tears prompt Alkinoos to ask him who he is, and this time he answers honestly:

> I am Odysseus, son of Laertes, known to all men for my cunning;
> my fame has gone up to heaven. My home is Ithaca . . . a rough land,
> but a good nurse of real men. For myself, I cannot imagine anything
> sweeter than one's own place.[21]

There has been an endless quest to pinpoint the historical and geographical 'reality' of Odysseus' travels. Yet even ancient geographical writers such as Eratosthenes and Strabo were sceptical; the problem is that once the North Wind blows him off course, we only get vague information. In any case, some of Odysseus' adventures are borrowed from the tale of Jason and the Argonauts, and we have serious difficulties making sense of the places that *do* seem historically authentic. However, the search for Homer's Ithaca continues apace, with geologists and classicists recently suggesting that Odysseus' homeland was on a part of Kephallenia, which could have been a separate island in the Bronze Age. This is fascinating and impressively argued, but has zero literary importance.

The 'Great Wanderings' are now told by Odysseus in flashback. After leaving Troy, Odysseus reaches Ismaros in Thrace, a city of the Kikones, which he pillages, sparing only Maro, a priest of

Apollo who gives him splendid presents, including twelve jars of red wine, in return for his and his wife's lives. From there, Odysseus sails to the country of the Lotus-eaters in North Africa. When some of his crew taste the 'honey-sweet fruit of the lotus', which makes them forget everything and want to stay with the Lotus-eaters, Odysseus has to drag them back to the ships by force.

Odysseus' itinerary then takes him to the land of the Cyclopes, where we witness his defining quality of *metis* ('cunning intelligence'). One of his stock epithets is *polymetis* (= 'of much cunning intelligence', often rendered as 'wily' or 'resourceful'), and, as such, he is tricky, adaptable and a brilliant improviser, possessed of what the Italians call *furbizia*: if he were a footballer he would dive to win a penalty, and applaud Maradonna's 'hand of God' goal. It's just not cricket, but it does mean that he can survive by outwitting violent and lawless adversaries. The episode begins with Odysseus taking just one ship and landing with twelve companions. The adventure is immediately given a social context:

> We came to the land of the Cyclopes, a fierce, uncivilized people who never lift a hand to plant or plough but put their trust in Providence. [They] have no assemblies for the making of laws, nor any settled customs, but live in hollow caverns in the mountain heights, where each man is lawgiver to his children and his wives, and nobody cares a jot for his neighbours.[22]

The Cyclops Polyphemus is a son of Poseidon, and while he is out tending his flocks Odysseus and his comrades enter his cave, taking with them a skinful of the priest Maro's wine. In the hope of receiving gifts, they make themselves at home, but the return of the monstrous one-eyed creature puts a very different slant on the situation: Polyphemus brings in his flocks and puts a massive stone across the entrance, and only then realizes that he has visitors:

> 'Strangers!' he said. 'And who may you be? Where do you hail from over the highways of the sea?'[23]

This violates the protocol for entertaining guests: Polyphemus should entertain first and ask questions afterwards. He rejects Odysseus' appeal for hospitality, boasts that the Cyclopes do not concern themselves about Zeus and the Olympians, and then grabs two sailors, smashes their brains against the ground, and eats them, bones and all. He has two more men for breakfast before heading to his pastures, sealing the cave. He consumes two more on his return. Odysseus uses his *metis* to formulate a plan to blind the Cyclops with a huge olive-wood stake, and he succeeds in getting him drunk on Maro's potent wine. At this point Odysseus tells Polyphemos that his name is 'Nobody', and asks for a guest-gift, so the Cyclops promises to eat Odysseus last of all – a stomach-churning parody of the rules of hospitality that removes any sympathy for him whatsoever. Then he slumps to the ground, drunk and vomiting in his sleep.

Sleep usually brings release from pain, but not here. Odysseus shoves the stake into some cinders, and when it glows 'terribly incandescent' his comrades seize it and drive it into the monster's eye:

> So seizing the fire-point-hardened timber we twirled it
> in his eye, and the blood boiled around the hot point, so that
> the blast and scorch of the burning ball singed all his eyebrows
> and eyelids, and the fire made the roots of his eye crackle . . .
> He gave a giant horrible cry and the rocks rattled
> to the sound, and we scuttled away in fear. He pulled the timber
> out of his eye, and it blubbered with plenty of blood.[24]

The description is riddled with technical difficulties: the stake is hardened and holds its heat like metal, not wood; the Cyclops' eye would not burst into flames; and he would surely have reacted and crushed Odysseus instantaneously. But the narrative is so wonderfully engaging that none of this matters; we simply enjoy seeing Odysseus at his *polymetis* best.

Polyphemus screams to the neighbouring Cyclopes for help, but when they ask who is hurting him, he answers 'Nobody', and they think it is a false alarm.

The seven survivors are still blocked in the cavern. So Odysseus tethers rams together in threes, and straps his men underneath them, tying himself below the finest beast in the flock. At dawn, as the animals head out to pasture, Polyphemus feels their backs, but misses the men underneath. Odysseus releases his comrades, drives the rams to the ships, and sails off hurling taunts at Polyphemos, who hurls back a massive rock, which almost wrecks Odysseus' ship. Odysseus at last divulges his identity:

> You were blinded by Odysseus, sacker of cities,
> Laertes is his father, and he makes his home in Ithaca.[25]

Polyphemos had actually received a prophecy that he would be blinded by Odysseus, but he expected a handsome, tall, powerful man, not the 'little, feeble person' who incapacitated him with wine. So, again, we see the power of *metis*. Polyphemos prays to his father Poseidon to prevent Odysseus' homecoming, or, if that is impossible:

> Let him come late, in bad case, with the loss of all his companions,
> in someone else's ship, and find troubles in his household.[26]

Polyphemos heaves one final gargantuan missile at Odysseus' vessel, narrowly missing it and creating a tsunami that carries it to the safety of a neighbouring island.

Odysseus' next port of call is the island of Aeolia, ruled by Aeolus, the keeper of the winds. He presents Odysseus with an oxhide bag containing all the winds apart from the West, which blows Odysseus homewards. At the point when Odysseus can make out the men of Ithaca tending the fires, he falls asleep. His idiotic crew, thinking that the bag contains treasure, undo it. The terrible storm that follows drives them back to Aeolia, but Aeolus denies hospitality to a man that he now thinks must be hateful to the gods.

Sailing on, Odysseus reaches the land of the Laistrygones. He dispatches a reconnaissance party, who are led to King Antiphates' residence. Unfortunately the Laistrygones are giant cannibals, and Antiphates eats one of the crew for dinner. The others flee back to the ship pursued by tens of thousands of Laistrygones, who smash the ships with man-sized rocks, and eat the sailors. Odysseus severs the cable of his ship, which is now the only surviving one out of the original twelve, and puts to sea.

The sole vessel makes landfall at the Aiaian isle, home of the enchantress Circe, who is very adept at *pharmaka* ('drugs'/

'enchantments'/'charms'). Eurylochus and twenty-two others go
to check out Circe's house, a weird place where doped lions and
wolves behave like domesticated dogs. All except Eurylochus
accept her offer of a potion of cheese, honey, barley, wine and drugs,
whereupon she turns them into pigs. Eurylochus reports back to
Odysseus, who sets off for Circe's house. En route he encounters
Hermes, who gives him a plant called moly, plus some useful
instructions that enable him to subdue Circe, and make her
unmetamorphose his men. He then accepts her invitation to sleep
together, which turns into a year-long sensual interlude, before his
'nostalgia' (*nostos* = 'homecoming' and *algos* = 'pain') resurfaces.

Acquiescing to his departure, Circe tells Odysseus to go into the
home of Hades and consult the prophet Teiresias. So he heads north
to the land of the Cimmerians, where the sun never breaks through
the darkness, digs a pit, and performs blood-sacrifices to Teiresias
and the dead. This *nekyia* ('calling-up of ghosts') summons the dead
to him: Elpenor, who had fallen from the roof of Circe's palace in
a drunken stupor; Teiresias, who predicts Odysseus' homecoming
'in bad case, with the loss of all your companions, in someone else's
ship, and finding troubles in your household'[27], and also his death;
and his mother Antikleia, who describes the situation in Ithaca. It
is a desperately emotional meeting:

> Three times
> I started towards her, and my heart was urgent to hold her,
> and three times she fluttered out of my hands like a shadow
> or a dream, and the sorrow sharpened at the heart within me.[28]

Odysseus then tells of various females, including Heracles' mother
(Alcmene) Oedipus' mother (Epicaste), Leda, Phaedra and
Ariadne, until he is interrupted by Alkinoos and Arete. Tales then
follow of encounters with the ghosts of his comrades at Troy:
Agamemnon, who tells of his death at the hands of Aegisthus 'with
the help of my sluttish wife',[29] Achilles and 'Great' Aias (Ajax),
who refuses to speak with him. We are then told about Minos, the
judge of the dead; the mighty hunter Orion; Tityos, whose liver
was constantly devoured by vultures; Tantalus, hungry and thirsty,
but 'tantalized'; Sisyphos, rolling an enormous stone up a hill; and
Heracles, who empathizes with Odysseus' tribulations. In the end

Odysseus is overcome with 'green fear' and returns to his ship.

After a brief return to Circe's island, they sail past the Isle of the Sirens, the singing enchantresses who would seduce sailors to their deaths with their music. Homer does not describe them, although he uses a grammatical form of 'Sirens' known as the 'dual', indicating that there were two of them. Not wanting to miss out on their singing, Odysseus follows Circe's advice and blocks up his comrades' ears with wax, and has himself lashed to the mast. The Sirens' song lives up to expectations, but Odysseus' begging only persuades Perimedes and Eurylochus to bind him tighter still, and he sails away safely.

Further navigational hazards then appear in the shape of a choice between the Wandering Rocks, and Scylla and Charybdis, which lie on either side of a narrow strait. Scylla is a ghastly monster, with twelve feet and six long necks, each with a horrible head with three rows of teeth. She lurks holed up inside a cavern, but with her heads poking out. In the other cliff is the equally terrifying Charybdis, a whirlpool that makes the sea boil up in turbulence, spattering the pinnacles of the rocks with spume and sucking down the water so that the sand shows at the sea's bottom. On Circe's advice, Odysseus takes the channel between Scylla and Charybdis, but despite standing fully armed on the foredeck, he cannot prevent Scylla snatching six of his comrades and eating them alive.

Odysseus' last surviving crewmen die at the island of Thrinakia, the grazing ground of the sheep and oxen of Hyperion/Helios, the sun god. Odysseus has already continually warned his companions about the consequences of harming these animals, but when adverse winds maroon them on the island for more than a month, and they run out of provisions, the men slaughter some oxen while Odysseus is sleeping. When the winds eventually turn and Odysseus puts to sea, Zeus blasts the ship with a thunderbolt. All the crew are lost, but Odysseus ties the mast and keel together and clings to them. He is driven back towards Charybdis, but when the wreckage gets sucked down he grabs an overhanging tree, hangs like a bat until the timbers shoot back up again, drops down into the water, mounts the wreckage, and paddles to safety. Ten nights later he is washed up on Calypso's island, bringing his narrative of his travels to an end.

The poet of the *Odyssey* resumes the story in the land of the Phaeacians. Alkinoos bestows generous gifts on Odysseus and a

Phaeacian ship returns him, still sleeping, to Ithaca. Athene pours a mist over everything, which initially prevents Odysseus realizing where he is, but then, masquerading as an Ithacan shepherd, she tells him the truth. She teases him for not recognizing his own home, yet she introduces a hint of ironic humour by telling him that the name of Ithaca has spread even as far as Troy; the depreciatory tone that Telemachus used in Sparta is gone. Odysseus responds by lying about who he is, which Athene enjoys (she is the daughter of *Metis*, 'cunning intelligence'). She then reveals her true identity, disperses the mist, and shows Odysseus his homeland. He kisses the 'grain-giving' earth.

Odysseus is unquestionably brave and adaptable, but will he have the mental, verbal, technical and social intelligence to prevail? He certainly thinks so. Experience has equipped him well, and if disguise and violence can defeat the Cyclops, they should also be able to overcome Penelope's suitors.

Athene disguises Odysseus as a crusty old beggar, and when he arrives at the shelter of his aged, loyal swineherd, Eumaios, he tells a false story of his life. Athene prompts Telemachus to come home, and his first stop is also at Eumaios' hut. When he sends the swineherd to announce his return to Penelope, Odysseus takes the opportunity to reveal himself. His disguise miraculously fades, and father and son are overwhelmed with tearful emotion.

Meanwhile, the suitors as they plot their revenge, realize that their scheme to ambush Telemachus has misfired. Antinoos proposes murdering Telemachus, but Amphinomos vetoes him. Telemachus returns to the palace, followed by a redisguised Odysseus and Eumaios. Odysseus has to exert considerable self-control when the goatherd Melanthios provokes him, although the disguise fails to deceive his old dog, Argos. The once magnificent creature is terribly neglected, but, as he recognizes his master, he wags his tail, lays his ears back, and dies happy. Odysseus surreptitiously wipes away a tear.

Arriving at the palace, Odysseus gets to experience the suitors' behaviour in person, and particularly to ascertain which of them lack *themis* (i.e. does not acknowledge any rules, divine or human). Regardless of this, however, Athene is not going to save any of them: they might be *agathoi* (noble/powerful/rich/good), but they will be treated as though they were *kakoi*, its opposite. Antinoos hurls a footstool at Odysseus, which even offends the other suitors, and Penelope asks Eumaios to summon the stranger to her presence. Odysseus says he will wait until sunset: it is essential that he and Penelope talk in private.

Meanwhile Odysseus gets embroiled in a turf-war with Iros, a rival down-and-out who rashly challenges him to a boxing match. One fatal blow from Odysseus is enough to account for him:

> He dropped, bleating, in the dust, with his face set in a grimace,
> and kicking at the ground with his feet.[30]

When Penelope makes an appearance the suitors go weak at the knees with passion, and they each pray for the privilege of lying beside her. She drops some hints about marriage, and implies that nice presents would facilitate her decision making. Her husband adores her for this:

> Odysseus was happy
> because she beguiled gifts out of them, and enchanted their spirits
> with blandishing words, while her own mind had other
> intentions.[31]

Melantho, a maid who is sleeping with the suitor Eurymakhos, is disrespectful to Odysseus, and he is nearly hit by another footstool, but when Telemachus attributes the bad behaviour to too much food and alcohol, and suggests that everyone goes to bed, the suitors agree. Odysseus and Telemachus hide all the weapons that are in the house, and Penelope and Odysseus meet. She tells him her story; he tells her another false one, although he does affirm that Odysseus is alive and about to return. Pessimistic Penelope – one of her epithets is *periphron* (= 'very thoughtful/careful', 'circumspect') – orders Eurykleia, who had been Odysseus' nurse, to wash his feet. She notices a distinctive scar, and recognizes him instantly. Swearing her to silence, he resumes his conversation with Penelope, during which she dreams up the idea of having a contest with Odysseus' bow. This involves setting up twelve axes in a row and firing an arrow through them, like Odysseus used to do. Whoever can take his bow, string it and shoot an arrow clean through all the twelve axes will win her hand.

The next day Penelope announces the contest. Odysseus has to prevent Telemachus from stringing the bow himself, before Leiodes makes an unsuccessful attempt, after which Odysseus reveals himself to Eumaios and Philoitios. Eurymakhos tries to shoot the twelve arrows but fails, after which Odysseus asks for a turn. Penelope overrules the suitors' objections; Telemachus sends her away, but details Eurykleia and Philoitios to bar the exits from the palace. The suitors have their last laugh at Odysseus' expense, but when he strings the bow without the slightest difficulty they blanch with fear, and Zeus sends portentous thunder.

Odysseus' first arrow flies straight through the axes and out the other end; his second pierces Antinoos' throat. Now, finally, he announces his identity. He catalogues the suitors' transgressions – despoiling his household, forcibly taking his serving women to sleep beside them, seeking to win his wife while he was still alive, and having no respect for gods or men.

Now upon all of you the terms of destruction are fastened.[32]

The next arrow hits Eurymakhos in the chest; Telemachus spears Amphinomos; Odysseus slays suitor after suitor until he runs out of ammunition; Melanthios secures some weaponry for the suitors, but he is captured and tied to a column; Athene appears on Odysseus' side in the guise of Mentor, and makes a simultaneous volley of six spears; four more suitors fall; more spears are deflected by Athene; Telemachus and Eumaios suffer flesh wounds; another six suitors bite the dust; Athene spreads panic with her *aegis*; Leiodes is decapitated by Odysseus, but the singer Phemios and the herald Medon are spared on Telemachus' intervention. Not one suitor survives. Everyone involved is an *agathos*, a 'real man', but the suitors are *hyperenoreon*, 'excessively manly': they deserve to die.

Two grisly acts complete the massacre: twelve serving women who have behaved immorally with the suitors are forced to clean up the bloody mess, before Telemachus supervises their execution.

Their heads were all in a line, and each had her neck caught
fast in a noose, so that their death would be most pitiful.
They struggled with their feet for a little, not for very long.[33]

Melanthios is then hideously mutilated before Odysseus fumigates the palace.

Penelope continues to be 'circumspect' when Eurykleia tells her that the stranger is Odysseus. Her response oscillates between total disbelief and semi-belief; Odysseus' filthy appearance hinders her acknowledgment of the truth (despite him taking a bath), and she will only trust a recognition by special signs. These centre on the marriage bed that Odysseus built, incorporating a living olive tree into the structure. No one else knows this. So when Penelope tells Eurykleia to bring out the bed, Odysseus is outraged: 'What man has put my bed in another place?' Penelope's circumspection evaporates, and he falls weeping into her arms. They make love, and then talk, she of her troubles, he of his travels, until sweet sleep overtakes them.

Hermes conveys the souls of the suitors down into the Underworld, while Odysseus makes his way to his father Laertes' farm, where he puts him to the test by telling another of his false stories, which has a devastating emotional effect on Laertes, before Odysseus says who he really is. When the shocked old man demands a sign, Odysseus reveals his scar, tells of the fifty trees that his father once gave him, and the two of them embrace. Their joy is curtailed when the suitors' relatives advance on the palace seeking revenge. The three generations of Odysseus' family confront them. Athene puts a stop to the conflict, but, when Odysseus ignores her advice, Zeus throws a thunderbolt at her, which terminates the violence. The *Odyssey* ends with pledges being given by each side, and ratified by Athene.

The Afterlife of the Epics

Homer's poems have generated constant fascination since antiquity. On a Hellenistic relief in the British Museum known as the *Apotheosis of Homer*, the great man sits amid the Muses and is crowned by Time and the Inhabited World, with the *Iliad* and *Odyssey* personified as his children. The Roman poet Virgil wore his influences on his sleeve by opening his *Aeneid* with *arma uirumque cano* ('I sing of arms and the man'), where 'arms' stands for the *Iliad* and 'man' for the *Odyssey*. In the Byzantine Era, Homer was read by the educated elite, and generated romances set in Troy like the much imitated *Roman de Troie* by Benoît de Sainte-

Maure (c.1160), but when the Renaissance rediscovered Homer, it did not always like him. The translations of Homer by George Chapman (c.1559–1634) influenced Shakespeare's *Troilus and Cressida*, and were greatly admired by Keats:

> Oft of one wide expanse had I been told
> That deep-browed Homer ruled as his demesne,
> Yet did I never breathe its pure serene
> Till I heard Chapman speak out loud and bold.[34]

However, the scholar J.C. Scaliger (1484–1558) was less impressed – 'It is ridiculous, it is stupid, it is Homeric' – and John Dryden (1631–1700) felt that Virgil's Aeneas was a much better role-model than any Homeric hero.

In the eighteenth century important translations appeared, in German by Johann Heinrich Voss (1781) into 'megalithic hexameters', and by Alexander Pope (1720 and 1725), although the classical scholar Richard Bentley famously told Pope, 'it is a pretty poem, Mr Pope; but you must not call it *Homer*', and Keats still preferred Chapman. Robert Wood published *An Essay on the Original Genius of Homer* in 1767,[35] which applauded Homer's direct simplicity, and influenced Goethe, who wrote his *Achilleis* (1808, translated as *Achilleid*, 1890), picking up from the last line of the *Iliad*.

Meanwhile, Flaxman's design of *The Apotheosis of Homer* had graced a Wedgwood vase in 1778, and Ingres painted the same theme in 1827, depicting Homer surrounded by the likes of Apelles, Raphael, Dante, Virgil, Plato and Socrates.

In the nineteenth century Homer occupied a central place in Victorian public school education, just as he overshadows Shakespeare, Milton and Dante in the centre of the poetry frieze on the Albert Memorial in London; and Tennyson (1809–1892) took Odysseus' inspirational story to his heart as he launched his great literary journey.

As the twentieth century dawned, the Alexandrian Greek poet C.P. Cavafy made effective use of the duel between Achilles and Hector in his 'Trojans' (1905):

Our efforts are like those of the Trojans.
We think we'll change our luck
by being so resolute and daring,
so we move outside ready to fight.
But when the big crisis comes,
our boldness and resolution vanish;
our spirit falters, paralysed,
and we scurry around the walls
trying to save ourselves by running away.

He also used the *Odyssey* as the inspiration for his wonderful
'Ithaca' (1911):

When you set out for Ithaca
ask that your way be long,
...
But do not in the least hurry the journey.
Better that it last for years,
so that when you reach the island you are old,
rich with all you have gained on the way,
not expecting Ithaca to give you wealth.
Ithaca gave you the splendid journey.
...
And if you find her poor, Ithaca has not deceived you.
So wise have you become, of such experience,
that already you will have understood what these Ithacas mean.[36]

James Joyce, who regarded the story of Odysseus as 'the most
beautiful, all-embracing theme – greater, more human, than that of
Hamlet, Don Quixote, Dante, Faust',[37] used the myth in *Ulysses* 'as
a way of controlling, of ordering, of giving shape and significance
to the immense panorama of futility and anarchy which is
contemporary history'.[38]

In the poems of Rupert Brooke, Homer came face to face with
the onset of the First World War, particularly since Troy is so close
to the Gallipoli peninsula:

They say Achilles in the darkness stirred ...
And Priam and his fifty sons

Wake all amazed, and hear the guns,
And shake for Troy again.[39]

Patrick Shaw-Stewart fought at Gallipoli with the *Iliad* in mind:

Was it so hard, Achilles,
So very hard to die?
Thou knowest and I know not –
So much the happier I.
I will go back this morning
From Imbros over the sea;
Stand in the trench, Achilles,
Flame-capped, and fight for me.[40]

There are times when Homer has seemed just too raw: in John Buchan's words, 'to speak of glory seemed a horrid impiety. That was perhaps why I could not open Homer.'[41] Perhaps this is because Homer never shies away from addressing the horrors of war, and remains sharply aware of the victim as well as the victor. Drawing parallels between modern wars and Homer's work remains fashionable, most recently in the comparisons that are readily made between Wolfgang Petersen's 2004 film *Troy* and the Iraq war. It seems unlikely that Petersen intended it that way, and the harder the analogies are forced, the less convincing they appear, yet the willingness even to look for these correspondences is eloquent testimony to the enduring relevance of Homer's poetry.

5

GREEK HISTORY TO THE END OF THE FIFTH CENTURY BCE

When Greeks joined Greeks, then was the tug of war!
Nathaniel Lee, *The Rival Queens* IV.ii

Geography, Climate and History
The history of Ancient Hellas (Greece), as the Hellenes (Greeks)
called it, is inextricably entwined with weather and landscape. After
a colonizing movement in the eighth century BCE, driven largely
by a combination of increasing population and land shortage, the
Greek world encompassed Greece itself, the Aegean Sea, the coast
of Asia Minor (modern Turkey), some very prosperous cities in
Sicily and southern Italy (often referred to as *Magna Graecia* 'Great
Greece'), with outposts in the Black Sea, North Africa, and France.
Aristotle believed that this controlled their destiny: Europeans are
spirited, but lack skill and intellect, and so remain relatively free;
the Asiatic nations possess both intellect and skill, but lack spirit,
and therefore remain enslaved; but:

> the Hellenic race, occupying a mid-position geographically, has a
> measure of both, being both spirited and intelligent. Hence it
> continues to be free, to live under the best constitutions, and, given
> a single constitution, to be capable of ruling all other people.[1]

But Hellas is mountainous and communication was never
easy, communities tended to remain resolutely separate; *autarkeia*

(= self-sufficiency) was highly prized and so the Hellenes never lived under a single constitution. They inhabited a large number of fiercely independent *poleis* (sing '*polis*'). The conventional translation 'City States' is somewhat misleading, since the word *polis* covers the urban settlement, the Acropolis ('high city' – the fortified stronghold at its heart), the outlying villages and farmland, the residents and their way of life.

Greece has many small fertile plains but only a few large ones, although the jagged, indented coastline means that nowhere is more than about 80 km from the sea. This led many Greeks to become first-rate sailors, despite the capriciousness of the Aegean Sea, where winter sailing was out of the question. The many islands acted like stepping-stones to Asia Minor, and Hellenic mariners were enticed eastwards, making the Aegean basin a hub of exchange for goods and (perhaps more importantly) ideas between Europe, Asia and Egypt. As Perikles reputedly said: 'How can mere farmers, with no knowledge of the sea, achieve anything worthy of note?'[2]

Monarchy, Aristocracy, Tyranny and the World's First Democracy

In the Homeric world, monarchy was the normal way of things in the Greek states, but over time a transition to aristocracy took place. The aristocrats were hereditary groups, and as *Eupatridai* ('Sons of Good Fathers') they dominated all the political, legal, military, social and religious aspects of the *polis*. The *poleis* themselves were organized tribally, with political administration depending on kinship groups, and the system was stacked in favour of anyone of noble descent.

The status quo was challenged as the colonizing movement led to the generation of wealth among enterprising non-aristocrats, who started to resent their lack of influence. At the same time, some Eupatrid families exploited popular discontent in order to subvert the dominance of their rivals. Disaffected nobles, or wealthy non-nobles, emerged as 'champions' of the masses, and manipulated the situation to seize personal control.

In some cases this shift in power may have been based on the new hoplite soldiers. These heavy-armed infantrymen fought shoulder-to-shoulder in a fighting system that diminished the pre-eminence of the individualistic military prowess of the old nobility.

Such usurpations were replicated right across the Greek world, and the word used for someone who took over like this was *tyrannos*, 'tyrant'/'dictator'. The word *tyrannos* did not initially carry the overtones that 'tyrant' now does (although it came to do so later): it simply distinguished this type of monarch from a hereditary king.

Greece's 'Age of the Tyrants' conventionally begins with the takeover of Corinth by Kypselos in *c*.650 BCE. A representative example is Theagenes of Megara, who got hold of a bodyguard, exploited the unrest caused by land shortage, seized power ostensibly as champion of the oppressed peasants, and carried out a massive slaughter of the cattle of the rich (and presumably hosted a free feast for the poor). Typically, after the revolution, Theagenes introduced an ambitious programme of public works. There was normally a honeymoon period where the interests of the tyrant and the newly influential classes coincided, and often an economic boom based on increased trade, with agriculture making a shift towards '*agora* (market) culture'.³ The sixth-century poet Theognis clearly disliked this topsy-turvy world:

> Unchanged the walls, but, ah, how changed the folk!
> The base, who erstwhile knew nor law nor right,
> But dwelled like deer, with goatskin for a cloak,
> Are now ennobled; and, O sorry plight!
> The nobles are made base in all men's sight.⁴

At the city of Megara Theagenes then married his daughter to Kylon, the would-be tyrant of Athens, but then the nobles fought back. It was the usual pattern for the people, who had got what they wanted, and the aristocracy, who had not, to become drawn together by a common hatred of the tyrant, who would in turn become more 'tyrannical' in order to hang on to power, and Theagenes was ousted by such a coalition. Few tyrannies lasted for more than one generation, none for more than three.

At Athens the prospect of tyranny materialized just after 640 BCE when the aforementioned young Athenian noble Kylon tried to perpetrate a *coup d'état* with Athenian accomplices and Megarian troops. However, most Athenians rallied against him. Kylon himself escaped, but his followers took sanctuary in a temple, only to be executed by Megakles, of the Alkmaionid family.

This sacrilegious act brought pollution on the entire *polis*, and the Alkmaionidai were condemned before a court of 300 aristocrats, cursed and exiled (although they were back by the time of Megakles' son, Alkmaion).

Some twenty years later Drakon was appointed by the *Eupatridai* as *thesmothetes* (law-recorder), to defuse the discontent on which Kylon had hoped to play. Drakon's laws were proverbial for their severity ('draconian') and included debt laws that allowed the creditor to seize the debtor and his family as slaves. His legislation still supported the interests of the power-holding class, even if it did now define those interests in writing, but it became apparent that more comprehensive measures were needed to rectify Athens' difficulties.

The man ultimately appointed by the *Eupatridai* in *c.*594/3 BCE to reconcile these tensions was Solon, a man of good birth, respected for his integrity and moderation, who had written poems in which he 'everywhere lays the blame for the strife on the rich'.[5]

Athens had two types of landowner: the *orgeones* (members of guilds), whose property was alienable, and members of the *gene* ('clans'), whose estate was inalienable. This meant that the latter could not use land as collateral on a loan, but could use its produce, and if they became bankrupt they were forced to pay one-sixth of this to the creditor, and became known as *hektemoroi*, ('sixth-parters'). The *orgeones* could mortgage both their property and their families, but bankruptcy for them could result in slavery. So, in a package of measures known as the *seisakhtheia* (= 'shaking off of burdens'), Solon made it unlawful to secure loans on the personal freedom of the debtor, abolished the status of *hektemoroi*, cancelled debts and liberated those enslaved for debt. No longer would Athenians be kept as slaves at Athens.

On the economic front, Solon offered Athenian citizenship to foreign craftsmen, notably Corinthian potters whose expertise helped Athens to dominate the ceramics markets. Solon also decreed that no son was obliged to support his father in old age unless he had been taught a trade, and introduced an export ban on all agricultural produce except olive oil:

> The export of figs was prohibited . . . and those who informed against such exporters were called *sycophants*, or 'fig-declarers'.[6]

With home-grown corn kept at home, famine prices were avoided, and the olive oil trade stimulated.

On the political level, Solon broke the monopoly of the *Eupatridai* by dividing the Athenians into four census classes with graduated privileges, whose criteria were based on income in kind (the number of *medimnoi* [= 52-litre measures] of corn or oil that a man's land produced), shifting Athens from an aristocracy to a timocracy (i.e. where there is a property/wealth qualification for office). The highest political offices were open to the *Pentakosiomedimnoi* (whose estates produced more than 500 *medimnoi* per annum) and the *Hippeis* (= knights) (wealthy enough to equip themselves as cavalry and generating 300 *medimnoi*). Minor offices were available to the *Zeugitai* (200 *medimnoi*, wealthy enough to equip themselves as hoplites); and everyone else, known collectively as the *Thetes* or 'labourers', who comprised the vast majority, had what Aristotle dubbed 'a bare minimum of power'.

Athens' highest magistrates, the nine *arkhontes* (arkhons), were no longer necessarily nobles, and it is likely that they were selected by the Assembly of Citizens (*ekklesia*) by *klerosis ek prokriton*, i.e. the election of a pool, followed by selection by lot.[7] The *ekklesia* dealt with legislation, matters of war and peace, and key questions of public policy – and all classes had a vote. The *arkhontes* became accountable to the *ekklesia*, since only if their actions in office were acceptable were they granted admittance to the Council of the Areiopagos. The Areiopagos had been a very powerful and exclusively aristocratic institution, but Solon converted it into the protector of the constitution, guardian of the laws and the chief homicide court. Its pre-eminent constitutional place was taken by the new *boule*, the Council of Four Hundred, chosen by lot from members of the four Athenian tribes. This council handled the discussion and presentation of business for the *ekklesia*. Finally, Solon granted a right of appeal from the magistrates' courts to the *heliaia* (People's Court), which was the *ekklesia* sitting as a court. This was a major step towards democracy: as Aristotle observed, when the people control the judicial system, they control the State.

Solon had initiated some major improvements at Athens, yet even he was aware of his shortcomings; by attempting to avert a tyranny, he actually created a new kind of political unrest in which the old aristocratic inter-family rivalries became blended with class struggles.

We hear that Athens broke up into three factions: the Plain, led by Lykourgos, comprising *eupatridai* who favoured oligarchy; the Coast, led by Megakles, formed from the *orgeones*, who sought a 'middle form' of constitution; and the Hill, led by Peisistratos, made up of poor countrymen, which aimed at democracy. Peisistratos seized power *c*.560 BCE by pre-packing the Assembly with his supporters, claiming to have been wounded by a political opponent, being voted a bodyguard, and taking the Acropolis. However, this success simply united Lykourgos and Megakles, who drove him out, until the latter joined him to play what Herodotus described as 'the silliest trick which history has to record'.[8] They dressed up a tall beautiful woman as Athena, and drove her into Athens in Peisistratos' chariot, saying that the goddess was bringing Peisistratos home. Apparently the Athenians fell for this. Unfortunately, although Peisistratos had married Megakles' daughter, he didn't want to add to his sons from a previous union, and 'lay with her in an unnatural way'.[9] Outraged, Megakles reunited with Lykourgos and again expelled Peisistratos. Peisistratos spent ten years planning another *coup d'état*, and in *c*.546 BCE he returned, backed by foreign mercenaries. It was third-time-lucky for him, and he defeated his enemies at the Battle of Pallene.

Opponents were murdered, exiled or kept as hostages, and the appointment of the *arkhontes* was tightly controlled, but in other respects Peisistratos observed Athenian legal protocols. His rule became known as 'The Age of Kronos' (a mythical Golden Age): like a good tyrant, he made agricultural loans to the poor; promoted trade and industry; instigated a major programme of public works; and was a high-profile patron of the arts.

When Peisistratos died in 527 BCE, his sons Hippias and Hipparkhos took over. The cultural and building programme flourished, as top-class poets were invited to Athens; recitations of Homer became part of the remodelled Great Panathenaia festival; and new silver coins known as 'Athenian Owls' enhanced Athenian trade and prestige. But then things started to unravel. Hipparkhos had a same-sex crush on the beautiful Harmodios, but, having been spurned twice, the tyrant insulted Harmodios' sister by denying her the honour of being a basket-bearer at the

Panathenaia of 514/3 BCE. So Harmodios and his (male) lover Aristogeiton plotted to assassinate Hippias and Hipparkhos at the festival. Unfortunately for them, things went wrong: Hipparkhos was murdered, but Hippias got away; Harmodios was killed; and Aristogeiton was tortured to death.

In a distortion of historical reality, drinking songs in honour of the 'Tyrannicides' said that Harmodios and Aristogeiton 'slew the tyrant and made Athens a land of equal rights'. In fact, Hippias instituted a hard-line regime, again expelling the Alkmaionidai, who rebuilt the Temple of Apollo at Delphi, thereby winning the support of the Oracle, which constantly pressurized the Spartans into 'liberating Athens'. This they did in 510 BCE when King Kleomenes invaded Attika (the 'Greater Athens' area) and captured some of the Peisistratids' children as they were being smuggled away. The Peisistratids came to terms with the Athenians in order to get them back, and left the country in July. Hippias spent the next twenty years in the Troad cultivating friendly relations with the King of Persia.

Ironically, by replacing the aristocratic in-fighting and class struggle with stable government, the Peisistratid tyranny created a situation in which democracy could flourish. First, however, there was an aristocratic backlash. Kleisthenes, leader of the Alkmaionidai, found himself frustrated by Isagoras, a close friend of Kleomenes, who also had connections with Hippias. When Isagoras was elected *arkhon* for 508/7 BCE, Kleisthenes 'joined the people to the company of his followers',[10] and proposed radical reform of the constitution. Isagoras appealed to the Spartans to step in, and Kleomenes invoked the 'Curse of the Alkmaionidai' from the time of Megakles to exile 700 households of Kleisthenes' supporters. However, when he occupied the Acropolis, and tried to replace Solon's *Boule* with a junta of Isagoras' supporters, the Athenians rose up and expelled him. He left in ignominy, taking Isagoras with him, while Kleisthenes returned with the 700 families, and exploited Isagoras' failure by equating oligarchy with subservience to a foreign power.

Kleisthenes is said to have established three great rights for the Athenian people: *isonomia* (= 'equality under the law'); *isegoria* (= 'equality of speech'); and *isokratia* (= 'equality of power'). Athens had become a democracy (*demokratia* = 'rule of the people').

Demokratia was achieved by creating ten new tribes for political purposes, and making small localities called 'demes' (*demoi*, sing. *demos*) the basic unit of local government. There were 168 of these, each with its own Assembly, *Boule*, Chief Magistrate and Treasurers. A group of contiguous *demoi* from each of the three areas of Attika (i.e. the coast, inland and city) was amalgamated into a *trittys* ('a third'), and these three (non-contiguous) *trittyes* were then united to form a tribe. Each tribe therefore contained *demoi* from across the coastal, inland and urban areas, in theory giving it a cross-section of the community and eradicating party-strife based on local differences. *Demos* and tribe membership was hereditary, and citizenship became dependent on your *demos*. Every Athenian male was identified by three names: given name, patronymic and *demos* – Perikles Xanthippou Kholargeus ('Perikles, son of Xanthippos, from the deme of Kholargos').

Membership of the *Boule* was increased to 500, with 50 councillors selected from each of the 10 tribes by election, then lottery. Councillors had to be thirty years old, but all classes were eligible, and they could serve on the *Boule* twice in their lifetime. It effectively became the supreme administrative authority of the State, preparing the agenda for the Assembly, ensuring that the Assembly's decisions were implemented, examining all new magistrates before they took up office, handling its own internal discipline, practically controlling all the State finances, and dealing with foreign officials and envoys.

The impracticality of keeping together the entire *Boule* around the clock, twenty-four hours a day, seven days a week, led to the establishment of the Prytany system, where a 'standing committee' was authorized to act for the whole group in certain circumstances. Its members were called the *prytaneis*, and each tribe took it in turn to act 'in prytany' for one of the ten months of the year. Each day they selected one member by lot to act as *epistates* ('chairperson', in effect, Head of State for the day), and he presided over any meetings of the *Boule* or Assembly that might take place.

Aristotle also attributes a remarkable innovation to Kleisthenes: ostracism. This was an optional, annual 'unpopularity contest', at which all Athenian citizens could write the name of one person on a piece of broken pottery known as an *ostrakon*. Subject to a rule of 6,000 votes, the person who polled the highest had to leave the State

Figure 5.1 The Athenian Constitution

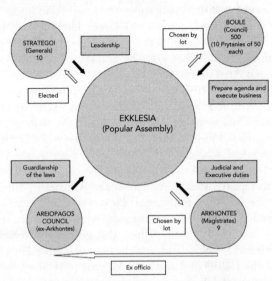

for ten years. Ostensibly to prevent tyranny, ostracism eventually became a tool of party politics. Hipparkhos, son of Kharmos, was the first man to be ostracized in 488/7 BCE.

Whether Kleisthenes was cynically exploiting the people for selfish ends or truly committed to widening participation in the running of the State remains difficult to assess. Nevertheless he established the world's first, and some would say only genuine democracy, and in the context of the ancient world this was a staggering innovation. Nothing remotely like this had existed anywhere ever before. There was still plenty of room for improvement and refinement, but the average Athenian citizen already had far more political power than any citizen of a modern democracy.

The Persian Wars

To the east of Athens' fledgling democracy, some very disturbing events were taking place. The Persian Empire, ruled by Darius I (521–486 BCE), had become one of the most powerful in the ancient world, and it included the sophisticated Ionian Greek communities of Asia Minor. The Persians installed local tyrants; they levied tribute and taxes, but did not put this money back into local circulation; Ionian trade was up against serious outside competition; and the Greeks resented being subject to a barbarian (quite literally someone whose speech sounds to a Greek like 'bar, bar, bar . . .') monarch and ruled by tyrants at a time when tyranny was patently out of fashion. So in 499 BCE, led by a couple of adventurers called Histiaios and Aristagoras, they rebelled.

Aristagoras went to Greece to garner support and, although he got short shrift at Sparta, the Athenians and Eretrians agreed to send ships. The campaign started promisingly, with the Ionians burning Sardis in 498 BCE. Herodotus says that when Darius learnt of this, he asked who the Athenians were, then cried: 'Grant, O God, that I may punish the Athenians', and commanded one of his servants to repeat, 'Master, remember the Athenians', three times, whenever he sat down to dinner.[11] However, the Persian king had greater resources and time on his side, whereas the Ionians were disunited and ineptly led. When the going got tough, both Aristagoras and Histiaios fled, and the issue was settled in a huge sea battle off the island of Lade near Miletos (494 BCE), where the rebels, rent apart by mutiny and desertion, were overwhelmed. Miletos was sacked, and Darius was left seeking further revenge.

Armed with 'just grievances', Darius moved to subjugate Greece itself. Herodotus tells of his wife Atossa wheedling him into invading Greece: (a) to prove himself as a man; and (b) to bring back exotic Greek slave girls to wait on her. In reality, however, expansionism was the default position of the Persian Empire. Two years after an abortive invasion attempt led by Darius' son-in-law Mardonios in 492 BCE, in which the Persian fleet was devastated in a storm off Mount Athos, Darius demanded earth and water as tokens of submission from the Greeks. The Athenians threw his messengers into a pit; the Spartans pushed them down a well, and told them they could find earth and water there; but many Aegean islands submitted, including Aigine, which was near to, and at war with, Athens, and the Spartan king Demaratos defected to Persia.

The Persian force, commanded by Datis and Artaphernes, was said to be 600 ships strong, and included Hippias, the ex-tyrant of Athens. For Hippias, democracy was worse than collaboration with Persia: people like him were ruthlessly ambitious, hated being governed by other factions, objected to democracy putting their social 'inferiors' on a par with themselves, had no ideological objection to monarchy, were perfectly happy to side with a rival state to regain power, and did not feel that collaborating with the enemy was acting against the people, because their 'people' were their family, relatives and friends. The leading lights of the anti-Persian party were Themistokles, who as *arkhon* in 493 BCE had begun the fortification of Peiraieus, 5 km from Athens, in order to create a new naval base and commercial harbour, and Miltiades, a swashbuckling aristocrat who became *strategos* in 490 BCE after a spell as a tyrant in the Chersonese.

Avoiding Mount Athos, the Persians started at Samos, burned Naxos, spared Delos, took hostages, requisitioned troops, conquered Karystos and sacked Eretria. At this juncture the Athenians sent the first of their two 'marathon runners', Pheidippides, to Sparta to seek help. He covered the 260 km from Athens to Sparta in under two days, but the Spartans were genuinely unable to respond immediately, because of a religious festival.

In summer 490 BCE the Persians landed at Marathon, some 40 km north-east of Athens. They expected either that the Athenians would confront them there and lose, or that fifth-columnists would betray the city. It looked like a win–win situation. Miltiades is said to have persuaded the *boule* and the *polemarkhos* ('war-*arkhon*') Kallimakhos to march out to Marathon, and most sources say that there were 9,000 to 10,000 Athenians, plus 1,000 Plataians, mainly hoplites.

A stand-off then ensued. The Persians, who were not as heavily armoured as the Greeks, wanted to fight on the plain, where their formidable cavalry and archers would be most effective, but the Hellenes realized this, and remained in the hills covering the roads to Athens. The battle was precipitated when Miltiades was informed that, under cover of darkness, the Persians had started to embark their cavalry. He immediately ordered his men to attack 'at a run'. This is an extraordinary testament to their strength and fitness, given the weight of the hoplite equipment and the distance they had to cover (some 1500 m), but the speed of their onslaught negated the effect both of the Persian archers and their cavalry. The Greeks were still vastly outnumbered, so to match the length of the Persian line they deliberately thinned the centre of theirs. Although they were pushed back in the centre, the Athenians on one wing and the Plataians on the other were both victorious. Having got the upper hand, they drew the two wings together, turned their attention to the Persians who had broken through in the centre, pursued the fugitives to their ships, where Kallimakhos was killed, and inflicted casualties reported at 6,400 dead; the Athenian losses were 192.

The danger was not over, though. The surviving Persian ships set sail for Athens, and the Athenians dispatched the man whose amazing running is commemorated in the modern marathon race. According to Plutarch, the herald, Eukles (or Thersippos) was somewhat late, and so ran to Marathon, fought in the battle, and afterwards 'ran in full armour all the way to Athens hot from the battle, and bursting into the City Hall, could only say, "Good news! We've won!" and almost at once fell down dead'.[12] The Greek forces managed to get to Athens before the Persians, at which point the invaders gave up and sailed for Asia. Miltiades, the Marathon-men and Athens revelled in the glory; Darius yearned for revenge; the Spartans arrived late, surveyed the battlefield, and went home.

Miltiades died of gangrene the following year, having been wounded in an ill-fated military expedition against Paros, but in 483 BCE the Athenians struck a rich vein of silver at Laureion. By adept use of political spin, Themistokles persuaded the people to ostracize his rival Aristeides, and to spend the windfall on building 200 state-of-the-art warships called 'triremes'. It was one of the most significant decisions the Athenians ever made.

Darius died in 486 BCE and was succeeded by his son Xerxes. Egged on by Mardonios, Demaratos of Sparta and the Peisistratids of Athens, the new king assembled a vast multinational force (5,283,320, including 10,000 of the elite Immortals, if we believe Herodotus), accompanied by a massive fleet. He constructed a bridge of boats across the Hellespont; bridged the Strymon River; installed supply depots along the coast; dug a canal through the Mount Athos peninsula; and sent envoys all over Greece, except to Athens and Sparta, with a demand for earth and water. Many of these states sided with the Persians and thus, remained neutral or dithered. The Delphic Oracle delivered prophecies so pessimistic that the Athenian oracle-seekers refused to go home until they got better ones. The new improved version, reports Herodotus, told them that 'the wooden wall only shall not fall'[13] and that 'Divine Salamis' would bring death to women's sons. The key Greek states met at the Isthmus of Corinth and created an anti-Persian league. Later, thirty-one communities added their names to the Serpent Column, a victory monument in the form of three intertwining snakes, which was dedicated at Delphi and is now in the Hippodrome in Istanbul, having been taken there by the Roman Emperor Constantine.

Never before and never again did the Greeks display even such limited unity: Athens and Aigine buried their differences and combined their large navies; the Athenians recalled their exiles; and Sparta was given the high command in both the military and naval spheres.

The Greek strategy was to confine the Persian forces in restricted areas like mountain passes and narrow waterways, and threaten their supply line. Having rejected the valley of Tempe in the north, the Greek army made its stand with 7,000 hoplites under the Spartan king Leonidas at the pass of Thermopylai in central Greece, while the fleet took up a position at nearby Artemision to stop the Persians landing forces in their rear.

Xerxes' frontal assault was a disastrous failure, until a traitor, Ephialtes, showed him a mountain track that led round to the rear of the Greeks. Leonidas dismissed the troops, remained in the pass with his 300 Spartan warriors, and was overwhelmed in a heroic last stand that earned him an immortal place among military heroes. The courage of the Spartan warriors is exemplified by Dienekes, who, on being told that when the Persians shot their arrows there were so many of them that they hid the sun, responded: 'This is pleasant news. If the Persians hide the sun, we shall fight in the shade.'[14]

Meanwhile, indecisive naval actions were conducted at Artemision until a storm inflicted significant damage on the Persian fleet. However, the setback at Thermopylai forced the Greek fleet to retreat south. Those Athenians who interpreted the 'wooden wall' oracle as meaning they should defend themselves on the Akropolis, eventually lost their lives when the Persians sacked the city in September 480 BCE; Themistokles allegedly argued that the 'wooden wall' was the navy, and that 'Divine Salamis' would bring death to the Persians, and he convinced the allies that the best place to fight was in the narrow waters by that island. Tradition also has it that Themistokles sent a slave with a message to the enemy that the Greeks were at daggers drawn with each other, had many pro-Persians amongst them, and were about to row for their lives under cover of night.

Assuming the authenticity of the tale, the deception worked. Herodotus, Aeschylus and Plutarch all show pro-Athenian bias, and it is difficult to get at the truth underlying the Greek tactics. There were valid reasons for *not* wanting to engage: the Greek fleet was pretty inexperienced; the Persian fleet included highly regarded Phoenician and Egyptian contingents; the last time the Greeks and Persians had fought at sea was at the Battle of Lade – a comprehensive Persian victory; the Greek fleet had not been keen to seek a showdown at Artemision; and hindsight is always 20/20. It may be erroneous to assume that this had been the Greek plan all along.

The Persian-Egyptian squadron was probably sent to surround the Greeks via the western exit from the bay of Eleusis, while from the base of Mount Aigaleos, Xerxes watched his mammoth fleet move into the confined space between Salamis and the mainland. As the Persians advanced they lost formation, while Themistokles exploited local knowledge by waiting for the wind to whip up a heavy swell. The taller Persian vessels became awkward to manoeuvre, whereas the Greek ships were comparatively small and lay low in the water. Aeschylus, who may have fought in the battle, dramatized the scene brilliantly in a speech by a Persian messenger to Xerxes in his tragedy *The Persians*:

At once ship into ship battered its brazen beak.
. . . But soon, in that narrow space,
Our ships were jammed in hundreds; none could help another.
They rammed each other with their prows of bronze; and some
Were stripped of every oar. Meanwhile the enemy
Came round us in a ring and charged. Our vessels heeled
Over; the sea was hidden, carpeted with wrecks
And dead men; all the shores and reefs were full of dead.
Then every ship we had broke rank and rowed for life.
The Hellenes seized fragments of wrecks and broken oars
And hacked and stabbed at our men swimming in the sea
As fishermen kill tunnies or some netted haul.[15]

With his plans in tatters Xerxes returned to Asia Minor, but left the land forces in Greece under the control of Mardonios. The Spartans eventually put together the largest force ever to leave the

Peloponnese under the regent Pausanias. With the combined Hellenic army numbering around 100,000, Mardonios withdrew to a defensive position near the Boiotian town of Plataia (479 BCE). The terrain there suited his cavalry, and the armies stood facing one another for days. Eventually, though, disputes within the Persian high command prompted Mardonios to attack in conditions favouring the Greeks. The battle was a close-run thing, but the discipline, fighting ability and weaponry of the Greek hoplites prevailed; Mardonios was killed.

Herodotus also relates that the Persians suffered another defeat on the same day at Mykale on the Ionian coast. The Persian threat to the Greek mainland was over.

The Pentekontaetia

The period from 479 to 431 BCE is called the Pentekontaetia (= 'Fifty Years', even though it isn't exactly fifty years). To Sparta's annoyance, Themistokles got the Athenians to rebuild their walls, reinforcing this symbolic rejection of the Spartan's traditional hegemony by telling them that it was only on the basis of equal strength that fair discussions on the common interest could be held. In some regards, the two states were polar opposites: Athens was an Ionian democratic sea power known for its energy, artistic innovation, and creativity; Sparta was a Dorian oligarchic land power with a reputation for austerity and lack of initiative. However, there was no direct clash of interests at this stage, since Sparta's formidable alliance (the Peloponnesian League) was not geared up for extensive overseas activity, while Athens' focus was on the Aegean Sea.

After the Battle of Mykale the allies then sailed to the Hellespont to destroy Xerxes' bridges, only to find that this had already been done. The Spartan king Leotykhidas wanted to head home, while the Athenians wanted to regain the Chersonese area because of its significance to their corn routes; so they parted company. The Athenians laid siege to Sestos, and its fall in 478 BCE virtually ended the war in Europe. That summer, Pausanias commanded successful operations against Cyprus and Byzantium, but he started to behave like a Persian tyrant, which prompted the allies to appeal to the Athenian admiral Aristides for protection. When Pausanias was recalled to Sparta, the allies refused to accept another Spartan as leader, and Aristides emerged as commander. The Spartans then debated their options and, since it was looking like the leading light in Athenian politics would not be Themistokles, whom they distrusted, but Kimon, who was more sympathetic towards them, they allowed the *ephor* (Spartan 'official') Hetoimaridas to persuade them to opt for compromise solution entailing acquiescence to Athenian sea power but expansion of Spartan interests outside the Peloponnese on land. In the light of these events, a new voluntary confederacy, under Athenian leadership, was constituted in the winter of 478/7 BCE on the island of Delos. What is now called the 'Delian League/Confederacy' was then known as 'Athens and her allies', and comprised around 150 members drawn from the Ionian cities of Asia Minor, the Hellespont and the Propontis, plus most of the islands in the Aegean. No mainland Greek states were founder members of the League, nor were any states to the west. An oath was taken that they would have the same friends and enemies, and to confirm this they sank wedges of red-hot iron in the sea. Only when the metal floated to the surface would the alliance lapse. The immediate aim was to recoup their losses by ravaging the territory of the King of Persia, but the longer-term objective had to be to preserve Greek freedom from any future Persian aggression.

League policy was decided at meetings held on Delos on a one-state-one-vote basis, although in practice Athens dominated: ten Athenian officials called *Hellenotamiai* supervised the contributions to the League's finances, and Athens decided who should contribute ships and who *phoros*, or 'tribute'. The first financial assessment, totalling 460 talents, was conducted by Aristeides, and after 454 BCE the *phoros* was paid to the *Hellenotamiai*, who deducted one-sixtieth of each state's contribution (called the *aparkhe*) and dedicated it to Athena, recording the figures on marble inscriptions. Right from the beginning the Athenians had the wherewithal to turn this alliance into an empire, but, with the Persian threat still the main worry, no one seems to have considered that eventuality.

Everything went smoothly at first, despite Themistokles being ostracized around 472 BCE and, after a brief stay in Argos, ending up, ironically, with the King of Persia. His place was taken by Kimon, son of Miltiades, and under his leadership the Delian League scored some impressive successes, although not just against

Persia – there also were actions against its own members, and coercion of other Greek states. The maverick Spartan Pausanias was expelled from Byzantium; Eion, the last major Persian stronghold west of the Hellespont, was captured, followed by Skyros, a pirate base in the north Aegean, which the Athenians colonized – it was on their corn route from the Black Sea. Here a large skeleton was discovered, which, it was claimed, was the remains of the Athenian hero Theseus. Karystos was made to join the Delian League by force in c.472 BCE, and Naxos was the first League member to be 'enslaved'[16] when it tried to withdraw in 469 BCE. The island was forced back, lost its fleet and was made to contribute money, which the Athenians spent on their own navy, presumably justifying their response on the basis of the permanence of the alliance and the ongoing war against Persia. Still, the war was undoubtedly progressing well: Kimon won a resounding victory at the river Eurymedon on the south coast of Asia Minor in 468 BCE, effectively destroying both the Persian fleet and with it any threat to the Aegean. The nearby city of Phaselis was 'persuaded' to join the League, and by around 466 BCE the Delian League had achieved unquestioned command of the sea, and acquired vast quantities of booty.

At Sparta things were not so good. There was no king from either of its two royal dynasties to provide positive leadership at this period. Pausanias governed on behalf of the Agiad king Pleistarkhos, who was a minor, but after being expelled from Byzantium for a second time, and unsuccessfully conspiring to change the Spartan constitution, he ended up walled up in a temple to die. When Pleistarkhos came of age he promptly died childless, and was succeeded by his nearest male relative, Pleistoanax, who was a boy of only nine or ten. To make matters worse, Leotykhidas King of the Eurypontid dynasty was exiled after an unsuccessful military expedition in 477 BCE, and, since his son was dead, his grandson Arkhidamos, who was only a boy, assumed the throne. Not surprisingly, the Spartans gave less consideration to Athens than they might have done, especially as they also had to cope with a number of other challenges from within the Peloponnese. When their long-standing enemy Argos effected a constitutional reform from oligarchy to democracy, there was great alarm at oligarchic Sparta. There was also unrest that resulted in all the Arcadian communities (except Mantineia) making an alliance with Argos. Democracy was gaining impetus elsewhere, too: at Elis there was a 'synoecism' of the surrounding villages in *c.*470 BCE, and a walled city with a democratic constitution on the Athenian model was set up; and Sparta's loyal ally Mantineia underwent a similar process.

By the mid-460s BCE, though, the unrest in the Peloponnesian League had subsided and Sparta's kings had reached maturity. Focusing on Athens again, the Spartans disliked what they saw and, when the island of Thasos seceded from the Delian Confederacy, they promised to invade Attika, although the promise was never fulfilled because a violent earthquake struck Sparta in 464 BCE. By the following year the Athenians had forced the island back into the League, and Sparta had a Helot revolt on its hands. Although they forced the rebels to take refuge on Mount Ithome in Messenia, the Spartans still appealed to Athens for help, and in 462 BCE the pro-Spartan Kimon persuaded the Assembly to send a force, led by himself. Unfortunately for him, they were almost instantly dismissed from the siege because of Athenian *neoteropoiia* (= 'subversive tendencies'), and the consequent loss of face led to Kimon's ostracism in 461 BCE. The beneficiaries of this were Ephialtes, who had opposed sending help to Sparta, and Perikles. The immediate result was the First Peloponnesian War (461–446).[17]

Thucydides wrote that:

> Perikles, by his position, intellectual ability and manifest incorruptibility, exercised a free control over the commoners: he led them instead of being led by them . . . Theoretically Athens was a democracy; in practice power was in the hands of the first citizen.[18]

Paradoxically Perikles rendered the Athenian democracy 'theoretical' by maintaining the confidence of the electorate. He ultimately served as one of the ten *strategoi* (= 'generals'), who were elected, not selected by lot, and could be reappointed annually, fifteen times in succession. In 461 BCE he was associated with Ephialtes in stripping the Areiopagos of its key judicial and political powers, and when Ephialtes was assassinated Perikles further radicalized the democracy by introducing state payment for jurymen and other officials, thereby enabling participation for all, regardless of their background. He also introduced tighter restrictions on Athenian citizenship, which actually excluded his third son (also called Perikles): his mistress, the glamorous, exotic, morally dubious Aspasia of Miletos, who had a high reputation for her seminars on public speaking, and a low one because she trained prostitutes, gave birth to Perikles junior after the law was passed – having a foreign mother disqualified the boy from citizenship. However, the Athenians waived the rules – a clear indication of the esteem in which Perikles was held.

He also masterminded the impressive 'Periklean Building Programme', with the aim of glorifying Athens, and providing employment for the masses. The buildings included the Parthenon, the Hephaisteion, the Temple of Poseidon at Sounion and the Propylaia, the seminal influence of which on world art remain unquestioned. Perikles himself said:

> Mighty indeed are the marks and monuments of our empire which we have left. Future ages will wonder at us as the present age wonders now.[19]

Prophetic words indeed.

Hostilities broke out between Athens and certain Peloponnesian states in 461 BCE. Megara reneged on its alliance with Sparta because of a border dispute with Corinth and joined the Delian League, giving Athens control of Megara's ports, but contributing to Corinth's *sphodron misos* (= 'bitter hatred') for Athens. In 459 BCE the Athenians overcame their long-standing rival Aigine, 'the eyesore of the Peiraieus',[20] and deployed Delian League contingents when they themselves were defeated at the Battle of Tanagra in Boiotia in 457 BCE. However, the Athenians later defeated the Boiotians at Oinophyta, then forced Boiotia and Phokis to join the Delian League. They also began the construction of two 'Long Walls' joining Athens to its ports, from where Athenian ships sailed to burn the Spartan dockyards at Gytheion, capture the Corinthian city of Khalkis, attack Sikyon, gain control of the south side of the Gulf of Corinth, and bring the cities of Akhaia into their alliance, along with Segesta and Leontinoi in Sicily, and Rhegion in Italy.

This probably represents the zenith of the Athenians' power, but in c.460 BCE they had got embroiled in an expedition to Persian-controlled Egypt. King Inaros of Libya had fomented a revolt there, and the Athenians sent a force to help. Initially they had the upper hand, but the Persian government eventually defeated the Delian League forces in the summer of 456 BCE, and blockaded them on the island of Prosopitis on the Nile, which fell after eighteen months. This may not have been the gigantic disaster that Thucydides implies, but nevertheless there was no more Athenian intervention in the affairs of Egypt. A knock-on effect of this was that in 454 BCE the Delian League treasury was moved to Athens, which became the de facto headquarters of the League. Kimon was recalled from ostracism, a five-year truce was signed with Sparta, and Athens turned its focus to Persia.

In 451 BCE Kimon fell ill and died while campaigning in Cyprus. It is possible that a treaty known as the Peace of Kallias was signed between Athens and Persia in spring 449 BCE, effectively ending hostilities and freeing Athens to concentrate on its own empire, but it may be that no such agreement ever existed – scholarly debate revolves around the possibility of a notorious 'missing' entry for 449/8 BCE on the first *stele* of the tribute quota lists that record the *aparkhe* paid to Athena from 454/3 to 440/39 BCE – but, if it did, it stipulated that the Aegean Sea was to belong to the Delian League, while Egypt and Cyprus were to belong to Persia, with the Asia Minor seaboard as a sort of 'demilitarized zone'. So now the Athenians faced a dilemma: the Delian League's objectives had essentially been fulfilled, yet the alliance was forever. Should they disband it and lose their tribute, or insist on its permanence at the cost of goodwill of the allies? It was a no-brainer. Their democratic system was based on the principle of payment for those who served – on the Council, as magistrates, on juries or in the fleet – and someone had to fund the Periklean building programme. There were too many vested interests, and seventeen years later they justified themselves with brutal honesty:

> We have done . . . nothing contrary to human nature in accepting an empire when it was offered to us and then in refusing to give it up. Three very powerful motives prevent us from doing so – security, honour and self-interest.[21]

However, by the early 440s BCE the Athenian land-Empire was on shaky ground: in 447 BCE the Boiotians defeated them in battle at

Koroneia; the following year Euboia revolted, as did Megara; and with the five-year truce with Sparta coming to an end, King Pleistoanax briefly invaded Attika. Peace negotiations followed, and in 445 BCE Perikles and Pleistoanax signed the Thirty Years Peace (which actually lasted for only fifteen years). It appears that Athens agreed to give up its land empire, but was allowed to keep Naupaktos and Aigine despite Corinthian protests. Athens recognized Spartan supremacy on land, and Sparta acknowledged Athens' hegemony of the Delian League. Neither side would assist revolts by states in the other side's sphere of influence, and neutral states were to be free to join either bloc.

A kind of 'Cold War' thus developed. Not everyone at Sparta was in favour of the treaty, and there were serious reservations about it at Corinth, but the Athenians were pleased: the Delian League was inexorably shifting away from an equal partnership between the *hegemon* (= 'leader') and its allies towards authoritarian rule (*arkhe*) over subjects.

It was all a question of 'attitude'. The Athenians used their allies in wars that had little to do with the Delian League, imposed garrisons on disloyal (or potentially disloyal) members, and installed endless officials in the process; Athenian citizens were settled in allied territory, either in colonies or in 'cleruchies' (*kleroukhia* = 'a holding of plots of land'), where Athenians had the option of going to live, or staying in Athens and leasing out the land; certain religious cults were promoted, notably the worship of Athena Queen of Athens (*Athena Athenon Medeousa*) and the hero Ion (a mythical King of Athens); offerings of barley and wheat, cows, panoplies and phalluses were demanded at some Athenian festivals; legal cases between Athenian citizens and members of allied states were probably heard in Athens, and cases involving death or exile penalties (defacing Athenian imperial decrees or not paying tribute certainly were heard); the Athenians banned the minting of silver coinage by the allied states, and imposed an embargo on all non-Athenian coins; Athenian weights and measures were foisted on the allied states; and Athens generally preferred democracies and did not flinch from regime change in cases of revolts (or before possible ones). On the plus side, the allies achieved revenge and better protection against Persia, the benefits of peace, democratic governments and prosperity through increased trade.

Unsurprisingly, various states became disaffected, and Samos revolted in 440 BCE. In violation of the Thirty Years Peace, the Spartan assembly voted for war, but Corinth, which would have borne the brunt of any fighting, persuaded the Peloponnesian League to reject the proposal. The Athenian fleet, under the command of Perikles and others, including the playwright Sophocles, brought the Samians to heel. Thucydides (an Athenian) had little sympathy with them:

> Because of their reluctance to face military service, most of them . . . had assessments made by which, instead of producing ships, they were to pay a corresponding sum of money. The result was that the Athenian navy grew strong at their expense, and when they revolted they always found themselves inadequately armed and inexperienced in war.[22]

But it was precisely this (over)confident imperialism that led Athens into the terrible Peloponnesian War with Sparta.

The Peloponnesian War (431–404 BCE)

> Never before had so many cities been captured and then devastated . . . never had there been so many exiles; never such loss of life.[23]

Despite Corinth's refusal to go to war over Samos, its relations with Athens were not good. Decades of Athenian encroachment on areas under Corinth's sphere of influence had generated that *sphodron misos* that Thucydides thought made war inevitable. He was really the first historian to analyse seriously the causes of a war:

> I propose first to give an account of the causes of complaint (*aitiai*) which they had against each other and of the specific instances where their interests clashed . . . But the real reason (*alethestate prophasis*) for the war was, in my opinion, . . . the growth of Athenian power and the fear which this caused in Sparta.[24]

The first of these *aitiai* really had nothing to do with Sparta or Athens. In 435 BCE civil strife had arisen between democrats and oligarchs at Epidamnos, a colony of Kerkyra (Corfu), which in turn was a colony of Corinth, albeit with an attitude problem towards its mother city. The Epidamnian democrats appealed to Kerkyra, which refused to help, and then to Corinth, which did get involved. So the Kerkyraians sided with the oligarchs. The rival forces engaged in a naval battle that the Kerkyraians won, but, when the Corinthians threatened retaliation, Kerkyra appealed to Athens, which agreed to an alliance. Technically this was not a violation of the Thirty Years Peace, but the combined size of the Athenian and Kerkyraian fleets was extremely threatening to Corinth. Hostilities escalated when Athens sent ten ships to help Kerkyra. This was nominally in a defensive capacity, but when the Corinthians engaged the Kerkyraians at the Battle of Sybota (433 BCE), the Athenian ships inevitably got dragged into the fighting. Corinth accused Athens of breaking the Thirty Years Peace.

The following year a convoluted dispute arose involving Poteidaia, a Corinthian colony in north-eastern Greece that was also a member of the Delian League. Concerned that the Poteidaians might revolt and take the other cities of the area with them, the Athenians demanded that they dismantle their seaward walls and get rid of the magistrates who they still received from Corinth. Sparta threatened to attack Attika if Athens attacked Poteidaia; the Poteidaians revolted; Athens and Corinth both sent troops; and the Athenians won the battle that took place outside the city.

A debate then took place in Sparta; in practice, war could only be declared if Corinth and Sparta were united on policy, which they now were, especially since Corinth also threatened to 'join a different alliance' if Sparta did not act; some Athenians who happened to be in Sparta at the time urged the Spartans to seek arbitration under the terms of the Thirty Years Peace, and the moderate Spartan king Arkhidamos warmed to this proposal; the belligerent *ephor* Stheneliadas argued that the Athenians were the aggressors and that the Spartans should defend their allies; and the Spartan Assembly voted for war. The Peloponnesian League then ratified the decision, but Sparta still felt the need to establish a firm pretext for war, and delivered a series of ultimata, which Athens rejected. Among the issues they raised was the 'Megarian Decree' (or Decrees), which excluded the Megarians from all ports in the Athenian Empire and from the market in Attika itself, probably dating from the 430s BCE. In Aristophanes' comedy *The Acharnians* (426/5 BCE) Dikaiopolis says:

> It was Athenians . . . who started the whole thing . . . Some young chaps got drunk and, for a lark, went to Megara and kidnapped their tart Simaitha. Well, this raised the Megarians' hackles, and they stole two of Aspasia's girls in retaliation. And that, gentlemen, was the cause of the war . . . it was all on account of three prostitutes. Olympian Perikles . . . began making laws written like drinking songs [banning the Megarians from our markets]. Well, pretty soon the Megarians were starving by slow degrees, and not unnaturally asked their allies the Spartans to try and get the decree reversed.[25]

In *Peace* (421 BCE) Aristophanes depicts a Megarian farmer trying to sell his daughters dressed as piglets, which, as well as providing a rich source of double-entendre (in Greek 'piggy' carries a similar connotation to the English 'pussy'), may also illustrate the effects of the Athenian embargo. Sparta may have feared that these bully-boy tactics would lead to Athens picking off her allies one by one, and, although Perikles seemed willing to submit to arbitration, he attached so many conditions that negotiations were replaced by hostilities when the Thebans attacked Athens' ally Plataia in 431 BCE.

The Peloponnesian War was a ghastly conflict. Like many warring states, Athens and Sparta entered the fray without a clear vision of what the war would entail. Perikles' strategy was to avoid direct confrontation with Sparta on land, keep the sea lanes open, harass the enemy and maintain Athens' grip on the empire. The Spartans thought that all they had to do was to invade and devastate Attika, which would lead either to the Athenians surrendering or to a battle, which they were confident of winning. However, the Athenians simply sheltered behind the Long Walls, sent their livestock to Euboia, imported their necessities by sea, and retaliated by invading Megara's territory and ravaging the Peloponnesian coasts. The drawbacks of this policy were the astronomical cost of keeping the navy at sea; the competing vested interests between the farmers and landowners who lost their livelihoods, and the urban population who even benefited financially from naval service; the demoralising nature of the strategy; and worst of all the plague that hit Athens in 430 BCE, which may have killed 30 per cent of the population, including Perikles in 429 BCE. After Perikles' death, a much more aggressive, but less coherent, strategy was promulgated by Kleon (of whom most of our sources disapprove deeply). More tribute was levied from the allies (almost a 300 per cent increase by 425 BCE), and revolts were handled uncompromisingly. At home Kleon increased the fees of jurymen, who could be useful allies in politically motivated court cases, from two to three obols, and conducted a zealous campaign to ensure that democracy was respected by the magistrates.

The fighting of 429 BCE took place mainly in north-west Greece, although the Athenian admiral Phormio won sea battles in the Gulf of Corinth. The following year Mytilene revolted from Athens but was forced to surrender in 427 BCE. Influenced by Kleon, the Athenian Assembly dispatched a ship with orders to execute the entire adult male population of Mytilene and enslave the women and children, but then had second thoughts: the dramatic 'Mytilenean Debate' followed, with Kleon pushing to keep the death penalty. Still, the Athenian people reversed their decision, and sent a second vessel that arrived in the nick of time to prevent the massacre. But, in general, 427 BCE was a particularly grisly year. It witnessed a vicious example of civil strife between the oligarchs (looking to Sparta) and democrats (looking to Athens) at Kerkyra, and the fall of Plataia, where the Spartans perpetrated what the Athenians had shrunk from doing at Mytilene. Meanwhile, Athens sent a small fleet to Leontinoi in Sicily, and their general Demosthenes defeated the Spartans at Olpai in 426 BCE, destroying all Spartan credibility in the north-west and underlining that the Corinthian colonies there could not rely on Spartan support.

In 425 BCE, when a storm forced the Athenian fleet to take refuge on a promontory at the bay of Pylos in the south-west Peloponnese, Demosthenes established a fortified base there. When the Spartans encamped on the promontory and landed troops on the island of Sphakteria opposite, he sent home for reinforcements. These managed to cut off the contingent on Sphakteria. Negotiations for the release of these men were scuppered by Kleon, but as winter approached it began to look as if the Athenians might not achieve anything. Losing popularity, the adept demagogue put the blame on Nikias, one of the generals, and boasted that if he were in command he would easily capture the Spartans. Nikias called his bluff, and Kleon got lucky. The Spartans found themselves blockaded, asked their leaders what to do, and were told: 'Make your own decision about yourselves, so long as you do nothing dishonourable.'[26] To everyone's astonishment, they surrendered. The Athenians used their 120 prized hostages to prevent further attacks on Attika. So the Spartans adopted a strategy suggested by their brilliant commander Brasidas, and tried to stir up revolts amongst Athens' allies on the northern Aegean seaboard.

Kleon's domination lasted until 424 BCE, when a scheme to conquer Boiotia came to grief, and Amphipolis was captured by Brasidas, who also detached thirteen states from the Delian League. These setbacks shocked the Athenians, and Kleon appears not to have been elected for the following year. By the spring of 423 BCE the Athenians and Spartans had made a one-year truce, but then news arrived that Skione had defected to the Spartan commander Brasidas, who refused to hand over the city. Kleon's fortunes benefited from the outburst of warmongering that resulted at Athens, but only until a major battle fought outside Amphipolis in 422 BCE, in which he and Brasidas were killed. Nikias and Pleistoanax then negotiated the 'Peace of Nikias'. This was to last for fifty years, but Corinth and Boiotia were against it, and Athens' allies were never consulted. Its prospects were not good.

One persistent opponent of the treaty was a young Athenian aristocrat called Alkibiades. In 420 BCE he facilitated a new alliance with the anti-Spartan Peloponnesian *poleis* of Argos, Elis and Mantineia. The Spartans responded by defeating the coalition in battle in 418 BCE, effectively reducing the Peace of Nikias to a meaningless hunk of marble.

In 416 BCE Athens demanded that the neutral (though probably pro-Spartan leaning) island of Melos should join the Delian League. When the Melians refused, the Athenians slaughtered the adult males and enslaved the women and children. Having given a chilling insight into the 'might is right' ethic of their imperialism:

> This is no fair fight, with honour on one side and shame on the other.
> It is rather a question of saving your lives and not resisting those
> who are far too strong for you.[27]

The next year Alkibiades persuaded the Athenians to launch a massive naval invasion of Sicily. He preyed on the Athenians' fear that the rich and mighty city of Syracuse posed a security threat to them; Nikias opposed the idea, but, in an example of Greek democracy at its chaotic worst, the *Ekklesia* voted to send the greatest naval force ever to have left Greece, under the command of Alkibiades, Lamakhos and, of all people, Nikias. No sooner had it sailed than Alkibiades was recalled to face accusations of profaning the Eleusinian Mysteries (initiation ceremonies) and being involved in the 'mutilation of the *Hermai*', rectangular stone pillars with a bust of Hermes on the top, feet on the bottom and a set of erect male genitals in the middle. Whether as an act of sacrilege, political subversion or just as a 'schoolboy prank', someone had hacked off the statues' phalluses. Guilty or not, Alkibiades was not willing to face trial; he defected to Sparta.

The Athenian fleet put Syracuse under siege, but Lamakhos got killed, the sickly, dithering Nikias lost the initiative, Alkibiades persuaded Sparta to send their general Gylippos to advise the defenders, and the Syracusans built a counter-wall that turned the Athenian besiegers into the besieged. Nikias asked for massive reinforcements, and to be relieved of the command, hoping that the scale of his request would induce the Athenians to abandon the expedition altogether. Yet the *Ekklesia* authorized the relieving force. Led by Eurymedon and Demosthenes the new troops tried to act quickly, but a night attack on the Syracusan counter-wall went catastrophically wrong. The Athenians decided to depart, but on the very night when they were going to leave, 27 August 413 BCE, there was an eclipse of the moon. The diviners decreed that the Athenians should wait 'thrice nine days', during which the Syracusans defeated them, killed Eurymedon in the harbour, blocked them in with boats, chains and bridges, and finally crushed them on 9 September. Nikias was forced to surrender, and he and Demosthenes were undoubtedly executed. Some 7,000 PoWs were incarcerated for months in Syracuse's stone quarries, although there are stories of some Athenians winning their liberty through reciting excerpts of Euripides to their appreciative captors.

Sicily was a shattering defeat for Athens. Even while the expedition was under way the Spartans had established a fortified base at Dekeleia only a few kilometers from Athens, on Alkibiades' advice. Because of this, agricultural work was now prohibitively dangerous, Athens became far more dependent on imported food, and the economy suffered a blow as some 20,000 slaves from the silver mines at Laureion ran away to the Spartan camp. Also, the Persian *satraps* (governors) Tissaphernes (Sardis) and Pharnabazus (Hellespontine Phrygia) started to foment unrest among Athens' allies and to fund a new Peloponnesian League fleet. Egged on by Alkibiades, numerous states revolted from the Delian League, threatening Athens' cornroutes to Egypt and the Black Sea. To make things worse, under the Treaty of Miletos the Spartans granted the Persian king dominion over all the territory that had belonged to him and his forefathers: Ionia was back to where it had been before the Persian invasions.

Yet the Athenians were nothing if not resilient. They dipped into their emergency reserve funds, rebuilt their fleet, trained new crews and by 411 BCE they were generally holding their own along the Anatolian coast. Domestically, though, they were in turmoil. An oligarchic-leaning group, including Antiphon, Peisandros and Phrynikhos, asserted that they could handle Athenian policy more effectively than the democracy, and Alkibiades promised that he would broker an alliance with Tissaphernes on condition that Athens become an oligarchy. A return to Athens was becoming rather urgent for Alkibiades because the negotiations with the Persians were making the Spartans suspicious of him, especially King Agis, with whose wife Alkibiades was having an affair. The oligarchs ratcheted up the fear, manipulated the *Ekklesia*'s lust for Persian gold, and in 411 BCE they got it to replace all the existing magistracies with 'the Four Hundred', who would have absolute authority. The Four Hundred were supposed to choose 5,000 men as an Assembly, but they never did.

This oligarchic regime only lasted from June to September. The Athenian fleet was stationed at Samos and its democratic sailors, urged on by Thrasyboulos and Thrasyllos, who also brought Alkibiades on board, threatened to restore the democracy by force. Before this could happen, though, a 'moderate democracy/mixed oligarchy and democracy', dubbed the Five Thousand Legislators, was set up. The system was championed by Theramenes, who earned himself the nickname *Kothornos* ('Buskin' – a boot that fits either foot).

The incoming government voted to recall Alkibiades, but he delayed returning. Under him, Thrasyboulos and Theramenes, the Athenian fleet defeated the Spartans and Pharnabazus in 410 BCE at Cyzicus, killing the Spartan commander, and intercepting a typically (and literally) laconic dispatch from the defeated Spartans: 'Ships lost. Mindaros dead. Men starving. Don't know what to do.'[28]

The victory resulted in the restoration of democracy at Athens. Its most prominent leader was Kleophon, an uncompromising imperialist who instituted the famous 'two-obol payment' (for what, we do not know), restarted the building programme on the Akropolis, and rejected a Spartan peace proposal. In retrospect, the Athenians should have accepted this. Alkibiades finally made his long-awaited return to Athens in the summer of 407 BCE, but his honeymoon period was brief. With Persian finance the Spartans constructed the biggest fleet they had had for years, and in spring 406 BCE their commander Lysander captured fifteen Athenian ships at Notion, near Ephesus, and Alkibiades was held accountable. Again he went into exile. Konon took over, only to be defeated and blockaded in the harbour of Mytilene. The Athenians melted treasure from their temples, promised slaves their freedom and resident aliens citizenship, sent out 150 triremes, and won an amazing victory off the islands of Arginousai. And then it all went horribly wrong. Adverse winds prevented the rescue of some crews; a blame-culture arose; politicians got involved; popular hysteria took hold; and all eight Athenian commanders were condemned to death (even Perikles' son was among those executed).

Again the Spartans offered peace; again the Athenians rejected it. Lysander negotiated further money from Persia, practically became *satrap* of Sardis, and rampaged over the Aegean before reaching Lampsakos on the Hellespont in the late summer of 405 BCE. Konon's Athenian fleet beached at Aigospotamoi across the strait, but Lysander surprised his complacent and predictable adversaries while they were eating. The mighty Athenian navy was destroyed practically without a fight.

Athens did not fall immediately, but famine eventually forced the issue. The surrender came in the spring of 404 BCE. The Spartans installed a collaborationist regime of anti-democratic Athenian aristocrats, who became known as the Thirty Tyrants. Repressive and unpopular, they were ousted by a pro-democracy movement led by Thrasyboulos in 403 BCE, which quite remarkably then proclaimed the most famous ancient 'amnesty' (arguably the first in Western history).

Athens was again a democracy, but was economically and militarily shattered. The city remained a centre of intellectual creativity, although it was not always tolerant of its creative intellectuals. In 399 BCE Socrates was impeached on nebulous charges of 'refusing to honour the gods honoured by the state, introducing new divinities, and corrupting the youth', found guilty, and met his end by drinking hemlock. Revolutionizing Greek thought had cost him his life, and, with the death of the man that Plato dubbed 'the best man of his time in wisdom and justice',[29] we come to the end of an era.

6

GREEK SOCIAL LIFE

Plato gave thanks to nature, first that he was born a human being
rather than a dumb animal; second that he was a man rather than a
woman; then that he was a Greek not a foreigner; finally that he
was Athenian born in the time of Socrates.

Lactantius, *Divine Institutions* 3.19

Citizens, Metoikoi *and Slaves*

Aristotle defined a *polis* as 'a compound made up of citizens', and
a citizen as 'a man who shares in the administration of justice and
in the holding of office'.[1] The citizenship issue was very clear cut:
if you were not a citizen, you always remained an outsider,
regardless of whether you were a free man (be this a foreigner
[*xenos,* pl. *xenoi*] or a resident alien [*metoikos,* 'metic', pl.
metoikoi]), a woman or a slave. Statistics are hard to come by, but
although it is not the same as the total population of the state (we
need to factor in women, children, slaves and foreigners) it is likely
that there were never more than 50,000 citizens in Athens.

The concept of citizenship was crucial. Losing your citizen rights
(*atimia* = the deprivation of *time*) – a penalty imposed at Athens
for crimes such as embezzlement, bribery, cowardice in battle,
perjury, violence against your parents and anti-democratic activity
– barred you from speaking in the Assembly or the law courts,
holding any public office, sitting on the *Boule,* acting as a juror or
entering temples or the *agora.* Also, as Athens' democracy became
more radical, the citizen body became more exclusive. Initially
Athenian citizenship depended simply on having a citizen father –

Kleisthenes, Themistokles and Kimon had non-Athenian or even non-Greek mothers – but after 451/50 BCE only males with an Athenian citizen father *and* an Athenian mother from a citizen background were eligible. Very occasionally *metoikoi* or *xenoi* could be voted to receive citizenship as a reward for some extra-ordinary service to the democracy, but this was rare.

Economic distinctions affected the citizens' political and military roles because there was always a direct link between their wealth and their function in the army, which in turn determined how much political power they might have. Only the very wealthy could afford to equip themselves as cavalry, and the moderately wealthy as hoplites, meaning that the poor majority played a very subordinate role in land warfare. However, once sea power became the basis of Athens' military might, the poor Athenians who manned the fleet started to play key roles. Democracy and naval empire went hand in hand.

For the Athenian, citizenship brought both inalienable rights and clearly defined duties. The English word 'idiot' is derived from the Greek '*idiotes*' (= 'private person/individual', i.e. someone who does not get involved in politics). The right to vote for, initiate and amend legislation, make decisions on war or peace, elect officials and generals, and speak in the Assembly, entailed an obligation to take an intelligent and active interest in the city's affairs. The privilege of being able to stand for election to the various magistracies, councils and committees, and being paid for service, went hand-in-hand with an acute sense of political responsibility and participation. State subsidies were granted to various groups, such as those who were unable to afford tickets for the theatre during religious festivals, or the orphans and widows of those killed in action and invalided in war, but rich citizens had to perform 'liturgies' such as the outfitting, maintenance and command of a trireme, or the funding of a tragic or comic chorus, and everyone had to contribute a war tax (*eisphora*) in time of emergency (though income tax was not normal). To maintain everyone's right to national security, citizens were required to fight for their gods, homes and laws; the *Hippeis* had to provide their own horses; all *epheboi* ('ephebes', boys of 18–20) had to complete military training involving frontier duty; and all citizens between 20 and 60 years had to provide their own armour and equipment, and report for duty with three days' rations if called up.

And, finally, the right to worship obliged everyone to participate in and respect religious observances.

The *metoikoi* were free Greeks or non-Greeks who lived in Athens or in Attika. After a stay of (probably) one month, *xenoi* had to register as a *metoikos* or face being sold into slavery, and even then they had to comply with certain obligations that symbolized their inferior status. Every *metoikos* had to find a *prostates* (legal protector) – an Athenian citizen who would undertake legal representation if necessary – and the penalty for neglecting this obligation was also to be sold into slavery. Metics also had to register as being domiciled in one of the demes of Attika, and they are easy to identify on inscriptions: citizens' names are followed by their *demos* name; metics' names are followed by 'domiciled in the *demos* of . . .'; slaves' names by the name of their master or nothing at all. The accounts relating to work on the Erekhtheion shows citizens (28 per cent of the work force), *metoikoi* (50 per cent) and slaves (22 per cent) working side by side on its sculptures, here being paid the same rates of 60 *drakhmai* per figure, or 18 *drakhmai* for work on the fluting of the columns:

> Phyromakhos of the *demos* of Kephisia [i.e. citizen] – the youth beside the breast-plate: 60 *dr.*
> Praxias domiciled in the *demos* of Melite [i.e. metoikos] – the horse and the man appearing behind it and hitting it in the flank: 120 *dr.*
> Antiphanes of the *demos* of Kerameis [i.e. citizen] – the chariot, the youth, and the two horses being harnessed: 240 *dr.* . . .
> Ameiniades domiciled in the *demos* of Koile [i.e. *metoikos*]: 18 *dr.*
> Aiskhines [i.e. slave]: 18 *dr.*
> Somenes, slave of Ameiniades: 18 *dr.*[2]

Depending on their personal wealth, the *metoikoi* were subject to liturgies in the same way as citizens were, and they were also liable to call-up for the military. They had, on pain of being sold into slavery, to pay the *metoikion* ('metic-tax'), which was not much (12 *dr.* per annum for adult males, 6 *dr.* for adult women living on their own), but citizens did not pay poll taxes like this. They also had to pay tax for the right to trade in the *agora*. Yet in Aristophanes' play *The Acharnians*, Dikaiopolis says that the citizens are the flour of the Athenian corn, the *xenoi* are the worthless chaff, and the *metoikoi* the bran that the Athenians incorporated into their bread: nutritionally inferior, but nonetheless essential companions. When Nikias addressed the *metoikoi* in the Athenian navy on the eve of the Sicilian disaster, he was similarly inclusive:

> Through your knowledge of our language and imitation of our manners [you] were always considered Athenians, even though not so in reality.[3]

For all this, metic status entailed a number of limitations: crucially they had no political rights; they had no right of intermarriage with citizens, which meant there was no possibility (except in the case of a special grant) of obtaining citizen status; the murder of a *metoikos* was treated as unpremeditated homicide; furthermore, only a citizen could normally acquire, own and alienate land, which meant that *metoikoi* could not borrow or lend money on the security of land. This limited the types of economic activity that they could get involved in, yet despite this they seem to have conducted a wide range of occupations, and some of them became very wealthy.

An inscription dating from 401/400 BCE listing metics who had performed extraordinary services to the democracy, gives us an interesting snapshot of ordinary working-class people:

> Leptines, a cook; Demetrios, a carpenter; Euphorion, a muleteer; Kephisodoros, a builder; Hegesias, a gardener; Epameinon, an ass driver; . . . Opos, an oil merchant; . . . On, a nut seller; . . . Bendiphanes, a bath maker (?); Emporion, a farmer; Paidikos, a baker; Sosias, a fuller; Psammis [an Egyptian name] a farmer; . . . Eukolion, a hired servant; Kallias, a statuette maker.[4]

Trying to put numbers on the *metoikos* population is fraught with difficulty. The only overall figure available comes from the census Demetrios of Phaleron carried out at the end of the fourth century BCE, which counted 21,000 citizens and 10,000 *metoikoi* (although it is unclear whether metic women were included). Demetrios' Athens was a very different beast to Perikles', but considering the emotive nature of immigration in modern politics, this still raises the issue of why, if there were about half as many resident aliens as citizens, the Athenians allowed them in. The sources are unanimous: they needed their economic services, the revenues they brought in, and their service in the military. The 'Old Oligarch', writing *c.*430 BCE, has some shrewd insights to make in among his overt prejudices:

> As far as slaves and *metoikoi* are concerned, it is in Athens that you see them behaving with the greatest insolence; you may not strike them there and the slave will not stand out of your way. The reason ... is this: if there was a law allowing the free man to strike the slave, the *metoikos* or, the freedman, he would often have struck an Athenian thinking he was a slave. For the common people there are no better-dressed than the slaves and the *metoikoi* [But] the city needs the *metoikoi* on account of the multiplicity of trades and because of the fleet.[5]

So the presence of metics was actively encouraged, and the citizens tended to regard them not as economic rivals but as indispensable to Athens' economy.

Another group that was a key element in the *polis* structure was the slaves. Like every other ancient society, the Greeks treated slavery as a basic fact of life. Slaves were a form of property, and if you could afford to buy them, you did:

> Of property, the first and most necessary kind, the best and most manageable, is man. Therefore, the first step is to procure good slaves.[6]

There is no uncontroversial evidence about the number of slaves in Athens, or about what proportion of Athenians owned slaves, but even the very lowest estimates add up to approximately one slave per citizen. Slaves not only lacked the privileges of citizens, but they had no legally enforceable rights whatsoever: they did not do military service (the Athenians did not use 'galley-slaves' – service as a rower was the prerogative of the free man), and, because they were property, they could be bought and sold in a market. They were also tortured if summoned as witnesses in the courts – how else, the Athenians thought, could it be guaranteed that they would tell the truth? However, a slave did have the right of sanctuary if he or she were being ill treated, and could take refuge in a temple, but it was up to the priests to decide whether to send the slave back or sell him or her to a new master.

After Solon banned Athenians being kept as slaves at Athens the main sources of supply of slaves was capture. The women and children of any *polis* defeated in war were liable to be enslaved (and the grown men put to death), after which they would either be sold in the conquering city, or exported. Slave dealers also obtained prisoners from piracy. 'Pirate' is a Greek word (*peirates*). Plato was said to have been captured and only saved from slavery by payment of a large ransom, and many heroines of Greek New Comedy went down this route into slavery. Generally, though, the dealers acquired slaves from outside Greece, and the words 'slave' and 'barbarian' became practically synonymous. Both citizens and *metoikoi* could own slaves, and an inscription recording an auction allows us to see the range of their backgrounds, the high prices that they fetched, and what you could get for your money: 170 or 115 *dr.* would buy a Thracian male; a Thracian woman cost between 220 and 135; a Syrian up to 301; a Carian 105, a Carian boy 174, or a Carian infant 72; 121 or 161 got you an Illyrian; 144 a Scythian; 153 a Colchian; and 85 a Lydian woman.[7] In the same auction, you could have bought two female work oxen for 100 *dr.*, 67 goats and their young for 710, a bed for 9, a table for 4, and a bench for 1 *dr.* 1 *obol*. Roughly speaking, a slave represents the kind of outlay that a modern person might make on a car.

Another source of slaves came from the sale or 'exposure' of unwanted children, although our sources also mention that the chance to have children is offered to good slaves, who:

> will love us the better for it; but those, who through subtlety will endeavour to gain their ends with any of the women without consent, will be always contriving and practising ways to our disadvantage, to compass or carry on their lewd designs.[8]

Slaves were employed to carry out pretty much every conceivable kind of task, be this in an urban, rural, private or public setting. They often worked alongside their masters, and, in a world without pension plans or an NHS, a slave provided security against old age or misfortune, as one disabled Athenian tells us:

I have a trade, which brings me in a little, but I can barely work at it myself and I cannot afford to buy someone to replace myself in it.[9]

More fortunate individuals might own larger numbers of slaves. The *metoikos* Kephisodoros had at least sixteen, and Demosthenes' father had more than fifty, split between two businesses:

> One was a sword-factory, employing 32 or 33 slaves, mostly valued at 5 or 6 *minai* and none at less than 3. From this he received a net income of 30 *minai* a year. The other was a bed-factory, employing 20 slaves, offering a security of 40 *minai*, and bringing in a net income of 12 *minai*.[10]

The sums of money he is talking about are very substantial: 1 *mina* = 100 *drakhmai* (see Table 6.1, below). Some slaves, called 'pay bringers' or 'those living apart', lived separately from their masters, and were contracted out. These might sometimes be allowed to keep a portion of their wages, although that privilege probably did not apply to the 1,000 slaves who Nikias rented as mine workers to a Thracian called Sosias (presumably a *metoikos*) for 1 *obol* per day per man, thereby generating an enormous income of 166 *dr.* per day for Nikias, and allowing Sosias to undercut the price of free labour by a considerable margin. Slaves might even supervise other slaves, and we hear that Nikias paid the staggering sum of 1 talent to buy a slave to manage a silver mine.[11] Presumably he was worth it.

It is clear that slave labour was used in farming. Smallholders tended to work their own land, but those with medium-sized holdings, such as Gorgias in Menander's *Old Cantankerous*, would have had slaves working alongside them. Larger estates were more dependent on slave labour, but Greece had nothing like the massive *latifundia* that came to characterize Roman agriculture.

Table 6.1 Athenian currency

Currency	Equivalent
6 *obols*	= 1 *drakhma*
[literally 'metal spits', but in practice small coins]	[i.e. a bundle of 6 spits]
100 *drakhmai*	= 1 *mina*
60 *minai*	= 1 talent
Daily pay for jurymen	= 2 or 3 *obols*
Daily pay for a skilled artisan	= 1 *drakhma*

The state kept public slaves, ranging from well-educated secretaries, to criers, gaolers, an executioner and a 'police force' of Scythian archers. The Scythians became stereotypical buffoons on the comic stage, but in reality they must have had the power to arrest free men. Policing seems to have been a job that no Athenian citizen wanted to do.

At the opposite end of the slave hierarchy came the likes of mine workers. Archaeological excavation of the mine shafts vividly illustrates how cramped the conditions were and how stale the air. When the Spartans occupied Dekeleia in 413 BCE some 20,000 slaves ran away – eloquent testimony to their desperation. Yet, despite these defections, there were no slave revolts in Classical Athens to compare with those of Spartacus in Roman times, or of the Helots against the Spartans, and neither was it expected that there would be: Sparta's Helots were Greeks enslaved by other Greeks, whereas Athens' slaves were largely from diverse barbarian backgrounds. Plato felt that this was essential:

> The revolts . . . in Sparta, and in the states where a lot of people speak the same language, have shown the evils of the system often enough . . . If the slaves are to submit to their condition without giving trouble, they should not all come from the same country or speak the same tongue; they should also be properly treated, not only for their own sake, but more so in the master's interest.[12]

Most sources agree: good but firm treatment is what slaves needed, and it is extremely difficult to generalize about slave conditions. The majority of them lived among the general population, and because every slave had a price, the less unfortunate might be able to save up enough money to buy their freedom. There was no special process ('manumission' is derived from Latin, not Greek), but ex-slaves became *metoikoi*, and continued to owe various obligations to their liberators as patrons. Manumission might also occur in their master's will, and we hear of some slaves being liberated as a reward for giving information about serious crimes or for distinguished service in war. In Aristophanes' *The Frogs*, Charon, the ferryman of the dead, refuses to take the slave Xanthias over the Styx because he had not 'fought in the sea-battle' – a reference to the battle of Arginousai, which the Athenians won with the help of slaves, who were rewarded with their freedom. In the fourth century BCE consortiums even lent slaves the money to buy themselves out:

> Bion, gem engraver, domiciled in the *demos* of Melite, having 'defeated' Khairippos, son of Khairedemos of the *demos* of Halai, and an association of contributors headed by Khairippos of Halai, [has dedicated] a bowl worth 100 *drakhmai*.[13]

Bion's ex-master loaned him the money to buy his freedom!

The highly charged term 'freedom' (*eleutheria*) became enormously important because it was this that divided the citizens from the slaves. In the Homeric poems the basis of slavery was pure force, and a slave was not necessarily regarded as an inferior being, except in so far as she or he was under someone else's power: Eumaios in the *Odyssey* is a man of the highest virtue. But after the Greeks defeated the Persians, they began to consider themselves superior to barbarians, who also readily submitted to absolute monarchy, which the newly democratic Greeks regarded as tantamount to slavery. Freedom made people truly human; forced labour made them little better than animals. Freedom allowed people to develop reason, self-control, courage, generosity and high-mindedness; slaves exercised no mental or spiritual faculties at all and so were irrational, undisciplined, cowardly, selfish and pusillanimous. This led to two conclusions: (a) barbarians were naturally fitted to slavery; and (b) given that it was morally right to help your friends and harm your enemies, it was the duty of the Greeks to enslave them:

> So, as the poets say, 'It is proper that Greeks should rule non-Greeks',[14] the implication being that non-Greek and slave are by nature identical.[15]

Plato believed that those who are not inhabited by divine wisdom are better off when controlled by those who are, and that if wisdom and control do not come from within, they must be imposed from without. Aristotle argued that good or bad character is not the *result* of freedom and slavery, but the *cause* of it. Those who are slaves *by culture* are so precisely because they are slaves *by nature*.

Such an ideology makes it seem natural that those who are free should govern those who are not. It is to everyone's benefit, especially the slaves':

> It is clear then that by nature some are free, others slaves, and that for these it is both just and expedient that they should serve as slaves . . . Whereas the one must be ruled, the other should exercise the rule for which he is fitted by nature, thus being the master.[16]

Aristotle does, however, disapprove of instances where people become slaves for the wrong reason (military conquest, for example): this is an unnatural type of enslavement, since those enslaved are not slaves by nature.

So slavery itself was unquestioned and had a central economic and social function in many Hellenic *poleis*. From the Greek perspective, any moral issues surrounding the ownership of slaves were practically non-existent. One regular modern criticism of Athenian democracy is that it was not democratic: the time that the citizens needed to participate in it was created at the expense of slaves. But the Athenians would not have seen the logic of the complaint because: (a) Athens had always had slaves, but had not always been a democracy; and (b) other Greek states had slaves and were not democracies.

It is similarly objected that Athenian 'democracy' was confined to the adult, male, native, freeborn community, a minority of the total population. It was. But equally, an Athenian would have looked at our society and seen people heading off to work each morning and being told what to do by their employers, and concluded that pretty well everyone was a slave. An Athenian aristocrat would take this view one step further. He saw his social and economic activities as a form of self cultivation, undertaken for honour rather than material benefit, and liked to think that what he did was never subject to any form of compulsion. To him, work for any form of material gain was a pointless and disgusting form of slavery.

A Woman's Place is in the Oikos

The basic social unit of the *polis* was the *oikos* (pl. *oikoi*), 'household', although the word can be used both of the building ('house') and the people who lived in it. Aristotle tells us that a complete household consists of slaves and free men, and that its key elements – in which the male *kyrios* (head of the *oikos*) holds the dominant position – are master and slave, husband and wife, father and children, plus 'the so-called art of getting wealth'.[17]

Only a man could be *kyrios*. At birth an Athenian male had to be accepted by his father and, after the reforms of Kleisthenes, registered in his hereditary *deme*; a woman remained part of her *oikos* until she married, after which she joined her husband's. Even 'citizen' women had no political rights, but the Greeks would have baulked at the glib modern assertion that they 'treated women just like slaves'. That, says Aristotle, is a barbarian thing to do: in Greek society, 'Nature has distinguished between female and slave', and the husband's relationship with his wife is defined as 'in the position of a statesman governing fellow citizens', even though 'the male is more fitted to rule than the female, unless conditions are quite contrary to nature'.[18] When Socrates asks a friend, 'Which are better, your free women or Keramon's slaves?' he gets the reply, 'My free women, of course.'[19]

On his father's death, a legitimate son would automatically take possession of the inheritance. If there was more than one legitimate son they shared equally, and a man without a legitimate son might adopt an heir during his lifetime or in his will. This would normally be an adult with Athenian parentage on both sides, usually a relative. A daughter only inherited, in a very technical sense, if there were no sons, sons of predeceased sons, or adopted sons. Such a girl was called an *epikleros*, but she had to marry either the man named by her father, or her nearest male relative, who would then claim the estate. All this was aimed at preserving the individual *oikos*, and there was a focus not just on the transmission of property, but also on the heir's obligation to take responsibility for all members of the *oikos*.

In order to fulfil what Aristotle calls the 'procreative relationship', there would have to be a marriage. The prospective husband was usually chosen by the bride's father or guardian. Betrothal took place in front of witnesses, and a dowry had to be agreed upon. Husbands were often about fifteen years older than their brides, and since there was a 'surplus' of girls as a result of deaths in battle, a dowry was indispensable in order to keep the bride in the style to which she was accustomed. Athenian law stated that the *kyrios* who had a woman's dowry in his possession was obliged to support her; if there was a divorce the dowry had to be repaid, which might provide the woman with a degree of security.

Athenian women could divorce their husbands, but the procedures made this practically impossible if the husband was reluctant. The virtuous and affectionate Hipparete became sick of her husband Alkibiades' liaisons with various courtesans, but the law demanded that she lodge her petition for divorce with the magistrate in person. When she did this, Alkibiades simply carried her home again. Plutarch comments that this was not regarded as inhuman or illegal.

> Indeed, it would appear that the law, in laying it down that the wife who wishes to separate from her husband must attend the court in person, is actually designed to give the husband the opportunity to meet her and recover her.[20]

The wedding, presided over by the household gods, and attended only by parents and friends, took place when the bride was transferred to the bridegroom's *oikos*. Much of our information about weddings comes from special long-necked vessels used to draw water for the nuptial bath, called *loutrophoroi*. One example by Polygnotos[21] shows the bride being greeted by her husband, who gives her a pomegranate, a many-seeded symbol of fertility that emphasizes that the birth and upbringing of children was the main purpose of marriage. *Loutrophoroi* were sometimes placed on the graves of girls who died unmarried.

An insight into a husband's expectations from his marriage were, appears in a conversation between Socrates and the affluent Iskhomakhos in Xenophon's *Oikonomikos*. Iskhomakhos has not married for love – he wants someone to handle his domestic arrangements, bear his children, and bring them up – but the relationship would not necessarily be loveless. Greek literature is full of tales of the power of love: Hector clearly adores Andromache; there is electrifying passion between Jason and Medea; Aristophanes' *Lysistrata* is built around the reciprocal lusts of husbands and wives; and Xenophon's Socrates seems to understand the demands of motherhood:

The wife conceives and bears her burden. She suffers pains and endangers her life; she gives away the food that sustains her. She goes through a period of labour, gives birth and brings up the child with care . . . The baby does not know its helper, and cannot convey its needs. She has to guess what is good for it and will satisfy it, and tries to provide these to the full. She cares for the baby night and day laboriously for a long period, with no expectation of reward.[22]

Perikles, on the other hand, became disenchanted with his wife, arranged for her remarriage by mutual agreement, and developed a relationship with Aspasia that was clearly sexual, but affectionate too:

He took Aspasia and loved her dearly. Every day on leaving for his public business and on returning he would kiss her.[23]

But Aspasia was not typical. Not only was she not Perikles' wife, she was a *hetaira* (= courtesan). Men like Perikles and Iskhomakhos might fulfil their extramarital physical yearnings with other women, or indeed men, if they wanted. One option was a one-off liaison for cash with a *porne* (prostitute, hence the English 'pornography'). Alternatively a long-term and exclusive relationship with a *pallake* ('concubine', although the English word has more pejorative tone than the Greek), possibly Athenian, but more likely a foreigner or a slave, might suffice. Or again a *hetaira* ('companion'/courtesan) might be a possibility. She would accept successive clients, often two or more at once, and might be a slave belonging to a pimp, hired or sold at a price commensurate with her 'talents', a free but poor woman turning whatever tricks she could, or an educated, beautiful and successful creature who could cherry-pick her lovers, and get rich doing so. A description of how prostitutes are treated and presented by their pimp comes from a fragment of the *Fair Measure* by the comic poet Alexis: short ones have cork soles stitched into their shoes; tall girls wear thin slippers, and hold their heads on one side; ones with blonde eyebrows paint them with lampblack; dark-complexioned ladies are smeared with white-lead; those that are too pale apply rouge; and those that are beautiful – in part – reveal that part naked.[24]

Greek same-sex relationships are the subject of ferocious scholarly argument, but it is crystal clear that 'Greek love' formed an integral part of the accepted pattern of life for men, and sometimes women. But the Greeks did not categorize anyone as 'a homosexual'. They don't have a word for this, although they do give us ours: the 'homo-' part is Greek (*homos* = 'one and the same'), and so is the 'hetero-' in heterosexual (*heteros* = 'other'). Their vocabulary centres on the *erastes* ('lover') and the *eromenos* ('beloved'). The *eromenos* is generally someone at the specific life-stage between late teenage and early twenties. He was not expected to be liberal with his favours, and making sexual advances towards under-age boys was both morally unacceptable and illegal. Some commentators regard the *erastes* as a predatory older man looking for anal sex with a submissive young person, but stymied both by the law and strong social disapproval of penetrating a free man of any age, and hoping at best for a bit of excitement between the boy's thighs. Greek males often had sex face to face, not bending over, and much male-on-male sexual activity was 'intercrural' (i.e. between the legs), rather than penetrative. Others dismiss this, seek evidence for a reciprocal same-sex disposition, regard the *erastai* simply as gawping admirers whose behaviour was totally baffling to the *eromenoi*, and interpret depictions of sexual activity on vases as warnings against this sort of behaviour. The debate rages on.

Demosthenes famously said:

> We have courtesans for pleasure, concubines to look after the day-to-day needs of the body, wives that we may breed legitimate children and have trusty wardens of what we have in the house.[25]

Iskhomakhos and his wife (who is never named) need legitimate children to ensure the continuing prosperity of the *oikos* and to care for them in their old age. The importance of a child's legitimacy is underlined by the fact that adultery with a married woman was both a public and private offence: it is the *woman's* marital status that counts, whereas a man's relations with *pornai*, *pallakai* and *hetairai* do not really affect this issue. However, it is notable that killing an adulterer caught in the act was considered justified, even if the frivolity with which adultery is sometimes treated could indicate a mismatch between the law and reality. In Homer's *Odyssey*, when Aphrodite, goddess of love (or, more properly, sex), and her lover Ares are cunningly caught in the act and trapped under an unbreakable net by her husband Hephaistos, much to the delight of the male Olympian deities (the goddesses, 'constrained by feminine modesty', stayed at home), Apollo asks Hermes:

'Would you care, though held in those unyielding shackles, to lie in bed by golden Aphrodite's side?' To which the Giant-slayer replied: '. . . There is nothing I should relish more. Though the chains that kept me prisoner were three times as many, though all you gods and all the goddesses were looking on, yet would I gladly sleep by golden Aphrodite's side.'[26]

In Aristophanes' *Wealth* we hear that money can enable a detected adulterer to escape ritual humiliation,[27] and in the *The Clouds* Pheidippides learns how to escape using the power of words:

WRONG ARGUMENT: Supposing you get caught with some-body's wife, you can say to him, cool as a cucumber, 'What have I done wrong? Look at Zeus; wasn't he always the slave of his passions, sexwise? And do you expect a mere mortal like me to do any better than a god?'
RIGHT ARGUMENT: Ah, but suppose the man doesn't take any notice? Suppose he starts applying the carrot and ashes treatment? Then you'll have bugger's arse for the rest of your life. [*To WRONG ARGUMENT*] Get out of that one, clever guy![28]

The Wrong Argument's mention of Zeus refers to the frequency with which he succumbed to extramarital sexual temptation, and abused his supernatural powers to have sex with lots of mortal females. The Right Argument's worries centre on the way in which to humiliate the adulterer, and symbolize his feminization and rape by the husband, his pubic hair was burnt off with hot ash (a similar fate to that avoided by the affluent aduterer in *Wealth*), and a root vegetable (usually a *rhaphanis*, a very large radish) was forced up his anus. The Greeks despised any male who enjoyed submitting and called him '*katapygon*' ('a down-into-the-arse man') or '*euryproktos*' ('having a wide anus'), the latter term being the one rather misleadingly translated 'bugger' here.

Adultery not only potentially confused the issue between the husband's children and the adulterer's, it also resulted in legal attitudes that regarded rape as less serious than seduction, on the premise that a woman hates a rapist, but not a seducer. So the pre-marital virginity of Iskhomakhos' wife was incredibly important. She was married at the age of fifteen, and had lived an incredibly sheltered existence before then. Iskhomakhos' advice that she exercise by 'moving around the house and supervising the house-work' suggests that her movement outdoors was restricted. Even within the house the women's accommodation was segregated from the men's. We hear of women who were so obsessed with their modesty that they were embarrassed even to be seen by their male relatives,[29] and that respectable wives did not accompany their husbands to banquets or dine with strangers. This cocooned environment is reflected in Aristophanes' *Lysistrata* where the women have difficulty in attending a meeting:

> It's not easy for women to get away. We're always dancing attendance on our husbands, or getting the maid moving, or putting the baby to bed, bathing it, feeding it.[30]

The house itself could have had the characteristics of the Hellenistic merchants' houses excavated on Delos, where the small but tastefully simple 'House of the Lake' was fairly typical. You entered from the street by a double door leading into a small forecourt, on the right of which was possibly a *thyroreion* (doorman's lodge). A door led from the forecourt to a peristyle courtyard, which was surrounded by twelve columns. It is from here that the house derives its light and air. There are no ground-floor exterior windows, making the house cool, quiet and secure. In the centre of the peristyle was a square space covered with mosaic for the reception of rainwater that was drained off into a cistern below, and surrounding it were the reception rooms, ancillary areas, slaves' rooms and storerooms. A large room with three doors that opened on to the peristyle was probably the *andron* (room for entertaining male guests) facing south to give maximum light in winter and shade in summer; beyond it were two smaller rooms probably used as male sleeping chambers. There was probably a kitchen and a latrine off the secondary entrance, and a common feature of these houses was an open recess (*exedra*), which was probably used as a summer sitting room. The women's and children's quarters would be on the upper storey, accessed by wooden or stone stairs.

Within this environment, the standing of 'Mrs Iskhomakhos' would increase significantly once she had given birth, preferably to males. As one Athenian puts it:

> When my son was born, I began to trust [my wife], and put all my possessions in her hands, presuming that this was the greatest proof of intimacy.[31]

Gravestones prove that childbirth was very dangerous for mother and baby. The question – 'What about contraception?' – reflects modern concerns rather more than ancient ones. The womb was considered to have a life of its own, making it anxious to become pregnant to stop it wandering about inside a woman's body to the detriment of her health. Therefore sex was the only cure, early marriage was essential, and contraception was less important than conception. However, we hear of a substance called *misy* (copper ore?), which supposedly had the power to prevent conception for one year. Various general gynaecological remedies may have been effective as contraceptives or early-stage abortificients: sponges soaked in vinegar or oil were commonly used as barriers, and cedar resin was applied to the mouth of the womb. Pomegranate skin, pennyroyal, willow and the squirting cucumber, which forcefully ejects its seeds, could be taken orally or used as pessaries, while amulets and other magical techniques were deployed, along with 'non-fertile' sexual positions, although the use of coitus interruptus does not appear in the sources. The ancient physician Soranus recommended sneezing after sex, washing the vagina, and drinking cold water. Since it was erroneously believed that the most fertile time of the month was just before or just after menstruation, using the rhythm method could result in having sex at exactly the wrong time. Although the Hippocratic Oath included a vow not to give a pessary to cause an abortion, other Hippocratic writings discuss both herbal and mechanical methods of achieving the same result, and the first ban on abortion did not appear until c.211 CE in Rome. The exposure of unwanted babies was a common enough alternative to termination.

Girls were taught household skills such as cooking, weaving and spinning in the home; poorer boys generally learned the trade of their fathers. A good citizen was expected to be *kalos k'agathos* ('beautiful and good'), which entailed being honourable, physically fit and well mannered, with the Homeric heroes providing essential role models. Enormous emphasis was placed on good behaviour and self-control:

> Nurse, mother, *paidagogos* [a slave responsible for a child's education, who would later escort the boy to and from school and ensure discipline in the classroom] and the father himself vie with each other to make him as good as possible, instructing him through everything he does or says, pointing out: 'this is right and that is wrong, this honourable and that disgraceful, this holy, that impious: do this, don't do that.' If he is obedient, well and good. If not, they straighten him with threats and beatings, like a warped and twisted plank.[32]

Formal education, which was neither compulsory nor free, started around the age of six if the parents could afford it. A wealthy boy might be taught at home by a tutor, as were Achilles (in myth), Perikles and Alexander the Great, but most children were taught in groups in schools: the city of Priene had a schoolroom, whose walls still bear the graffiti of the boys who had marked out their territory: 'the place of Dionysios', etc. Laws attributed to Solon imposed strict regulations on teachers:

> The teachers are not allowed to open the school before sunrise and are bound to close it before sunset . . . The law is extremely suspicious of allowing a teacher alone with a boy, especially in the dark.[33]

The basic curriculum at this stage comprised: reading and writing, taught by the *grammatistes*, which was then used as a vehicle for studying morally inspiring poetry; music, taught by the *kitharistes*, because the study of rhythm and harmony was thought to make children better adjusted, and because music was a leisure activity fit for free men; and physical education, taught by the *paidotribes*, which encompassed activities like javelin and discus throwing, jumping, running and combat sports. The latter took place either in the *palaistra* or the gymnasium and, despite some philosophers' misgivings ('the labour of the body prevents the progress of the mind, and the mind of the body[34]), the whole process was seen as essential to developing good citizens.

More formal training in the duties required of a citizen-soldier took place in the *ephebos* groups, where, from the ages of 18 to 20, young Athenian men eligible for hoplite status did military service patrolling the frontiers with light-armed troops.

Around the middle of the fifth century BCE, educational practice at Athens was shaken to the core by the arrival of the Sophists. The word *'sophistes'* originally meant simply 'wise man', but gradually it acquired the sense from which we get our words 'sophistical' and 'sophistry'. Our evidence about the Sophists comes primarily from hostile sources, who regarded them as verbal tricksters who charged outrageous fees for turning their pupils into immoral know-it-alls, but their teaching really developed in response both to the practical demands of democratic life and to a new atmosphere of inquiry and scepticism in Greece.

Persuasion had become a crucial art: in democratic Athens it was the key to political power. Protagoras of Abdera said that his students came to him to learn how to become 'a real power in the city, both as speaker and man of action'.[35] So although many Sophists had their own specialities, such as mathematics or astronomy, they were primarily tutors of rhetoric. Like Protagoras, Hippias of Elis and Gorgias of Leontinoi, they tended to be *metoikoi*, and they had to make a living. What concerned their critics was the fact that rhetoric could easily be used for selfish ends rather than the greater good. At the heart of the whole debate was *arete* (often translated 'virtue', but also covering 'goodness', 'excellence' and 'social effectiveness'), which many Sophists claimed to be able to teach, as Protagoras did when Socrates quizzed him about his curriculum:

> 'Do I follow you?' said I. 'I take you to be describing the art of politics, and promising to make men good citizens.'
> 'That,' said he, 'is exactly what I profess to do.'[36]

However, Xenophon felt that while the Sophists professed to direct the young towards virtue, they actually did the exact opposite,[37] and Socrates told Protagoras: 'I do not believe that *arete* can be taught.'[38]

This burning issue found its way on to the comic stage in Aristophanes' scintillating play the *The Clouds*. Here we meet two personified characters: the Right Argument, who represents the Establishment, champions the old-style of education and the older generation, distrusts the new, and has pederastic obsessions; and the Wrong Argument, who is immoral, clever, subversive, stands for the Sophists and the new, uses subtle arguments to win the debate, and completely converts the Right Argument to his viewpoint. This deliberately manipulates popular (mis)conceptions about the Sophists as people who can win legal cases regardless of right and wrong, engage in trivial and irrelevant scientific research, have bohemian habits, and deny the existence of the traditional gods.

Some Sophists did indeed question the nature of the gods: 'Concerning the gods I am unable to discover whether they exist or not, or what they are like in form.'[39] Many of the Sophists were also at the cutting edge of a movement that believed that human beings ought to be at the centre of our view of the world. Protagoras' famous statement, 'Man is the measure of all things',[40] sounds like a manifesto for the whole Sophistic movement, and leads on to a position that rejects absolute truths and embraces relativism: a bucket of lukewarm water feels warmer to a man coming in from the snow than it does to one coming in from the sunshine; beauty is in the eye of the beholder; and both religion and morality are the result of custom and tradition, which vary according to where people live. In *The Clouds* Aristophanes ascribes such views to Socrates, but this was an outrageous falsehood: he had nothing to do with atheism, physical science or rhetoric, and taught that truth, justice, beauty, *arete* and so on were non-negotiable and were the same the whole world over. He felt that a person's duty was to learn what *arete* was, since once you knew this you would act accordingly: evil was simply due to lack of knowledge. What disturbed him most was the thought of the Sophists' students exploiting their new-found skills regardless of what was right and good.

When it came to what was right and good for women, Perikles stated the received wisdom on the subject of female *arete*:

> Great will be your glory in not falling short of your natural character; and greatest will be hers who is least talked of among the men whether for good or for bad.[41]

Many sources reflect this attitude. Andromache in Euripides' *Trojan Women* says, 'there is one prime source of scandal for a woman, when she won't stay indoors',[42] and in Xenophon's *Memorabilia* Aristarkhos also accepts the convention that his sisters, cousins and nieces, who have come to him in a time of economic crisis, must remain within the house. He is prepared to set them to work making clothes, but only within the confines of the *oikos*. Apparently:

> frowns gave way to smiles, grumbles to contentment. They loved him as a protector, he was satisfied with them as being of practical use. Finally he went to Socrates and told him with a laugh that their only grouse against him was that he was the only person in the house who didn't work for his food.[43]

However, the notion that women's seclusion was total is bogus. There were religious festivals especially for women, such as the Thesmophoria and the Arrephoria. In Aristophanes' comedy *Ekklesiazousai* Blepyros wakes up to find his wife Praxagora missing, but is surprised not that she has gone out but that she has taken his clothes. Then she rehearses a speech she is going to deliver to a male gathering, pretending to be a man but praising women in ways calculated to appeal to men, which descends into a series of stock jokes against women, and so reveals some interesting social attitudes:

> It will not take me long to demonstrate the superiority of their methods to ours. In the first place, they all, without exception, continue to use hot water when dying wool, as has always been the custom. I mean, you won't find them experimenting with other methods, such as the use of cold water. Whereas, if the City had some institution that worked well, do you think *you'd* try to preserve it? You wouldn't rest, I tell you, till you'd thought up something different. Women still sit down to do the roasting, as they've always done. They carry things on their heads, as they've always done. They hold the Thesmophoria Festival, as they've always done. They bake their cakes, as they've always done. They infuriate their husbands, as they've always done. They conceal lovers in the house, as they've always done. They buy themselves

little extras on the side, as they've always done. They drink their wine neat, as they've always done. They enjoy a bit of sex, as they've always done.[44]

There was a generally held Greek view that women enjoyed sex more than men. Teiresias, the mythical prophet who had been both a man and a woman in his lifetime, asserted that, of the ten units of pleasure involved in making love, the man got one and the woman got nine.

As regards the poorer women, the ones who had no slaves and had to do their own domestic work, help their husbands work the land, or even go out to work themselves: 'Who could prevent the wives of the poor from going out when they want to?'[45] According to conventional values, this was frowned upon, but needs must, and women were of course in demand as dancers, music girls and prostitutes. These were usually from non-citizen backgrounds, but we also have evidence of a wide range of occupations undertaken by poor citizen women, who seem to have found outlets in the retail trade (like Euripides' mother, if we can believe Aristophanes), as midwives (like Socrates' mother) or as wet nurses, woolworkers and fruit pickers.

So, although we might expect the men of the privileged classes to be particularly concerned with their honour and public reputation, and their wives to be more likely to be kept secluded to safeguard this, the sources suggest that for ordinary citizens there was a gap between the notion of what a woman's idealized role should be and what was often the reality. But nevertheless, as Socrates said, it was still definitely better to be a man rather than a woman in ancient Athens, and the Athenians knew it.

7

SPARTA: THE ALTERNATIVE MODEL

Molon labe (= 'Come and have go if you think you're hard enough!')

King Leonidas of Sparta[1]

Sparta's Development

Ancient Sparta ('the Sown Land'?) has an awesome reputation for terrifying, violent, xenophobic totalitarianism. Thucydides rather prophetically compared it with Athens:

> Suppose that the city of Sparta were to become deserted and that only the temples and foundations of buildings remained, I think that future generations would find it very difficult to believe that the place had really been as powerful as it was represented to be . . . Since . . . the city is not regularly planned and contains no temples or monuments of great magnificence, but is simply a collection of villages, its appearance would not come up to expectation. If, on the other hand, the same thing were to happen to Athens, one would conjecture . . . that the city had been twice as powerful as in fact it is.[2]

The cliché that 'history is written by the winners' simply does not apply to Sparta – its power took a while to grow. At some point in the post-Mycenaean period, four adjacent villages of Doric dialect speakers were founded in the fertile Eurotas valley in Lakonia in the south-east Peloponnese. The plain is surrounded by the imposing mountain ranges of Taygetos, Panion and Arcadia, and has a rugged coastline to the south; the natural strength of these frontiers negated the need for a city wall. Around 900 BCE there was a *synoecism* (= 'amalgamation') of these villages into the single city of Sparta. The state became known as Lakedaimon, and its inhabitants as Lakedaimonians – 'Spartans' are really a specific sub-group, although in normal usage Lakedaimon/ Lakedaimonians and Sparta/Spartans are interchangeable.

A century or so later, a fifth village was incorporated into the city, and by *c.*750 BCE Sparta had become the mistress of all Lakonia, reducing the non-Doric-speaking population to the status of *helots* (serfs), and making the other communities (the *perioikoi* = 'dwellers round about') politically subservient. As other Greek states were embarking on the colonizing movement, Sparta conquered Messenia – 'good to plough and good to plant'[3] – to the west and made the Messenians into *helots*.

Lakedaimon flourished, and so did its culture: the quality of its ceramics, sculpture, architecture, music and poetry was high, and there was widespread trade with the east. But in *c.*650 BCE the Messenians revolted, and Sparta found itself embroiled in a 17-year conflict. Inspired by the gritty verses of their great poet Tyrtaios, they won the war, (re-)enslaved the Messenians as *helots,* and divided the land into *kleroi* ('allotments') for the Spartiates (i.e. the true Spartans, as opposed to the *perioikoi* and *helots*), who were always a small and elite minority of the overall population.

The Spartan way of life thus altered dramatically. The new austerity, discipline, devotion to duty, diminishing foreign imports and signs of artistic decay are attributed to Lykourgos, who outlawed 'all needless and superfluous arts'.[4] However, the cultural sacrifice was counterbalanced by military success, and by around 550 BCE, Sparta had become the head of a loose confederacy of Peloponnesian states, which is known as the Peloponnesian League.

True Spartans, Helots and Perioikoi

The true Spartans called themselves the *homoioi* ('the peers'), and they almost completely rejected economic activity. Xenophon says that at Sparta:

> There is no point in making money even for the sake of clothes, since it is physical vitality which gives these men a distinctive appearance, not lavish dress. [Lykourgos] instituted currency of such a type that

neither master nor servant could ever be unaware of a tiny amount coming into a house: indeed this would require much space and a wagon for transport.[5]

This was because the money was in the form of huge iron bars, not coins. The *homoioi* therefore depended on the *perioikoi* and the *helots* for their economic needs, while devoting themselves exclusively to military training. As a hereditary group of professional warriors, their main goal in life was to turn themselves into Greece's finest soldiers. To be one of the *homoioi* you had to be the son of a Spartan father and mother; to have undergone the Spartan education; and to have been elected to a 'mess-company'. Your dedication to the state was reciprocated by a grant of state-owned land in Lakonia or Messenia, which was worked by *helots*, whose body-shattering labours supported you throughout your life.

The mess-companies, which the Spartans called *sysskania* or *pheiditia*, each comprised fifteen members who would contribute barley-meal, wine, cheese and figs, plus a small amount of money for fish or meat. Boys would attend the messes, where they could hear political discussion, experience entertainments appropriate for free men and get used to joking without becoming obscene, as well as developing the very Spartan ability to take a joke. The procedure for vetting new members was rigorous, and any would-be entrant had to be elected unanimously.

By the time a Spartan was accepted into his mess-company he had already undergone the *agoge* ('education system'). This was designed to produce instant obedience to authority, an ability to endure pain and hardship, and to instil courage. It was quite literally the survival of the fittest:

> The father of a new-born child . . . brought it in his arms to a particular spot where the elders sat. If the baby proved well-built and sturdy they instructed the father to bring it up. But if it was puny and deformed, they despatched it to 'the place of rejection', a precipitous spot by Mount Taygetos.[6]

The first six years of a boy's life were spent at home, brought up by his mother and a nurse. They trained him not to be fussy about his food, not to be scared of the dark or of being left alone, and not to cry or throw temper-tantrums. Then, at the age of seven, he left home to live in the barracks with other boys (*paides*) of the same age. Until they finished their education, they were under the control of a *paidonomos* (= 'public guardian of education'), who had a group of young adults equipped with whips, who helped him deal with any misdemeanours. In fact, though, boys were under constant supervision, because every citizen had the right to discipline them.

At around the age of thirteen, Spartan boys were made to go barefoot all the time; they received one garment, which had to last for an entire year; they learned only the barest minimum of reading and writing; they cropped their hair; and they exercised naked: 'their bodies were rough, and knew nothing of baths or oiling: only on a few days in the year did they experience such delights'.[7] These hardy, athletic boys, who were predictably successful in the great athletic festivals, did their own housekeeping, plucked reeds by hand to make their beds, and only received small amounts of food. The thinking behind this was to make them better able to go without while they were on active service, but stealing to supplement their diet was acceptable – providing they weren't caught.

Thieving was bad; incompetent thieving was unforgivable. This attitude is graphically illustrated by the story of the boy who had stolen a fox cub and had it concealed inside his cloak: to escape detection he was prepared to have his insides torn to shreds by the animal. Indeed Plutarch commented that, even in his day, Spartan youths practised stealing and were then seen to die from lashes they received at the altar of Artemis Orthia. This particular bizarre endurance test/initiation ritual is mentioned by authors of the Roman period who speak of a ceremony where youths were flogged at the altar, although for the Classical period we hear that:

> after making it a matter of honour for them to snatch as many cheeses as possible from Orthia, [Lykourgos] commanded the others to whip them, wishing to demonstrate thereby that a short period of pain may be compensated by the enjoyment of long-lasting prestige.[8]

Plutarch informs us that at around this age the boys were courted by lovers from among the older men, and Xenophon also passes comment about 'men's love for boys' at Sparta:

If out of admiration for a boy's personality a man of the right character should seek to befriend him in all innocence, Lykourgos would consider it the finest training. On the other hand if someone was obviously chasing after a boy for his body, he regarded that as an absolute disgrace and laid it down that at Sparta lovers should refrain from molesting boys.[9]

This tone seems to pervade Spartan attitudes to the intimate personal relationships of both sexes. Plutarch adds that sexual relationships of this type were so highly valued across society that even respectable women would initiate love affairs with unmarried girls. Yet we also hear that there was no rivalry; instead, if two males found that their affections had the same object, they made this the basis for mutual friendship and pursued joint efforts to perfect their loved one's character.

From age eighteen to nineteen, the Spartan entered the class of youths (*paidiskoi*) and could be called up for military service. Xenophon says that at this stage of life youths become very self-willed, cocky and subject to intense cravings for pleasure, so this was the age at which Lykourgos felt they should be kept as busy as possible. The *paidiskoi* were required to observe specific rules relating to their public behaviour, such as keeping silent and gazing down at all times when walking in the streets. This gave rise to Xenophon's characteristically chauvinistic comment: 'In consequence it has become absolutely clear that by nature the male sex possesses greater strength than the female even in matters of self-control'.[10]

At age twenty the young men (*hebiskoi*) were permitted to marry, although they still lived in the barracks and only visited their wives in secret. This resulted, we are told, in some husbands having children even before they saw their own wives in daylight. The sources again stress the moralistic side of this:

Such intercourse was not only an exercise in self-control and moderation, but also meant that the partners were fertile physically, and always fresh for love, rather than being sated and pale from unrestricted sexual activity.[11]

At the age of twenty-four the Spartan male became a front-line combatant, and at thirty he became a full citizen with the right to participate in the Assembly. From then on he lived at home with his wife and family, although he was still obliged to dine every night in the mess. The citizens were also allowed to let their hair grow:

> They took particular care over it in the face of danger, making it look sleek and combing it. They bore in mind one of Lykourgos' statements about long hair, that it renders handsome men better looking, and ugly ones more frightening.[12]

On the eve of the Battle of Thermopylai, Leonidas and his 300 Spartans took care arranging their hair, and the baffled Persian king Xerxes was informed that it was common for the Spartans to pay careful attention to their hair when they were about to risk their lives.

The education of girls was also aimed at producing healthy bodies, and Lykourgos made them run, wrestle and throw the discus and javelin. The purpose of this was so that:

> their children in embryo would make a strong start in strong bodies, while the women themselves would . . . meet the challenge of childbirth in a successful, relaxed way.[13]

The girls' physical regime was intensive. Perhaps their most strenuous workout was *bibasis*, jumping up and down touching their buttocks with their heels. This features as part of Aristophanes' caricature of Spartan women in *Lysistrata*:

> LYSISTRATA: Welcome Lampito my dear. How are things in Sparta? Darling, you look simply beautiful. Such colour, such resilience! Why, I bet you could throttle a bull.
> LAMPITO: So could you my dear, if you were in training. Don't you know I practise rump jumps (*bibasis*) every day?
> LYSISTRATA: And such marvellous tits, too![14]

They participated in choral performances at festivals' clad in basic slit-sided tunics – a mode of dress that some regarded as indicating healthy-minded purity, others as the exact opposite. Lykourgos was supposed to have done away with prudishness, sheltered upbringing and 'girliness', and a fragment of the writings of the philosopher Herakleides Lembos tells us that Spartan women were deprived of make-up, not allowed to have their hair long or to wear gold. Lykourgos also made young girls participate in processions in the nude, as well as dance and sing at festivals with the young men looking on: sometimes the girls would make fun of the young men and criticize their failings; or they might sing their praises. Those who received the girls' accolades went off feeling good, whereas the barbs of the girls' playful humour were no less effective than more serious warnings. Plutarch says there was no hint of immorality about the girls' nakedness. Rather, it encouraged simple habits, enthusiasm for physical fitness, and imparted a touch of masculine gallantry. A typical attitude is reflected in the anecdote about Leonidas' wife Gorgo: when a foreign woman said, 'You Lakonian women are the only ones who can rule men,' Gorgo replied: 'That is because we are the only ones who give birth to men'.[15]

Spartan girls were usually married at a later age than their Athenian counterparts:

> The custom was to capture women for marriage – not when they were slight or immature, but when they were in their prime and ripe for it. The so-called 'bridesmaid' took charge of the captured girl. First she shaved her head to the scalp, then dressed her in a man's cloak and sandals, and laid her down alone on a mattress in the dark. The bridegroom first had dinner in the mess, then would slip in and carry her to bed.[16]

A rather colourful version states that young men were locked up in the dark with girls of marriageable age, and each married the one he caught. In either case, she would not appear in public as a wife until she was pregnant, and she wouldn't share a household with her husband for the first ten or so years of marriage. So important was it to produce children that it was said that an older husband would lend his young wife to a well-bred childless young man to bear him a child. However, children remained in essence the property of the state, rather than of their parents, and Lykourgos supposedly regarded non-Spartan attitudes to these issues as stupid:

> Such people have their bitches and mares mounted by the finest dogs and stallions whose owners they can prevail upon for a favour or a

fee. But their wives they lock up and guard, claiming the right to produce *their* children exclusively, even though they may be imbeciles, or past their prime, or diseased.[17]

The end result of these customs was that the Spartans, allegedly, had no notion of adultery.

Spartan women were noted for their intense patriotism, too: they famously told their sons, as they went off to battle, to return 'with your shield or on it'. The death of a son in battle became a cause for celebration; Spartan women bore sons to die for Sparta, so it was a positive thing when it happened. Other Greeks were often critical of Spartan women, though: Aristotle complained that they lived 'intemperately, enjoying every kind of licence and indulging in every luxury,'[18] and in Euripides' *Andromache* Peleus rages against their lack of morals:

No Spartan girl could grow up modest even if she wanted to. They go out of the house with bare thighs and loose clothes to wrestle and run races with young men – intolerable behaviour![19]

Essentially the Spartans were taught a way of life. Their upbringing certainly produced very courageous and loyal citizens, but it didn't encourage adaptability. During the fourth century BCE the Spartans were unable to cope with changing conditions: although they won the Peloponnesian War, they never made the most of that victory, and soon afterwards fell victim to innovative battle tactics developed by the Thebans.

One of the reasons for this inflexibility was the existence of the *helots* (serfs). Tyrtaios gives us a very vivid picture of their economic conditions:

Like donkeys worn out with huge burdens, compelled by a terrible necessity, they bring their masters a half of all the fruits of the earth.[20]

Although the Spartan authorities frequently enrolled *helots* in the army, sometimes giving them freedom, they never trusted them: they had an institution called the *Krypteia* ('Secret Police') in which young Spartans were sent out into the countryside to hide by day and kill the most active *helots* by night.[21] The relationship between

Sparta and the *helots* involved an awkward contradiction: Sparta needed the *helots* for military purposes, but even lightly armed *helots* were a huge risk. Yet, as ever, Sparta found a solution: on one occasion, those *helots* who thought they had particularly distinguished themselves in battle were invited to claim their freedom, on the premise that the first to do so would be the most liable to revolt. Some 2,000 *helots* came forward and immediately 'disappeared'.

Slavery of the Athenian type ('chattel slavery') was a more 'modern' institution than keeping *helots*, and by the Classical period it was the normal type. The *helots* were different. You didn't buy them at a slave market. They were a homogeneous, self-reproducing native people who all spoke Greek, and who had become dependants through conquest. The problems this engendered were evident to Plato, who felt this was a recipe for disaster, and indeed *helot* revolts were a constant factor in Sparta's history. One individual to challenge the system was Kinadon, a young man who was not one of the *homoioi*, and who claimed that the majority of the *helots* were of one mind with him. He told someone, who ultimately informed against him, that those who had to do military service had all the weapons they needed, and that the quantities of daggers, swords, axes, hatchets and sickles in the iron market could easily equip everyone else. The Spartan authorities were very alarmed, but decided to send Kinadon on a mission to arrest a beautiful woman who had the reputation of corrupting all the Lakedaimonians who came to her village (he had carried out assignments like this before), and when he got there he was arrested.

> When asked what was his aim in acting as he did, he replied: 'I wanted to be inferior to no one in Lakedaimon.' Thereupon his hands and neck were tied in a collar, he was scourged and stabbed and led around the city with his accomplices.[22]

Kinadon's final comment is relevant to the class of individuals at Sparta called the *hypomeiones* (= 'the inferiors'), who ranged from the upwardly mobile *Neodamodeis* (*helots* granted freedom in return for some act of courage or service to the state) to the *Tresantes* (= 'tremblers'), *homoioi* demoted (temporarily) for cowardice.

The people of Lakedaimon who most closely approximated to the citizens of 'normal' Greek states were the *perioikoi*. They resided in communities that had some degree of local autonomy, but were liable for military service, and had no independent foreign policy. Although they served in the army, the *perioikoi* were not bound by the code of values of the Spartan warriors, and so could engage in all the economic activities that the Spartiatai spurned. They cultivated the land, carried on manufacture, and enjoyed a fairly secure position. We seldom see them showing disaffection towards the Spartiatai, and in general they were one of the essential elements in the stability of Lakedaimon. Indeed, the official designation of what we call the Sparta was not 'the Spartiatai' (cf. 'the Athenians' = 'the Athenian State'), but 'the Lakedaimonians', which expressly included the *perioikoi*.

Sparta's Constitution

If Sparta had an unusual social structure, it also had an extraordinary constitution. Its main elements were two kings, a council of elders, a popular assembly and five officials known as *ephors*. This curious mixture of monarchy, oligarchy and democracy made it difficult for ancient writers to classify: Plato couldn't decide whether it was a democracy or a tyranny; Aristotle described it as a happy mixture of oligarchy and democracy; and the Roman writer Cicero described it as 'mixed'.

Why there were two kings and two dynasties at Sparta remains a mystery, although Herodotus recounts the story of King Aristodemos' wife Argeia giving birth to identical twins just before Aristodemos died. The Spartans wanted to make the elder child king, but they had no idea which of them to choose. Argeia knew perfectly well which was which, but pretended not to, in the hope that both of them might be made kings. The Delphic Oracle told the Spartans to let that happen, but to give the elder one the greater honour. In order to ascertain which baby had been born first, a man called Panites suggested that they should observe the mother and see which of them she fed and washed first. If she varied the order it would be clear that she knew no more than they did, but if she always kept to the same routine, that would tell them everything they needed to know. Apparently Panites' scheme worked.

The kings were the supreme military commanders and, although Aristotle defined the Spartan kingship as a 'perpetual hereditary generalship',[23] it could be far more than that. The advice of a successful warrior carried great political weight, and Sparta's history falls naturally into a series of influential kings, who left their imprint, be this positive or negative, on their country's fortunes.

Sparta's council of elders, the *Gerousia*, consisted of twenty-eight life-members, who had to be sixty years old or over, plus the two kings. The system of election was by 'acclamation', which Aristotle described as 'childish': an assembly was called; judges were confined in a windowless room nearby; the candidates came forward; the people shouted; and whoever got the loudest cheer was elected.[24]

The *Gerousia* was the criminal court, and operated as the guiding committee of the Assembly. It called the Assembly at fixed periods and put motions before it, which were then either rejected or confirmed, although it could also veto decisions of the Assembly of which it disapproved. Many ancient historians represent the *Gerousia* as being virtually the governing body of Sparta.

The Assembly of Citizens comprised all male Spartiatai from the age of thirty. Tyrtaios speaks of how the Delphic Oracle decreed that:

> First in the debate shall heaven's favourites, the kings, the guardians of fair Sparta's polity, speak, and the elders. After them the commoners shall to direct proposals make response with conscientious speech and all just consequence, making no twisted plans against our realm; and commoners majority shall win the day.[25]

How far they enjoyed the right of free debate is rather doubtful: Aristotle implies that the Assembly could simply vote yes or no on motions that were presented to it.

The final pieces in Sparta's constitutional jigsaw were the five *ephors*, who, as representatives of the people, had formidable powers. They were elected by acclamation; any Spartiate over the age of thirty was eligible; the term of office was one year; no one could be *ephor* twice; they assumed office on the full moon after the autumnal equinox, and issued a proclamation to all citizens to 'shave their upper lips and obey the laws'; every year they declared war on the *helots* (who could then be killed without incurring religious impurity) and could execute them without trial; they had disciplinary powers over all citizens; they virtually conducted Spartan foreign policy; they presided in the *Gerousia* and the Assembly; they oversaw the training and discipline of the young; the *Krypteia* (Secret Police) was under their orders; and they had interesting powers in relation to the kings, with whom they exchanged a monthly oath, 'for the kings that they would rule according to the established laws of the city, and for the city that if he were true to his oath they would maintain his kingdom unshaken'.[26] In the presence of the kings all rose, but the *ephors* remained seated. And they could fine a king, as they did Arkhidamos for marrying a short wife: 'for she will not bear us kings but kinglets.'[27]

Sparta's Afterlife

In 1834, very soon after Greek independence, a new Sparta was laid out close to the ancient site. It was a symbol of the rebirth of Greece. Admirers of Sparta include many of the big names of political science, including Machiavelli and Montesquieu. In *The Commonwealth of Oceana* (1656) James Harrington urged Oliver Cromwell to imitate Lykourgos; Rousseau praised the Spartan system in *Du contrat social* (1762); according to the classical scholar Meyer Reinhold, 'American leaders judged Sparta as a model of freedom and order, a stable, long-lived commonwealth, its people distinguished by virtue, simple life-style, patriotism, vigour';[28] and Samuel Adams looked forward to Boston becoming 'a Christian Sparta'.[29]

Degas' *Young Spartans Exercising* (1860) depicts Lykourgos standing among a group of mothers as naked boys and topless girls work out in what is intended to be a utopian, naturalistic view of Sparta. The great French romantic Chateaubriand was more ambivalent: 'If I hate the manners of the Spartans, I am not blind to the greatness of a free people, and neither was it without emotion that I trampled on their noble dust'.[30]

As the nineteenth century progressed, however, Athens took over as the model to be admired. The democratic tradition that dominates modern western thought still tends to favour Athens, although Walter Pater's *Lacedaemon* bucks the trend with its positive assessment of the 'half-military, half-monastic spirit which prevailed in this gravely beautiful place'. In Proust, the Baron de Charlus reflects on the First World War: 'Those English soldiers who at the beginning I dismissed as mere football-players . . . well, they are . . . Spartiates'.[31] Later in the twentieth century the similarities between the education of Spartan boys and the Hitler Youth are not coincidental. Admiration for Sparta reached an astonishing climax under the Nazis:

> Many of the plans and ground rules which the Spartans had about how to build a state and how to train its ruling class are of relevance to us . . . We want to help the Führer to build a great Reich. Sparta should be a rousing example.[32]

Hitler himself, according to his *Table Talk*, often praised the Spartans, and their subjugation of the *helots*. As Tobias Hill wrote in his 2009 novel *The Hidden*, which is set in Sparta, 'all extremisms are alike and in Sparta all are prefigured'.[33]

8

COMMUNICATING WITH THE GODS: SACRIFICE, ORACLES AND ATHLETICS

(Prometheus) Know: although seeing they did not see, although
hearing they did not hear, ephemeral men apparitions of dreams,
under the earth they lived like ants, until I showed them dawn and
sunset.

Luigi Nono, *Prometeo*, II, First Island

Greek Worship

The moment that twenty-first-century people start to look into the
world of Greek religion, they find themselves in a very alien
environment where modern value-systems cease to apply. A
religion is like a game of cricket: totally incomprehensible to
outsiders, unless they have learned the rules from childhood and
are *au fait* with the apparent inconsistency and weirdness that the
participants take for granted. And so we find that the Classical
Greeks were more concerned with rituals than with 'beliefs': they
lacked concepts such as sin and faith, and they did not *believe* in
their gods, so much as *acknowledge* them through prayer, sacrifice,
erecting temples and making them the focus of cult. Their divinities
were not omnipotent, and did not create the universe; there were no
sacred texts equivalent to the Bible or the Qur'an or the Torah; no
Ten Commandments, Five Pillars or Thirteen Principles; no creed
or *shahadah*; no Talmud; no *sharia*; no covenant; no orthodoxy, and
therefore no heresy; no *jihad*; and (perhaps incredibly to modern
readers) no wars of religion.

The large numbers of men and women who kept religious activity ticking over were very often simply public officials selected by lot for a limited term, although some priesthoods were hereditary and others could be bought. Priests and priestesses usually assumed responsibility for overseeing some communal religious activity, but they generally lacked any spiritual sense of vocation, special training or particular expertise.

Unlike synagogues, mosques or churches, Greek temples were seldom places of congregational worship. They are usually described as houses of their deity, where a cult image and often a good deal of treasure were stored. Strictly speaking, the temple building was an optional extra. What was needed was a clearly defined sacred space, called the *temenos*, and an altar (usually in the open air), where sacrifices would be made. But the Greeks also worshipped by means of hymns, dances, processions and competitions in athletics, music and drama, in contexts that were unique to each individual *polis*.

Greek literature is full of people saying prayers, which shows us that they understood and interacted with their deities in much the same way as they did with their fellow human beings: in many ways they regarded their gods as being fundamentally just like themselves. In Herondas' *Mime* 4, an ordinary woman called Kynno prays to Asklepios:

> Hail to thee, Lord Paieon, ruler of Trikka, who hast got as thine habitation sweet Kos and Epidauros, hail to Koronis thy mother withal and Apollo; hail to her whom thou touchest with thy right hand, Hygieia, and those to whom belong these honoured shrines, Panake and Epio and Ieso; hail ye twain which did sack the house and walls of Leomedon healers of savage sicknesses, Podaleirios and Machaon, and what gods and goddesses soever dwell by thine hearth, Father Paieon; come hither with your blessings and accept the aftercourse of this cock whom I sacrifice, herald of the walls of my house . . . paying the price of cure from diseases that thou didst wipe away, Lord, by laying on us thy gentle hands.[1]

She talks to Asklepios courteously and precisely, using his formal titles, naming his ancestry, powers and attributes, and including a 'catch all' phrase at the end: he will not hear her prayer if she gets his identity wrong. Also noticeable is the notion of reciprocity: Kynno's humble offering is 'votive', made in fulfilment of a vow for recovery from illness, although in other contexts she might have made the offering first, hoping that the deity would reciprocate in kind. This practice of vows allows us into a deeply personal aspect of Greek religion, revealing genuine anxieties, hopes and prayers.

Kynno supplements her prayer with an animal sacrifice, a ritual with a very clearly prescribed procedure. First the victim, which must be a domesticated animal (goat, sheep, ox, chicken, etc.), is festively prepared for slaughter: it has to look like it is going to its death willingly. The venue for the sacrifice is then defined as sacred by carrying a sacred basket round in a procession and by sprinkling water over the worshippers and the victim. In the basket is barley grain, which everyone throws at the victim, and (out of sight) the sacrificial knife. Whoever is acting as priest cuts a few hairs from the animal's forehead before its head is pulled back and its throat slit. Up until this point there has been ritual silence, but now the women scream a ritual cry. The animal's *splankhna* (vital organs: heart, lungs, liver and kidneys), are removed, kebabbed and roasted; the tail, gall bladder and thigh bones are wrapped in fat and burnt on the altar as the god's share; and feasting ensues when the lean meat is cooked, which everyone gets a share of once they have tasted the *splankhna*. In Herondas' poem a slimy temple warden appears to announce the success of the offering, and to try to join the meal.

The Greeks made their gods in the image of man, which the philosopher Xenophanes thought was inevitable:

> If cattle, horses and lions had hands, or could draw and do what men do, horses would draw gods like horses, and cattle gods like cattle.[2]

But gods who are exactly like humans are pretty pointless. They need to combine the human with the non-human, surpass humanity and have some kind of 'otherness'. The Greeks inhabited an extremely precarious world, characterized by famine, fatal illnesses, earthquakes, warfare, and death in childbirth. Life-expectancy was low, but if, as many argue, religion tries to give people a sense of security in a frightening world, then the Greek gods enabled their worshippers to articulate in a complex and subtle way what they thought the world was like, and to provide a set of responses for dealing with life as it was actually lived, rather than as they would have liked it to have been lived. And it worked for them for hundreds of years.

At the core of the system were the twelve Olympian gods and goddesses (see Table 8.1, below). Being polytheists, though, the Greeks had far more than these twelve divinities – at Athens more than a hundred days of the year were assigned to one festival or another. The primordial 'chthonic' deities of the Underworld, such as Hades, needed to be appeased; trades had their own patron gods, such as Prometheus (potters), Kastor and Polydeukes (sailors); personifications such as Tykhe (Fortune) and Eros (Love) were felt to be at work in the world; Pan and the Nymphs were active in the countryside; and every home had its own shrine to Hestia, the goddess of the hearth. However, some intellectuals looked for a less anthropomorphic (*anthropos* = man; *morphe* = form/shape) concept of god: according to Thales, the ultimate basis of nature was water; according to Herakleitos, it was fire; later Plato saw god as the 'divine architect'; and his pupil Aristotle saw god as the 'unmoved mover' of the universe.

Table 8.1 Major Greek and Roman Deities

Deity	Roman equivalent	Attributes	Sphere of Activity
Zeus	Jupiter	Thunderbolt; eagle; sceptre	'The father of gods and men'; sky; weather; hospitality; supplication; oaths
Hera	Juno	Sceptre; crown; peacock	Wife of Zeus; the integrity of marriage
Poseidon	Neptune	Trident; often surrounded by sea-creatures	The sea; earthquakes; horses and bulls
Athena	Minerva	Helmet, spear and shield; the snake-fringed *aigis* with the Gorgon's head; the owl; virginity	Domestic arts; warfare
Apollo	Apollo	Bow and arrows; the lyre; laurel	Music; divination and prophecy; purification and healing; the sun
Artemis	Diana	Bow and arrows; hunting outfits; virginity	Hunting; wild animals; childbirth

Aphrodite	Venus	Girdle; doves; sparrows	Sex; love
Ares	Mars	Helmet, spear and shield	War
Hephaistos	Vulcan	Lameness; axe; anvil; blacksmith's tools	Brilliant artisan; fire; metallurgy
Demeter	Ceres	Torch; corn	Corn and fertility of the land; the Eleusinian Mysteries
Hermes	Mercury	Herald's staff; winged boots/sandals; traveller's broad-brimmed hat	Messenger of the gods; guide of the souls to the Underworld; protector of travellers; fertility of flocks; thieves
Dionysos	Bacchus	Ivy; vines; panthers; the thyrsos	Intoxicated ecstasy; wine; drama

These cults gave little reassurance about life after death. Homer's Underworld (Hades) is a grim, grey, depressing environment, and fear of death was a fact of life. But, as Plutarch says, the polytheist found strategies for coping with this:

> [Many people] think that some sort of initiations and purifications will help: once purified, they believe, they will go on playing and dancing in Hades in places full of brightness, pure air and light.[3]

This was achieved through 'mystery cults', voluntary, personal, secret initiation rituals that aimed at some form of salvation through closeness to the divine. These represented an 'optional extra', and did not entail conversion to a new religion, or the rejection of the old one. A prime example is the Eleusinian Mysteries, celebrated only at Eleusis, twelve miles from Athens, which offered people from all classes of society, even slaves, the promise of salvation and a blessed after-life. They were organized by the *polis* of Athens and supervised by the *arkhon basileus*, but, although our sources provide us with much information, the central 'mystery' remains just that – all we know is that the 'hierophant' revealed 'the holy things'.

In the autumn, a procession went from Athens to Eleusis and culminated in a nocturnal celebration in the Hall of Initiations, the Telesterion, which could hold thousands of initiates. The Eleusinian Mysteries were devoted to the 'Two Goddesses', Demeter the goddess of grain and her daughter Persephone, who is often just called Kore, 'The Maiden'. In mythology, when Kore had been abducted by Hades, god of the Underworld, the Eleusinians had helped Demeter in her search. This was successful. However, Persephone had eaten a pomegranate seed, thereby binding herself to Hades for eternity, so a compromise was eventually reached in which she would divide the year between Hades in the Underworld and Demeter on Mount Olympus. While she was parted from her sorrowing mother, the earth was barren, but, when the two were united, it was fruitful. The myth explains the seasons, but because crops die and are 'reborn' every year, the same could apply to people: Demeter's gift was rebirth after death, and therefore immortality. The prospect of a happy afterlife makes this life much more bearable.

The Riddle of the Delphic Oracle

The gods could also assist in important decision making. The number-one shrine of Apollo, god of prophecy, and the site of Greece's most famous oracle, was Delphi. The term 'oracle' can refer both to the responses given by a god when consulted, and to the place where they were delivered, which the Greeks called a *khresterion* or *manteion*. The Romans called it an *oraculum*, so we call it an oracle. The prime function of the Delphic Oracle was to give people *nemertea boulen* (unfailing advice the Greeks consulted oracles on a broad range of personal, religious and political matters), not, crucially, to foretell the future.

The sanctuary at Delphi comprised a *temenos*, defined by a wall and entered by a Sacred Way, inside which were a vast number of monuments and inscriptions erected by various Greek states, plus around twenty treasuries, a theatre and a temple of Apollo. There was also a stadium, with various ancillary athletic facilities, and a separate sanctuary of Athena Pronaia.

The mythical tradition claimed that Agamedes and Trophonios constructed the first temple of Apollo. When this was destroyed by fire in 548 BCE, its replacement was funded by donations from foreign rulers such as Croesus of Lydia and Amasis of Egypt, and was supervised by the Alkmaionidai, who were living at Delphi in exile from Athens. That temple was destroyed by an earthquake in 373 BCE and another one was erected, the remains of which can still be seen on the site. The Roman Emperor Nero pillaged the sanctuary in the first century CE; the historian Plutarch was a priest there, giving us some excellent primary source material; and in around 350 CE the Emperor Julian tried to revive the sanctuary and sent the priestess Oreibasios to consult the Oracle, only to have her prophesy her own demise:

> Go tell the king – the carven hall is felled,
> Apollo has no cell, no prophetic bay
> Nor talking spring; his cadenced well is stilled.[4]

In the last decade of the fourth century CE, Theodosius closed Delphi in the name of Christianity.

In Delphi's heyday, Apollo gave his prophetic responses monthly throughout the year, apart from the three winter months when he relocated to the land of the Hyperboreans. His priestess, the Pythia, was dedicated to his service for life. She was an ordinary local peasant with no special training, had to be over fifty years old and, once selected, remained chaste and irreproachable. Prior to a consultation she bathed in (and probably drank) the waters of the Kastalia spring. You had to pay a consultation fee and sacrifice a goat on the altar outside the temple – if it had shivered from head to foot when it had been sprinkled with holy water, Apollo was ready to prophesy.

Then, having entered the temple, you would approach the *adyton*, the sacred area where the oracle would be given, which contained the *omphalos* ('belly-button'), which marked the centre of the world, and a laurel tree sacred to Apollo (and perhaps two statues of Apollo, one wood, one gold). The Pythia would already have entered the temple, which was fumigated with barley-meal and laurel leaves on the sacred hearth. In the *adyton*, over a round opening in the ground, a tripod cauldron was set up, and the Pythia sat on its lid. She probably drank the waters of the spring Kassotis, which Pausanias was told had numinous powers, flowed underground into the *adyton*, and gave the Pythia prophetic abilities. You would probably go with the *prophetai* ('interpreters') and cult officials into a special room which prevented you from seeing directly into the *adyton* itself, and your enquiry would be put to the Pythia either orally or written on a tablet. Then she would prophesy.

It is often said that she munched laurel leaves, became intoxicated by exhalations from the chasm, uttered obscure, equivocal, frenzied, incoherent babblings, which were transcribed by a poet, and left the inquirer totally bemused. She did no such thing. You undoubtedly didn't have a normal conversation with her, but the image of her ranting and raving was fabricated by pagan and Christian writers seeking to discredit Delphi, although it has recently been the subject of a media-friendly hypothesis that the Delphic prophecies were made by a substance-abusing priestess. Essentially Apollo entered into the Pythia and used her voice as if it were his – Delphic utterances were always in the first person – but the Pythia's psychological state remains obscure: the preliminary ritual is bog-standard magical procedure, and her trance could have been autosuggestively induced, although occasionally things could still go horribly wrong:

> [The Pythia] went down into the *adyton* unwillingly . . . and at her first response it was at once clear from the harshness of her voice that she was not responding properly and was . . . as if she was filled with a mighty and baleful spirit. Finally she became hysterical and with a frightful shriek rushed towards the exit and threw herself down.[5]

She actually died a few days later. Clearly the incident shows that under normal circumstances her voice did not change in this uncanny and extreme way: the Pythia would not usually rant and rave. Furthermore, the business about her chewing of laurel is only attested by two late authorities who were attempting to bring the Oracle into disrepute, one of which is Lucian, writing satirically about Apollo, who was not an omnipresent deity, having to run from one oracle to another:

> Now he has to be in Delphi, and soon after he runs to Kolophon and from there crosses to Xanthos, and then back on a run to Klaros, then to Delos or to Brankhidai, in a word wherever the [female] *promantis* (= 'representative of the god and the organ of his prophecies'), after drinking from the sacred spring and chewing the bay and shaking the tripod, bids him be present.[6]

His account contains a number of factual errors: Klaros had a male *mantis*, and Delos never had an oracle at all. This is not a sound passage from which to extrapolate.

And what about the vapours that rose from a chasm in the rock and induced the Pythia's utterances? Diodoros relates a myth that some goats discovered a hole in a mountainside, leaned in and started to shriek bizarrely. So did the goatherd, who also started to prophesy the future. Hence the oracle was established. Plutarch talked a great deal about the *pneuma* (= wind/breath/breath of life/odour/divine inspiration/spirit of god), and describes a delightful fragrance that sometimes emanated from the *adyton*. More recently a team of scientists has tried to argue that, because Delphi stands on the intersection of two geological faults lines, hydrocarbon vapour – largely methane, ethane and ethylene – rose into the *adyton*, and that the Pythia's trance-like state resulted from inhaling ethylene or an ethylene/ethane mix. This would match the effects of the ancient prophetic vapours, they say. The theory appealed to positivist inclinations in the science-reading public, but, given that it is impossible to measure the actual ethylene levels present at the temple site more than two millennia ago, the explanation was always speculative, and now has been conclusively refuted.[7]

The problem with 'rationalizing' theories like this is that their authors don't accept the power of Apollo, whereas the Greeks did. And, contrary to the popular misconception, Apollo spoke very straightforwardly. Of the 535 Delphic responses that survive, only 14 per cent are attested by contemporary sources. The questions are pretty direct: 'Shall I do x?', 'How shall I do y?', 'Shall I succeed in z?' The main concerns include portents, civic welfare, religious questions, worship, proposed enterprises and interstate relations. The responses were usually just commands and sanctions; predictions are rare, and of questionable authenticity. For instance, when Khairephon quizzed the Delphic Oracle about whether there was anyone wiser than Socrates, it delivered an unambiguous, 'No'. The bemused philosopher didn't feel that he was extraordinarily clever, so he decided to challenge those who thought they were, found their views confused and opinionated, and concluded that, paradoxically, his superiority lay in admitting his own ignorance. A typical enquiry came from the city of Halieis, which asked about a snake that had been carried there in a wagon that had brought home a recovered invalid from the sanctuary of Asklepios at Epidauros. Should they send it back, or let it stay in Halieis? The Oracle said that it should stay in Halieis, and that a sanctuary of Asklepios should be inaugurated there.[8] On a personal level, Plutarch tells of a priest who had violated his priesthood by having sex with a woman when he was drunk. Asking whether his offence could be absolved, he was told that 'deity forgives all uncontrollable acts'.[9] It is only when we get into responses allegedly spoken in historical times but attested by people who were born later, mythical responses and deliberately invented fictional ones that we get the 'ambiguous oracle' stories. Any ambiguity that we do find seems designed to force the questioner to reconsider their position on an issue to which there was no straightforward answer.

The Olympic Games

In addition to the oracular activities conducted at Delphi, there was also the site of the Pythian Games, one of the four pre-eminent athletic festivals of the Greek world. All four sites were religious sanctuaries, and the quartet was completed by the Nemean Games at Nemea, the Isthmian Games at Corinth, and the Olympic Games at Olympia, which were the most prestigious. The Greeks believed that the Olympic Games were first held in 776 BCE, and that the only event held on that occasion was a foot-race, which was won by a local cook called Koroibos. As with Delphi, the Olympic Games came to an end in the reign of the Christian Roman Emperor Theodosius.

Olympia was not a town, but a religious precinct in the territory of Elis; the Olympic Games were primarily a religious activity held in the *altis*, the sacred area. This was a male-only event, sacred to Zeus, and held every four years. The central day of the festival coincided with the second or third full moon after the summer solstice, which may indicate some original connection with a fertility cult linked to the end of harvesting. Certainly, holding an athletic festival at the hottest time of the year seems an odd choice, particularly in a stadium that held 40,000 spectators and when the prize for winning (at least on the day) was merely a wreath of wild olive.

One scholar has gone so far as to suggest that sport in ancient Greece can be regarded as the ritual sacrifice of physical energy, but we instantly encounter a problem with this, since there is no ancient Greek word for 'sport' as we understand it (or in any other language apart from English: you have to use 'sport', or modify the word to suit the language, if you want to express the idea). What the ancient Greeks were interested in was *competition*; their word *athletes* means 'someone who competes for a prize'. They did not play for fun; they played to win. Philo wrote that, 'athletes who are always beaten should give up',[10] and Pindar's description of an athlete returning after failing is typical: 'Even his mother will not smile on him.'[11]

So when Bill Shankley, manager of the mighty Liverpool football team of the 1970s, was asked whether he thought football was a matter of life and death and he replied, 'Oh no. It's much more important than that,' the crowds at Olympia would have stood and applauded. The fact that the games were a religious activity meant that cheating and bribery were sacrilegious, although that didn't necessarily stop the highly competitive athletes trying to get away with doing such things: bronze statues called *zanes* were erected on inscribed plinths along the approach to the Olympic stadium, paid for by fines paid by competitors who had defiled the games.

The events contested varied over time, but the core of the competition revolved around running, *diskos*, jumping, javelin, combat sports and equestrianism. Cultural and religious activity completed the picture. The track on which the running races were held was one *stadion* ('stadium', sometimes rendered 'stade') long, i.e. 600 Greek feet (198.27 m) at Olympia. The *stadion* race was a straight sprint from a standing start, and its winner had the Olympics named after him. Over the years other races were added, always multiples of the *stadion*, including the *dolikhos*, a long-distance race of probably 24 *stadia* (just over 5,000 m) added in 720 BCE, and a race in armour (*hoplitodromos*) introduced in 520 BCE, in which the athletes wore a helmet and greaves and carried one of 25 bronze shields that were kept at Olympia for their use. There was, however, no marathon race, even though it is derived from a classical Greek precedent.

One other feature of the ancient Olympic festival is that, by and large, the athletes competed naked. There is a story that this practice was initiated after an athlete called Orsippos was leading a race, probably in 720 BCE, but tripped over his loincloth (*diazoma*), which had come undone. This may, however, be a fabrication based on Aias (Ajax) in the funeral games in honour of Patroclus in the *Iliad*, who was just about to win when he slipped on a pile of dung, allowing Odysseus to snatch the victory. But Homer's heroes wore loin cloths in that competition, and in the fifth century Thucydides wrote:

> In ancient times, even in the Olympic festival, athletes performed with loin cloths . . . and it is not many years since they stopped wearing them.[12]

Diskos, long jump and javelin were not usually held as separate events, but as part of the pentathlon, with a run (usually assumed to be a *stadion*) and wrestling completing the set. Quite how the winner was decided is heavily disputed, but if an athlete won the first three events he would be declared the victor, and the running and wrestling would be cancelled. The physique of a pentathlete was greatly admired, and *erastai* were attracted to the gymnasia to ogle at their sun-bronzed skin and fine muscular development, although celebrity athletes also came in for some criticism:

> There are thousands of things wrong with Greece, but the athletes are the worst of all. Living properly – they don't know about it and they don't care. How could any man be a slave to his jaw and a servant to his belly, and outstrip his father's glory? . . . When young they're famous and add to their country's repute. When old age comes grimly on them, they're like cloaks with frayed ends. I blame Greek practice. We make a fuss of them, do them honour, give them free meals. Wrestlers, sprinters, discus-throwers, boxers – what good do their crowns do their country? Will they fight the enemy with discuses? Drop their shields and repel the invader by sprinting? Oh no; they've more sense than to face cold steel.[13]

The 'heavy events' as the Greeks called them, were: wrestling, where you grappled with your adversary and tried to force him to the ground three times; boxing, where there were no rounds, the fighters wore straps of leather to protect their hands (rather than boxing gloves to protect their opponents), punching was allowed but not grappling, and hitting a man when he was down was perfectly acceptable; and the *pankration*, a combination of the two, where the bout simply ended when one of the contestants could not, or would not, continue. There were no weight divisions, so big men usually did well.

The equestrian events (horse and chariot racing) were always extremely popular, but horses were incredibly expensive, which limited participation either to very wealthy individuals, or even to cities. A racehorse could cost 1,200 *dr.* in 421 BCE, but in 416 BCE, to ensure victory, Alkibiades entered seven chariot teams at Olympia and got 1st, 2nd and either 3rd or 4th place at a time when he was seeking high political office. Jockeys rode bareback and without stirrups, and were usually paid servants, as were chariot drivers, although it was the owner who collected the prize. This meant that several women were able to win prizes at the Olympic Games, even though they were not permitted to attend. The most infamous competitor of all was the Roman Emperor Nero, who postponed the festival from 65 to 67 CE so that he could compete during a tour to Greece: he was thrown from his chariot, and, despite being helped back in, failed to finish, although the diplomatic Greeks still proclaimed him the victor, on the grounds that he would have won if he had completed the race.

The modern Olympic Games are one of Ancient Greece's most obvious legacies. Interestingly, this has also given rise to a myth of amateurism that still seems to permeate many people's ideas about ancient athletics. In fact, however, the Hellenes had neither the ideology nor the vocabulary of amateurism; they didn't know what it was. Their athletes accepted as much prize-money as they could. This is a classic example of how judging ancient cultures from modern ideological perspectives can lead to the misinterpretation of the ancient evidence.

9

GREEK TRAGEDY

It's fun, tragedy, isn't it?

Rita, in Willy Russell's *Educating Rita,* Act I, Scene vi

How to Stage a Greek Tragedy

Drama is a Greek word (= 'an action/doing') and it is one of the
Greeks' (specifically the Athenians') finest contributions to world
culture. Yet the space and context in which dramatic performances
originally took place were radically different from today's. First,
they formed part of a public act of worship to honour Dionysos;
second, these events were competitive. So the ancient theatre
complex included an altar and various ancillary religious buildings
– it was more than just an entertainment venue and still less a
commercial profit-making venture.

The Greek theatre was an open-air structure designed to give the
spectators easy access to and from their seats, unimpeded sight lines
and clear acoustics, and to provide the production team with a space
for actors and a chorus, somewhere to display scenery, and
changing facilities. At the centre of it all was the *orkhestra*, a flat
circular area of hard beaten earth around 20 m across, often with an
altar to Dionysos in the centre. The seating area (*theatron* or *cavea*)
was, if possible, built into a hillside to give the seats a natural rake
and provide space for an audience that could well number up to
15,000.

The Theatre of Dionysos at Athens, where the plays of
Aeschylus, Sophocles and Euripides were all performed, is very
difficult to assess archaeologically, since it has been altered radically

over the centuries, but it was pretty basic: the spectators would simply congregate on the hill slopes or possibly use temporary wooden 'grandstands'. By the time of Aeschylus' *Oresteia,* more substantial structures were needed, but stone seating only started to be utilized in the fourth century BCE, and true architectural monumentality did not arrive until the Hellenistic era. Once stone construction was used, the *theatron* was often divided into upper and lower tiers by a concentric horizontal gangway (*diazoma*) and into wedge-shaped sectors (*kerkides*) by stairways that fanned out radially, thereby facilitating circulation around the theatre and the division of the audience into constituent groups. If the terrain allowed, the *theatron* formed more than a semi circle, wrapped around the *orkhestra*, allowing the audience to see each other, and allowing the theatre to retain an organic relationship with the landscape: its religious, democratic and social functions did not belong indoors.

Looking to either side of the *orkhestra*, the audience could see the *parodoi* (sing. *parodos*) or *eisodoi*, walkways leading into (or out of) the *orkhestra*. Defined by retaining walls on the *theatron* side, they were essentially spaces between the auditorium and the *skene* (from which we get our word 'scene'), a free-standing structure that served as a changing room for the actors and as a place to put the scenery, which often depicted an architectural facade with three doors. At the height of fifth-century BCE Athenian drama, the *skene* was wooden with painted scenery, although it eventually became constructed of stone and grew to a height of two storeys. A deeply controversial question concerns precisely where the actors of the fifth century BCE performed: they may have used a low platform in front of the *skene*, but if so it did not encroach on the *orkhestra*.

Two important mechanical devices were also deployed from the *skene*: the *ekkyklema* (= 'something which is rolled out'), a low, wheeled platform that could be brought through the central doors to display a tableau, which the audience imagined as being an *indoor* scene; and the *mekhane*, a crane-like device that could swing flying figures into view and land them on the stage, giving us the term *deus ex machina* (or *theos apo mekhanes* in Greek).

During the Hellenistic era a *proskenion* was developed. This was a one-storey addition of a row of pillars attached to the front of the *skene*, joined to it by stone or wooden beams, and with wooden planking on top. This allowed the actors to perform at ground level, using the *proskenion* as a backdrop, or to use the *proskenion* platform as the stage with the upper storey of the *skene* as the background. When the role of the chorus started to diminish after the fifth century BCE, the *orkhestra* gradually became obsolete and was often used as a seating area – hence the 'orchestra stalls' (usually just 'stalls') in a modern theatre.

Greek theatres have astonishing acoustics: the resonance of the stone gives power and presence to a speaker's voice (like singing in the shower) and, as tourist guides at Epidaurus gleefully demonstrate with actions that have no connection to ancient theatrical practice (tearing paper, dropping Euros, lighting matches), from the altar (the one place where no performer could have stood), the softest sounds can be clearly heard from the back row. Although the corollary of this is that any fidgeting or heckling by an audience that habitually ate and drank throughout the performance would be highly intrusive, the theatre was unquestionably fit for its purpose.

Greek tragedy itself is a bizarre concatenation of drama, poetry, music, dance, religion, politics, high art and popular culture, the origins of which are elusive: 'Two words on the origins of Greek tragedy: unknown and irrelevant.'[1] The primary context for tragedy was the Great (or City) Dionysia festival in honour of Dionysos Eleuthereus in late March/early April. The poet Thespis (from whom modern actors call themselves 'Thespians') is credited with winning the first prize for tragedy in *c.*534 BCE and with adding the first actor to what had hitherto been a purely choral performance. The very word 'tragedy' creates difficulties: the Greeks used the words *tragoidia* and *tragoidoi*, which both have something to do with a goat (*tragos*) and a song (*oidos*), although how and why these elements belong together is unclear. So it is hard to put Greek tragedy in a nutshell, although Aristotle's definition has been influential:

> A representation [*mimesis*] of an action that is worth serious attention, complete in itself, and of some amplitude; in language enriched by a variety of artistic devices appropriate to the several parts of the play; presented in the form of action, not narration; by means of pity and fear bringing about the purgation [*katharsis*] of such emotions.[2]

Katharsis can be physical, spiritual and emotional, and the phrase *pathei mathos* (= 'learning through suffering') used in Aeschylus' *Agamemnon*[3] seems quite pertinent here.

Aristotle asserts that the quality of a tragedy is governed by plot, character, diction, thought, spectacle and song, and, although the performances were highly stylized, written entirely in verse, and accompanied by music, the audience clearly became closely involved with the characters. The concepts of an overturn/change of fortune (*peripeteia*) and recognition (*anagnorisis*) are also stressed, and although nowadays we tend to use 'tragedy' to signify something sad or distressing, an ancient 'tragedy' does not have to be – the change of fortune can be positive, and the recognition might facilitate a happy outcome. In Willy Russell's *Educating Rita*, Frank explains to Rita the difference between 'tragic' and 'tragedy':

> FRANK: A woman's hair being ruined, or – the sort of thing you read in the paper that's reported as being tragic, 'Man Killed by Falling Tree', that is *not* a tragedy.
> RITA: It is for the poor sod under the tree.
> FRANK: Yes, it's . . . absolutely tragic. But it's not a *tragedy* in the way that *Macbeth* is a tragedy . . . Tragedy in dramatic terms is inevitable, pre-ordained. Now, look, even without ever having heard the story of *Macbeth* you wanted to shout out, to warn him and prevent him going on, didn't you? But you wouldn't have been able to stop him would you?
> RITA: 'Cos they would have thrown me out of the theatre.[4]

At the City Dionysia, the *arkhon eponymos* 'granted a chorus' to three tragedians, who entered four plays each: three tragedies followed by a 'satyr' play. There could have been some kind of audition process, but, as comic poets were quick to point out, having a politician make cultural decisions did not guarantee first-rate work. The *arkhon* also chose the 28 *khoreghoi* ('chorus-bringers'), wealthy citizens who financed the choruses as part of their *leitourgia* (public duty). This involved recruiting the personnel, hiring a trainer, providing rehearsal space, and housing and feeding everyone. One *khoregos* claimed to have spent 3,000 *dr.* at a time when a skilled artisan was paid around 1 *dr.* per day, and the fee for jury service was ½ *dr.* But, as with sponsorship today, there were paybacks in terms of the kudos this brought. The *arkhon* also allocated the actors to the poets, and arranged the payment of the leading actors and poets. What their fees were is unknown, but after 449 BCE a prize was established for the best actor.

Ten judges (*kritai*, from which we derive 'critic') were appointed by lot to choose the winning playwright, even though they had no specifically pertinent qualifications. Certain officials and the priest of Dionysos Eleuthereus received special seats and 'complimentary tickets', whereas the majority of the audience paid two *obols* per day to attend, until Perikles arranged for the state to fund the admission price for citizens. In all probability the Athenians sat by tribe, with the generals and the priest of Dionysos at the front, and separate sections for the *epheboi*, the *metoikoi* and visitors from other states. There is, however, much dispute over whether, at this date, women and children were permitted to attend, and, if they were, whether or not they had to sit in a segregated area at the back.

Two days of preliminary activity set the Great Dionysia under way, starting on the 8th day of the month of *Elaphebolion* ('Deer-Hunt') with the *proagon*, a kind of 'trailer', where the poets would present their actors and chorus. The following day the *eisagoge* took place, which involved taking the statue of Dionysos from the temple precinct to another temple on the outskirts of Athens, and then bringing it back, in commemoration of the god's first arrival from Eleutherai; when the Athenian men resisted the god's worship they suffered (probably) a continual erection, which only lessened once they promised to worship Dionysos by making and carrying phalluses.

The main events kicked off on the third day with a procession that led the audience through the city and down the Street of the Tripods, where monuments commemorating past winners were displayed, and into the theatre. Women were basket-bearers at the front, groups of men sang hymns and a bull was led in the place of honour. It culminated in a feast in the sanctuary.

The first competitive phase of the festival concerned dithyrambs, cult songs in honour of Dionysos, sung by *kyklioi khoroi* (= 'circular choruses'), groups of fifty singers from the same tribe. Dithyrambs are first mentioned in connection with drunken revelry in celebration of Dionysos in the mid-seventh century BCE: 'I know how to start the lovely round of singing lord Dionysos' dithyramb when the wine has blitzed my brains in.'[5] Around 500 BCE, Lasos of Hermione helped institute dithyrambic competitions in Athens, and three great poets became particularly associated with the genre: Simonides, Bakkhylides and Pindar, who wrote two 'books' of dithyrambs, won a victory in 497/6 BCE, and was noted for his 'austere harmony':

> Come to the chorus, Olympians,
> and send over it glorious grace, you gods
> who are coming to the city's crowded, incense-rich navel
> in holy Athens
> and to the glorious, richly adorned agora.
> Receive wreaths of plaited violets and the songs plucked in
>   springtime
> and look upon me with favour as I proceed from Zeus
> with splendour of songs, and secondly
> to that ivy-knowing god,
> whom we mortals call Bromios and Eriboas
> as we sing of the offspring of the highest of fathers
> and of Kadmeian women.[6]

From around the mid-fifth century BCE, dithyramb became the favoured vehicle of the musical avant-garde.

The day after the dithyrambs came the comedy competition and, after that, three days of tragedy: one author per day. At some point before the performance, the sons of citizens killed in battle were paraded in full armour in the theatre, as was the tribute brought by Athens' allies.

The tragedies were acted by a maximum of three male character actors (the term is *hypokrites* = 'one who responds/answers/ interprets') in conjunction with a chorus, their leader (the *koryphaios*) and sometimes some mute extras. In order of importance the actors were the *protagonistes* ('protagonist' – the 'star'), *deuteragonistes* and *tritagonistes.* They took all the speaking parts between them, including the female roles; cross-dressing was part of the experience. The tragic chorus was played by twelve ordinary citizens (increased to fifteen by Sophocles), who visually represented a pretty anonymous single-sex group. *Khoros* means 'a dance', but they do much more than that: their speech and song is a core element of the drama, and crucially they serve to make the play's events *public* – Greek tragedy was popular, not elitist:

> Their constant and essential presence (they are not an optional part of [the tragic] fiction), creates a collective, and in some sense 'communal', dimension for 'the tragic' and sets the tragic experience ... apart from those of Hamlet, Othello, Macbeth or Lear.[7]

They function as an 'emotional bridge' between the actors and the audience, but their role is not to manipulate the audience's feelings. They have been pertinently described as:

> like groups of people standing on the bank and following with their eyes someone who is being snatched away by the current. That is how the chorus stands in safety and watches, participating, but outside.[8]

Once they enter the arena they remain until the end, but they may have made themselves as inconspicuous as possible when not actively involved – they are not a naturalistic stage crowd.

Tragedy's aesthetic is conventional, not realistic. The actors and the chorus usually wore colourful, long-sleeved robes from neck to ankles, calf-length boots with thin, flexible soles called *kothornoi,* and masks with an open mouth. This meant that, with some spectators more than 50 m away, the actors had to express emotions by large gestures and/or by words. Much of their spoken verse was delivered in iambic trimeter,[9] which was used for both set-piece speeches and dialogue, which can accelerate into alternating single lines called *stichomythia* when it becomes heated. The actors also spoke or chanted trochees[10] (less solemn) or anapaests[11] (more rhythmic), or sang complex lyric metres as solos, duets or with the chorus. Song was accompanied by a double-pipe player (*auletes*).

The chorus used normal speech, most likely delivered by the *koryphaios* alone, but its song and dance routines comprised lyrics arranged into matched pairs of stanzas known as *strophe* and *antistrophe* (which signify a break in the action and the passage of time); speech and recitative/song alternating between itself and the actor/s (*amoibaia*), which exists in the same time frame and intensifies the emotion; non-strophic stanzas; or chanted anapaests. The music and choreography are almost totally lost: we just have a few fragments of musical notation from the whole of antiquity.

Much has been made of the 'three unities' of tragedy: unity of time, place and action. This comes from a Renaissance critic's misinterpretation of Aristotle's *Poetics*. Aristotle insists that the *action* of the play should contribute to a single overarching idea, but he only mentions *time* when he says that tragedy *tries as far as possible* to keep within a 24-hour period, and nowhere does he say that the action should be confined to a single place.

To select the winning play, each of the ten judges wrote his choice on a tablet and dropped it in an urn. The *arkhon eponymos* then drew five tablets – a system that could potentially deny victory to a poet who got seven out of the ten votes, or result in a tie (settled we know not how). Still, the winning poet and *khoregos* were crowned with ivy. If cash prizes were given they were probably not very much, and anyway it was the glory that counted. An after-party followed, and it was pretty much obligatory for the winning *khoregos* to dedicate an expensive bronze tripod in the Street of the Tripods, as did Perikles in 473/2 BCE: 'Tragedy: Xenokles of the deme of Aphidna was the *khoregos*, Aeschylus the *didaskalos*.'[12]

Aeschylus: The Agamemnon

Born into a Eupatrid family at Eleusis in Attika *c.* 525/4 BCE, Aeschylus went on to write between seventy-three and ninety dramas and score between thirteen and twenty-eight victories. This represents both a prodigious output and, considering that each victory was for a group of four plays, a high success rate. However, less than 10 per cent of his output has survived, and this all comes from the last fifteen years of an eventful life, which included fighting at the Battle of Marathon, but which ended, according to tradition, in 456 BCE when he was sitting by the roadside at Gela in Sicily. An eagle flying above with a tortoise in its talons saw the sunshine reflected on his bald head, mistook it for a stone, dropped the tortoise to crack its shell, and cracked Aeschylus' skull instead.

Aristotle credited Aeschylus with increasing the number of tragic actors from one to two, and making the dialogue crucially important,[13] although by the time of the production of the *Oresteia* three actors were available (an innovation of Sophocles, says Aristotle). Aeschylus is the heavyweight champion of tragedy: his poetry, allegedly described by himself as 'mere slices from Homer's rich banquets',[14] is crammed with similes and grand compound adjectives, his imagery is bold and complex, and his Greek is tough to translate: as Robert Yelverton Terrell wryly remarked: 'the original Greek is of great use in elucidating Browning's translation of the *Agamemnon*'.[15] Aeschylus was sometimes mocked for his use of silent characters, the inordinate length of his choral odes, the militaristic flavour of his dramas, and the repetitiveness of his lyrics, yet his visual effects were stupendous, and the awesome Erinyes (Furies) appearing on stage in *Eumenides* were allegedly so scary that children fainted and women had miscarriages.

The only complete trilogy of Greek tragedies that survives is Aeschylus' *Oresteia*. Its subject is the misfortunes of the house of Atreus, who got embroiled in a bitter feud with his brother Thyestes. Atreus had married Aerope, who bore him Agamemnon and Menelaus, known as the *Atreidai* ('Sons of Atreus'), but she was also having extramarital sex with Thyestes, whom she supported in his struggle with Atreus to establish control over Mycenae. Zeus backed Atreus, who banished Thyestes and drowned his unfaithful wife. He then lured Thyestes back, slaughtered his sons, cooked them and served them to Thyestes at a banquet. Thyestes called down the terrible 'Curse of the House of Atreus', and then followed an oracle that said he could exact revenge by having intercourse with his own daughter Pelopia and fathering a son. Pelopia exposed the child to die, but it was found by shepherds, suckled by a she-goat, and taken in by Atreus, who named him Aegisthus (*Aigisthos* in Greek: *aix*, genitive *aigos*, = goat). Agamemnon married Tyndareus' daughter Clytemnestra, with whom he had a son, Orestes, and daughters, who included Elektra and Iphigeneia; Menelaus wed Clytemnestra's sibling Helen, but, when Paris abducted her, Agamemnon led the assault on Troy to get her back. However, when the Greeks were held up at Aulis, the only solution was for Agamemnon to sacrifice Iphigeneia, which he did. In Agamemnon's ten-year absence, Clytemnestra took a lover: Aegisthus. A complicated back-story, but Aeschylus' audience knew it well.

So we start from a situation where, for different reasons, Aegisthus and Clytemnestra both want revenge on the man who avenged the rape of Helen. In a society where 'helping friends and harming enemies' was a fundamental principle, revenge could become a social norm; its circularity meant that the avenger immediately became the next object of revenge: 'The one who acts must suffer.'[16] And so it is in the *Oresteia*'s opening play, *Agamemnon*.

It is just before dawn, and a grumpy watchman on Agamemnon's palace roof at Argos is looking out for the beacon that will signal the fall of Troy. The myth usually locates the events in Mycenae, but 'Argos' can mean 'the Argolid region' (including Argos and Mycenae) – as it does in Homer – or just the city of Argos – as it usually does in the fifth century BCE. However, about four years before the *Oresteia* was produced, Mycenae had been destroyed by Argos, which had become an ally of Athens, and this may have had an influence on Aeschylus' choice of setting. When the watchman mentions Clytemnestra, he says she 'commands' (*kratei*, a word associated with *male* power (*kratos*)). This is abnormal: she should be subject to male authority, but instead she is described as *androboulon*, 'plotting like/against a man', which is essentially the same thing – to plot *like* a man, and so aspire to *kratos*, she has to plot *against* a man. Something is rotten in the state of Argos.

The watchman sees the beacon and exits in a cheery mood, although not without hinting that things have not been entirely perfect during the decade of Agamemnon's absence. He gives way to the chorus of twelve 'old, dishonoured, broken husks of men', who sing a very lengthy song, about the senseless misery of the Trojan War, which they were too old to fight in. They also tell of the circumstances in which Agamemnon sacrificed Iphigeneia, mentioning an omen in which two eagles swooped down and sank their talons into a pregnant hare. This was deeply offensive to Artemis (although Aeschylus never tells us why), and the seer Khalkas interpreted the omen as indicating that Iphigeneia should be sacrificed. Human sacrifice violated every rule of normal behaviour, yet Agamemnon could not shirk the choice: unacceptable option 1 – abandon the expedition to avenge Paris' adultery; acceptable option 2 – sacrifice his daughter. He knows that if, rightly, he takes revenge for Paris' transgression, he himself has to transgress that is how revenge works. Of the two impossible choices, he goes for the military one. The chorus are critical in their judgement:

> And once he slipped his neck in the strap of Fate,
> his spirit veering black, impure, unholy,

once he turned he stopped at nothing,
seized with frenzy . . .
Yes, he had the heart
to sacrifice his daughter,
    to bless the war that avenged a woman's loss.[17]

Aeschylus does not make it easy for us to reach a definite conclusion about Agamemnon's dilemma and responsibility, although we know that Zeus ordered the expedition to Troy, Artemis demanded Iphigeneia's sacrifice, and Agamemnon is not being punished for *previous* wrongdoing. His gut reaction is to consider disobeying, but that would be pointless, since not only would the other Greek chieftains carry out Artemis' wishes, but it would be contrary to the will of Zeus. Agamemnon knows that he must slaughter what is dearest to him, and then pay the penalty. That is what makes his action truly tragic.

While the Chorus have been singing heartrendingly of Iphigeneia's sickening fate, Clytemnestra has made a powerful, silent entrance. The Chorus say:

We respect your power (*kratos*).
Right it is to honour the warlord's woman
Once he leaves the throne.[18]

But as a woman Clytemnestra should not be wielding *kratos*, even though Agamemnon is away. When she finally speaks, she does so authoritatively and impressively, initially describing the transmission of the beacon from Troy to Argos, and then, because the Chorus are not convinced, describing the sack of Troy, but from the Trojan perspective. Of course, she has no idea precisely what happened at Troy – she invents the entire scenario – but the manipulative effect that words can have is starting to become significant. The fact that a woman has just used the quintessentially Athenian male art of rhetoric to make a group of men believe what she wants them to is shocking.

In the first *stasimon* (song) the Chorus sing about how the dead bodies are coming home, the public is questioning the validity of the war, and Agamemnon is losing popularity. He must beware:

God takes aim
At the ones who murder many;
The swarthy Furies stalk the man
gone rich beyond all rights – with a twist
Of fortune grind him down.[19]

The second episode starts when a Herald arrives. He announces Agamemnon's imminent triumphant return, and then digresses on the unpleasantness of military life. Clytemnestra responds with lies and dramatic irony (where the ignorance of the characters is played off against the audience's knowledge): she professes her love for her husband, contemplates 'the best way' to welcome him home, and then exits, leaving the Herald to deliver more depressing news. Menelaus and his ships have gone missing in a storm. This is crucial: Agamemnon is on his own.

The Chorus now sing a vitriolic hymn directed at Helen, whom they blame for the Trojan War. The *hel-* prefix can mean 'destroy', and they make her *helenas,* 'ship-destroyer', *helandros,* 'man-destroyer', and *heleptolis,* 'city-destroyer', as well as comparing her to a lion cub, who grows from being a cute pet into a murderous beast. They conclude by stressing that success and wealth are useless without goodness.

As the Chorus are singing, Agamemnon arrives on his chariot. Aeschylus has been building up to this moment for almost 800 lines, and Agamemnon's speech underlines that he has no doubts about the justice of the Trojan War:

For their mad outrage
of a queen we raped their city – we were right.[20]

But the pomp and circumstance is disturbing: the audience realize that the gods are jealous of the success that Agamemnon embodies, and that he has sacrificed his own daughter.

Clytemnestra comes out to welcome him, but, bizarrely, given his ten-year absence, she addresses the Chorus for a good twenty lines before speaking to him. She lies again about her distress at his absence and her delight at his return, and about how inaccurate reports of his death have upset her. Her deceptive words are all about deceptive words, and they are powerful enough to lead

Agamemnon to his doom. She orders her maids to bring out fabulously opulent crimson tapestries and spread them up the steps from Agamemnon's chariot to the door, and invites him to walk over them into the palace.

> Let the red stream flow and bear him home
> to the home he never hoped to see – Justice,
> lead him in![21]

Agamemnon is uneasy. He is aware that trampling on these tapestries could be a transgressive act, and he tells his wife not to fawn over him as though he were a barbarian tyrant, or pamper him like a woman. When he pointedly asks: 'And where's the woman in all this lust for glory?'[22] – it is because he thinks she is assuming a male role. She is. And as the dialogue accelerates into *stichomythia*, her powers of persuasion give her the upper hand. The (mis)use of rhetoric had become a big issue in Aeschylus' day, especially because of the Sophists, but apart from in some religious contexts, women had no business speaking in public at all. Clytemnestra is completely out of order, and the fact that she is such an awesome speaker makes her utterly terrifying to Athenian males. When the sacker of Troy complies with her wishes, he turns from punisher into transgressor, victor into victim.

As Agamemnon alights, the audience become aware of a female PoW in his chariot. He enters the palace, Clytemnestra follows him, and the Chorus sing of their fears, which are entirely justified.

The fourth episode opens with Clytemnestra reappearing to talk to the prisoner, who we discover is Priam's daughter, the prophetess Cassandra. No one is ever persuaded by her, even though she always speaks the truth; Clytemnestra, who lies and persuades everyone, tries to make her go into the palace. But the Trojan keeps silent. Only after Clytemnestra has given up in frustration and gone inside again does Cassandra speak – in highly articulate Greek, and in song. Using extraordinarily allusive and metaphorical language, she predicts Agamemnon's murder, and refers to the ghastly tale of Atreus and Thyestes. She sees Furies who have drunk human blood sitting in the house; Aegisthus, 'a lion who lacks a lion's heart', laying a trap for Agamemnon; and Clytemnestra, a 'raging mother of death'. Cassandra tries desperately to get the Chorus to realize that Agamemnon is going to be murdered, only to be confronted by infuriatingly bland platitudes (in speech, not song): they cannot comprehend. Yet we can recognize what in many ways is the core of the tragedy's exploration of social order when she cries: 'What outrage – the female is the slayer of the male!'[23] Cassandra ends by predicting her own death, which is also integrated into the process of revenge and reversal:

> When the queen, woman for woman, dies for me,
> And a man falls for the man who married grief.[24]

She exits, leaving the Chorus alone in the *orkhestra*, Clytemnestra in the palace with her victims, and the audience on tenterhooks.

Having made us wait 1,343 lines, Aeschylus finally releases the tension as Agamemnon screams in pain from inside the palace. The conventions of Greek tragedy do not permit the spectators to watch the murder happen. What they do see is a gory tableau of its aftermath, possibly staged using the *ekkyklema*. Clytemnestra is magnificent, completely in her element, gloating over the corpses of Agamemnon and Cassandra, and still manipulating the process of communication:

> I have said many things before to suit the occasion; now I will not be ashamed to say the opposite. It makes me proud.[25]

Clytemnestra is not just transgressive in her words, though. Her sexual behaviour is far more menacing to a fifth-century BCE Athenian male than it is to us. Adultery is a social threat. Helen's adultery is so subversive that it requires a massive military task force to exact revenge; a real-life Athenian woman's adultery undermines the process of inheritance within a patriarchal social system; the 'misuse' of the female body threatens the social position of the male; 'patriarchy requires sexual control of women';[26] and Clytemnestra is way outside of that control, brazenly challenging the fundamental relationship at the heart of Athenian society. She is a monstrous reversal of the true female role.

The men of the Chorus are appalled. They threaten her with banishment (it is highly abnormal for a Chorus to do this), but she retorts that they have double standards: why did they never demand similar treatment for Agamemnon when he sacrificed Iphigeneia? Speaking from a position of unassailable strength, she justifies the murder:

> You try me like some desperate woman.
> My heart is steel, well you know. Praise me,
> blame me as you choose. It's all one.
> Here is Agamemnon, my husband made a corpse
> by this right hand – a masterpiece of Justice.[27]

Clytemnestra cows the old men by sheer force of personality, and, when they try to put the blame on Helen, she will have none of it: it was the curse that was responsible. She insists that Agamemnon will remain unmourned, and imagines Iphigeneia's ghost rushing to meet him at the River Styx:

> She'll fling her arms around her father,
> Pierce him with her love.[28]

At this late stage, Aegisthus emerges. It is entirely in his character to show up when the danger is over yet claim credit for the murder, which he sees as justified revenge for what Agamemnon's father did to his. Atreus' son could not escape his family history: the one who acted had to suffer.

Aegisthus revolts the Chorus, who question his manhood and address him as 'woman', a feminized foil to his lover's 'maleness'. But he is still menacing: he announces his intention of ruling as king, and it will be a tyrannical regime. Clytemnestra intervenes to prevent a massacre as the feisty old men prepare to fight Aegisthus' stormtroopers with their sticks. She calls off Aegisthus and tells the Chorus to go home:

> What we did was destiny.
> If we could end the suffering, how we would rejoice.
> The spirit's brutal hoof has struck our heart.
> And that is what a woman has to say.
> Can you accept the truth?[29]

This is hard for them. Stating their hope that Agamemnon's son Orestes will return to avenge him, they leave the *orkhestra*. As Clytemnestra and Aegisthus make for the palace, she has the last word: 'Let them howl – they're impotent. You and I have power now.'[30] The first part of the *Oresteia* trilogy is over.

The second play, the *Khoephoroi* (Libation Bearers) continues the theme of 'the one who acts must suffer' into the next generation. Orestes and Elektra have to decide between killing their mother or letting their father's death go unavenged. They decide on the former, and Orestes slays both Clytemnestra and Aegisthus. For doing this he is hounded by the Furies, the supernatural bringers of retribution, and in the final play in the trilogy, *Eumenides*, they pursue him from Delphi to Athens, where he becomes the defendant in the first murder trial in the court of the Areiopagos. He is acquitted thanks to Athene's casting vote, and the Furies put aside their anger against Athens (persuasion has to take the place of violence to create a better future) and take up residence there, complete with a new name, *Eumenides* = 'the Kindly Ones'.

So, in the end, Aeschylus has created a 'brave new world' where vengeance is replaced by *dike*, which can, amongst other things, mean 'justice', 'right', 'retribution', 'punishment', 'law-court' and 'court-case'. Trying to define *dike* was a hot topic in democratic Athens, and it appears all through the *Oresteia* with a strong link to revenge: Paris 'kicked the altar of *dike*'; Troy is destroyed by 'Zeus who brings *dike*'; Agamemnon saw himself as the agent of *dike* in the sacking of Troy; Clytemnestra thinks the same about her killing of Agamemnon;[31] and, although in Homer Nestor has no doubt that Orestes was right to murder Clytemnestra, tragedy finds the issue far less cut and dried.

Sophocles and Oedipus the King

Sophocles was born at Colonus near Athens in either 497/6 or 495/4 BCE, and combined his literary career with prominent public service, holding the office of *Hellenotamias* ('Treasurer of the Greeks') in 443/2 BCE, and *Strategos* (General) in the campaign against Samos in 441/40 BCE. He made a winning debut in 468 BCE, beating Aeschylus, and went on to produce more than a hundred plays, of which only seven are fully extant: *Ajax*, *Antigone*, *Elektra*, *Oedipus the King*, *Oedipus at Colonus*, *Philoktetes* and

Women of Trakhis. His number of recorded victories fluctuates between eighteen and twenty-four, and he never came last in the competitions, which represents a highly impressive strike-rate that neither Aeschylus nor Euripides could match. He died in 406/5 BCE, allegedly from choking on a grape sent to him by an actor.

Stylistically speaking, Sophocles is often said to occupy the middle ground between Aeschylus' rugged simplicity and Euripides' precision and urbanity. His poetry was admired for being majestic, highly tragic and euphonious in its phrasing.[32]

His tragedy *Oedipus the King* (also referred to as *Oedipus Rex*, or by its Greek name, *Oidipous Tyrannos*, shortened to 'the *O.T.*') is generally regarded as his masterpiece. The Oedipus myth is a DIY concoction of common motifs – exposure, the coming of age of a prince, the combination of parricide and incest – and the earliest version that we have appears in Homer's *Odyssey*:

> I [Odysseus] saw the mother of Oedipus, the fair Epicaste, who committed an enormity in ignorance, marrying her son. He married her after killing his father. But in time the gods made matters known to men . . . and she went to strong-gated Hades, after stringing a high noose from the top of a room, gripped by her own misery, leaving behind for him many causes of pain.[33]

In Sophocles' version, however, it is Oedipus himself who 'makes matters known to men'.

Behind the play lie two predictions from the Delphic Oracle: Oedipus' father Laios, King of Thebes, was told that he would be killed by his own son, prompting him to expose the child on Mount Kithairon; Oedipus was later told that he would kill his father and marry his mother, prompting him to leave Corinth, where he had grown up. When the play starts, both these prophecies have already come true.

Thebes had also been oppressed by the Sphinx, who had learned a riddle from the Muses:

> There walks on land a creature of two feet, of four feet, and of three; it has one voice, but sole among animals that grow on land or in the sea, it can change its nature; nay, when it walks propped on most feet, then is the speed of its limbs less than it has ever been before.[34]

The Thebans were told that solving this riddle would rid them of the Sphinx, but she ate anyone who guessed wrongly. They decreed that whoever could solve the riddle would be rewarded with both the kingdom and marriage to Queen Jocasta, widow of Laios, who had recently met a violent death. Oedipus, whom everybody thought was the son of King Polybos and Queen Merope of Corinth, happened to be travelling towards Thebes, and came forward with the answer: 'man'. The Sphinx hurled herself from the citadel; Oedipus claimed his reward, and became a celebrity: 'you all know me, the world knows my fame: I am Oedipus'.[35]

As the play opens, he is receiving a delegation. A terrible plague is afflicting the city, rather like the one that struck Athens at the beginning of the Peloponnesian War. There is also a significant literary model in the plague inflicted on the Greeks by Apollo at the start of Homer's *Iliad*, and although Sophocles never specifies *who* sent the plague or *why* it has struck, Apollo's shadow constantly looms over the play.

Oedipus' response to the delegation is sympathetic:

> I know well that you are all suffering, and although you suffer, there is not one of you who suffers as much as I do . . . My spirit is grieving for the city, for myself and for you all at the same time.[36]

These words are laden with dramatic irony, as is the case with practically everything Oedipus says. His search for a solution is driven by positive qualities and motives that make him appear in a very favourable light, but he has no idea that he himself is the problem. There is a common tendency to dumb down the play to 'the world's first detective story', 'a psychological whodunit'. Except we already know whodunit.

Oedipus has already sent his respected brother-in-law Kreon to Delphi to seek advice, and now he arrives with the Oracle's response, which Oedipus tells him to deliver publicly. It says that the plague will end when the Thebans banish or take revenge upon the murderer of Laios, who is still in Thebes. Oedipus promises to do this 'on behalf of this country and on behalf of Apollo'.[37]

Some commentators interpret the play as an enactment of an ancient scapegoat ritual in which plague or famine could motivate the killing of a king and the selection of another ruler to restore fertility to the land. Others see Oedipus' overconfidence as *hubris*, a 'tragic flaw' or 'transgression' (*hamartia* in Greek) that justifies his fall. But that is really missing the point. Aristotle did say that tragic action should come about through *hamartia*,[38] but the word is associated with missing the target in archery – it is an 'error' rather than a 'character flaw', and it has nothing to do with arrogance. Comparison with Shakespearean tragedy has influenced some to see pride (*hubris*) as the error (*hamartia*), but this Christianizes Greek tragedy in an inappropriate way: *hubris* is more than an attitude – it manifests itself in violent or arrogant *actions* (it was the Greek word for GBH). Pride was an *appropriate* feeling for an aristocratic male to display, humility was not; and in any case Oedipus has already fulfilled his destiny.

Oedipus declares that he will bring the murdere to light himself, and he summons the Thebans to his palace. The Chorus of Theban noblemen then enters the *orkhestra* and they sing a prayer to Zeus, Apollo, Athena, Artemis and Dionysos, in which they worry about the sacrifices that might have to be made to avert the horrors of the plague. By the time they have finished, the Thebans are assembled in front of Oedipus' residence, and, ironically describing himself as 'a stranger to the story, a stranger to the crime',[39] he invites anyone with information about who killed Laios to speak out. When no one does, he loses his patience and curses the murderer and anyone who might be sheltering him, pointedly including himself in all this, and asserting that he will fight for Laios as if he were his own father.

Oedipus is certainly on the case. In keeping with the play's intertwined themes of knowledge/ignorance, blindness/sight, he has summoned Teiresias, a blind old prophet. His speciality is predicting the future, but here Oedipus quizzes him about the past. The prophet sees the truth, and so initially refuses to help: 'I will never reveal my dreadful secrets, not to say your own.'[40] The ensuing stand-off reveals Oedipus' volatile temper. He accuses Teiresias of involvement in the murder; outraged, Teiresias retorts: '*You* are the curse, the corruption on the land! . . . I say you are the murderer you hunt.'[41] Oedipus, who genuinely believes that he has never met Laios, thinks this is a lie and taunts Teiresias with his blindness. Essentially this means he is rejecting prophetic power, a very dangerous position to adopt.

An element of insecurity in Oedipus' personality now comes out as he jumps to the conclusion that Kreon is plotting against him, and that Teiresias is complicit in the scheme:

> When the Sphinx . . . was here, how was it that you did not say anything . . . But I came, Oedipus who knew nothing, I put a stop to her, finding the answer by intelligence.[42]

The prophet responds in highly loaded vocabulary:

> I say, since you have taunted me for my blindness, that you have sight but do not see the evil situation you are in . . . A terrible-footed curse will drive you from this land: you who can see clearly now will then see darkness.[43]

The adjective 'terrible-footed', *deinopous* in Greek, plays on Oedipus' name: *Oidipous* = 'swollen-footed'. He was called this because his ankles had been pinned when he was exposed, although this is an odd motif in the myth, especially as Sophocles' Oedipus does not limp. Sophocles also exploits other aspects of the name: *dipous* means 'two-footed', echoing the Sphinx's riddle; and the first two syllables suggest *oida* = 'I know', with all the irony implicit in everything that Oedipus does *not* know. After a final savage exchange of *stichomythia* (single lines of dialogue), Oedipus heads for the palace and Teiresias exits having served his dramatic purpose: his actor will be needed for other characters.

The chorus now deliver the first *stasimon*, glorifying Apollo, and singing of how the 'dread voices of Delphi' will descend on Laios' killer. But their faith in prophecy is not unshakeable, and they opt for the compromise of honouring Apollo, while needing definitive proof from his prophet: after all, Oedipus saved them from the Sphinx, and they owe it to him to stay loyal unless the charges stick.

Kreon then arrives, hoping to clear his name. He states his case very effectively, but Oedipus has made up his mind and when Kreon eventually asks, 'What do you want? You want me banished?' Oedipus retorts: 'No, I want you dead.'[44] Their argument gets so heated that Jocasta comes out and gives them a telling-off. Oedipus sends Kreon away and tells his wife about Teiresias' accusation. She rejects this instantly because she does not believe in prophecy, primarily because her ex-husband once received an oracle saying that he would be killed by his own son. This, she says, was wrong on two counts: (a) Laios, so the report went, was killed by robbers at a place where three roads meet; and (b) their son had had his ankles fastened, and a henchman had flung him away on a barren, trackless mountain.[45]

Oedipus' 'swollen-footedness' might have been picked up on here, but the reference to the road-junction leads Oedipus to wonder if Teiresias could have been right after all. Oedipus had killed several people, including an old man that Jocasta said looked a bit like him, in a road-rage incident at that very crossroads. Oedipus had not given it a second thought since it had happened. Why should he? It arose from an affront to his *time*, and he had no reason to become fixated on it. What worries him, though, is the possibility that he killed Laios.

Oedipus recalls a banquet where an inebriated Corinthian said that he was not the son of Polybos and Merope, and that the fracas had happened when he was returning from consulting the Delphic Oracle about this. The Pythia had ducked the question of his parentage, but delivered a much more disturbing response:

> You are fated to couple with your mother, you will bring
> a breed of children into the light no man can bear to see –
> you will kill your father![46]

To avoid fulfilling this oracle, Oedipus had left Corinth. Jocasta reminds him that the story was that Laios died at the hands of a gang, not an individual, but even so Oedipus has the sole survivor of the incident summoned for questioning. He has to know the truth.

The survivor's back-story gradually emerges: he was a slave in Laios' household, worked as a shepherd on Mount Kithairon, was with Laios at the time of the massacre, delivered the news of Laios' death to Thebes, and when Oedipus became king he asked Jocasta to send him back to his shepherding, which she did.

While we anticipate the shepherd's arrival the Chorus sing of how they would prefer Oedipus to have killed his father and married his mother than that their religious beliefs should be shattered. For them, the truth of prophecy equals the existence of the gods:

> I will go to Delphi no longer
> To worship at the pure navel of the Earth,
> If these oracles never come true.[47]

The next episode opens with Jocasta, despite her scepticism, burning incense to Apollo in an attempt to allay Oedipus' fears about the prophecy that very god has given. She is interrupted by the arrival of a Messenger from Corinth, who announces the death, from natural causes, of Polybos. She immediately reiterates her views on prophecy – half the oracle is obviously false – and a relieved Oedipus gives his opinion about prophets and oracles: 'They're nothing, worthless.'[48]

However, he is still fretting about the possibility of incest with Merope. Jocasta brushes aside his worries:

> It's all chance,
> chance rules our lives . . .
> Better to live at random . . .
> Many a man before you,
> in his dreams, has shared his mother's bed.[49]

The Messenger, who has overheard the conversation, tries to make things better, only to make them infinitely worse. He informs Oedipus that he is not the son of Polybos and Merope: while working as a shepherd on Mount Kithairon the Messenger had been given the baby Oedipus by a Theban shepherd working for Laios. He then passed the infant to the childless Corinthian royal couple, who brought him up as their own. This Theban shepherd is, of course, the one who has been summoned to solve the question of Laios' death.

The news hits Oedipus hard, but Jocasta is one step ahead of him. She realizes that the prophecy has been fulfilled, and desperately urges Oedipus to abandon his inquiry. But he is unstoppable. When she exits screaming, Oedipus rather unkindly dismisses this as womanly shame at him being low born, which is now not an issue for him:

> I must know my birth, no matter how common
> it may be – I must see my origins face to face.
> . . . I count myself the son of Chance.[50]

Oedipus can always choose whether to find out the truth or not, and he exercises that freedom. He will bring about his own downfall; Oedipus' destiny has already been fulfilled, and if he does not continue to seek the truth, it will not be revealed (at least, not yet). He is not a helpless puppet of fate, but deploys the quintessentially human qualities of courage, intelligence and perseverance to try to find out who he really is. That is Sophocles' great contribution to the mythology of Oedipus.

While we wait for the Theban shepherd, the Chorus sings an ode to Mount Kithairon. When he arrives, he first becomes the victim of the Corinthian messenger's 'helpfulness', as he is forced to admit that he did give him the child, and then of Oedipus' temper. The shepherd knows what is coming, and initially refuses to supply the information that Oedipus wants, but, faced with threats of torture and death, he divulges that the baby came from the house of Laios. Aristotle was highly complimentary about Sophocles' combination of discovery (*anagnorisis* = 'the change from ignorance to knowledge') and reversal (*peripeteia* = 'a change from one state of affairs to its opposite') here: 'The best type of discovery is when it happens together with a reversal, like the one in *Oedipus* does.'[51] The discovery that Oedipus has already fulfilled the prediction is upon us. Both the shepherd and the king brace themselves:

SHEPHERD: Oh, no,
I'm right at the edge, the horrible truth – I've got to say it!
OEDIPUS: And I'm at the edge of hearing horrors, yes, but I must hear![52]

The shattering climax is one of the defining moments of world drama. Oedipus finally knows that he has killed his father and married his mother.

Oedipus rushes off into the palace, leaving the audience wondering what the consequence of such ghastly knowledge might be, and the Chorus reflecting on Oedipus' life. A Messenger then appears to impart the news that Jocasta has taken her own life, along with a blood-curdling virtuoso description of how Oedipus found the queen hanging by a noose, took the pins from her dress (ancient dress pins are not like modern safety pins:

Jocasta's would be heavy golden artefacts at least 10 cm long), and then perpetrated a horrifying act of self-blinding. Just as the messenger finishes the story, Oedipus emerges. It is worth noting that although the blind Teiresias foresaw Oedipus' blindness, this did not feature in Apollo's oracles, and the Messenger stresses the independence of Oedipus' action:

> Terrible things, and none done blindly now,
> all done with a will.[53]

Oedipus confirms this when the Chorus ask him about his self-mutilation. He acknowledges that Apollo ordained his agonies, but asserts that;

> the hand that struck my eyes was mine, mine alone – no one else –
> I did it all myself![54]

He explains that he could not bring himself to look upon his father, his mother or, even worse, his children in the Underworld after his death. He begs Kreon, who has become the *de facto* ruler of Thebes, to have him executed or banished – that is what Apollo's original decree demanded – but Kreon says that he will first consult the oracle. In the end, Sophocles focuses on Oedipus' anxieties about his daughters' futures, and, as he is allowed to embrace them one last time, the *katharsis* is complete. Oedipus exits, while the chorus laments his fall from greatness in clichéd, but apposite words: 'Count no man happy till he dies, free of pain at last.'[55] For them, Oedipus is a prime example of how precarious human happiness can be, yet there are those who are tempted to see his attitude as the embodiment of the inextinguishable human spirit, particularly when he says:

> No sickness can destroy me,
> nothing can. I would never have been saved
> from death – I have been saved
> for something great and terrible, something strange.
> Well, let my destiny come and take me on its way![56]

Oedipus has endured unimaginable physical and mental traumas at the hands of the gods and himself, yet, despite the personal cost, there is a sense in which he triumphs: he has discovered who he is. Aeschylus' *Agamemnon* fails in this and dies; Sophocles' Oedipus succeeds and survives.

Euripides and Medea

Euripides, the son of a woman who allegedly sold vegetables in the marketplace, was the youngest, most avant-garde and least successful of the 'big three' Athenian tragedians. Born in 485/4 or 480 BCE, he wrote a minimum of eighty-eight plays, but won just four victories, although he also had one posthumous success after his death in 407/6 BCE. We are told that he spent the last two years of his life at the court of the Macedonian king Arkhelaos, but we don't know why. The ancient biographers depict him as a recluse, composing his plays in a cave on the seashore, but other sources make him more sociable: apparently one of the Sophist Protagoras' works had its first reading at Euripides' house, and in Aristophanes' *The Acharnians,* Dikaiopolis drops in at Euripides' home, where he is working on a tragedy. Of his eighty-eight plays, eighteen have come down to us more or less intact, ten of them because they were included in a 'greatest hits' collection like those of Aeschylus and Sophocles, the others because of the chance survival of one volume of 'The Complete Plays' in two fourteenth-century CE manuscripts. There are also significant fragments of another nine plays on papyrus.

Aristotle famously writes that: 'Sophocles said that he drew men as they ought to be, whereas Euripides drew them as they are.'[57] However, 'the paradoxical and disconcerting multiplicity of Euripides' theatrical imagination'[58] makes him rather mercurial, and in antiquity he had a reputation for being a theatrical innovator, fond of portraying disabled characters and characters dressed in rags, an iconoclast, an atheist and a misogynist.

His astonishing tragedy *Medea* was entered in the competition of 431 BCE, where it came third to works by Euphorion (Aeschylus' son) and Sophocles. Yet its heroine is one of the finest creations of Greek drama. The play deals with life after the romance and adventure of Jason's quest for the Golden Fleece. Medea was a barbarian sorceress, the daughter of King Aietes, owner of the Fleece. She had fallen in love with Jason, provided him with drugs that enabled him to win the Fleece, and murdered her brother Apsyrtos to facilitate their escape. Back in Iolkos, King Pelias, who had sent Jason on the quest, had murdered Jason's father, Aison. Medea exacted terrible vengeance for this by persuading Pelias' daughters that they could rejuvenate their ageing father by boiling him. When this resulted in his agonizing death, she and Jason were expelled from Iolkos and went to Corinth, had children and lived happily until Jason decided to upgrade his marriage in favour of a wedding to Glauke, the daughter of King Kreon of Corinth (not to be confused with the Theban Kreon of the Oedipus story).

Medea stands to lose everything because of this, and the play opens with her old Nurse telling us how she rants and raves, invokes all Jason's vows and pledges, refuses to eat and spends long hours in tears. More disturbingly,

> She hates her sons:
> To see them is no pleasure to her. I am afraid
> Some dreadful purpose is forming in her mind. She is
> A frightening woman.[59]

These two young boys then appear with their cynical old tutor, who is far from surprised that Jason has spurned Medea. Rumour has it that Kreon intends to banish the boys and their mother and, as the nurse starts to pack off the children into the house, we hear Medea's voice offstage, 'giving incoherent voice only to pain and articulate only in universal cursing and damnation'.[60]

Drawn by Medea's cries, the Chorus of Corinthian women enter. They offer resigned, sympathetic consolation, but Medea continues to rave:

> Come, flame of the sky,
> Pierce through my head!
> What do I gain from living any longer?
> Oh, how I hate living! I want
> To end my life, leave it behind, and die . . .
> Oh, may I see Jason and his bride
> Ground to pieces in their shattered palace
> For the wrong they have dared to do to me, unprovoked![61]

When Euripides finally brings Medea onstage, rather surprisingly, and perhaps disturbingly, she appears completely in control of herself. Her barbarian roots would not be apparent from her voice, since she does not speak in dialect, but, if vase paintings illustrating the play are a reliable guide, she probably wore a foreign-looking costume. Still, she has a razor-sharp view on Greek women's place in society: no say in their choice of husband; a subservient position; and a set of double-standards to cope with:

> If a man grows tired
> Of the company at home, he can go out, and find
> A cure for tediousness. We wives are forced to look
> To one man only. And, they tell us, we at home
> Live free from danger, they go out to battle: fools!
> I'd rather stand three times in the front line than bear
> One child.[62]

She concludes with a subtly ironic twist, reminding the Chorus that they have a city and a home, whereas she is a complete outsider (yet Medea actually chose her husband). Awed by her eloquence, they fall silent, and she asks them to stay that way as she seeks her revenge. She has to do this for the practical reason that the Chorus cannot leave the *orkhestra*, but it also turns them into uneasy observers, and Medea's supernatural criminality will stand out more starkly against the background of these mundane women.

Kreon appears and confirms Medea's exile. He is aware that his position is morally dubious, but at least he is honest about his motivation: it is self-defence – he fears her cleverness and sorcery, and has heard reports that she has made threats against Jason, his bride and himself. Medea loathes the fact that her reputation is so damaging, but the Greek notion that women are more cunning than men, and are constantly up to no good, goes right back to Homer, and this type of characterization of women was particularly associated with Euripides. The grouchy old men of Aristophanes' *Lysistrata* praise his insight: 'There is no man more correct in his judgement than the poet Euripides. There is no creature so unreasonable as women!'[63]

Kreon is tough but fair, and he reluctantly but naively allows Medea twenty-four hours to organize the logistics of her exile. That will be ample time for her purposes, and the second he departs she turns from a grovelling suppliant into a scheming witch. Jason and his new bride must perish: poison is her preferred option, if she can find someone to protect her from any reprisals; plan 'b' is to kill them with her own hands and face the consequences. So she prays to Hekate, goddess of witchcraft, and reminds the audience that her grandfather was the Sun-god. She finds the idea of being laughed at by Jason and his new allies intolerable, but she is confident in her powers. As she confides to the Chorus:

> We were born women – useless for honest purposes.
> But in all kinds of evil skilled practitioners.[64]

They reply with the first *stasimon*, a lament full of uncanny images of the reversal of the natural order of the universe, which develops into a litany of complaints about the way women are portrayed in mythological tales. How can the tradition accuse women of lies and deceit, they ask, when men behave like Jason? They look forward to a time when the female sex is honoured, and male poets' tales of faithless women will no longer be fashionable. If Apollo bestowed inspiration via female understanding, they say, there would be a barrage of counter-epics against men.

At last Jason enters. Given that Euripides has only presented him from the perspective of people who are biased against him, we wonder how he might justify himself. But he doesn't even bother. In his arrogant, self-centred, self-righteous way he believes that because his new marriage is good for himself it must be right. And, in any case, he has offered Medea financial support in her banishment. He genuinely thinks that this has discharged his obligations. Medea is incensed, and responds with a brilliant display of rhetoric: every Argonaut knows he would never have won the Golden Fleece without her; she abandoned her home for him; she inflicted the most horrible of deaths on King Pelias; she has borne him sons; and in return he has turfed her out and got himself another wife. Jason is staggered by her ingratitude and tells her to count her blessings: she lives in Greece, the home of justice, where force yields to the law, and, he says:

> You are famous; if you still lived at the ends of the earth
> Your name would never be spoken.[65]

The irony of this completely escapes him – Medea doesn't want celebrity, and he is hardly a paragon of Hellenic justice – but, he continues, it's all down to petty sexual jealousy: if women have a satisfying sex-life, they have everything they wish for, but, if that goes wrong, it ruins everything. He wishes that children could be got without females.

Their argument degenerates into a slanging-match, and Jason stomps off to the palace with her angry words ringing in his ears. As was the case in Aeschylus' *Oresteia*, the combination of woman-and-*eros* (sexual desire) in the wrong context can have bad ramifications, especially since women's sexual desires, though obviously equal to men's, were more difficult to pursue. To compound the problem, as a result of being physically weaker, the usual way out was for the woman to resort to trickery, and the fact that feminine power was not overt made it seem all the more frightening. Soundbites taken out of context can easily be deployed to make Euripides into a misogynist or a 'feminist', but he was neither. He was a playwright with a deep interest in the problems and effects of male–female interrelationships, and we might note that the Chorus of ordinary women never once complain about men's oppression, or question their place in society. At this point, they sing of the mixed blessings of love, and stress the classic Greek maxim that moderation is best: they hope that Aphrodite will never cause their hearts to leave old love for new:

> But let her judge shrewdly the loves of women
> And respect the bed where no war rages.[66]

As they conclude, an old traveller now turns up seeking to clarify an oracle concerning his sterility. He is King Aigeus of Athens, and Medea instantly tells him her story, hints that she knows how to cure him, and begs him to shelter her. A couple of inconsistencies intrude here, since Aigeus speaks as if he knows Medea's plans, even though the Chorus are the only other parties to this information, and his circumspection about offending the Corinthians is odd, seeing that they are only too glad to be rid of her. But what matters is that he takes Medea's bait: she can have sanctuary at Athens if she can get away from Corinth unaided.

This is perfect, and Medea can proceed with her plan. First, she will send a robe and a golden diadem, impregnated with supernatural poison, as 'gifts' for Glauke. And then she will kill her own sons. The Chorus are aghast. In an effort to dissuade her they sing a lovely ode to the glories of Athens, and wonder how a city that is a byword for truth and justice will give sanctuary to a murderess. But the lady is not for turning. She has again sent for Jason and, when he returns, her role-play is chilling: she is immediately humble, reasonable, submissive and apologetic. She acknowledges Jason's wisdom and the folly of her own ways, summons her sons and tells them to hug their father. She just about manages to keep her emotions in check, and Jason is completely taken in. Then she asks if the boys can take the gifts to Glauke and plead to have their exile revoked, and, though Jason hesitates, he agrees, and the innocent, unknowing boys follow him home. If we wanted to nit-pick, we could point out that Medea has not had the chance to get the poisoned gifts ready, but we should not really expect 100 per cent naturalism from tragedy.

The Chorus lament the inevitable deaths, after which the Tutor hurries in and announces that Glauke has accepted the gifts and pardoned the children. Then the children themselves return, and Medea bids them farewell:

> All was for nothing, then – these years of rearing you,
> My care, my aching weariness, and the wild pains
> When you were born. Oh, yes, I once built many hopes
> On you; imagined, pitifully, that you would care
> For my old age, and would yourselves wrap my dead body
> For burial. How people would envy me my sons!
> That sweet, sad thought has faded now.[67]

Euripides expertly manipulates the conventions of tragic drama to ratchet up the pathos. The three-actor rule means the boys cannot speak, but their silence is unbelievably eloquent. They exit for the last time, heart-rendingly tangled up in issues they know nothing about.

Pathos is now supplanted by utter horror. Again, Euripides turns the dramatic conventions to his benefit: he cannot 'stage' the princess's death, but no restrictions apply to describing it. A Messenger now tells how Glauke put on the gown and the coronet, and started to preen herself in the mirror. The girl's sexy, almost prostitute-like behaviour should alert the listeners that something awful is about to happen. And it does. She staggers, collapses, froths at the mouth, rolls her eyes and goes completely pale. When she regains consciousness, the coronet discharges a stream of unearthly fire, while the dress corrodes her flesh. Her attempts to loosen the crown intensify its effects, until she falls to the ground, grotesquely disfigured, her flesh melted like drops of pine resin. When Kreon arrives and embraces her, he sticks to the toxic garment and expires too.

The jubilant Medea steels herself to murder her children, and goes inside the palace. The tense wait ends, just as in the *Agamemnon*, with cries from offstage – the first sounds the children have uttered. When Jason arrives from the scene of Glauke's death, the Chorus tells him the grim news. Euripides again makes brilliant use of tragedy's conventions: the dialogue focuses the audience's attention on the palace, and the Chorus use a standard formula in telling Jason to 'open the door', setting up an expectation that the *ekkyklema*, with the bodies on it, will appear at ground level. Instead, Medea's voice comes from above the roof: most likely suspended by the *mekhane*, she is riding in the dragon-drawn Chariot of the Sun. Most critics regard this as a stunning effect, although Aristotle felt it was unsatisfactory:

> The unravelling of the plot should arise from the circumstances of the plot itself, and not be brought about *ex machina*, as done in the *Medea*.[68]

Jason demands the children's bodies; Medea refuses; they taunt each other; she promises to create a festival at Corinth to expiate the murders; the *mekhane* conveys the chariot out of sight, leaving Jason a broken man and the Chorus reflecting on the precariousness of life.

Satyr Play: Sophocles' Trackers
At the Great Dionysia in the fifth century BCE, a 'satyr-play', which the original sources call *satyroi* ('satyrs'), was usually written by each tragedian to be performed by the same company after his tragic trilogy. At this period satyrs, or *silenoi* as the Athenians called them,

are male human/equine creatures, with bushy tails, pointy ears, snub noses, high foreheads and beards, who are generally represented naked with an enormous erect phallus. They are ambiguous beasts: full-on hedonists, but immortal companions of Dionysos; cruder than men, but wiser; mischievous and lewd, but fine musicians; and, although they are insatiable drinkers and womanizers, they are complete cowards. Together with nymphs and maenads, whom they lasciviously and unsuccessfully chase, they form the *thiasos* ('sacred band') of Dionysos, and they describe themselves like this:

> We are children of the nymphs, servants of Dionysos, companions of the gods. We are fit for every suitable trade: combat with a spear; contests of wrestling, riding, running, boxing, biting, testicle twisting. We have songs of music, oracles secret and not false, diagnosis of diseases; we can measure the sky, dance, and make noises down below.[69]

A *thiasos* of satyrs forms the chorus of the satyr plays, with Silenos (or 'Pappasilenos'), the father of the satyrs, appearing as a character in his own right.

Our surviving material includes one complete play, Euripides' *Cyclops*, plus over 400 lines of Sophocles' *Ikhneutai* ('*Trackers*'), large chunks of Aeschylus' *Net-Haulers* and *Spectators or Isthmians,* the Pronomos vase,[70] which displays the entire cast of a victorious play, and the monument adorned with scenes of satyr-plays that the victorious *khoregos* Lysikrates erected in 334 BCE in the Street of the Tripods in Athens. The themes were sometimes related to the trilogy they followed, sometimes not, and 'the recipe is as follows: take one myth, add satyrs, and observe the result'.[71] Although the earthy preoccupations of the satyrs may have undermined the dignity of heroes like Odysseus in the *Cyclops* – one source described satyr-play as *tragoidia paizousa* (= 'tragedy playing around') – Odysseus' speech is virtually indistinguishable from its tragic counterpart. That of the satyrs and Silenos, though, is lower in tone:

> Tragedy scorns to babble trivialities, and, like a married woman obliged to dance at the festival, will look rather shamefaced among the wanton satyrs.[72]

The plays have a standard set of motifs: the satyrs often find themselves in a situation where they are out of their element, in captivity or forced to work; their rescue/escape frequently involves monsters or evil humans; and cleverness/deceit often provides the means of their liberation. Marvellous inventions and creations (of wine, the lyre, fire, etc.) appear, along with riddles, magic, emergence from the Underworld, the birth and raising of divine or heroic infants, romance and athletics.

Satyric drama was probably formally instituted in the Great Dionysia festival around 501 BCE. It is a difficult genre to pin down: various theories make it attack, subvert, round off or reinforce the world of tragedy; look at it from a different point of view; serve up a kind of 'dessert' after the tragic feast; or simply generate escapist fun. What it did not do was offer comic relief to an emotionally exhausted tragic audience; comedy could have done that, but satyr-plays draw on tragic, not comic, subject matter. Neither do they feature the same freedom, colloquialism and obscenity as comedy.

The discovery of about 400 lines of Sophocles' *Ikhneutai* on papyrus fragments in Egypt in 1908 gave us pretty much all the first half of a play based on the myth of the birth of Hermes. In the *Homeric Hymn to Hermes,* Maia lay in love with Zeus, and gave birth to Hermes in a cave on Mount Kyllene. The god was born at dawn, played the lyre in the afternoon, and stole the cattle of Apollo in the evening. In Sophocles' play Apollo has been looking for these animals, and offers a reward for information leading to their recovery. Silenos says that he and the satyrs will join the search, providing they are paid up front. Apollo accepts, and the satyrs soon find cattle-tracks pointing in several different directions, which they sniff out 'like a monkey bending over to let off a fart'. As they make this discovery they hear a weird new sound that terrifies them. Silenos asks:

> Why on earth are you so scared of a sound? You mannequins moulded from wax, you dirty pieces of animal dung! You see terror in every shadow, you are afraid of everything. You are spineless, slovenly and slavish attendants, nothing but bodies, tongues and phalluses! If you're ever needed, you sound loyal, but run away from the action. And yet, you worthless beasts, you have such a father as

me – who, when young, graced the dwellings of the nymphs with many monuments to his manliness.[73]

Kyllene, the goddess of the mountain, explains that the noise is the sound of Hermes playing the lyre in the cave and gives the Satyrs a telling-off for shattering the pastoral peace. They are suitably contrite, but they still want to know about these bizarre sounds, so Kyllene tells them that Maia has secretly given birth to Hermes and that he has constructed the lyre out of a tortoise shell. Although confined in the cave on Zeus' orders, Hermes is in paroxysms of joy at the beauty of the sound. The Satyrs are unimpressed and accuse Hermes of cattle-rustling. Kyllene denies the allegation: the boy is not genetically predisposed to criminality, telling them to go and look somewhere else, 'you should know better at your age, with your long beards and bald heads'. The Satyrs are tenacious, though. They are certain Hermes has used leather to make lyre strings, so they put two and two together and stand firm until he is handed over. Then the text runs out.

It is likely that Sophocles' play ran along the lines of the *Homeric Hymn to Hermes*. The Satyrs were definitely on the right track: Hermes had stolen the cattle in Pieria, where Apollo was in charge of the herds of Admetos but preoccupied with a love affair with Hymenaios. Hermes had worked hard to avoid detection:

He reversed their hooves,
making the front hooves backward
and the back hooves forward
while he himself walked backwards.[74]

He drove the animals to Kyllene, where Apollo caught up with him. By this time Hermes had snuggled back into his swaddling clothes, and when he denied everything Apollo appealed to Zeus, who told them to seek the cattle together. Hermes eventually returned the animals, but Apollo was still enraged. He was on the verge of punishing Hermes when the young god started to play the lyre. Apollo was so entranced by its effect that he swapped the cattle for it. In all likelihood, in Sophocles' *Trackers,* the satyrs would not have received the reward they were hoping for.

The Tragic Afterlife

The influence of Greek tragedy has been felt across an extraordinary range of media from the fifth century BCE right up to the present day. Aeschylus' *Agamemnon* spawned the Classical scholar and poet A.E. Housman's magnificent parody 'Fragment of a Greek Tragedy' (1883),[75] which pokes fun at both the playwright's style and the way it has sometimes been translated. Sophocles' Oedipus has become one of the great celebrities of Greek mythology, although Freud must be credited with increasing his profile in the last hundred years or so. The Roman playwright Seneca produced a version in *c*.50 CE, which was adapted by John Dryden and Nathaniel Lee, who co-authored *Oedipus* (1678), for which Henry Purcell later wrote *Incidental Music from Oedipus* (1692). Sophocles' drama has also proved to be a rich source of inspiration to operatic and musical works, ranging from Stravinsky's highly regarded *Oedipus Rex* (1927), to George Enescu's operatic masterpiece *Oedip*, Op.23 (1936), Tom Lehrer's comic song 'Oedipus Rex' (1953), and 'The End' by Jim Morrison (released on the 1967 album 'The Doors'). In Ted Hughes' *Song for a Phallus* (1972), which is part of his 'vast folk epic' *Crow: From the Life and Songs of the Crow*, Crow cannot seem to escape suffering and death, just like Oedipus cannot escape his fate; Steven Berkoff's *Greek* (1980) transforms Oedipus into Eddy, a young English lad living in London; Mark-Anthony Turnage's opera *Greek* (1988) has a similar aesthetic, adapting the Oedipus story to show a skinhead progressing from racism and poverty to self-knowledge. Far less harrowing are *Oedipus Wrecks,* segment three of the film *New York Stories* (1989) directed by Woody Allen, and Salley Vickers' 2007 novel *Where Three Roads Meet*, in which the myth is retold via a series on engaging conversations between Teiresias and Freud.

Medea has also enjoyed a vibrant life outside Euripides, with Seneca again dramatizing the story. The image of Medea contemplating the murder of her children became popular in wall-paintings in Pompeii, well before Delacroix revisited the subject in *The Fury of Medea* (1862). In 1913, somewhat ironically, given Euripides' ancient reputation as a misogynist, excerpts from *Medea* were recited at suffragette meetings, because they seemed so relevant. Tony Harrison's libretto for *Medea: A Sex-War Opera,* commissioned by the New York Metropolitan Opera (1985), also used quotations from Euripides to explore a number of the gender issues. The controversial Dutch director Theo van Gogh's stylish and sexy TV mini-series *Medea* (released in 2005) made Mr Jason into a modern property-developer-turned-politician, and his partner Medea the daughter of the chairman of the Dutch Senate. Mr Jason is lured into a politically expedient marriage with the 'beautiful, horny and dangerous' Anne (= Glauke) as part of a deal with her father to enable Mr Jason to become prime minister. Medea kills Anne with a poisoned necklace, and then her and Mr Jason's own 'love babies' with poisoned baby milk. She then drinks the milk herself, giving a disappointingly weak dénouement: Anne's father survives unscathed, and Medea never gets to witness the impact of the boys' death on Mr Jason.

Satyr-play has its place in the tradition, too. Tony Harrison's remarkable play *The Trackers of Oxyrhynchus* had its world premier at the ancient stadium at Delphi in 1988. With its chorus of Yorkshire-style clog-dancing satyrs, ear-shattering rock music, a six-a-side football match played with papyrus, and Apollo speaking tiny fragments of Greek, it is a stunning example of how incongruity, subversion, irony and deliberate anachronism can turn ancient Greek drama into a dazzling, if weird, contemporary work.

10

GREEK ART AND ARCHITECTURE

When old age shall this generation waste,
Thou shalt remain, in midst of other woe.

John Keats, *Ode on a Grecian Urn*

Table 10.1 Archaic, Classical and Hellenistic Styles of Art

Styles and Chronology

*c.*650–480 BCE	ARCHAIC	
*c.*480–323 BCE	CLASSICAL	Early Classical (*c.*480–450 BCE)
		High Classical (*c.*450–425 BCE)
		Late Classical (*c.*425–323 BCE)
*c.*323–31 BCE	HELLENISTIC	

Neither the Greeks nor the Romans had an exactly comparable word for 'art' as we now use the term. The nearest Greek equivalent is *tekhne* – from which we get 'technology', etc. – which had a much wider frame of reference. It can be translated as 'craft', 'trade', 'art', 'skill', designate a system, a set of rules, or a treatise, and be applied to metalworking, ceramic production, painting, sculpture, the laying out of a city or an olive plantation, shipbuilding and soothsaying. The Latin word *ars*, from which the English 'art' is derived, had just as broad a range of meaning. That said, though this issue reinforces the gulf between modern and ancient attitudes. The constant discovery of new artefacts keeps the scholarship vibrant, while the legal and moral issues surrounding the collecting of antiquities are particularly topical, especially (and deliberately) with the opening of the New Acropolis Museum in Athens in 2009.

Vase Painting

The first problem that confronts us is that there is no ancient account of how Greek vases were made. All potters knew how to do it, so there was no need to write it down. However, by drawing inferences from the pots themselves,[1] it looks like the clay would first be 'wedged' to expel any air bubbles, and then the pot would be thrown on a wheel spun by hand. The vessel would then be put aside to dry in the air, and when it was 'leather hard' the surface would be trimmed on the wheel with a sharp tool. Handles were then added using a solution of clay as 'glue'.

The painter (who may or may not be the same as the potter) next applied *miltos*, a ferruginous red ochre, as a wash over the vase, before making a rough sketch, often using a stick of charcoal. The pots were decorated in 'red' (actually an orangey brown) and black. The red is simply the raw untreated surface of the pot; the black (known as the 'gloss') is not paint or a glaze, but is actually the same clay as the body of the pot, refined and thinned with alkaline water to give it a higher proportion of iron oxide, and applied as a 'slip'. Essentially the artist applied red on red, often using a more dilute solution that fired to a warmish brown for less important lines, and a much thicker solution for major lines, which sometimes stand proud of the surface. The tools were mainly brushes, although slight texturing could be applied with a quill or syringe, and in Black-Figure vases details such as hair, folds in drapery or patterns on dresses were depicted using incised lines. Details might be picked out in purple, which had a base of red oxide of iron, or in white, which was largely pipeclay.

Firing was done in a simple, roundish wood- or charcoal-fired kiln, about 1.5 m across. It had a lower fire chamber with a short stoking tunnel, separated by a perforated floor from a larger upper chamber in which the decorated pots were placed. The roof of this chamber was domed, with a closeable vent at the top.

Here, a little bit of chemical magic took place. The pot and the slip were both rich in iron oxide, Fe_2O_3, which in its natural form is the red, but if you heat it in a reducing atmosphere – an enclosed atmosphere hungry for oxygen – some of the oxygen is lost by the Fe_2O_3, and converted into FeO or Fe_3O_4, both of which are black. The trick is to get iron oxide reduced (black) in the slip but oxidized (red) in the rest of the pot. So you light the fuel in the stoking tunnel with a draught (oxidizing) and bring the temperature up to about 800 °C. Then you add fresh green wood, which will absorb oxygen, and close the stoking tunnel and the vent to shut off the oxygen supply. You now have a reducing atmosphere. As the temperature rises further, two things will happen: both the clay of the pot and the slip will go black; and above 825 °C the quartz in the clay will enclose particles of iron oxide, which insulates them against reduction or oxidation. This process, called 'sintering', works on the refined slip, but not on the coarser clay of the pot. Now you can open the stoking tunnel and the vent to create an oxidizing atmosphere again and let the kiln cool. The pot will absorb oxygen and return to red, but the slip, enclosed in the sintered quartz, will stay black.

Greek pots tend to have specific practical purposes, and there is now an internationally accepted vocabulary (see Table 10.2, below). Black-Figure vases are decorated with a black gloss on a red background. The technique really originated in Corinth, but by the end of the seventh century BCE, Attic (Athenian) artists had adopted the technique, and by the sixth century BCE had become the leading Black-Figure exponents.

Table 10.2 Pots and Containers

Type	Use
amphora (2 handles)	Olive oil or wine storage
pelike (2 handles)	Olive oil or wine storage
hydria (3 handles – a horizontal pair at the sides for lifting and a vertical one at the back for pouring)	Water storage
krater – volute, bell, column or calyx	Mixing bowl for wine and water (the Greeks drank their wine diluted with water – 2 parts wine to 3 parts water)
dinos	As for *krater*
oinochoe (wine jug with a handle at the back)	Serving wine
skyphos	Drinking cup
kylix (now more fashionably called a 'cup')	Stemmed drinking cup
kantharos	High-handled drinking cup
lekythos (a single handle at the back)	Olive oil for personal hygiene; its narrow neck prevented the oil flowing too freely

aryballos	Small flask in which athletes carried oil for their rub-down
alabastos/alabastros/alabastron	Perfume bottle
pyxis	Trinket or cosmetics box
phiale	Pouring libations
loutrophoros	Carrying water for a bride's ritual bath
white-ground *lekythos*	A *lekythos* covered with a white slip, used as a container for oil and presented as a gift to the dead

Greek art has been described as 'art without artists', but the first Attic painter to sign his work was Sophilos, whose signature *SOPHILOS M'EGRAPHSEN*, 'Sophilos painted me', appears on a *dinos* made around 575 BCE.[2] The vase is divided into several zones or friezes, the lower of which contain mainly monsters and animals, but Sophilos' primary interest was the continuous, meticulously labelled, mythological composition that goes all the way round the top of the bowl. This shows the wedding of Peleus and Thetis, to which nearly all the gods, with the key exception of Strife, were invited. Peleus is welcoming the approaching deities with a *kantharos* of wine; Iris comes first followed by several other deities including Dionysos (the perfect party guest), Hebe, wearing a gorgeous dress, and the good centaur Kheiron. The figures are very two-dimensional, with legs drawn in profile, torsos either in profile or fully frontal, and heads usually in profile but with frontal eyes. The spacing of the figures is interestingly varied (sometimes overlapping, sometimes isolated), and all are identified by name. Sophilos also makes effective use of colour, adding touches of purplish-red to the drapery, and picking out the women's flesh in white, which becomes the conventional way of defining female figures.

Kleitias, working at Athens just after Sophilos, produced a masterpiece called the 'François vase',[3] a volute *krater*, painted around 570 BCE. It is divided into seven friezes, five of which depict various myths: the Calydonian boar-hunt; the funeral games of Patroclus; the wedding of Peleus and Thetis again; the story of the death of Priam's son Troilos at the hands of Achilles at a fountain-house outside Troy; animals and monsters. On the foot of the vase the pygmies fight the cranes; and on the outside of the handles Aias is carrying the body of Achilles from the battlefield. There are around 200 figures on the vase, with inscriptions labelling people and things, and Kleitias draws them with brilliant narrative skill. The Troilos frieze depicts a young Trojan man and a girl filling their *hydriai*, and Achilles' mother Thetis, Hermes and Athena are all present, but the calm normality is violated by the ambush. Troilos is driving his horses in a vain dash for safety, with his hair blown back by his speed. He strains away from Achilles, but the right leg of his otherwise fragmentary 'swift-footed' assailant indicates the inevitable outcome. Troilos' sister Polyxena runs in front of her brother, while a discarded *hydria* rolls beneath the horses. Priam hears the terrible news from Antenor, while two of Troilos' brothers are belatedly coming out from the gates of Troy.

The excellent draughtsmanship of Athenian Black-Figure artists is beautifully exemplified by the work of the Amasis Painter. On a joyously exquisite 'neck *amphora*'[4] from the mid-sixth century BCE, he used just three bold figures. Dionysos, holding the obligatory *kantharos*, is greeting two maenads, whose flesh is not painted white but is outlined and left the natural colour of the clay. They skip towards him with their arms around one another, each holding a wild animal and an ivy branch. The artist adeptly exploits repeated geometric patterns and motifs: the maenads' profiles echo each other as they dance forward in perfect time, with their front feet raised together and their back feet poised on their toes; the shape and position of their arms are repeated as they encircle one another's shoulders; and carefully incised lines create enchanting patterns in the folds of Dionysos' clothing, the locks of his hair, the decoration of the maenads' dresses, and even the spots on the panther-skin that one of them wears. This is pure Dionysiac ecstasy.

Black-Figure vase painting really reached its apogee with Exekias, working at Athens under the tyranny of Peisistratos. His outstanding representation of Achilles and Aias playing dice, now in the Vatican[5], appears on an *amphora* that has been painted almost totally black, apart from the panel on the body. On this clearly defined field we see, identified by inscriptions, Achilles sitting on the left and Aias (Ajax) on the right. Their hair and their elaborately decorated cloaks are incised with unbelievable finesse. Although fully kitted out for battle, they are completely engrossed in a board game, and as they lean forward their bodies define the composition.

The curve of their backs echoes the outline of the vase; their shields, which are placed behind them, pick up the line of the handles; and their spears form a strong V-shape that makes our gaze follow that of the warriors. Achilles is winning: 'four', he cries, in response to Aias' 'three'. Interestingly, this incident does not occur in Greek literature: great art does not just reflect the mythical tradition – it drives it.

The Black-Figure brilliance of Exekias had raised the bar so high that vase painting now needed to move in a totally new direction, and a painter who we call 'the Andokides Painter' came up with a huge innovation: Red-Figure. The effect this has is obvious from a 'bilingual' *amphora* (i.e. one that combines Black- and Red-Figure) now in Munich (530–510 BCE).[6]

One side of the vase, probably by the Lysippides Painter, is a standard Black-Figure. Herakles or Dionysos is feasting at a small table in the presence of Athena. Hermes stands on the left, while a servant is occupied with a *dinos* on the right. There is also a vine laden with bunches of grapes. The figures are bold; the ornament is delicate; broad stripes of purplish-red enliven the drapery; and white paint originally picked out Athena's flesh and parts of the furniture. This would have made a fine vase in its own right, but the other side is revolutionary. Here the Andokides Painter has drawn practically the same picture (minus Hermes and the boy), but instead of painting the *figures* black, he has painted the *background* black, thereby allowing the figures to stand out in the natural red of the clay. His Red-Figure scene uses less colour (some purplish-red; no white), and is not as interested in the decoration (Red-Figure will eventually abandon this type of thing altogether), but he does try to imply layers of space – the table appears in front of the couch; one of Herakles'/Dionysos' legs is behind the other; his right hand is further back still; and the torso is in three-quarter view. Black-Figure work had been articulated by incision, but the internal detailing of the red figures is painted with a brush, which allows the artists greater precision, and here the softness of the drapery is implied by fluently painted folds, particularly those that fall from the male's arm and those at the bottom of Athena's dress. These challenges of depicting convincing drapery and plausibly foreshortened anatomy now become two of Red-Figure's big preoccupations. And the 'negativizing' of the traditional colour scheme was an instant hit: Black-Figure's days were numbered.

Red-Figure vase painters also started to explore how to convey emotions in a more subtle way, as did Euthymides, who painted an *amphora*, now in Munich, with *Three Men Carousing*.[7] The central figure of the half-drunk trio is adeptly depicted from behind: his feet point to the right, his head to the left, and the transition between them, which had caused great difficulty to both Sophilos and Kleitias, is handled with aplomb. On the two outer figures Euthymides uses strong black lines for the key elements of their musculature, but utilizes a light-brown slip for the less important ones like the 'six-pack' of the right-hand man. Euthymides was so pleased with himself that he wrote on the vase a challenge to his rival Euphronios.

Euphronios was a fine artist. His version of Herakles fighting the Amazons on a volute *krater*, now in the Museo Civico, Arezzo[8], highlights his capabilities. Herakles wades into the female warriors from the left, brandishing his club, and is confronted by three adversaries, two of whom march rhythmically together. Their back-up is provided by another Amazon wearing a skin-tight, stripy oriental outfit and firing an arrow. She is light on her feet, the more advanced of which is nicely foreshortened. In the middle of the combat zone lies a wounded Amazon, the top of whose left thigh conceals the rest of her leg. To the left is another Amazon casualty, mirroring the pose of her sister in the middle, although she wears the same costume as the archer Amazon on the right; Telamon, with his back to his comrade Herakles, is about to deliver the *coup de grace*. The whole composition is bold, vigorous, complex and exciting, making good use of foreshortening and heavily cross-referenced patterns and motifs. The end result is rather chaotic, though: sometimes less is more, and virtuoso draughtsmanship does not necessarily produce satisfying art.

One such minimalist approach occurs on a volute *krater*, now in the British Museum, by the Berlin Painter.[9] Practically all the body of his vase is covered with a black gloss, enhanced by some stunning geometric and floral ornament on the lip. Just four widely spaced, individually labelled figures are shown on the neck. Achilles and Hector, clearly in peak physical condition, are in combat. The youthful Achilles is on the offensive, moving in menacingly, his shield up and his spear poised; the mature, bearded Hector is already wounded, his weapon pointing harmlessly to the ground, and his shield out of position. He is staggering backwards, and his open-armed pose is desperately vulnerable. War is a young man's game. The inevitability of the outcome is underlined by the outer figures: Athena stands supportively behind Achilles, a spear in her right hand, and her left hand raised in a gesture that displays her dread aegis; at the opposite side Apollo turns away from Hector, leaving him to his doom with a wave of an arrow, the angle of which parallels that of Hector's spear. The Berlin Painter seems to capture both the horror and violence, and the beauty and pathos, of one of Greek mythology's greatest life-and-death struggles.

Hector's death hastened the sack of Troy, but the mythical tradition was always open to freshly nuanced interpretations, and the Kleophrades Painter exploited this in his early-fifth century version of the *Ilioupersis* ('Sack of Troy'), on a *hydria* now in Naples.[10] He lived in Athens during Xerxes' invasion, and here he depicts a scene of horrendous carnage: Priam is seeking refuge at an altar, holding his hands to his bleeding head in despair; the mutilated body of his son Polites is splayed across his knees; Achilles' son Neoptolemos grabs the king's right shoulder and prepares to send him down to Hades; Cassandra, a cloak ineffectually protecting her modesty, vainly grabs the Palladion, the *xoanon* (wooden image) on which the salvation of Troy depended; 'Lesser Aias' grabs her by the hair as he brandishes his sword; there are dead Trojans everywhere; women crouch in fear, tearing their hair, although one feisty individual assaults a warrior with some kitchenware; Aeneas is carrying his father Anchises and leading his son Ascanius to safety, but otherwise we are witnessing the bleak brutality and mindless destruction of an all-out war with no consideration for collateral damage.

In a sense, the Kleophrades Painter's generation represented Red-Figure's last hurrah: as the Persians were beaten back, and Athens built up her empire, the finest painters redirected their talents towards wall and/or panel painting. But none of their art survives.

Temples and Architectural Sculpture

If you said to a Greek architect, 'Build me a temple', with no further specification, you would probably end up with a building that had an east-facing central chamber (*naos/cella*), with a columned porch at the front (*pronaos*) and one at the back (*opisthodomos*). This central core would be surrounded by a colonnade (*peristyle*), the usual configuration of which would be six columns at the front and thirteen down the sides. The *naos* would be windowless, completely walled in with large ashlar blocks, and *antae* (rectangular columns engaged in the wall) would terminate its side walls. In between the *antae* would be two columns *in antis*. Access to the *naos* would be through a large door from the *pronaos*, providing the only source of natural light into the interior. The cult statue of the deity would be at the western end of the *naos*, facing the door. The *naos* might have a row of columns down the middle or, more usually, two rows, creating a nave and two side aisles. These columns might be erected in two tiers, and there could be a gallery approached by stairs. The ceiling of the *naos* would generally be wooden, and the peristyle ceiling might have marble coffers.

You would have to choose what 'order' of architecture you wanted: Doric, Ionic or Corinthian. Doric will give you a solid, massive, masculine (to Greek eyes) structure, and it might carry political associations of the physicality of mainland Greece. If you want something more graceful and feminine, with more of the intellectual flavour of the islands and the east, you should choose the Ionic order. From the late fifth century onwards you might also be offered a new type of order, the Corinthian, which first appears in the Temple of Apollo Epikourios at Bassai. Regardless of your decision, the temple will have sturdy foundations, completed by a 'levelling course' to create a flat surface to build on, and the whole edifice will stand on a three-stepped platform (*krepis*), the top step of which is called the *stylobate*.

If you have chosen Doric, the columns will not have bases, and will stand directly on the *stylobate*. They will normally be made up of several drums, have 'fluted' shafts (normally with twenty sharp edges called *arrises*), taper towards the top, and be surmounted by a *capital* consisting of a curved member (*echinus*) with a square block (*abacus*) above it.

On top of the *capital* will be the *entablature*, made up of the architrave, frieze and cornice. The architrave will be plain apart from a small horizontal moulding at the top (*taenia*) and decorated at regular intervals with a panel (*regula*), from which six little knobs called *guttae* will stick out downwards. The frieze will be made up of *triglyphs,* grooved mouldings with three vertical bands, alternating with rectangular *metopes*, which might be plain, painted or sculpted. A horizontal band will run along the top of the frieze, and generally there will be a *triglyph* over each column and over the middle of each *intercolumniation* (space between two columns). On top of the frieze will be the projecting ('jutting out') cornice. This has a moulding surmounted by a plain vertical member (*geison*), and along its lower surface (*soffit*), over each *triglyph* and *metope*, is a rectangular slab (*mutule*) with rows of *guttae*.

The roof will be double-pitched, and covered in terracotta or marble roof tiles, depending on your budget. The ends of the lowest cover tiles will be concealed by decorative floral *antefixes*. Your guttering (*sima*) might well have waterspouts in the form of lions' heads. The *pediment* (triangular space at each end) will be closed off by a wall and protected by a raking (sloping) cornice, and you will have to decide whether to install sculpture on its floor, or leave it plain. Finally your architect will finish off the temple by ornamenting the ridge of the roof with more antefixes, and the three points of the pediment with *akroteria*, either in the form of discs or sculptures.

If you take the Ionic option, your columns will be more slender, and stand on a base with several tiers. There will be a choice of base types, but a fairly typical one will have a *spira,* formed of three sets of double roundels, divided by two deep concave mouldings called the *scotiae* or *trochili*; the lowest pair of roundels will project most, the central pair least. Above this you get the *torus*, fluted horizontally on the under-surface of the curve. The foot of the column shaft will curve outwards like a pair of flared trousers, and will do this in three parts: the *roundel*, a convex moulding at the bottom; a vertical *fillet* above this; and the *apophyge*, which curves steeply upwards to the flutes of the shaft. The flutings of the shaft (usually 2twenty-four of them) will be separated by a narrow flat band. At the top of the shaft there will be another *apophyge,* flaring outwards again, crowned with another perpendicular *fillet*, and then a convex roundel that will probably be carved with the *bead-and-reel*. The joint between shaft and *capital* will be just above this *roundel*.

The Ionic *capital* begins with a flat-topped moulding with a profile like that of the Doric *echinus* (that is what it is called), which will normally be carved with *egg-and-dart*. On top of this will be the *volutes*, which look like a thin cushion (*pulvinus*) placed over the *echinus*, with its loose ends wound up in dropping spirals on each side of the shaft, and the cushion between the volutes sagging over the *echinus*. On the front and back faces there will be a wide shallow concave channel (*canalis*) between the *echinus* and the *abacus*: this channel curls round into the spirals of the *volutes*, which usually have 'eyes' (*oculi*) in their centres. Your architect will decide whether your columns will look wide-eyed like earlier temples often do, or cross-eyed like many Hellenistic ones.

The architrave will be articulated into three horizontal bands or *fasciae*, each sticking out a little beyond the one below it. Above the top *fascia* there will be, in turn, an *astragal* and *egg-and-dart* moulding. Then your architect will specify *dentils*, a row of small projecting rectangular members, or a continuous Ionic frieze, usually sculptured, or a combination of the two. Then comes the cornice, a plain band crowned by a small convex moulding and a flat *fillet*; from the front it looks similar to a Doric one. The roof, and its ornamentation, will resemble that of a Doric building in most of its key aspects, although the *pediments* will not normally carry any sculpture.

Corinthian is very like the Ionic in all its essential elements, except that it has a square *capital* usually enriched with a single or double row of acanthus leaf scrolls, out of which rise four thin, almost leaf-like *volutes*. Its entablature is like that of the Ionic order.

Stone will be the material of choice: worked limestone (*poros*) coated with stucco to obtain nice smooth surfaces, or marble if it is obtainable and/or affordable. No mortar will be used; instead, the stones will be held together by metal dowels (to fasten them vertically), C- or H-shaped metal cramps (to fasten them horizontally), and by their own weight.

Finally, parts of your temple will be painted in order to accentuate the various architectural elements: the backgrounds of the sculpted *metopes*, frieze and *pediments* – red (or blue); the *mutules*, *triglyphs* and *regulae* – blue; the *soffit* of the cornice, the top border of the *metopes* and the *taenia* – red; and it is likely that the flesh of any figured sculpture was polished and may even have been tinted, and the hair, eyes and clothing coloured appropriately. This sculpture might adorn the Doric *metopes*, an Ionic frieze or the *pediments*.

Sculptors swiftly became adept at handling *metopes*, where the restricted space meant they had to 'cut a long story short'. The solution was to use strong verticals and horizontal lines enlivened with diagonal accents, and integrate them into a composition that was highly symmetrical. A fine archaic example comes from Temple C at Selinus (mid-sixth century BCE) where a *metope* depicts Herakles striding to the right (legs in profile, torso fully frontal) with the rogueish Kerkopes brothers dangling upside-down from a pole over his shoulders. This, allied with their characteristic 'Archaic smiles', is typical of the period. Another tactic might be to use repetition and rhythm. This is used effectively in a mid-sixth century *metope* from the Treasury of the Sikyonians at Delphi, depicting a heroic cattle-raid. Here we see three parallel, vertical heroes taking up the full height of the *metope*. With their spears at the same angle, they walk in time, both with one another and with the rhythmically positioned cattle, whose beautifully aligned legs recede into the distance.

Ionic friezes offered sculptors more scope for narrative illustration, as long as suitable subject matter could be found. The Siphnian Treasury at Delphi, *c.*525 BCE, uses eye-catching patterns and repeated rhythmic motifs in rendering the *gigantomachy* (Battle of the Gods and Giants). An exciting battle scene shows one of Cybele's lions biting a chunk out of a giant; the matched figures of Apollo and Artemis fire their arrows at three opposing giants, who mirror them in serried ranks with overlapping shields; a giant flees in between them, legs to the right, head looking left and body swivelling in an anatomically impossible pose – much of archaic Greek art looks like 'work in progress', although it has brilliant energy.

More challenging was the awkward triangular space of the pediment. We can see the problems they confronted, and solved, on the Doric temple of Aphaia on Aigine, built between 500 and 490 BCE, right on the transition point between the Archaic and Classical periods. The Aiginetan sculptors opted for a single battle-scene, overlooked by a central deity at the apex, and with the triangle filled with standing, striding, kneeling, falling and reclining figures.

The Archaic west pediment shows the Trojan War, in which Aigine's mighty hero Great Aias fought. Athena takes centre-stage in her snake-fringed *aigis* with Medusa's head in its centre, wielding her usual weapons. Matched pairs of warriors fight on either side of her. The aim of two Trojan archers draws the eye towards the corners, where there are crumpled, dying fighters. The wounded warrior on the far right, still sporting an 'archaic smile', leans on his left arm, lifts up his right, and tries to pull a missile out of his chest. His head, shoulders and hips are all rendered frontally, and his profile right leg is folded over his frontal left in a pose that repeats that of his right arm: again symmetry and repetition are deployed to create a beautiful, albeit rather stiff, composition, and are further carried through into the hair and even the negative space between the arm, body, legs and ground.

The temple was damaged soon after it was erected, and a new east *pediment*, showing Herakles sacking Laomedon's Troy, an episode that featured Great Aias' father Telamon, was installed. By that time Greece was just entering the Classical era, and a suppler, more naturalistic Athena occupies the apex. This time inward movement from the periphery focuses the viewer's attention on the centre, and produces a much tighter composition. Herakles, who is crouching near the right-hand corner, fires an arrow inwards, with all the tension between his powerful muscles and the bowstring superbly rendered. In the opposite corner lies a dying warrior, struggling to raise his sword with his right hand, but unable to keep hold of his shield with his left. The 'archaic' smile is replaced by the almost expressionlessness of Classical faces, and he is completely absorbed in his last moments. Revolutionary compositional approaches are also at work, as the figure gradually, and convincingly, rotates from the profile right leg and the frontal left leg and hips, to the torso in three-quarter view, to the head in profile. A straight comparison with his counterpart on the earlier pediment shows how far sculpture had moved in the ten or so years that divide them.

The Persian invasions of Greece curtailed major temple-building activity for a while, but when the rulers of Elis in the north-west Peloponnese conquered their neighbours at Pisa, they used the war-booty to construct the temple of Zeus at Olympia, completing enough of it for the Spartans to display a gold shield on the *pediment* in celebration of their victory at the Battle of Tanagra in 457 BCE. Although big, the temple was austere, bog-standard Doric;

however, its sculptures were extraordinary, and one of them became one of the Seven Wonders of the Ancient World.

On the east *pediment*, Pelops' chariot race to win the hand of Hippodameia from her father Oinomaos is just going to start. These magnificent sculptures are somewhat over life-size, splendidly integrated into the *pediment's* triangular frame, and, within the parameters of Classical blank-faced calm, full of nuances of character and personality. Zeus looms authoritatively over a central group that crackles with tension: Oinomaos cockily stands hand-on-hip; his spouse Sterope has her arms folded over her Doric *peplos* (a simple body-length garment); Pelops is pensive; and Hippodameia is tugging at the shoulder of her *peplos* with her left hand in a bridal gesture. This group is flanked by chariot horses that fit naturally beneath the rake of the pediment, and sundry sitting or kneeling attendants, including a bored boy playing with his toes, and a seer – balding, wrinkled, saggily out of condition – who knows the impending unpleasantness and fiddles with his beard. In the corners, the river gods Kladeos and Alpheios locate the scene of Olympia.

The design's use of the descending heights of the god, men, women, horses, crouching extras and rivers-gods works perfectly; the naturalistic drapery conceals the anatomy but allows us to see the underlying pose; the musculature is confident yet simple; faces are clearly defined, with elegant, sweeping lines; Pelops' *contrapposto* pose, dropping his hip to shift his weight on to one leg and so giving a gentle s-shaped swing to the line of his body, in which the hips and shoulders slant in opposite directions, is a significant departure from archaic rigidity, as is the way in which he encroaches on the space that surrounds him: he no longer looks like a figure carved from a rectangular block of stone.

The west *pediment* shows the fight between the Lapiths and Centaurs (*centauromachy*) that broke out at the wedding of Peirithoos. As the forces of barbarity and chaos challenge those of order and civilization, Apollo presides as a serene representative of the latter, extending his right arm in an authoritative gesture, with not a hair of his elaborately coiffed, exquisitely proportioned head out of place. We know who will win. Around him is a tumultuous tangle of men, women and monsters: hair is grabbed, although the clothing is barely ruffled; the bride shoves her elbow into the face of a centaur as she tries to detach his hand from her left breast, yet while her body-language vividly expresses the desperation of her struggle, and despite being groped by a terrifying mythical beast, her face remains expressionless. This is pure artistic convention. Classical artists could render emotion very effectively: the centaurs have scowling, wrinkly faces, but the representatives of civilized Greece behave with perfect serenity, thereby accentuating the cultural divide between the adversaries.

The external *metopes* were plain, but over the entrances to the *pronaos* and *opisthodomos* were twelve sculpted *metopes* depicting the 'Twelve Labours of Herakles'. These were produced by a highly competent school of sculptors (you can just see minor differences in the rendering of hair, eyes and faces), probably working under an inspirational (though unknown) master. Rather than giving us the triumph of an invincible super-hero, he portrays a man confronting unfavourable odds and paying a high price for his victories. The beardless youth who slew the lion becomes the man with a lifetime's experience etched on his bearded face as he holds up the sky; remarkably, his immortal protectress Athena appears to age in empathy with him.

Both the compositions and the narratives of the *metopes* are crystal clear, rejecting obvious symmetry and repetition in favour of powerful geometrical designs: strong parallel horizontals and verticals give a calmness to scenes where the Labour has been successfully completed; where a Labour is in progress, the compositions tend to feature more dynamic X or + shapes, pyramids or combinations of verticals and obliques. These twelve *metopes* may well have become so famous that they came to represent *the* 'Twelve Labours of Herakles' from now on.

The temple's *pièce de résistance* was added when the great sculptor Pheidias was commissioned to produce a 13 m high chryselephantine (i.e. gold and ivory) statue of Zeus, sometime after 432 BCE. Pausanias says that Zeus sat on a throne of gold, gems, ebony and ivory, which itself stood on a platform adorned with golden figures; his flesh was ivory; his drapery was gold; and he held a life-size statue of Nike (Victory) in his right hand, and a staff surmounted by his eagle in his left. This work was admired as *the* great masterpiece of classical sculpture. The orator/metorician Quintilian says that it 'added something to human religion'; the

Roman Emperor Caligula sent workmen to transport it to Rome, although the statue supposedly emitted a cackle of laughter that made the workmen flee; but it was eventually taken to adorn a palace in Constantinople, where, in 462 CE, it was destroyed in a fire.

Pheidias' involvement at Olympia came after he had made his name at Athens as the creative impetus behind Perikles' building programme. The centrepiece of this was the Parthenon, a temple to Athena Parthenos on the Acropolis, constructed between 447/6 and 433/2 BCE. Two architects are associated with its construction: Kallikrates, who was fired by Perikles for what were probably political reasons, and Iktinos, who brought the project to fruition. It was staggeringly expensive: whereas the Aigine and Olympia temples had used marble to enhance their roofing and decoration, the Parthenon was made entirely of marble. Over 22,000 tonnes of it, quarried on Mount Pentelikon 16 km away or (for the roof) imported from Paros. Perikles was rumoured to have used the works of art on the Parthenon to seduce women; Pheidias was accused (and acquitted) of corruption.[11]

The visitor to the Acropolis undergoes a carefully manipulated process of preparation, tension and release. As you approach from below, the Parthenon drops out of your field of vision. You are enveloped by the projecting wings of the Propylaia (the ornamental gateway to the Acropolis), pass the small Temple of Athena Nike, move through the doorway, and finally re-emerge into the daylight to be presented with the Parthenon in all its glory, standing above you, slightly to your right, and displayed in three-quarter view, so that you can see all its interrelated proportions to their best advantage.

You are looking at the back of a temple with a peristyle (30.5 m × 70 m) of 8 × 17 large Doric columns. The entablature is standard, except that every single one of the ninety-two *metopes* is sculpted, and each side tells a different story: the Amazonomachy (Greeks v Amazons), Greeks fighting Trojans, a Gigantomachy and a Centauromachy (the best-preserved *metopes*). The battle scenes are significant: Athena was a war goddess, but selecting eastern foreigners or monsters as opponents stresses that the struggle is not good versus evil, but Greek civilization and order versus chaos and barbarity. And we all know who won in the end. Your eye is also drawn up to the pediments and their sculpture, and with Pausanias' guidebook in your hand, you can discover that:

> all the figures in the gable over the entrance to the temple . . . relate to the birth of Athena. The back gable contains the strife of Poseidon with Athena for the possession of the land.[12]

If you move round to the east end of the building, ascend the front steps, and look up once you are inside the peristyle, you will see a long, sculpted Ionic frieze some 10.5 m above you and running right around the entire *naos*. You access the *pronaos* via two steps and through a porch of six Doric columns, pass through an enormous doorway (4.25 m × 9.75 m) into the *naos* (19.2 m × 29.9 m), the centre of which was enclosed by a three-sided, two-tiered Doric colonnade, at whose far end, beyond a shallow pool, was the 14.6 m high chryselephantine cult statue of Athena Parthenos:

> The image of Athena stands upright, clad in a garment that reaches to her feet: on her breast is the head of Medusa wrought in ivory. She holds a Victory about four cubits [2 m] high, and in the other hand a spear.[13]

This statue had cost as much as the temple building itself. Finally, if you were to wander round the back, you would find a separate room reached from the *opisthodomos*, the ceiling of which was supported by four Ionic columns, but you would probably be refused entry: this housed the tribute from Athens' allies.

What initially looks like straight geometrical lines is in fact a complex of subtle curves, modulations, and 'refinements'. These are what turn the building into the masterpiece that it is. The *stylobate* rises in a gentle curve from its four corners, as does the entablature. This might be for one of several reasons: a long, flat surface appears concave when you stand on it and look along it, so if it is made slightly convex, it will appear perfectly flat ('compensation theory'); by the same illusion, however, the entablature will look *more* curved when you look up at it ('exaggeration theory'); or the fact that your brain interprets as flat what your eyes see as curved creates tension between them, which makes the building subliminally more interesting to look at ('tension theory'). In addition to this, the corner columns are placed closer together, possibly to correct an optical illusion that would make them otherwise seem further apart; the columns themselves have *entasis*, a slight swelling of the shaft; and they all tilt imperceptibly inwards.

Whatever the purpose of these refinements (which are not unique to the Parthenon, but are not present to the same degree elsewhere), the end result is a building that is vibrantly alive. Additionally, the Parthenon is rhythmically interesting. Greek temples are constructed on modular systems based on the lower diameter of the column. Here, the ratio of the lower diameter of the column to the distance between the centre of one column and the next is 4 : 9 (easy enough to set up using 3 : 4 : 5 Pythagorean triangles); the ratio of the front of the temple to its sides is 4 : 9; the ratio of the height of the order to the width of the temple is 4 : 9.

All this would be enough to establish the Parthenon as one of the world's great buildings. But the sculptural programme takes it to another level entirely. The *metopes* were the first pieces to be completed, and we can see that the team of artists hadn't been together quite long enough to have developed a 'house style'. However, the compositions betray the innovative influence of a master designer – Pheidias. Strong diagonals permeate the scenes; heads are boldly placed at the extreme edges of the frame; the panels are rendered in such high relief that figures are carved almost fully in the round. South 27, a fabulous piece of technical mastery, depicts a Lapith who is only attached by his right shoulder and buttock, his left calf, and his (missing) right foot; South 4 uses circular shapes to contrast with the square frame, and generates great excitement from the powerful downward diagonal movement that the centaur's pot is about to make before it smashes into the Lapith who is collapsing into the corner.

The frieze, 1 m high and 160 m long, depicts a procession, whose interpretation is still a problem: it relates to the Panathenaia procession, celebrated in honour of Athena's birthday. It stresses the aristocratic elements (heavy on horsemen, light on hoplites); the Olympian gods are present, but few mortal women, who were prominent in the actual procession; and there is an interesting coincidence in that the number of male figures is 192, the total of Athenian dead at the Battle of Marathon.

The composition starts on the west side with horsemen getting ready while others attend to dress and tack. These slabs are self-contained, with no overlap, whereas the rest of the composition runs from one block into the next. The procession then proceeds in two parallel branches running down the south and north sides. An exciting cavalcade thunders along, with the horses and riders brilliantly portrayed in very low relief. The depth of the carving is only around 5 cm, and yet there is often the illusion of three or even four horses side by side. The overlapping figures create the illusion of a seething crowd, and the strong diagonals of the galloping horses generate real energy. They seem to be organized in overlapping ranks, probably ten on each side, often distinguished by their hats, helmets, cloaks, tunics, armour, footwear and so on. In front of the horsemen are chariots whose occupants sometimes perform stunning feats of prowess. Among all this appear some solitary marshals. In front of the chariot action the pace becomes more stately: old men, musicians, water-jar carriers and tray-bearers are preceded by men with sheep and cows for sacrifice on the north, and just cows on the south. The two streams turn inwards fairly symmetrically as they reach the east side. Here we see girls and women, many of them carrying the jugs and *phialai* necessary for libations, then male figures who are sometimes interpreted as the 'Eponymous Heroes' of the Attic tribes, and then the twelve Olympian gods, seated facing outward to greet the procession. Finally, over the main entrance to the temple is a group comprising two girls holding cushioned stools on their heads, a woman, probably the priestess of Athena, and a man, most likely the *arkhon basileus*, handling a folded *peplos* and helped by a young person. The *peplos* is the robe presented to Athena every year at the Panathenaia festival.

If the iconography and interpretation of the frieze pose is challenging, the appreciation of its aesthetics is not. It is carved in a much more uniform style than the *metopes*, it exudes a strong Classical atmosphere, dictated by the faces, which, though differentiated, share a timeless solemnity despite the intensity of the action.

The crowning glory of the Parthenon's exterior was the two pediments. On the west was the contest between Poseidon and Athena for possession of Attika. Drawings made by Jacques Carrey in 1674 CE, just before the Parthenon was badly damaged by an explosion in 1687 CE, show that the two deities dominated the composition in an X-shape, while chariot-horses reared up on either side. Their motion and conflict impacted on all the attendant deities, kings, heroes and local river gods. The surviving figure of Iris (goddess of the rainbow) has flimsy, flying drapery that clings to and emphasizes her youthful form in the 'rich' or 'wind-blown' style that became dominant in the later Classical period. Cold, hard stone has become warm living flesh.

The more fragmentary east pediment showed the birth of Athena from the head of Zeus, assisted by Hephaistos' axe-wielding 'midwifery'. The surviving figures themselves are naturalistic, with solid, weighty musculature. A nude Dionysos lolls on a rock; Demeter and Persephone (probably) turn in response to the action; a running girl (Hebe?) dashes away from the miracle in a flourish of flying drapery. On the other side, Aphrodite (probably) reclines languorously in clothing that simultaneously conceals and reveals her sex-goddess figure. At the very edges, the chariot horses of Helios (the Sun) rise from the pediment floor on the left, and that of Selene (the Moon) sinks in marvellous equine exhaustion on the right.

If the Parthenon was there to generate shock and awe, the building that had the strongest connection with some of the oldest, weirdest and most fundamental Athenian cult practices on the Acropolis was the Erekhtheion, started in 421 and completed, after a gap between 415–3 and c.409, in 405 BCE. It is built across two levels, on the higher of which is a porch of six Ionic columns at the (east) front, with a doorway between a pair of windows in the wall behind the columns, giving access to the main *naos* of Athena Polias. A small false porch with an Ionic frieze supported by six 'karyatids' (supporting columns in the shape of female figures) projects from the west end of the south side, while at the lower level, reached by steps to the right of the east porch, is the north porch. Its configuration is four Ionic-columns-wide by two deep, and it overlaps the west end of the main block by one column. It covered the mark made by Poseidon's trident in the contest with Athena, which was lit from above by a special opening in the roof. A doorway at the end of the porch's back wall led into an open-air precinct that housed Athena's olive tree, the tomb of Athens' first king, Kekrops, and the shrine of Kekrops' daughter Pandrosos.

The west facade starts with a plain wall at the lower level, above which were four partly engaged columns between pilasters, the bases of which were above ground level. The spaces between these columns were probably filled with bronze lattices (except for the southernmost one, maybe). The precise interior layout is very uncertain, although Pausanias tells us that there were altars to Poseidon, Erekhtheus and Butes, and Hephaistos, as well as the 'holy of holies', a wooden image of Athena Polias that legend said had fallen from heaven.

The architectural ornament on the building was gorgeous and expensive: the Ionic columns generate a feeling of spacious elegance; they are beautifully worked, with finely carved bases and elaborate capitals ornamented with deep bands of lotus and palmette. This motif is carried right round the top of the wall, and there is also a row of carved ornament between architrave and frieze, while another crowns the cornice; each porch had an elaborately coffered ceiling; and the frame of the north door was decorated with relief rosettes fitted with bronze flowers.

There were two friezes, one on the entablature of the north porch, and one surrounding the central block. Both of these had a background of dark Eleusinian marble on to which figures of white Parian marble were attached. The Karyatid porch had dentils rather than a frieze, and the Karyatids themselves are handsome women with emphatic hips and legs that suit their architectural function, as do the flute-like folds of their clinging drapery, which enhance their columnar quality, although the fact that they rest their weight on their outer legs adds an attractive swing to their bodies.

Free-Standing Sculpture

It is clear that the marble sculpting techniques in the fifth century were impressive, whether applied to static architectural features, the movement of figures, the transparency of drapery, the modelling of human forms, or some combination of these, but by the beginning of the fourth century BCE many Greek artists were seeking to push things further. Kephisodotos' serene figure of Eirene (Peace), sculpted around 375 BCE, wears simple, heavy, opaque drapery that falls in straight, natural folds. But the simplicity of the figure belies its innovative qualities: she is part an allegorical group. Eirene is holding a baby, Ploutos (Wealth), and the interaction of the figures represents an abstract concept: 'peace gives birth to wealth'. Furthermore, the manifest tenderness between mother and child falls in with two further trends: the exploration of a greater range of emotions; and the 'humanizing' of the gods.

Another magnificent ensemble of an adult with an infant was Praxiteles' Hermes holding the baby Dionysos, dating from the third quarter of the fourth century BCE. There are now doubts about the authenticity of the work that graces the Olympia Museum – when the Romans pillaged a famous work of art, they sometimes commissioned a replacement copy – but the original, whether this is it or not, was utterly revolutionary, not just because Praxiteles' rendering of the indolently relaxed deity showed how even hard marble can be made to convey the softness of flesh, or because of its proportions, which make Hermes appear taller and more slender than his fifth-century BCE counterparts, but because he is *off-balance*: his weight is on his right leg and his right arm is raised to tease Dionysos with a bunch of grapes, resulting in supple, swinging curves and counter-curves.

Roman copies are incredibly valuable to the study of Greek art, and those of Praxiteles' notorious marble *Aphrodite of Knidos* (which definitely no longer survives), give further insights into his radicalism, partly because this work gained celebrity as being the first large-scale Greek representation of a female nude (Aphrodite is about to take a bath). Here Praxiteles applied *contrapposto* to the female form, making the goddess look to her left, as if she has been disturbed; she rests her weight on her right leg, raising the hip on that side; her right shoulder is lowered as she attempts to protect her modesty; the right-hand side of her torso is contracted, while the left is extended; the slant of her shoulders (downward to our left) contrasts with that of her hips (downward to our right); her weight-bearing right foot is slightly in advance of her left; and her knees are held together, making her thighs and hips expand from quite a narrow base. Poets sang the alluring statue's praises. Suggesting that the likeness was so perfect, Aphrodite asked: 'Where did Praxiteles see me naked?' Bathing, despite its ritual connotations, also makes this awesome goddess seem rather human, and 'humanizing' divinities, while still maintaining allusions to their superhuman status, was very typical of Praxiteles.

Fourth-century BCE artists also developed a much greater interest in exploring human emotions and character, and Skopas, from the island of Paros, was the acknowledged master of passion. Although the original is lost, his famous *Raging Maenad* exists in a Roman copy that allows us to experience the drama that he could generate. Her frenzy is vividly expressed by her body-language (violently turning head; arched back; twisted torso), but in other works Skopas explored the possibilities of dramatic facial expression, sculpting squarish faces with deep-set, yearning eyes and parted lips that contrast sharply with Praxiteles' more tranquil pieces: when the Megarians modernized their temple of Aphrodite, they hired both men – Praxiteles to create *Persuasion* and *Consolation*; Skopas to do *Love*, *Desire* and *Yearning*.

The mid-fourth century BCE produced some other stunning works, including the *Apollo Belvedere*, which, after the discovery of a marble copy of Leokhares' bronze original that has resided in the Vatican since 1503 CE, became one of Greek sculpture's 'greatest hits'. The Roman copy still captures the lightness, grace and elegance of Apollo's svelte physique, depicting him in mid-stride, turning to one side in the direction of his extended hand. He invites comparison with the Apollo from the west pediment at Olympia, but, whereas that figure is composed using emphatic verticals and horizontals, the *Apollo Belvedere* is supple, deliberately arranged to eschew geometrical precision.

The more recently discovered *Bronze Youth* from Antikythera, now in the National Archaeological Museum in Athens, offers a contrasting physical ideal: athletic and robust, his beautifully defined muscles ripple under his well-toned skin, and his *contrapposto* stance is further enlivened by his right arm, which reaches forwards and so gives him a much more intimate relationship with the space surrounding him, and hence a more immediate involvement with the spectator.

These trends towards naturalism, redefining ideal proportions and exploring new spatial possibilities, culminated in the work of Lysippos of Sikyon, who became the court sculptor to Alexander the Great. Alexander employed him as a portraitist, but paradoxically his most influential work – the *Apoxyomenos*, the *Man Scraping Himself* – took a very mundane subject, an athlete removing the oil, sweat and dirt from himself after a workout. Lysippos always worked in bronze, and none of the marble copies make it easy to appreciate the real finesse of his work, but, even so, we can see the brilliant mobility of the stance of the *Apoxyomenos*': his weight is on his left leg, yet he seems to be in the process of shifting it on to his right; his extended arms almost take possession of the surrounding space; his proportionally small head makes him look tall and slender; and, although there is no single point of view that is perfect, the statue is interesting from various aspects – you have to walk round it to appreciate its full spatial complexity. Lysippos stands at the transition to the Hellenistic era: his patron Alexander ultimately created a new world for the Greeks, and Greek art had to move with the times.

11
GREEK COMEDY

It's an odd job, making decent people laugh.

Molière, *La critique de l'école des femmes*

Greek Old Comedy: Aristophanes' The Frogs

Comedy is a Greek word (*komoidia*) the origins of which are as mystifying as the weird, hybrid art form that was performed in the same venue as tragedy – to the same audience, and in the same festival context. Aristotle says that the Megarians and the Sicilians claimed that they invented it, on the grounds that comedians take their name from touring the *komai* ('villages').[1] However, modern scholarship tends to favour a link with *komazein* (= 'to revel'), interpreting *komoidia* as 'a song to do with a *komos*.' A *komos* can be a group (or procession) of men singing, dancing, drinking and generally behaving exuberantly, or the revelry itself, or the ode sung at one of these processions. *Komoidoi* (= 'komos-singers') is also used as the Greek word for a comic performance.

Aristotle goes on to say that Comedy originated with the leaders of phallic songs/processions.[2] In Aristophanes' *The Acharnians*, Dikaiopolis celebrates such an event on stage, and sings a phallic hymn to the pleasures of sex and alcohol, and describing Phales, the personification of the processional phallus, as a companion of Dionysos, a fellow-reveller, night-rover, adulterer and pederast.[3] The players of Old Comedy usually went barefoot, and their costumes included exaggerated bellies and bottoms, plus the highly distinctive limp leather *phallus* for male roles. Semos of Delos (*c.*200 BCE) speaks of 'phallus bearers' who picked on their audience, and it may be that elements of Old Comedy evolved out of verses mocking the public, delivered by those who accompanied the phallus in the procession. A number of sixth-century BCE vases depict dancers, whose dress occasionally includes a super-size phallus, and also hirsute, phallic satyrs. One Corinthian *krater*,[4] dating from between 600 and 575 BCE, also shows a masked dancer and various strange beings, one labelled *komios* (= 'reveller') and another *paikhnios*, which might be derived from *paignion* (= 'jest'/'comic performance'), engaged in a vigorous dance and some activity with large jars. Their skin-tight costumes, with padding on the stomach and buttocks, resemble the characters in Athenian Old Comedy.

A further facet of the 'comic hybrid' is the fact that many choruses appear as animals (wasps, birds, frogs, etc.), suggesting that animal masquerades may also have had an important influence. One Attic vase[5] that predates the surviving comedies by more than a century depicts men disguised as horses, with riders on their backs, accompanied by a flute player; an Attic *oinochoe* contemporary with the earliest known official Athenian comic productions, shows men dressed as birds leaping into the air to the music of an *aulos* player;[6] and an Attic *kalyx krater*, 415–410 BCE, with a scene from *The Birds* by Aristophanes, has bird-men with avian heads, wings on their backs and feet, feathery costumes and erect phalluses, shaking their tail-feathers to *aulos* music.[7]

Old Comedy is also part of a tradition of invective and sexual humour that would send any twenty-first-century 'celebrity' straight to the libel courts. Archilokhos of Paros (seventh century BCE), where there was a tradition of *iambos* – exceedingly sexual and scatological songs performed at fertility rituals – bragged about his erotic conquests:

> Up and down she bounced, like a kingfisher flapping on a jutting rock . . . Like a Thracian or Phrygian drinking beer through a tube she sucked, stooped down, engaged too from behind . . . And his dong flooded over like a Prienian stall-fed donkey's.[8]

Hipponax, writing in the late sixth century BCE, also deployed iambic elements, humorously portraying himself as a scurrilous low-life addicted to violence, crime, alcohol and sordid sex. He had a favourite enemy, the sculptor Boupalos, with whose mistress Arete ('Virtue'!) he was carnally acquainted:

> On the floor . . . undressing . . . we bit and kissed . . . She was eagerly . . . while I was fucking . . . pulling out to the tip, like skinning a sausage, saying to hell with Boupalos.[9]

All these elements coalesced into Old Comedy as the improvisatory nature metamorphosed into something more regularized and official. Aristotle does not know who introduced masks, prologues or a plurality of actors, but says that proper plot-lines originated in Sicily with Epikharmos and Phormis, while at Athens, Krates was the first to reject the lampoon format and use more coherent stories and plots.[10]

Comedy became an official fixture in the Great Dionysia festival at Athens in 488/7 or 487/6 BCE, and was added to the Lenaia festival c.445 BCE. Five comedies were normally performed at each festival, although this may have been reduced to three during the Peloponnesian War. Old Comedy was a very democratic art-form – challenging to compose, expensive to produce (the same man who spent 3,000 dr. on a tragic chorus says he spent 1,600 dr. on a comedy), and reliant on freedom of speech. It blossomed, flourished and withered in synch with Athens' imperial power.

No complete plays by any Old Comedy playwright other than Aristophanes still survive. There are eleven of these, from the long and distinguished career of an acknowledged genius, although they were preserved because scholars were more interested in the dialect he was writing in than in the quality of his comedy. We do not know the exact dates of his life (c.450–c.385 BCE are usually given), although his aristocratic name (= 'Conspicuously the Best'), and that of his father Philippos (= 'Lover of Horses'), give hints about his background, and he might have lived, or owned property, on Aigine. All but two of his extant works were performed during the Peloponnesian War.

Aristophanes' plays tend to have a generic overall pattern under-pinned by a standard plot-structure based on six formal elements:

1. The Prologue: the actors warm up the audience with often irrelevant and farcical routines, and introduce themselves. The

hero is faced with a predicament and he or she comes up with a big idea, frequently violating the laws of nature and taking no account of logical objections, to solve it.

2. The *Parodos*: the moment everyone has been waiting for – the entry of the Chorus. It is usually the starting point of the main action, out of which the play's essential conflict develops as the big idea runs into opposition.

3. The *Agon*: a formal contest/discussion/debate, in the form of alternating speeches and songs. In its full form it has nine elements:

   - *Ode*: a short lyric stanza from the Chorus;
   - *Keleusmos*: the Chorus-leader encourages one of the contestants to begin in a couple of lines that establish the poetic metre that the speakers will use;
   - *Epirrhema*: the first contestant states his or her case, and deals with frequent interruptions;
   - *Pnigos*: a 'stifler', meant to be sung all in one breath (climactic or humorously anti-climactic);
   - *Antode*: we now repeat the whole process as the second contestant has his or her say: -
   - *Antikeleusmos*;
   - *Antepirrhema*;
   - *Antipnigos*;
   - *Sphragis*: the Chorus-leader puts the 'seal' on the contest by announcing the winner.

4. The *Parabasis*: the Chorus 'come forward' (Greek: *parabasai*) and perform an interlude purporting to give serious advice that might be entirely unconnected with anything in the play. It, too, has a highly structured form:

   - *Kommation*: a short prelude;
   - *Anapaests* (or *Parabasis* proper): the Chorus-leader, using anapaestic tetrameters and with musical accompaniment, has a rant about a topical issue;
   - *Pnigos*: as in the *agon*;
   - *Ode*: often a lyric invocation by the Chorus;
   - *Epirrhema*: the Chorus-leader speaks again;

- *Antode*: matching the ode, and building on what has gone before;
- *Antepirrhema*; matching the *epirrhema*, and building on what has gone before.

5. A series of self-contained scenes, punctuated by choral interludes, playing out the ramifications of the big idea's success, frequently in the form of a blatantly male fantasy.
6. The *Exodos*: the all-singing, all-dancing finale, which is all about eating, drinking and priapic sexual gratification.

This formalized structure was by no means restrictive to Aristophanes, whose plays are amazingly varied: *Peace* opens with its hero Trygaios flying up to Olympus on a massive dung-beetle in order to free the goddess Peace from captivity; *The Wasps* satirizes the Athenian legal system, portraying the trial of a dog that tries to elicit sympathy for itself by bringing a litter of cute puppies on stage; *The Clouds* parodies the philosopher Socrates in his crazy 'Thinking Shop'; *The Birds* is a scintillating fantasy of some disillusioned Athenians who try to live with the birds in 'Cloudcuckooland' (the word is Aristophanes' invention); and in *Lysistrata*, the heroine stops the Peloponnesian War by means of a sex-strike.

Politicians were always fair game for Aristophanes, and so were other famous poets, musicians, scientists and philosophers, and so was any form of artistic or intellectual innovation, especially if it appeared a little left field. Quite how the victims and the audience responded is not known: legislation was occasionally enacted to restrict comic attacks on individuals, but the evidence for its scope and effect is scanty. Aristophanes certainly did not do 'political correctness' – race, gender, sexuality, religion, class, politics, education, the military: no topic is off-limits, and hardly anyone is exempt. Perhaps surprising to modern sensibilities, given the type of reaction that greeted *Monty Python's Life of Brian* or Kurt Westergaard's Mohammed cartoons, is the blatant irreverence with which Aristophanes treats the gods, particularly Dionysos. Yet there is no evidence of comic playwrights being prosecuted for impiety, or of great offence being taken. After all, Dionysos is, after all, the god of comedy: he can take a joke, and the comedies were religious events performed in his honour.

Aristophanes moves easily between the humorous and the solemn, the delicate and the filthy, and the verbal ethos of the plays is highly imaginative. He uses puns (sometimes deliberately feeble); word-plays where one character uses a word that another takes in a different sense; hyperbole (exaggeration for the sake of effect); bathos (where serious sentiments are undercut by trivial comments, or a character makes a deliberately anti-climactic statement); invents amazing new words; revels in surreal nonsense and illogicality; sends up the dialects spoken by people from different parts of Greece; and is a virtuoso exponent of parody (ridicule by imitation), selecting the distinctive features of tragic, epic, philosophical, scientific, political or everyday language, and then exaggerating them out of all proportion.

Neither does he shy away from transgressive humour, be this scatological ('toilet humour'); the breaking of taboos (e.g. sacrilege, insults); references to physical abnormalities; personal abuse; *Schadenfreude* (pleasure gained through witnessing someone else's discomfort); or sexual. The latter can range from smutty innuendo to crass obscenity: in Aristophanes' surviving work there are 204 terms for genitalia and other erogenous bodily parts (e.g. figs, valleys, soup-ladles, boat-poles, swords, snakes, resin, the letter delta, mouse holes, sausages, boxes and 'piggy'), plus 190 for sex (explicit or euphemistic, with imagery drawn from nautical, agricultural, and sporting activity), 69 scatological ones, 91 referring to homosexuality, and 4 to autoerotic behaviour (seen as characteristic of male rustics, slaves, foreigners and lecherous females).

There is a wide range of characters in the average comedy: deities, heroes and mythological personalities; contemporary celebrities. 'Types', such as Xanthias (the clever slave) and Aiakos (the irascible doorman) in *The Frogs*; animals; natural phenomena; personifications (*Demos* = 'The Athenian People' in *The Knights*; reconciliation in *Lysistrata*); figures characterized by a personal obsession that is also their name (Prokleon and Antikleon in *The Wasps*); and minor characters and silent extras, often introduced just to make a one-off gag. The 'three-actor rule' does not seem to apply to Aristophanes, and his choruses were made up of twenty-four members who can be humans, animals, personifications or natural phenomena, although they always talk as humans.

The performers' masks were somewhat bigger than life size, with grotesque facial features – deep furrows on balding foreheads, abnormally large eyes, hooked noses, large open mouths, protruding chins, etc. Some masks may have been lifelike caricatures: in *The Knights* we are jokingly told that the property-makers were too afraid to provide a portrait-mask of Kleon. Aristotle says that comedy represents the worst kinds of men, in the sense that 'the ridiculous' is a species of ugliness or badness, but he adds that although the comic mask is distorted and ugly, it causes no pain.[11] The masks also facilitate cross-dressing: all the characters, women included, were played by men, but also in the plays men dress up as women, and women dress as men, opening the richly comic possibilities of a-man-dressed-as-a-woman-dressed-as-a-man.

Aristophanes' plays need actors with an impeccable sense of comic timing and considerable mime or clowning skills. Although most comic antics have to be inferred from the text, which contains no stage directions, it is still clear that Aristophanes uses a huge array of visual techniques to get laughs: he deploys props and stage machinery very effectively; exploits mistaken identities; puts his characters in ludicrous, bizarre or difficult situations where they have to improvise; conspiratorially informs the audience about a character's misconception; or mystifies them by showing elaborate preparations for some as yet unknown purpose. All this can vary from the surreal to the downright silly, and the various comic devices are seldom used in isolation. Aristophanes doesn't sit down and think: 'I'll put in some situational/transgressive/visual humour here'; rather, he batters the audience with every comic weapon he can lay his hands on, all at the same time, and nowhere did he do this better than in *The Frogs*.

This play was staged at the Lenaia festival of 405 BCE, a time when the Athenians were in deep crisis politically, socially and militarily. It was not an easy time to make them laugh, so, without shirking the serious issues, Aristophanes adjusted his focus to another sad contemporary event, the recent death of Euripides. Unusually Aristophanes practically inverted the play's usual structure by putting the disconnected farcical scenes before the *parabasis* and staging the *agon*, which is rather more intellectual and has far less obscenity, after it. But it was a risk that paid off: *The Frogs* took the 1st prize, and gained the unparalleled honour of a second performance in 404 BCE.

The appearance of two bizarre characters raises a laugh even before anyone utters a word. One, who is wearing a lion skin over a long yellow dress (*kothornoi*), and brandishing a club, is a very effeminate Dionysos, badly disguised as Herakles; the other, who is riding a donkey while carrying a load of baggage, is Xanthias ('Blondie'), Dionysos' rascally but loyal slave. After a series of gratuitously lavatorial jokes and a nice parody of sophistic arguments they arrive at the house of Herakles. The great hero is a traditional comic favourite: a massive, boisterous, dim-witted glutton, slavering in anticipation of an enormous dinner that he never gets. When Herakles answers the door, and sees Dionysos' get-up, he collapses in paroxysms of hilarity. Dionysos explains, by making use of a wide range of tragic language and quotations, and exploiting Herakles' notorious fondness for food, that he has developed an insatiable craving for the recently deceased Euripides.

Dionysos is on his way to retrieve the great tragedian from the Underworld because the living poets are either untried, out of the country, or atrocious. He wants:

> A poet who can produce something really audacious, like 'Ether, the residence of Zeus', or 'the foot of Time', or that business about the tongue being able to perjure itself and the heart not being committed.[12]

Dionysos knows his tragedy. The first distorted quotation comes from Euripides' *Melanippe*; the second indicates a ridiculous personification; the third is a clumsy paraphrase of a line of Euripides, which taken out of context had become notorious: 'my tongue it was that swore, but my heart is not under oath', from *Hippolytus*. Yet the drama-god's taste is dubious: although he yearns for a poet who is *gonimos* (= 'full of productive energy', but also 'sexually potent'), even the philistine Herakles realizes that the choice of Euripides is odd.

Nevertheless, Dionysos needs Herakles' advice because he went down to the Underworld to bring Kerberos, the guard dog of Hades, back to the world above. Rejecting the hero's macabre suggestions that he can gain access to the Underworld by killing himself, Dionysos says he wants to use the same route as Herakles. This will entail getting Kharon, the ferryman of the dead, to take him. Traditionally the fare was one obol, but in a gag that is related to the various doles and payments made to Athenian citizens of the time, Herakles says it will cost two, the daily pay for soldiers and sailors, or the fare from Peiraieus to Aigine. Herakles then gets on a roll, describing the filthy environment and unsavoury characters of the Underworld, before telling Dionysos that he will emerge into brilliant daylight, and meet happy bands of Mystic Initiates, who will give him the final directions to Pluto's (= Hades') residence.

So they set off, and immediately encounter a corpse on its way to burial. Dionysos tries to hire it to carry the luggage, but when it wants too much money, Xanthias resignedly agrees to carry it himself.

They arrive at the lake, and while Xanthias has to run round it, Dionysos embarks. Quite how the crossing was staged is not known, but the fact that Dionysos has no nautical experience – he starts by sitting on his oar – makes for good comedy. He rows to the accompaniment of 'songs of swan-frogs'.[13] This scene, from which the play takes its title, has caused controversy for centuries: do the frogs actually appear, or are they only heard? Kharon only refers to them being heard; Dionysos never comments on their appearance. (It is argued that using two choruses in the play would not be financially viable; but the main chorus of Mystic Initiates are dressed in rags 'for laughter and economy',[14] which may indicate that Aristophanes had blown his chorus-budget on the frogs, who would be a costume-designer's dream-come-true).

In the poetic duel that ensues, punctuated by their *brekekekex koax koax* refrain, they make use of marvellous invented words, like *pompholygopaphlasmasin* (from the words for 'bubble' and 'splash'), and Aristophanes creates comedy by using different poetic metres: Kharon establishes Dionysos' original rhythm (dactyls); the frogs disrupt it with iambic and trochaic metres; Dionysos gets the hang of this; they revert to dactyls. Eventually though, Dionysos turns the frogs' refrain against them and wins out.

Dionysos and Xanthias regroup on the other side, and they make their way through darkness, until Xanthias says that they have made it through safely. In doing so, he exploits a moment from the production of Euripides' *Orestes*, when an actor accidentally turned *galén' horô* ('I see calm things approaching') into *galên horô* ('I see a ferret approaching') – the difference is in the pitch accent of the Greek words – to the great hilarity of the audience. Dionysos wonders whether 'Ether, the residence of Zeus' or the 'Foot of Time' was behind their recent experience, before, as promised, they encounter the chorus of Mystic Initiates.

Dionysos and Xanthias have now arrived at the palace of Pluto. Dionysos is still dressed as Herakles, but, when the doorkeeper Aiakos appears, speaking in the style of Aeschylus, it is clear that he is not welcome because of the abduction of Kerberos:

> Hah! I'll have you flung over the cliff, down to the black-hearted Stygian rocks, and you'll be chased by the prowling hounds of Hell and the hundred-headed viper will tear your guts out and the Tartessian lamprey shall devour your lungs and the Tithrasian Gorgons can have your kidneys and – just wait there a moment while I go and fetch them.[15]

Dionysos is so terrified he defecates. Here Aristophanes distorts a religious formula associated with making libations – 'It has been poured out (*ekkekhutai*): Call the god' – into: 'I have shat myself (*egkekhoda*)'.[16] When Xanthias offers his master a sponge, Dionysos suggests instead that the slave should take the club and lion-skin, while he carries the luggage, but no sooner have they made the exchange than Persephone's Servant comes out and tells 'Xanthiherakles' how pleased her mistress is that he is coming. A sumptuous banquet, plus a pretty flute-girl and some dancing-girls, are waiting for him, so Xanthias gratefully accepts and peremptorily orders 'Dionysoxanthias' to bring the luggage.

Dionysos, of course, now insists on having the Heraklean accoutrements back, but immediately he is wearing the lion-skin two Landladies enter. These feisty ladies catalogue Herakles' gluttonous and raucous behaviour and want reparations, so inevitably Dionysos asks to change costume again.

After some serious grovelling, he persuades Xanthias to take the lion-skin, whereupon Aiakos returns, with numerous slaves carrying whips, ropes, fetters and instruments of torture. The nimble-witted Xanthiherakles makes a 'gentlemanly' offer to prove his innocence. Under Athenian law, a master could allow his slave to be tortured in order to test the truth of an allegation, so Xanthias suggests that Aiakos do precisely that to Dionysos. The god protests that he can't be tortured because he is an immortal; Xanthias suggests that if he is a god he won't feel anything; Dionysos counters by saying that as a god Xanthias should be flogged too; and Xanthias, who as a slave is used to being beaten, agrees: whoever squeals first isn't a god at all. They each bend over – but after three inconclusive (and noisy and painful) blows each, Xanthias has noticed that Aiakos always needs to remind himself who to hit next, and tricks him into having one more go at Dionysos. Aiakos still cannot tell which of them is the god, so he decides to leave it up to Pluto and Persephone.

So they enter the palace, leaving the Chorus to deliver the *Parabasis*, which is abnormally serious, as Aristophanes argues for an amnesty for the citizens who were involved in the oligarchic revolution of 411 BCE.

Having got this off his chest, Aristophanes turns back to the action of the play, with plot taking a surprising new turn: there is a big dispute between Aeschylus, the current incumbent of the 'Tragic Throne' occupied by the finest non-living poet, and Euripides, who is laying claim to it. Preparations are being made for a contest, which, as the god of Drama, Dionysos has been asked to adjudicate. We immediately witness the dispute at first hand: Euripides accuses Aeschylus of being unsubtle and pretentious; Aeschylus casts aspersions on Euripides' ancestry, and attacks the banality of his tragedies.

As the contest looms Aeschylus prays to Demeter, goddess of the Eleusinian Mysteries; Euripides invokes Ether, 'Pivot of my Tongue', and Nostrils; and the *agon* (contest) gets underway, punctuated by Dionysos' comically inept commentary. Euripides launches into a critique of Aeschylus' use of silent characters, long choral odes, unintelligible speeches and grandiose vocabulary. The younger tragedian then praises himself: he has slimmed tragedy down; added clarity; no one stands idle; everyone talks; his plays are 'Democracy in action'; he taught his audience how to talk; and he wrote about familiar themes.

It is now Aeschylus' turn to speak. He kicks off by asking what are the qualities that make a good poet. Euripides suggests technical expertise, allied to the ability to make people into better citizens, and so presents Aeschylus with the opportunity to boast of how he presented 'real heroes', dealt with martial themes, had a useful lesson to teach, and generally to claim the moral high ground:

> AESCHYLUS: *I* didn't clutter my stage with harlots like Phaidra or Stheneboia. No one can say I have ever put an erotic female into any play of mine.
> EURIPIDES: How could you? You've never even met one.[17]

Aeschylus turns to the didactic obligations of the poets – the characters should speak in dignified language, and should be dressed suitably, not in rags, like many in Euripidean dramas. This is a stock criticism of Euripides' plays, but slightly incongruous here, given that Aristophanes has dressed *his* chorus in rags.

Dionysos deflates the tone with a joke about a fat, unfit, flatulent man; the Chorus sing another ode; and the tragedians now attack one another's prologues. This episode makes use of a great deal of verbatim quotation – Aristophanes' parody is based on intimate knowledge – but practically all the serious points are accompanied by extraneous comic business. So, when Euripides starts with some fastidious nit-picking of a few lines from Aeschylus' *Libation Bearers*, Dionysos plays the buffoon: 'Brilliant! Brilliant! Wish I knew what you were talking about!'[18] Then, as attention turns to Euripides' prologues, Aeschylus alleges that the banal phrase *lekythion apolesen* (= 'lost his bottle of oil') can be interpolated into their first sentences, and goes on to do so in a way that both fits the metre and subverts the sense. As Euripides makes genuine quotations, Aeschylus completes the third line of three plays, the second line of two, and the first line of the last one. When Euripides has a second attempt at the last one, Aeschylus puts the phrase into its second line instead:

> EURIPIDES: 'Tis said that Oineus –
> AESCHYLUS: – lost his bottle of oil.
> EURIPIDES: You might at least let me finish one line.
> 'Tis said that Oineus, offering to the gods
> First fruits of harvest –
> AESCHYLUS: – lost his bottle of oil.
> DIONYSOS: What, in the middle of a sacrifice? How very awkward for him.[19]

Assuming a keen sense of comic timing on the part of Aeschylus'
actor, this works well, as the phrase is inserted earlier and earlier.
There might also be an opportunity for audience participation, once
they pick up on what is happening, and an extra layer of comedy
might be generated by the phallic shape of the bottle.

The next phase of the contest focuses on each writer's use of
lyrics. They each recite lines by the other, presumably with
grotesque exaggeration of their faults, and it could be that music
played a major role here, but sadly it does not survive. Euripides
goes first, again quoting directly from Aeschylus, but using a
nonsensical refrain to indicate the monotony of Aeschylus' lyrics:

> The twin-throned kings in muted mockery send
> *Tophlattothrat tophlattothrat*
> A fox to dog the Sphinx, a Sphinx to fox the dog
> *Tophlattothrat tophlattothrat.*[20]

When Aeschylus takes his turn, 'The Muse of Euripides' takes the
stage, beating time with bits of broken pottery and, doubtless,
dancing comically. Dionysos makes an interestingly scurrilous
comment: 'This Muse wasn't playing the Lesbian part. No way!'[21]
The word he uses is *elesbiazen,* but 'Lesbian' did not have the
connotations that it now does: it was the standard comic word for
fellatio, but can also imply that the Muse didn't sing in the dignified
musical Lesbian modes that Aeschylus imitated. The parody of
Euripides' lyrics is brilliantly astute in terms of style, sensation-
alism, metres and weird musical effects, as a poor woman uses
extravagant tragic and Homeric language to make drama out of a
minor domestic crisis:

> O black-lit darkness of Night,
> what direful dream is this
> thou sendest me, come forth from obscure Hades
> with a life that is no life,
> a child of black Night,
> a fearsome sight to make one shudder,
> in black corpse-raiment,
> with murderous murderous gaze
> and with big claws? . . .

> Behold these wonders! My cockerel –
> Glyke has snatched it and made off with it![22]

Much of this consists of new verses written in Euripidean style, but the grandiose lamentation descends into bathos with a sudden lapse into colloquial speech as the woman's neighbour ('Sweetie') steals her pet cockerel. You don't need to be an expert on tragedy to get the message.

At this point Aeschylus suggests settling the competition by weighing their words on a huge set of scales. The contest is gloriously farcical, but because Euripides always goes first, Aeschylus trumps him every time. Euripides quotes the first line of his *Medea*, whose allusion to the *Argo* is outweighed by the river of Aeschylus' lost *Philoktetes*: 1 – 0 to Aeschylus. Death then beats Persuasion: 2 – 0. The Aeschylean hat-trick is completed by the unstoppable: 'Chariot on chariot, corpse on corpse was piled.'[23]

But Dionysos *still* can't separate the contestants. Pluto now reminds him why he originally came to the Underworld, and gives him permission to take one poet back to Athens, and by now Dionysos has something much more serious in mind: Athens must survive and go on holding choral festivals in his honour. So he decides to take the one who gives the best advice and starts with the burning question of the day: what should they do about Alkibiades? Again their responses leave Dionysos at a loss, and, frustratingly, our understanding of the text starts to become problematical at this point, but at last Dionysos makes his judgement: he chooses Aeschylus.

> DIONYSOS: Come, Aeschylus . . .
> EURIPIDES: Can you dare to look me in the face after playing such a low-down, shameful trick?
> DIONYSOS: I appeal to the audience.
> EURIPIDES: 'Oh, heart of stone, wouldst leave me here to die?' Well, to go on being dead, anyway.
> DIONYSOS [*quoting that other fatal line*]: 'Who knows if death be life and life be death.'[24]

This is brilliantly done: when Euripides protests, Dionysos quotes his own work back at him, beginning with the line 'My tongue it was that swore . . .', from *Hippolytus*, that he said he admired so much earlier in the play. He then justifies his decision by altering just two Greek letters of 'What is shameful if the doers think it not so?' – a line that had caused outrage when a Euripidean character used it to justify raping his own sister – and so turns 'doers' (*khromenois*) into 'audience' (*theomenois*). Dionysos' judgement really takes no account of poetic skill or political *nous*: the worst criticisms levelled against Euripides were that he filled his plays with slutty women and that his characters were always arguing and getting new ideas, but he does not deserve to lose.

Pluto tells Aeschylus to save the city and educate the fools (i.e. the audience), and gives him a sword, nooses and some hemlock in order to hasten the arrival in the Underworld of various politicians. Aeschylus accepts the assignment, entrusts the Throne of Tragedy, to Sophocles, and ends on an upbeat note with hopes being expressed for an end to the war. It was, after all, part of Aristophanes' brief to make his audience feel good.

Greek New Comedy: Menander's Old Cantankerous
The year after *The Frogs* was produced Athens was forced into surrender by the Spartans, and the consequences for comedy were immense: freedom of speech was curtailed, the personal wealth to fund elaborate choruses dried up, and new artistic trends started to surface. We enter a period known as Middle Comedy, whose exponents Antiphanes and Alexis produced more than 500 plays, and, although not one single scene has survived, we can still perceive some important changes: the chorus became less prominent; the *parabasis* pretty much disappeared; the language moved nearer to that of everyday speech; there was less obscenity; there was a greater focus on plot-construction; characters were given ordinary citizens' names; the titles (*The Miser*, *The Doll-maker*, etc.) indicate an increasing interest in social types and everyday life; and love stories were popular.

By the time Alexander the Great died (323 BCE) Athens had fallen under Macedonian domination. Around that time a poet called Menander (*Menandros*) made his debut with *Orge* (*Anger*). He was born in 342/1 BCE to the respectable Athenians Diopeithes and Hegistrate, learned his trade from Alexis, studied with the philosopher Theophrastus, squinted, had a sharp mind, was crazy about women, and died by drowning in the Peiraieus somewhere around 290/89 or 293/2 BCE, having written just over 100 plays. Although never especially popular in his lifetime, his posthumous fame was enormous, and he came to be regarded as the pre-eminent author of New Comedy.[25]

Menander never became part of the medieval manuscript tradition, which is why it is only in the last century or so that we have got to know his work at first hand. The big break came when Martin Bodmer, a Swiss bibhophile, scholar and collector, got hold of a codex that had been smuggled out of Egypt that contained *Dyskolos* (*Old Cantankerous*) practically complete. The play was published in 1958, and is still the only whole work to be recovered.

Menander's plays were mostly performed in the Theatre of Dionysos, although it had undergone some modifications since Aristophanes' day, especially in the *arkhon*ship of Lykourgos (338–324 BCE). The *skene* was now made of stone, and it is probable that the 'stage' was a low platform in front of it. The *skene* had three openings, which could represent the doorways of houses, and it was flanked by *paraskenia*, projecting open colonnades with Doric columns, through which actors approaching from the *parodoi* could pass. The *parodoi* themselves now had stone retaining walls: the eastern one (stage right) was conventionally taken to lead to the harbour or from the country, while the western one (stage left) led to the *agora* or town. The seats were also now constructed from stone.

The grotesque costumes of Old Comedy had been replaced by more realistic clothing, although the actors continued to wear masks, some of which caricatured the features of the old and of slaves. Academics disagree over whether a 'three-actor rule' applied. No scene of Menander's *needs* more than three speaking parts at any one time, but the fact that a play can be performed by just three actors doesn't prove that it actually was.

The structure of the plays had also changed. Menander uses a five-act structure with an expository prologue (no *parabasis*, no *agon*), although why he does so is not known. The act-breaks represent a variable period of time and are covered by choral interludes whose text is not preserved – all we get is one word, *KHOROU* = 'of the Chorus'. We do not know whether the Chorus sang and/or danced and, if so, what it sang or danced; how many members it had; or what it did and where it went during the acts.

In comparison with Aristophanes, there is very little evidence about contemporary events, and Menander followed Middle Comedy trends and took on its stock characters, while adding his own individual twists. Plutarch commented that Eros (love/ passion/desire) ran through all his plays, and there are interesting parallels with the approach to the study of character in works like Theophrastus' *The Characters*, where personality is illustrated by a series of typical acts:

> Boorishness I would define as uncivilized ignorance. The boor is the sort of man who drinks barley-brew before going into the Assembly; who asserts that garlic smells as sweet as any perfume; wears shoes too big for his feet; and can't talk without bellowing... He sits down with his clothes hitched up above the knee, exposing his nakedness ... he drinks his wine neat ... he feeds his horses while still eating his own breakfast ... he sings in the public bath; and he drives hobnails into his shoes.[26]

Menander presents subtly observed, lifelike characters with identifiable human emotions, and his plays are driven by words and actions consistent with those characters. His realism was much vaunted: the ancient scholar Aristophanes of Byzantium wrote: 'O Menander and life, which one of you imitated the other?'[27] Modern critics often object that Menander isn't realistic: he represents a restricted area of domestic life; relies on coincidence; and his work is full of clichéd motifs. Yet, his work *seems* realistic in the context of the comic stage.

Old Cantankerous was produced at the Lenaia of 316 BCE with Aristodemos of Skarphe as *protagonistes*, and won 1st prize. It is set in Phyle, about 23 km from Athens. Stage right is a house inhabited by Knemon, his daughter and a maidservant Simike; opposite them live Knemon's estranged wife Myrrhine, Gorgias (her son by an earlier husband), and their slave Daos. Between the two houses is a shrine of Pan and the Nymphs.

Pan speaks the prologue, putting the audience in possession of the basic facts, and describing Knemon, the old misanthropic farmer (*dyskolos*) of the play's title, his marital arrangements, and how reclusive he is. Knemon is very much an established comic type, although his name is unique – a kind of nickname applicable to anyone who has unusual shins. He has never spoken a civil word to anyone in his life, although he hates vice as well as people. His daughter, however, has turned out innocent and pious, and Pan is looking after her. Specifically, there is a fashionable young man called Sostratos: he lives in town; his father Kallipides owns a valuable farm nearby; and he has fallen in love with Knemon's daughter.

The god then exits never to be seen again, and the action gets under way with the entrance of the love-struck Sostratos and his friend Khaireas, who, he hopes, will help him out. In language typical of the comic parasite, Khaireas says he will. If she were a *hetaira* (courtesan), Khaireas would grab her, carry her off, get drunk, and burn the door down – 'quick action produces quick relief'[28] – but as something more long term and respectable is at stake he is more serious. He will have to perform checks on her family, finance and character. Sostratos has fallen in love without taking these factors into account, but this should not surprise us, since social conditions in Athens made it difficult (or at least dishonourable) for a young man to meet a marriageable girl in private. His problem is that he can only make her acquaintance through her father, and to that effect he has already sent his hunting slave, Pyrrhias, to see Knemon. Unfortunately, the interview has gone badly. Pyrrhias enters playing the stock role of the 'running slave', breathlessly shouting at imaginary people to get out of his way, but correspondingly sluggish at getting his message out. Knemon has chased him away, slinging clods, stones and even pears at him.

Khaireas' brash self-confidence evaporates, and he slopes off. As Knemon comes into view Sostratos comments on the uselessness of his friend and assumes that Pyrrhias must have provoked the old man. Pyrrhias leaves; Sostratos faces the advancing Knemon on his own; and when Knemon finally speaks, it is exactly what we were expecting: he wishes he were Perseus, who could fly, so he never had to meet anyone, and was armed with the Gorgon's head, so that he could turn anyone who annoyed him into stone.

Sostratos is not ready to face such a monster yet. His attempt to deflect the old man's rage by lying about why he is there only provokes a coruscating tirade of sarcasm before Knemon exits, catching his household unawares by his unscheduled return.

Having been failed by Khaireas and Pyrrhias, Sostratos now decides to get his father's slave Getas to help him: 'He's a real ball of fire', says Sostratos, 'and he's very experienced.'[29]

At this point the plot takes on a new element. Knemon's daughter (who remains anonymous throughout) enters in search of water. Her opening line is drawn straight out of tragedy, although the scenario she describes is rather mundane: her Nurse has dropped a bucket down the well. Smitten by her loveliness, Sostratos utters a string of oaths, composes himself and offers to help. He takes her jug into the shrine of the Nymphs and fills it up. Just before the act ends, Menander deploys a soap opera-style 'cliffhanger': Gorgias' slave Daos comes out of the other house and sees Sostratos give the jug to the girl, and, while the young lover goes off to get Getas, Daos reveals his suspicions about the situation and heads off to tell Gorgias that someone is inappropriately interested in his half-sister. As he exits, the Chorus of inebriated Pan-worshippers deliver the first of their interludes.

The second act opens with Gorgias, who is on his way to see Knemon, giving Daos a hard time for not looking after the girl better. However, Sostratos now appears, having failed to find Getas, who has been sent out to hire a cook by Sostratos' fussily religious mother, who is planning to make a sacrifice. Sostratos is now ready to confront Knemon, but he is himself confronted by Gorgias, who delivers a pompous, but rather illogical, moralization in a thirteen-line sentence that doesn't really come to the point. Sostratos, though, catches his drift: Gorgias thinks he is planning to seduce a respectable man's innocent daughter, which takes the young urban lover aback. He tells his rustic assailant that he is pontificating without knowing the facts, explains that he has fallen in love and that it's her father he wants to see, not the girl. He adds that he is free, solvent and prepared to marry her without a dowry, and he swears always to love and cherish her. His words have the desired effect. Gorgias not only becomes more conciliatory, but even agrees to help, formulating a plan for Sostratos to win Knemon over by pretending to be a hard-working farmer: they will work together in the field and, when Knemon shows up, they will broach the possibility of marriage.

It is remarkable how carefully Menander manages the entrances and exits at this point. Daos goes off first to build a wall; Gorgias wishes Sostratos good luck and then departs; Sostratos soliloquizes briefly before setting off to work himself; Daos' actor reappears as Sikon at the start of the next scene; then Gorgias' actor comes back as Kallipides' slave Getas. An experienced actor would not need long to change his mask and costume – modern catwalk models do this type of thing incredibly quickly – although getting from one side of the Theatre of Dionysos to the other might involve a short sprint. The 'clock time' also becomes distorted here: when Getas enters, he has already walked from Kallipides' estate near Phyle to the Athenian *agora* to hire a cook, and then back again – a round trip of about 45 km. Assuming that he set off at around dawn, he would arrive on stage roughly in the middle of the afternoon, and yet, just ten lines before, Sostratos has gone off to Gorgias' field, judging from the other activities of his day, at somewhere around 10 a.m. But, even if five or six stage hours pass in ten lines, the audience never notice the anomaly.

The two new characters treat us to some stock comic buffoonery. The cook Sikon comes on dragging a sheep, followed by Getas with a pile of rugs, for the sacrifice in the cave. This is happening because Sostratos' mother has had a bad dream involving Pan putting fetters on her son, giving him a leather jacket and a mattock, and telling him to dig on the land next door. In tragedy dreams often prefigure catastrophe, but here the audience can relax – Pan is directing the events positively, and Menander is cleverly combining his three-plot elements of Sostratos' love, Knemon's misanthropy and the dream that motivates the sacrifice. The act ends as they all go into the shrine, and the Chorus perform another interlude.

The irrelevance of the Chorus is apparent when Knemon emerges and sees the sacrifice party, which includes Sostratos' mother, her daughter (or possibly a musician) Plangon ('Doll') and a flute girl called Parthenis. He makes no mention of the Chorus, who would undoubtedly have irritated him, but does have a rant about the worshippers using sacrificial rituals as flimsy pretexts for feasting. Knemon might well have a point, but it is also just the kind of thing that a grumpy old man *would* say, and he decides to work at home. He tells his servant to unlock the door (a locked door in daytime is unusual – another sign of his misanthropy) and scurries back inside.

Unfortunately the sacrifice party has forgotten to bring a cauldron, so Getas has to borrow one. He hammers on Knemon's door. The old man answers it and gives Getas pretty short shrift. Sikon mocks Getas' failure, boasts of his prowess in borrowing cooking pots, knocks at Knemon's door, and predictably receives a fiercer verbal and physical onslaught.

At this point Sostratos returns, spontaneously drawn to the place where his love resides, but aching from digging all day in the sun, and frustrated that Knemon never turned up. Getas comes out of the shrine and tells Sostratos about the sacrifice, and much to the slave's chagrin the young man sees this as an opportunity to invite Gorgias, in the hope that such hospitality will help his wedding plans.

Things then take an unexpected turn. Simike ('Little Snub-nose'), Knemon's elderly slave, appears in the style of a tragic messenger, and says that in trying to retrieve the bucket she has dropped Knemon's mattock down the well. He threatens to lower her down into it to retrieve his things, but then decides to do it himself. As he goes inside, Sostratos arrives with Gorgias and Daos. When Sostratos starts giving orders to his guest's slave and inviting him to dinner, Gorgias immediately countermands the invitation and tells Daos to go and look after his mother. The Chorus then deliver their third interlude.

Act 4 opens with Simike again appearing like a tragic messenger, and when she announces that Knemon has fallen down the well, her tragedy becomes Sikon's delight. He recommends dropping something heavy on top of Knemon, but Simike pleads with him to go down and rescue him. He refuses, and although the stock characters remain hostile to Knemon, the more individualized Sostratos and (primarily) Gorgias step in to rescue him. Sostratos describes the scene: Gorgias jumped down into the well, with Sostratos standing up top with the girl. She was tearing her hair and crying while he just stood there gawping at her gorgeousness and hanging on to the rope. Gorgias got Knemon out, though.

Knemon is brought out in the style of a tragic victim by Gorgias and his daughter. He acknowledges that his misanthropic way of life, even though it was based on his experience of human behaviour, was founded on mistakes: he was wrong to think that he could be 100 per cent self-sufficient, or never even to imagine that anyone would ever do an altruistic kindness to someone else. He then adopts Gorgias as his heir, tells him to find his daughter a husband, and concludes with a final justification of his solitary behaviour. Yet in the end, he cannot change his ways: 'If everyone was like me, there'd be no law-suits or dragging one another off to gaol, and no wars.'[30]

Gorgias immediately sings the praises of Sostratos as a potential husband and (although the papyrus is badly damaged here) it seems that Knemon assents to the marriage, although when Kallipides shows up late for the sacrifice Sostratos decides to let his father eat before raising with him the subject of his impending wedding.

Sostratos' first words after the final choral interlude suggest that Kallipides has made objections to the marriage, but it becomes clear that he has not – he has simply rejected a further proposal that Gorgias should marry his daughter. Sostratos ultimately wins him round, but Gorgias, who has been eavesdropping on the discussion, is himself yet to be convinced: living off the proceeds of other people's hard work does not automatically appeal to him. However (again in a passage where the text is damaged) Sostratos manages to bridge the divide between city and country, and Gorgias agrees to a formal betrothal:

> KALLIPIDES: I now betroth my daughter to you, young man, for the procreation of legitimate children, and I give you with her a dowry of three talents.[31]

The formula 'for the procreation (literally, 'ploughing') of legitimate children' emphasizes the aspect of their marriage that interests the wider community. The dowry was important: (a) because its absence might raise the suspicion that the girl was a concubine, not a wife; and (b) because she brought expenses to her new family, making it reasonable that she should make a contribution. But the dowry also imposes a moral obligation on Gorgias to maintain the standard of living that she is used to, and, because the dowry had to be returned in the case of divorce, provides a financial incentive to keep the marriage going. Neither Knemon's daughter nor Sostratos' sister have any say in their marriages, and there is nothing in the text to indicate that they show any flicker of romantic interest in Sostratos or Gorgias. This would be the normal state of affairs.

It is then party time, for all except Knemon. He might be a bit less grouchy, but he is still a loner, and his decision not to attend the festivities leaves him defenceless as Getas calls Sikon out of the shrine and suggests having some fun at his expense. They carry him out of his house and, in a scene that directly mirrors their earlier unsuccessful confrontations with him, rag him by hammering on his door and making outrageous requests for cook-pans, a basin, wine-tables, dinner-tables, rugs, an oriental hanging 100 ft long and a big bronze mixing bowl. Finally they bully him into going to the party, and the play ends with a final direct address to the audience by Getas: 'You've enjoyed our victory over the old man, now please applaud us, young and old.'[32]

The direct influence of Greek comedy on later literature is far less than that of epic or tragedy, despite the fact that Menander became so highly regarded that Aristophanes of Byzantium ranked him second only to Homer. Quintilian also recommended him as a model for aspiring public speakers in Rome in the first century CE, and some of his lines have become English proverbs, including 'whom the gods love die young'. But, as the Classical Greek world moved into the Hellenistic period, and Rome ultimately became the dominant power in the Mediterranean, it was as a model for Roman Comedy that Menander's work exerted the most influence.

12

ROMAN COMEDY AND THE ROMAN THEATRE

Foul-jesting mimes always contain the sin of forbidden love, in which constantly a well-dressed adulterer appears and the artful wife fools her stupid husband. These are viewed by the marriageable maiden, the wife, the husband, and the child; even the senate in large part is present.

Ovid, *Tristia* 2, 495ff

The Roman Theatre

When Menander's plays were being performed in Athens, the Romans were not yet Italy's dominant power militarily, let alone culturally. There were indigenous Italian comic traditions, including *Atellana* (farces featuring masks, improvisation, and stock characters like Bucco, 'the Fool', and Maccus, 'the Clown'), *Planipedia* (mime) and *Togata* ('drama in a toga', usually a comedy set in Rome), but when Romans began to write their own works they turned to Greek models, especially New Comedy.

Men and women of all walks of life, from slaves to senators, went to the theatre, and the spectators idolized the stars of the stage: the medical writer Galen mentions a female patient suffering from unrequited love for the performer Pylades;[1] an affair between a famous actor called Paris and the wife of the emperor Domitian ended when the emperor had him murdered in the street; the comedian Mnester, who had a liaison with Caligula, subsequently began a relationship with Claudius' wife Messalina – until Claudius had him executed. Moralists pontificated: 'Let spectacles and plays that are full of scurrility and of abundant gossip, be forbidden', wrote Clement of Alexandria.[2] The public, however, loved them.

From the mid-third century BCE onwards the Romans started to produce some high quality works of drama. Livius Andronicus, who was possibly a captive Greek, presented a comedy in Rome at the *Ludi Romani* of 240 BCE, basing his plot and characters on Greek New Comedy. His example was seized upon by an Italian dramatist, Gnaeus Naevius, whose surviving fragments suggest that he, too, usually translated Greek works. Such plays generally preserved the Greek setting, costumes and character names, and so were dubbed *fabulae palliatae*, 'plays in a Greek cloak'. There are, however, lots of Latin jokes and Roman allusions, and there is a fundamental divergence from the Greek tradition because the Chorus is completely dispensed with. The Latin plays did, however, still feature lots of singing in the form of *cantica*. These were delivered with musical accompaniment, as opposed to the unaccompanied *diverbia* or *deverbia*, and can have an effect not unlike that of modern rap music, or operatic recitative, depending on the metre used.

The theatre building was adapted from Greek models to fit Roman requirements, but for a long time before it became a major feature of the Roman townscape it was an ad hoc assemblage of booths and staging, and it is in this context that the plays of Plautus and Terence would have been performed. Rome's first stone theatre was that of Pompey (*c*.55 BCE), where Julius Caesar was later assassinated.

Their use of arches and concrete allowed Roman architects to make their theatres into free-standing structures. There was no need for them to be built into hillsides (although many were), and the incredibly elaborate substructures, where vaulted passages ran both radially and concentrically under the tiered seating, which was accessed by staircases leading to individual zones, facilitated the movement of huge numbers of spectators both into and out of the auditorium. In essence a Roman theatre is made up of three interconnected elements: the auditorium (*cavea*); the semicircular *orchestra*; and the stage. Another feature that really sets the major Roman theatres apart from their Greek predecessors is the *scaenae frons*, the decorated facade of the building behind the stage that housed storerooms and the actors' dressing rooms, and provided an impressive background to the action. Its decoration might include marble facings, mosaics, superimposed tiers of columns, niches, entablatures, pediments and colossal statues. The *scaenae frons* rises to the same height as the auditorium, and usually has three doors in it, plus a slanting ceiling that both protected the stage and provided useful acoustic 'sound reinforcement'. It is joined to the auditorium by lateral returns, so that the interior of the building forms a self-contained unit. In a Roman theatre you are isolated from the outside world.

The *cavea* usually held thousands of spectators, whose social status was reflected in the seating arrangements. The various sectors of seating were often separated by walls and accessed by different entrances.

The *orchestra* was semicircular. It was not required for acting or dancing, and restricting it to a semicircle guaranteed a good view, even to spectators at the extreme edges of the *cavea*.

The stage was generally raised at least 1 m above the level of the *orchestra* and supported by a low wall called the *pulpitum*. It usually had a wooden floor, under which machinery for scene changes and special effects could be kept, and it might contain the curtain slot. The curtain was only about 3 m high and it dropped down into the slot at the beginning of the play and rose at the end.

The stage wall very often formed the theatre's external facade, and many theatres had rows of corbels (projections jutting out from the wall) pierced with holes to support the poles for the *velarium* (awning), which sheltered the spectators from the sun. With easy access, nice circulation spaces, good sight lines and carefully tuned sounding boards under the seats to act as loudspeakers, all the needs of the audience and the players were well catered for: the Roman theatre was very much fit for its purpose.

Plautus: The Swaggering Soldier

Our information about Plautus (*c.*254–184 BCE) is sketchy. He came from Sarsina in northern Italy, and may have been an actor before becoming a writer. Plautus is a genuine family name, but it also means 'flat-footed', as does *planipes*, which was the name for an actor in a mime. Furthermore, in various prologues he uses the names Maccus, and either Maccus and/or Maccius Titus. Again,

Maccius is a genuine name, but Maccus was a stock clown type in the *atellana*. Later generations believed he was called Titus Maccius Plautus; he may have been, but Titus Clown Flatfoot would be a fine professional name.

All twenty-one of Plautus' surviving plays are adaptations of Greek originals. On the whole he tends to stick to the general outline of the plot, to simplify the characters and their emotions, vary his style for comic effect, and aim squarely at broad amusement. Horace accused him of 'selling out': 'He's keen to pocket the cash; after that, who worries whether the play is a steady success or a hopeless flop?'[3] 'Bums on seats' was everything to him: if his plays flopped, he starved.

Plautus' audience particularly liked certain Greek stock characters, and these had their roles greatly extended, especially the *servus callidus* (ingenious trickster slave), who perpetrates bewilderingly elaborate intrigues, boasts extravagantly about how clever he is, and frequently orders about his despondent master. He delivers lots of *cantica*, uses lurid insults and Greek slang, and can become the dominant figure in the play. Other roles were also embellished, especially those of the *leno* (pimp), *parasitus* (parasite) and *meretrix* (prostitute), and there was still an obvious fondness for the 'running slave' (*servus currens*).

Conversely there were certain aspects of the Greek models that Romans found boring, particularly the clichéd happy endings and betrothals. Another modification that Plautus (perhaps) and Terence (certainly) made was the practice of interpolating material from a second Greek original into a play, a practice known as *contaminatio*.

The comedies are teeming with jokes, which often pander to the simpler tastes of Plautus' audience: there is a great deal of indecency, mostly sexual, which is often gratuitous and inappropriate to the characters who express it; Plautus deploys a rich colloquial vocabulary, as well as inventing new words; and there are many scenes in which characters insult or threaten one another to a ludicrously exaggerated degree. It is all about instant gratification, getting a laugh. As one scholar aptly said: 'Plautus made them laugh. And the laughter was Roman'.[4] This is entertainment for the *Roman* stage.

Plautus lived through Hannibal's invasion of Italy in an age of mercenary soldiers, so his early play *The Swaggering Soldier* (*Miles*

Gloriosus) is topical. There is a clue to the play's date when he alludes to a writer with his head supported on a stone block and two warders holding him down. This is Gnaeus Naevius, who famously attacked the powerful Roman family of the Metelli in one of his comedies, and was imprisoned between 206 and 204 BCE.

The play is an adaptation of the Greek *Alazon* (*The Braggart*) and is set in Ephesus in front of the adjacent houses of an aged bachelor called Periplectomenus ('Guardian') and Pyrgopolynices ('Tower-Many-Victories'), the stupid, conceited, lustful, boastful soldier of the play's title. Importantly, though, Pyrgopolynices doesn't know that Periplectomenus is a bachelor. The drama begins with the soldier bragging about his success on the battlefield and in the bedroom, while his oleaginous parasite Artotrogus eggs him on:

PY: I wonder if you remember . . . [*He seems to be vaguely calculating.*]
AR: How many? Yes, a hundred and fifty in Cilicia, a hundred in Scytholatronia, Sardians thirty, Macedonians sixty – killed, that is – in one day alone.
PY: How many does that make altogether?
AR: Seven thousand.
PY: Must be at least that. You're an excellent accountant . . .
AR: The women are all at your feet, and no wonder; they can't resist your good looks . . .
PY: It really is a bore to be so good-looking.[5]

Once we have been introduced to the soldier, his cunning slave (*servus callidus*) Palaestrio ('Wrestler') comes on and addresses the audience in the manner of a prologue speaker. Before the play began, he had been the slave of a man called Pleusicles in Athens, from where the soldier had abducted Philocomasium ('Party Girl'), Pleusicles' courtesan sweetheart, and shipped her back to Ephesus. Palaestrio had given chase, but had been captured by pirates, and then sold on to Pyrgopolynices. However, he had got word back to his master, who has just arrived in Ephesus, where Periplectomenus has made his home available to him. The neighbour is also in on a scheme to enable the lovers to meet by means of a secret passage between the two houses. Palaestrio is going to play a trick on the dim-witted slave who has been detailed to guard the girl:

> *One* girl is going to pretend to be *two* girls,
> One from this house and one from that: same girl
> But pretending to be a different one – all right?[6]

At this point Periplectomenus comes out with bad news. Someone from the soldier's household, who was chasing a monkey, has seen Pleusicles and Philocomasium kissing in the house next door. After some elaborate cogitations Palaestrio dreams up a scheme to persuade this person that he has seen Philocomasium's identical twin sister (who, of course, does not exist), who has just arrived from Athens with a man who is in love with her. Philocomasium will masquerade as her twin, and use the secret passage.

It emerges that the soldier's slave Sceledrus ('Rascal') saw the lovers kissing. It is odd that Palaestrio has told us about his plan to deceive his fellow slave *before* he knows that it is he that saw Philocomasium, but anomalies like this do not seem to have worried the audience too much as long as they were kept entertained. The spectators are also in on the secret, as Palaestrio accuses Sceledrus of lying and brings Philocomasium out of the soldier's house to prove it. When Sceledrus sticks to his story, Philocomasium introduces the twin sister idea, and in the next scene we see the 'twin' in the house next door. When Palaestrio addresses her by name she tells him that she is actually called Honoria, and that she has come to Ephesus to look for her twin. Sceledrus is still not convinced, but she evades him and scurries back into Periplectomenus' house. Palaestrio announces his intention of attacking the house, but when Sceledrus goes into the soldier's house to fetch a sword, he emerges having seen the 'real' Philocomasium lying on a bed. The neighbour Periplectomenus plays his part by storming out and threatening Sceledrus with severe punishment for assaulting his lady guest. Sceledrus *still* wants proof, though, which he receives thanks to the girl skipping through the secret passage once more to play the twin, and one final time when he goes back home and again sees Philocomasium herself. At last he accepts the trick.

As we enter Act III, the lovers' secret is safe, but they still need rescuing from the soldier. Simply using the secret passage as a means of escape would not be dramatically interesting, so Periplectomenus is made an important element in the second trick that Palaestrio then hatches, along with four other accomplices: Philocomasium;

Pleusicles, who will impersonate a ship's captain; Acroteleutium ('High End'), a courtesan who will become the fictitious wife of Periplectomenus, and pretend to be head-over-heels in love with the soldier; and her maid Milphidippa.

A light-hearted scene that is sometimes regarded as an example of *contaminatio* shows us a drunken slave of the soldier's called Lurcio, who tells us that Sceledrus is also inebriated and asleep. This allows Philocomasium access to the secret passage. Periplectomenus then comes out with Acroteleutium and Milphidippa, and Palaestrio goes over the details of the trick once more, even though he has already done this – not really because the characters are slow on the uptake, but because the audience are.

At the start of Act IV Palaestrio gives his master Pyrgopolynices a ring as a love token, explaining that a young, gorgeous admirer wants to have an affair with him (and to escape her ageing husband, who just happens to be Periplectomenus). The vain and lecherous soldier is so aroused by this that he is prepared to offload Philocomasium, along with all the 'jewellery and stuff' that he has given her, and to grant Palaestrio his freedom and let him go with her. Knowingly overheard by Pyrgopolynices, Milphidippa delivers a soliloquy outlining her mistress' desires. The soldier is deflected from lusting after the maid, and then falls headlong into the trap: he agrees to the request for a 'date', and tells Philocomasium to clear out back to Athens with her sister. Acroteleutium now plays her part to perfection, which, being a prostitute, comes easily. Milphidippa acts as intermediary, and adds the detail that Acroteleutium has already divorced her husband in anticipation of taking up with Pyrgopolynices; since the house next door was part of her dowry, she has the perfect venue for the affair.

The two women exit, to be replaced by Pleusicles disguised as a one-eyed ship's captain who is ready to set sail with Philocomasium. There is a moment when the deception is almost discovered, but the crisis is avoided, and the two lovers depart for the harbour while Palaestrio says one last lingering farewell to his ex-master. The act ends with a slave inviting the soldier to meet his new mistress.

The final act is short. Pyrgopolynices has walked headlong into an ambush and is dragged out of the house, humiliated, beaten and threatened with torture until he promises to mend his ways.

The final indignity is inflicted by Sceledrus, who returns from the harbour with the news that Philocomasium is gone and that the 'sea-captain' was in fact her lover. Pyrgopolynices acknowledges that it is a 'fair cop', and that justice has been done, and asks the audience for their applause.

Terence: **The Brothers**

According to tradition, Terence (Publius Terentius Afer), was born in Carthage in 184 BCE (or 195 BCE), brought up as a slave in the house of the Roman Senator Terentius Lucanus, and suffered a fatal accident in Greece or Asia Minor in around 159 BCE. A good-looking and talented man, Terence moved in very different social circles to Plautus, and is said to have established friendships with C. Laelius Sapiens and Scipio Africanus the Younger, who were both part of the philhellene 'Scipionic Circle'. *The Brothers* was first performed at the funeral games of L. Aemilius Paullus, the father of Scipio Africanus the Younger, in 160 BCE. This association with Rome's intellectual elite led to accusations that it was them, not Terence, who wrote the plays, but this seems unlikely.

Terence went in for much less broad comedy and buffoonery than Plautus, and adopted quite a serious and intellectually demanding approach, challenging the spectator to reflect on problems of behaviour and personal relationships. Most of his plays flopped.

Getting a mauling by the critics led to Terence dispensing with conventional prologues and replacing them with extra-dramatic, scholarly self-justifications. At the start of *The Brothers* he rejects the accusation of plagiarism, tries to fudge the issue of whether or not his eminent friends collaborate with him, and admits to inter-polating part of a second Greek play, the *Synapothneskontes* (*Joined in Death*) by Diphilus, to construct his own, which is based on an original by Menander (also called *The Brothers*). His removal of the divine prologues may be motivated by considerations of realism, a desire to keep the spectators in suspense, or simply to prevent them getting bored (a lengthy extra-dramatic prologue followed by a divine one would be boring): so he starts his plays proper with a dramatic dialogue or a monologue, and explains the plot's antecedents in the early scenes.

The Brothers is set in Athens and deals with the issue of how best to educate young men, and also with the 'Generation Gap'. Demea, who is of the 'harsh old man' (*senex durus*) and 'angry old man' (*senex iratus*) type, has two sons, Ctesipho and Aeschinus, who, in keeping with their 'young man' (*adulescens*) type, are both in love: Ctesipho with Bacchis ('Party Girl'), a music girl belonging to a pimp (*leno*); Aeschinus, who has been adopted by Demea's brother Micio, with a more respectable girl called Pamphila. Micio has raised Aeschinus with considerable tolerance, whereas Demea has been quite tough on Ctesipho. The older brothers are both concerned by the challenges of raising their boys: Terence presents them as both partly right, but each mistaken in the value of his method.

Micio enters the stage to express his anxiety that Aeschinus has still not come home from a party. He is a laid-back, unmarried urban-dweller who enjoys his leisure and fosters a liberal relationship with his adopted son. As a *senex lenis* (lenient old man), he advocates the use of affection and free will to train Aeschinus to choose the right course of action of his own accord: *pudor* (a sense of decency) and *liberalitas* (conduct worthy of a free man) permeate Micio's attitude to life. His dissimilarities with his brother become apparent when Demea joins him on stage. The latter is a married country dweller who saves his money, and he is livid to find out that Aeschinus has broken into a house and abducted a girl. Micio, who believes that 'boys will be boys', tells Demea to concentrate on bringing up his own son, who, incidentally, Demea thinks is a model of virtuous sobriety. Yet, once Demea exits, Micio confides that he is more concerned about Aeschinus than he is willing to admit publicly: Aeschinus has recently said that he will settle down and get married, so the abduction of a disreputable music girl is obviously worrying.

Aeschinus then enters with his 'thug slave' Parmeno and the abducted girl, hotly pursued by her hard-headed capitalist pimp Sannio. This is the scene introduced from Diphilus' *Joined in Death*, and the audience will doubtless have enjoyed watching the girl being safely delivered into Micio's residence and seeing Sannio getting a battering from Parmeno, even though Parmeno's role is ludicrously small (he speaks only two words in the Latin). Aeschinus tells the pimp that he will pay him the (relatively cheap) cost price of the girl, and Sannio has little choice other than to accept. (The downside of removing the divine prologue is that the audience will not realize until the next scene that Demea has got the wrong end of the stick: Aeschinus has abducted the girl for Ctesipho, not for himself.)

Aeschinus' *servus callidus* Syrus tries to persuade Sannio to accept the money for the girl, but the negotiations are interrupted by the arrival of Ctesipho, in fits of delight about his girlfriend and the help that his brother has given him. As it emerges that Ctesipho and Aeschinus are brothers, we have to adjust our opinion of them: Aeschinus is not doing the round of the whores, and Micio's education seems to be bearing fruit; Ctesipho lacks self-confidence but is not exactly a paragon of virtue, and Demea's system is not working as it should. So the situation has now developed into a 'dual plot', weaving together similar problems and complications involving two young men, two girls, two fathers and two educational systems.

Our opinion of Aeschinus changes immediately however, when a conversation between Pamphila's mother Sostrata and the nurse Canthara reveals that Pamphila is pregnant; Aeschinus is the father; and the birth is imminent. Aeschinus has raped Pamphila (not seduced her – if she had been a consenting partner, it would have damaged her reputation too severely), although the women still think pretty highly of him, and he obviously loves her. He just hasn't been able to tell Micio about it. This is understandable: Micio's consent to a marriage was essential because there was no way in Athenian society that a young man with no money could support a family; bringing a new member into Micio's household, and then offspring who might have claims on the estate, was an issue of great relevance to him. The new wife would need a reasonable dowry to contribute to these obligations; but Pamphila is poor and doesn't have a dowry.

From Pamphila and Sostrata's point of view (there is no father on the scene) the situation is also potentially very bleak. Taking the matter to court was practically impossible, since a woman could only conduct the case through her *kyrios* and, even if she won, the girl's future marriage prospects would probably be wrecked. It was better for them to get Aeschinus to apologize, promise to marry Pamphila and try to win over his father. Unfortunately, their predicament is intensified with the arrival of Sostrata's slave Geta, who performs a 'running slave' routine before announcing that Aeschinus has abducted the music girl and thus abandoned Pamphila. Rather than hush up the whole thing, Sostrata sends Geta to tell her relative Hegio about it, while Canthara goes off in search of the midwife.

Demea now returns, having found out that Ctesipho was involved in the abduction. He runs into Syrus, who exploits Demea's implicit faith in Ctesipho's virtue to fool the old man by telling him that Ctesipho has given Aeschinus a good telling off and is now back at the farm. Demea is just on the point of heading off there, when Hegio and Geta show up. Hegio is shocked by Aeschinus' behaviour, says he will stand by Sostrata, and proceeds to tell Demea about the rape and desertion of Pamphila. As Pamphila's birth-pangs are heard offstage, Hegio insists that Demea's family do the decent thing. Demea stomps to find his brother, followed by Hegio on the same mission.

Act IV kicks off with Ctesipho coming out of Micio's house with Syrus. He is anxious that his father might soon come looking for him, and makes a sharp exit when Demea does precisely that. Syrus, though, manipulates Demea's paternal pride by pretending that Ctesipho has given him a beating for being implicated in the abduction, and then sends Demea off on a wild-goose chase to the outskirts of Athens, where he says he can find Micio. Syrus then goes inside to enjoy some food and wine.

Syrus' place on stage is taken by Micio and Hegio, who are by now in possession of the full facts. Micio's response to Pamphila's pregnancy is honourable and he promises Hegio that he will do the right thing. They exit to Sostrata's house to make assurances to her, whereupon Aeschinus emerges in a state of utter distraction. He has found out that people think he has deserted Pamphila for the music girl, but he still can't bring himself to explain – because he wants to protect his brother. Finally he plucks up the courage to knock on Sostrata's door and set the record straight.

To Aeschinus' consternation, Micio answers the door. The old man enjoys teasing Aeschinus, although his aside, 'He's blushing; all's well'[7] shows his confidence in the boy's fundamentally upright character. He spins a story about Pamphila having to be married off to her nearest male relative, who will take her away to Miletus.

This is precisely the type of scenario that would apply under Athenian law, and the prospect reduces the boy to tears, but at this point Micio reveals that he knows the truth, and proceeds to give Aeschinus a dressing down for raping the girl, not telling anyone about it, and dithering for nine months. But then he lets him off, and tells him that he can marry her. Aeschinus has the humility to acknowledge the error of his ways. He gushes with praise, love and respect for his adoptive father.

Demea now returns from his fruitless search for Micio, and encounters him coming out of Sostrata's house. Always the last to learn what is going on, he is full of outrage about the 'new' information concerning Aeschinus' depravity. Micio puts him straight, explains about the impending marriage, and adds that the music girl (who Demea still thinks is Aeschinus' mistress) will stay in the house as well. Uttering all manner of expletives, Demea rails against the morality of the situation and its financial ramifications.

Syrus then reappears in a state of total inebriation, much to Demea's disgust, but when a slave calls out to him that Ctesipho wants to speak with him, Demea storms into Micio's house, where he finally learns the truth. The two elder brothers now end up face to face: Demea complains that Micio has broken their agreement by involving himself with Ctesipho; Micio says that, financially at least, no damage has been done and that he is prepared to cover the costs; Demea raises the issue of morality, to which Micio responds by asserting that the boys are fundamentally good and will turn out all right in the end; Demea finally agrees to come to the wedding, but is determined to remove his son to his farm the next morning and set the music girl to work there.

We have witnessed the reactions of Demea to successive reports about the behaviour, both good and bad, of his sons, but now he decides to take control. Like Knemon in Menander's *Old Cantankerous,* he learns from experience and modifies his attitude. When Syrus, Geta and Aeschinus appear he is uncharacteristically nice to them all, initiating acts of 'generosity' that are funded entirely by Micio. Demea persuades Micio to continue the unification of the households by marrying Sostrata, and then further exploits Micio's liberality by asking him to give Hegio the use of a piece of family property just outside the town, and adeptly turning his earlier platitude – 'the besetting fault of us all is that in old age we think too much of money' – against him when he objects. Finally Demea arranges for the manumission of Syrus, along with a financial loan.

Demea's role-play is designed to show that blind indulgence can be counter-productive, and it shows that Micio's popularity was due to excessive leniency. The characterization of the two elderly brothers is probably influenced by Aristotle's concept of the 'mean of liberality', which lies between the extremes of 'stingy rigour' and 'undiscerning prodigality',[8] and their presentation basically follows Theophrastus' stereotypes of the liberal and the stingy man.[9] Demea concludes by proposing a compromise that involves a moderate amount of restraint and advice, and this proves attractive to Aeschinus, who then asks what is going to happen to Ctesipho. Demea says that he has given his consent for him to keep his girl, on condition that she is his last, and on that positive note the play ends.

Later Influence

Plautus' Pyrgopolynices is perhaps the finest braggart warrior in Roman comedy, and his influence extended into the Renaissance: in the sixteenth century Lodovico Dolce based *Il Capitano* on *The Swaggering Soldier*; in France, Baïf used the play as the basis for *Le Brave*, as did Mareschal for *Le Capitan Fanfaron*; in England Nicholas Udall's play *Ralph Roister Doister*, the first real English comedy, was derived from *The Swaggering Soldier* (with additional material from Terence's *Eunuch*); and some think that Falstaff in Shakespeare's *The Merry Wives of Windsor* is ultimately derived from Pyrgopolynices. As far as Terence is concerned, Julius Caesar allegedly said he was a 'sort of watered down Menander'. Certainly, Terence is not an original dramatist by modern standards, but he is more than just a transmitter of Greek New Comedy to Republican Rome. The fact that Terence is seldom as funny as Plautus raises the fundamental question: 'does comedy have to be funny?' The answer, as Sam Goldwyn acknowledged after the making of *The Goldwyn Follies* in 1937 ('Our comedies are not to be laughed at'[10]), is 'no'. This is because 'comedy' meant something totally different to the Greeks and Romans than it does to us. They recognized three types of literary drama: tragedy, comedy and farce. Farce was intended solely to make the audience laugh, but comedy did more: it explored interpersonal relationships, analysed human nature and generally ended happily. But, just as tragedy did not have to be 'tragic', comedy did not have to be funny.

13

ROMAN HISTORY: FROM THE REPUBLIC TO THE PRINCIPATE

> Rome sits upon the nations with her all-powerful insatiable arms
> spread wide . . . She receives all the gods; she has opened the roads,
> freed the sea of pirates and the land of bandits, brought peace and
> order to the world. Above her is no one, not even God. Under her
> – everyone. Gods and men: all are citizens and slaves of Rome . . .
> What splendour, what immovable joy to be omnipotent and
> immortal, thinks Rome; and a wide fat smile flows over her fleshy
> rouged face.
>
> Nikos Kazantzakis, *The Last Temptation*, Ch. XXII[1]

The history of the Romans extends over more than 1,000 years and
is conventionally divided into three major phases. In legend
Romulus founded Rome in 753 BCE, and Rome was ruled by seven
kings until 510 BCE, when King Tarquinius Superbus was expelled.
Kingship became anathema to the Romans, who grew highly
sensitive to the difference between a *Regnum* ('Kingdom') and a
Res Publica ('Republic', literally 'the public thing'). During the
Roman Republic, which lasted from 509 to 27 BCE, the government
was (supposedly) controlled by magistrates elected for set terms.
The Republican era was a time of Roman expansion, first in Italy,
and then in the Mediterranean, but from the late second century
BCE Rome imploded in a series of internal struggles that resulted in
one-man rule (albeit in the guise of Republicanism). The period
from 27 BCE, the date of the 'First Settlement' of Augustus, to 476
CE, the end of the Roman Empire in the west, is known as the

Empire or 'Principate'. The first Emperor Augustus ruled as *Princeps* (= 'First Among Equals'), so to avoid confusion between the Roman empire (lower case 'e'; geographical) and the Roman Empire (capital 'E'; government under one man after 27 BCE), academics often use the world 'Principate'.

SPQR

A second-century BCE Roman could look back and see that the Greeks had ultimately failed in their political survival, and would conclude that the superiority of Rome was due to its institutions, way of life, religion and dealings with rival states. Quite remarkably, there was no real *coup d'état* in Rome from the establishment of the Republic until the first century BCE and, although internal differences certainly existed, they were seldom pursued in extremist ways. Yet one fundamental social divide that did exist was that between the Patricians and the Plebeians. The Patricians were a hereditary aristocracy of large-scale landowners who could be distinguished by their names: Claudius and Julius are patrician family names; Clodius and Licinius are not. Patrician rank was normally inherited, and the non-patricians, who formed the vast majority of Rome's population, were known as Plebeians (Latin *plebs* = multitude). The Patrician families jealously guarded their power, established strict limitations on the social and political movements of the plebeians, and monopolized all legal, political and religious posts.

In the Republican period Rome was governed by a combination of elected magistrates who held office for one year; a Senate; and the Popular Assemblies. Every (male) citizen could vote in the election of officials and on legislation in these Assemblies, but had to do so in person in Rome, meaning that the Romans had a 'direct' democracy, rather than the 'representative' systems that most western democracies use today. This was fair enough while Rome was a small town, but by the late Republican period many Roman citizens didn't live anywhere near Rome, and so could not exercise this right.

The Senate, or Council of Elders (*senes* = 'old men'), consisted originally of Patricians as life members, and the insignia SPQR (*Senatus Populusque Romanus* = 'the Roman Senate and People) shows how the Senate came first. Traditionally these men performed unpaid public service as legal advisers, judges, magistrates, diplomats, military officers and priests, and technically the Senate was an advisory body. Its membership generally ranged between 300 and 600 men, who had to possess a minimum property qualification of 1 million *sestertii* in the time of Augustus – an astronomical amount, given that around 50 BCE, a rank and file soldier was paid 900 *sestertii* a year. Two Censors had the power to remove anyone guilty of misconduct, and certain moral transgressions disqualified a person from admission. Members of the senatorial class or order (Latin *ordo* = 'class'/'rank') wore a broad purple stripe (*latus clavus*) on their togas, had special shoes and occupied prominent seats on major religious and public occasions.

Romans believed so strongly in tradition that, over the years, the Senate's advice had come to have the force of law, and the senators felt that their wealth and status justified their right to control Rome. They were ambitious and individualistic, and had a strong sense of their own self worth (*dignitas*). These attitudes were further reinforced by the fact that the Romans' respect for authority based on tradition meant that they usually voted for candidates or measures that the Senate endorsed. So the Senate's control over domestic and foreign affairs was seldom questioned: Rome was a Republic in name, but in fact was ruled by groups of families who occupied the political posts at Rome for generation after generation.

There were three Popular Assemblies at Rome. The Comitia Centuriata, which met in the Campus Martius, was arranged into 193 centuries ('constituencies') organized so that the richer ones dominated. It could pass *leges* (laws), and it elected magistrates with *imperium*. These magistrates (the Consuls, Praetors) had the authority to command in war, to interpret the law and carry it out, and were accompanied by *lictors*, who carried the *fasces*, bundles of rods enclosing an axe, symbolizing the right to inflict corporal and capital punishment. The Comitia Tributa, which met in the Forum, was based on Rome's thirty-five tribes, acted as a law-making body and elected magistrates known as *Curule Aediles* (magistrates) and *Quaestors*. The Concilium Plebis (Assembly of the Plebs), made up only of plebs, met in the Forum, could pass *plebiscita* binding on the whole community, and elected 'Tribunes' of the Plebs and Plebeian *Aediles*.

From the establishment of the Republic, Rome's top political post was the Consulship. The two consuls held almost kingly powers, but these were restricted by the duality of the post, a mutual veto (Latin *veto* = 'I forbid') and a one-year term of office. The Consuls organized the community religion, possessed great judicial powers, and led the army. The usual term for any magistracy was one year, but, because a war might go on for longer than that, the system of *prorogatio* was adopted in 326 BCE, whereby a Consul's military powers could be retained after his civic ones lapsed. He was then said to act *pro consule* (= 'on behalf of the Consul') and later the 'Proconsuls' became provincial governors.

Over time many plebeians came to acquire considerable wealth and with it a desire to have a voice in the leadership of the State; concurrently poorer plebeians wanted to redress their legal and economic disabilities. On two occasions the plebs resorted to *secessio* – separating themselves *en masse* and threatening to found a new city – to create a situation in which they could articulate their demands by forming a state within a state. Ten Tribunes of the Plebs, who came to be elected every year, were supposed to operate as the people's representatives in the Senate, but with their crucial powers of veto, personal inviolability and the right to propose legislation, they represented a way in which the Senate could be thwarted or bypassed.

By the fourth century BCE Plebeians were allowed to become consuls, and had received a written code of laws (the Twelve Tables), and by 287 BCE they had, in theory at least, obtained parity with the Patricians. Furthermore, as Rome acquired more wealth as a result of successful overseas wars in the third and second centuries BCE, opening up greater commercial opportunities, many wealthy Plebeians began to have the same interests as the Patricians. New political families came into being, and new terms were invented, such as *nobiles*, not now 'Patricians', but those men whose families had achieved the consulship: the senatorial class regarded the consulship as their own; over a period of 300 years only 15 non-nobles became consuls.

It was still possible to break into the political scene in Rome, and there was a term for anyone who did: *novus homo* (new man). Such a person tended to be 'Equestrian'. The *Equites* (Latin *eques*, plural *equites*, = 'horsemen'/'knights') belonged to the same social level as the senators, except that they normally chose not to pursue careers in politics. The key qualification for admission to the order (after 100 BCE) was a minimum property qualification of 400,000 *sestertii*. Their privileges included the allotment of special seats in the theatre, the right to wear a gold ring, and a narrow purple stripe on their togas. The *Equites* were not a middle class (Rome did not really have one in the modern sense): what distinguished them from the Senators was participation in politics; the difference between them and the Plebs was a financial gulf so enormous that upward social mobility was extremely difficult. The standard of living of the majority of the Roman population was far lower than that of the modern British, European or American middle or working classes, and the notion of 'poverty' in Rome needs careful definition: even the 'poor' still had to have a reasonably secure means of support, be this a trade, craft or some kind of connection with a wealthy family; if by 'the poor' we mean 'the destitute', there were hardly any – if you were destitute, you died.

Because the wealth of many eminent Romans was tied up in land, they borrowed heavily from Equestrian financiers to bankroll both their election campaigns and their duties as magistrates. There was a regularized progression of offices in Rome, known as the *Cursus Honorum*: after a spell of military and/or legal service, you would hope to be elected as *Quaestor*, with *potestas* (the power conferred on a magistrate to enforce the law by the authority of his office, which all the magistrates had), and financial and administrative duties. After this you might take an optional spell as *Tribune* – when you had the right of *veto*, could summon the Concilium Plebis and put resolutions (*plebiscita*) to it, and enjoyed sacrosanctity – and/or as *Aedile*, when you were expected personally to finance religious festivals, the upkeep of the streets, the water supply and so on, or to arrange public games and festivals. Either way, you would hope that your burgeoning fame and popularity might win you the office of Praetor. Since this conferred *imperium*, it took your power to a whole new level, and as Praetor you would then take up a provincial governorship for one year. 'Provinces' were what the Romans called their dependant territories (*provinciae* = 'spheres of duty assigned to a magistrate'), and now you could start to recoup your money: a 'good' province could be very lucrative even for an honest man; an unscrupulous man could make an absolute fortune. The Holy Grail was finally to secure one of the two Consulships. You would become Commander-in-Chief of the army, preside over the Senate, conduct the main elections and implement the Senate's decisions, before moving on to a better provincial governorship as Proconsul.

By the mid-third century Rome was effectively the ruler of the Italian peninsula, whose inhabitants fell into three main categories: Roman citizens; Latin allies; and other allied states. However, these allies began to resent their obligation to serve in the army when they didn't need to defend themselves, and didn't have any access to the corridors of power. Overseas, Rome's expansion accelerated dramatically: the First Punic War with Carthage (up to 241 BCE) brought them Sicily, Sardinia and Corsica; the Second Punic War (up to 200 BCE) gave them Spain; conquests in Greece (up to 146 BCE) and the final destruction of Carthage (also 146 BCE) brought the provinces of Macedonia and Africa.

This rapid expansion began to expose cracks in Rome's constitutional fabric. Long-term military commitments were dealt with by *prorogatio*, but this created the potential for a *coup d'état* if a provincial governor could build up a personal following amongst his troops, although the Senate tried to counteract the danger by forbidding any man to hold the Consulship more than once. But *prorogatio* also allowed pro-magistrates the time to squeeze a great deal of money out of the hapless provincials, and since the jury courts against corruption were comprised of Senators – men who had already done, or wanted to do, the same type of thing – corrupt governors were seldom convicted.

The foreign conquests brought a huge influx of slaves and wealth. Both Senators and *Equites* invested their capital in land, which could now be worked by cheap slave labour in preference to the more costly free peasant farmers. To buy out or even evict these people was easy, especially if they were away on military service, and the rich also began to acquire areas of public land (*ager publicus*), resulting in the creation of *latifundia*, vast estates worked by slave-gangs. The peasants could not compete, and many gravitated towards Rome to look for work, giving rise to what is rather disparagingly dubbed the 'urban mob'. They also fell out of the property class that obliged them to serve in the Roman army, leading to the growing recruitment of Italian allies.

Domestic Turmoil and Foreign Threats

One of the first Roman politicians to contemplate addressing the abuse of *ager publicus* was Gaius Laelius in 145 BCE, but he dropped the scheme in the face of the Senate's opposition, and was given the nickname *Sapiens* ('the Wise') as a result. The Senate made no attempt to confront Rome's growing problems, mainly because any faction that proposed measures benefitting the lower classes, army or provinces stood to gain politically, which meant that the default position of its rivals was to oppose them. Reformers were on a hiding to nothing. Still, in 133 BCE Tiberius Sempronius Gracchus, who had witnessed the bad service conditions of the Roman army at first hand, as well as the desolation caused by huge estates worked by slaves, came to the conclusion that if he could reverse the decline of the small farmer this would in turn solve the 'urban mob' situation and the military difficulties at the same time.

As Tribune of the Plebs in 133 BCE his solution was the *lex agrarian*, which proposed to cap the amount of public land that anyone could hold, redistribute the rest in small, inalienable allotments to the poor at low rent, and compensate the displaced 'occupiers'. The ancient sources are quite cynical about his motives, to the point of suggesting that he was seeking to become a tyrant, and he certainly ran into opposition that was motivated by greed, personal dislike and factional prejudice, as well as genuine reservations from landowners who had invested heavily in the land over a very long period.

In the midst of this controversy, Gracchus bypassed the senate and took his measure directly to the Concilium Plebis. A Tribune could do this, but it was against the spirit of the constitution, and the Senate got the proposal vetoed by another tribune, M. Octavius. Gracchus retorted with the unheard-of step of getting the Concilium Plebis to depose him, and the *lex agraria* was passed. When the Senate withheld the finances to implement it, Gracchus proposed that the unexpected bequest of his kingdom to Rome by Attalus III of Pergamum should be used to fund the project. The Senate were alarmed at the deposition of Octavius, resentful of Gracchus' interference in finance and foreign affairs, and scared of the 'urban mob', and when Gracchus stood for a second term, the Senate, who probably feared his methods more than his legislation, deployed an armed gang under P. Scipio Nasica on the eve of the elections. Tiberius Gracchus and 300 of his supporters died in the massacre.

The violence was shocking, but over the next decade the focus shifted to the treatment of Rome's Latin and Italians allies: Scipio Aemilianus emerged as their champion, but was found dead in his bed; when they started to agitate at Rome, M. Iunius Pennus proposed that all non-citizens should be expelled; and, when M. Fulvius Flaccus proposed granting full citizenship to every town in Italy, he was opposed by the nobles, because the new voters might not be dependent on them, and by the 'mob', because more mouths meant less cheap corn. His proposal was never put to the vote.

In 123 BCE Tiberius Gracchus' younger brother Gaius was elected Tribune. Motivated by a desire to avenge his brother, push on with the agrarian settlements, relieve the suffering of urban poor, curtail the power of ruling nobility, build up his own power base, (or any or none of the above) he aimed at getting citizenship for the Italian allies. Anticipating opposition, he put forward a number of measures aimed at winning support from the masses and the *Equites*. These included transferring the jury courts from Senatorial to Equestrian control (which gave the *Equites* political recognition for the first time, but failed to solve the corruption problem because the *Equites* had vested interests of their own) and a Corn Law subsidizing the price of corn for some Roman citizens by 50 per cent. So far so good, but when Gaius was elected to a second tribunate for 122 BCE and proposed full citizenship for the Latin allies, and Latin rights – basically a halfway stage to full citizenship – for the others, his support evaporated almost overnight: the Senate feared losing control over the Assemblies; the *Equites* feared commercial rivalry; and the Plebs didn't want to share the benefits of citizenship. When the Senate cynically introduced their own tame Tribune, M. Livius Drusus, to outbid Gaius with even more demagogic proposals, the fickle urban voters supported him instead. The Consul Fannius got the Senate to pass the *Senatus Consultum Ultimum* (*SCU* = 'Final Decree of the Senate'), under the authority of which Gracchus and Flaccus were killed, and 3,000 Gracchan supporters were later condemned and executed.

Actively siding with the underprivileged against the ruling oligarchy had become a very dangerous thing to do, but the political struggles within the ruling class itself also became more aggressive.

A new word came into use – *factio* (= 'a faction', with the same slightly pejorative sense as in English), and Rome's two factions were dubbed the *Optimates* and the *Populares*. Cicero explained the situation:

> Those who wanted everything they did and said to be pleasing to the masses were considered *Populares*; but those who conducted themselves so as to win for their policies the approval of all the best citizens were considered *Optimates* . . . All are *Optimates* who are neither malevolent, nor shameless in behaviour, nor insane, nor embarrassed by family problems.[2]

In fact, the *Optimates* were a powerful, determined, cohesive, ruthless and more or less permanent group who made up the majority in the Senate and defended the established traditions of political life because it was in their interests to do so. The *Populares* were also Senators, but they felt that they could achieve quicker results by whipping up popular feeling and sidestepping the Senate in order to gain personal advancement. They were not instinctive 'democrats', and although some *Populares* were undoubtedly genuine, many were merely demagogues. Political idealism was minimal in Rome.

In 113 BCE Rome suffered a disastrous military defeat to the north of Italy at the hands of the Germanic tribes the Cimbri and the Teutones. To deal with this, the Romans eventually turned to Gaius Marius, a *novus homo* who had worked his way up the *cursus Honorum* and forged his reputation in the Jugurthine War. Jugurtha was a talented, vigorous, warlike, unscrupulous prince of Numidia in North Africa. Aided by a liberal dose of bribery to keep the Roman government at bay, Jugurtha had killed his dynastic rivals and perpetrated a massacre of Italian merchants in Africa. The Roman response had only led to murders, military defeats and corruption scandals: in Jugurtha's famous judgement, Rome 'is a city put up for sale, and its days are numbered if it finds a buyer'.[3]

Marius, whose ambitions to stand for the consulship were being obstructed by his commander Q. Caecilius Metellus Numidicus, played on the increasing dissatisfaction to win over the soldiers, the *Equites* and the Plebs, and secured the consulship of 107 BCE on the promise to bring back Jugurtha dead or alive. The command of the war was transferred to him by special decree. In recruiting troops for the campaign, Marius waived the property qualification rules and enrolled many poor/unemployed men. He trained them up to legionary level, giving himself a loyal, professional army who looked to him, not the Senate, for maintenance, and in 106 BCE his Quaestor L. Cornelius Sulla secured the betrayal of Jugurtha, who was displayed in Marius' triumph before being executed in the Capitoline prison.

While Marius was occupied in North Africa, the Cimbri and the Teutones had inflicted humiliating defeats on Roman consular armies, including a massacre at Arausio that was the worst defeat since Hannibal's victory at Cannae more than a century before. So Marius was voted Consul for the second time *in absentia*, both aspects of which were illegal. He now reorganized the Roman army into the finest fighting machine of its day. Recruitment was voluntary; soldiering became a profession; discipline got stricter; promotion was won by merit, not by social background; the equipment and comfort of the soldiers became paramount; the outdated chequerboard system of *hastati, principes* and *triarii* was abolished; the Legion was established at 6,000 men in 10 cohorts of 600, each comprising 6 centuries; all ranks were now issued with entrenching tools, the *pilum* (a heavy, short-range throwing-spear) and a *gladius* (a short thrusting sword), and were trained in gladiator-style duelling; Rome's allies supplied the cavalry; and the eagle became the legionary standard.

This 'new model army' annihilated the Teutones (102 BCE) and the Cimbri (101 BCE), and Marius then granted citizenship to many non-Roman soldiers for achievements on the battlefield, even to those who held no property qualification. Landless men with nothing to lose now flocked to him, looked to him to guarantee their payment and equipment, and gave him the power to defy his colleagues, the Senate and the Comitia. He was elected to five consecutive (illegal) consulships from 104 to 100 BCE.

When Marius returned to Rome, hoping to fulfil a prophecy by becoming Consul seven times, the two main *Popularis* leaders were L. Appuleius Saturninus and C. Servilius Glaucia, both given to mob-violence and murder. Marius disbanded his army, and Saturninus then brought forward several measures on Marius' behalf, including allotments for his veterans in Gaul – the first time that allotments on a large scale had been given to discharged soldiers. Saturninus added a clause that every Senator should swear to obey his laws, and, typical of the spineless Senate, only one of them refused. However, when Glaucia's rival for the consulship of 99 BCE was openly murdered on the morning of the election, Marius had had enough. The Senate passed the *SCU* and called on Marius to 'safeguard the might and majesty of the Roman People'.[4] He forced the rioters to surrender, but, as the Senate debated their fate, a mob broke into the Senate house and pelted the prisoners to death with the roof tiles. The Senate was back in control, Marius lost his standing, Saturninus' legislation was declared invalid, and Marius went off to the East, hoping to provoke Mithridates VI of Pontus into a war.

Although these horrors caused everyone to take a step back, there was continuing unrest among the Italian allies at their failure to achieve the franchise, and there were grievances about the abuse of power by the Equestrian courts: whereas the Senate used to acquit guilty governors, the *Equites* condemned innocent ones. M. Livius Drusus (Tribune, 91 BCE) felt confident that the newly enfranchized voters would actually strengthen the Senate's control: in practice few Italians would use their vote because of the distances involved in getting to Rome; those who did would be those who could *afford* to; so they would share the interests of the *Optimates*. But the Senate were not convinced. In an attempt to please all of the people all of the time, Drusus proposed that membership of the Senate should be doubled by the inclusion of 300 *Equites*; the control of the courts should pass to this new body; the *Populares* should have fresh corn doles; and citizenship should be thrown open to all the Italian allies. Although the proposals were carried, they were then declared null and void on a legal technicality. Doubt set in, vested interests re-emerged and Drusus was assassinated.

The death of Drusus triggered the Italian War ('Social' War). About two-thirds of Italy rebelled from Rome, and even established a new capital, Italica. They minted coinage depicting the Roman wolf being gored by the Italian bull, and had the better of the early exchanges. It was a very bloody conflict – possibly 300,000 dead – but the Romans crushed the revolt. However, Rome also conceded what the allies wanted: the *lex Julia* (90 BCE), *lex Plautia Papiria* and *lex Calpurnia* (both 89 BCE) secured the franchise for the

Italians. L. Cornelius Sulla (Consul, 88 BCE) distinguishing himself in the south. The Senate also earmarked him to take command of the war against Mithridates of Pontus.

The Italians had achieved the franchise, but, in order to restrict their voting powers, they had been distributed in just eight out of the thirty-five tribes, and voted last. So a new *Popularis* leader, P. Sulpicius Rufus (Tribune, 88 BCE), proposed that they be registered in all thirty-five tribes, that the Mithridatic command be transferred to Marius, still yearning for his seventh consulship, and that all Senators owing more than 2,000 *denarii* should be expelled (to make them pay their debts to the *Equites*). Violence followed, but Sulpicius' proposals were passed. Taking a course that was to have momentous ramifications, Sulla gathered his six legions and marched on Rome. This was the first time a Roman, with a Roman army, had entered Rome under arms. Sulpicius was killed, his laws were repealed and Marius narrowly escaped to Africa.

Sulla then left Italy to confront Mithridates in the spring of 87 BCE, but no sooner was he gone than his colleague L. Cornelius Cinna revived Sulpicius' thirty-five tribes proposal. When he has was driven out and declared a *hostis* (= 'public enemy'), Cinna simply gathered an army of ex-rebels, Marius' son, Old Marius himself, assorted African exiles, slaves and brigands, and marched on Rome. He promised no bloodshed; what happened was five days of murder and looting by Marius' thugs. The violence finally ceased when Marius and Cinna were proclaimed consuls, giving Marius his coveted seventh consulship (although he died within a fortnight). Sulla became the *hostis* and his laws were repealed; the registration of the citizens in the thirty-five tribes was finally settled; and for three years (86–84 BCE) Cinna was virtual dictator with Cn. Gnaeus Carbo as his colleague.

The man Sulla had gone to confront was Mithridates VI Eupator, King of Pontus on the southern coast of the Black Sea. He had secured his throne in 120 BCE by imprisoning his mother, killing his younger brother and marrying his sister. He had a reputation for courage and athletic prowess, was a gargantuan eater and drinker, spoke several languages fluently, admired Greek culture and posed as a champion of the Greeks against the 'barbarian' Romans with some degree of success. Yet his Philhellenism was counterbalanced by the fact that he was also a suspicious, cruel and murderous monarch at heart. A series of conquests brought him into conflict with rulers who, like him, were 'allies and friends of Rome', but he treated the Roman senatorial envoys with disrespect.

When Rome was preoccupied with the Italian War, Mithridates had started to encroach on neighbouring territories, precipitating the First Mithridatic War (88–84 BCE). He swept through the Roman province of Asia, promising freedom to the Greek cities and cancellation of debts, and perpetrated the 'Asiatic Vespers', a massacre of the Roman and Italian residents that some sources say accounted for 80,000 lives in one single day. His forces then pressed on into Europe. Athens and most of the islands of the Aegean went over to him – compelling proof of the ill-feeling towards Roman rule in the region at the time.

Such was the situation when Sulla landed in Epirus in 87 BCE with five legions. The following year he took Athens by storm, and defeated the scythed-chariot-equipped Pontic army at Khaironeia in Boiotia and on the plain of Orkhomenos. These victories allowed Sulla to move to the Hellespont in 85 BCE but at this point his opponents at Rome sent out L. Valerius Flaccus and C. Flavius Fimbria to deal with Mithridates. Sulla thought they also had secret orders to turn against him, but Fimbria organized a mutiny, killed Flaccus and defeated Mithridates' reserve army in Asia Minor. Sulla then besieged Fimbria at Pergamum and, when his army deserted him, Fimbria killed himself. Mithridates and Sulla finally met at Dardanus in the Troad. Although Mithridates relinquished his gains, he remained King of Pontus, whereas a crippling indemnity was imposed on the province of Asia, causing financial ruin primarily because the provincials were forced to borrow from ruthless Roman businessmen at extortionate rates of interest. This deal created enormous problems for the future, but Sulla was itching to get back to Rome and take vengeance on his enemies.

The Big Beasts: Sulla, Pompey, Crassus and Caesar

Cinna and Carbo had intended to confront Sulla in Greece, but their troops mutinied, and Cinna was murdered. Sulla landed at Brundisium with five battle-hardened legions and some deep-seated grudges. Among those who joined him were Cn. Pompeius ('Pompey', a twentysomething leading three legions), and M. Licinius Crassus. Sulla closed in on Rome, emerging victorious at the Battle of the Colline Gate on 1 November 82 BCE, took the nickname *Felix* ('Lucky') and sent Pompey to mop up the resistance in Sicily and Africa (where the young man's successes led him to demand a triumph, which Sulla reluctantly granted). Then Sulla 'devoted himself entirely to the work of butchery'.[5] This consisted of massacring 4,000 prisoners, murdering many of the Marian faction, either devastating the lands of towns that had opposed him or settling veterans on it, and issuing the notorious proscription lists. These named his opponents, or people who had assisted them, and offered prizes to assassins and rewards to informers. The victims' property was confiscated; their sons and grandsons were debarred from holding any public office; the confiscated land was auctioned off, resulting in a crash in property prices; and there were ultimately thousands of names on the lists as personal scores were settled.

Sulla had his position formalized under the title of *Dictator legis scribundis et rei publicae constituendae* (= 'Dictator for the Purpose of Writing Laws and Restoring the Republic'), and proceeded to put Rome's political clock back 200 years, under the misapprehension that he could solve all of Rome's problems by removing all threats to the Senate's dominance. He enlarged the Senate with 300 new members, predominantly from Equestrian families (who, of course, owed their position to him). Its future recruitment would be from ex-*Quaestors*, and the number of *Quaestors* was raised to twenty. The Censorship, which had held the right to elect or expel senators, fell into disuse. Prior Senatorial approval was now essential before any legislation could be presented to the people, and the Senate was to decide all provincial commands. Election to the tribunate permanently disqualified anyone from any other office, so that no ambitious member of the nobility would want to hold it. Tribunes also needed prior senatorial permission for bills, and their power of veto was restricted. Sulla also redrafted the *lex Villia Annalis* whereby the *cursus honorum* was to be strictly enforced. He imposed minimum age limits for each office: thirty for *Quaestors*, thirty-nine for *Praetors* and forty-two for *Consuls*; the magistracies had to be held in strict sequence; and no one could hold the same office twice within ten years. Sulla wanted to avoid political 'whizz kids'.

A *lex de maiestate* (treason law) was passed that forbade governors to leave their provinces, march beyond the frontiers or initiate hostilities without authorization from the Senate. Yet, while there was no provision for the State to reward veterans with pensions at the time of their discharge, ambitious men with the backing of loyal armies would continue to be a menace, and no amount of strengthening of the Senate would help them deal with this.

Rome now ruled ten provinces: Hispania Citerior, Hispania Ulterior, Gallia Narbonensis, Gallia Cisalpina, Macedonia, Asia, Cilicia, Africa, Sardinia and Sicily. Sulla raised the numbers of *Praetors* to eight, so that with the two ex-Consuls there were sufficient pro-magistrates for governors.

The most abiding of Sulla's reforms was the setting up of seven special jury courts (the *quaestiones perpetuae*), to cover major offences against society: murder and poisoning; forgery; extortion; treason; electoral bribery; embezzlement of public funds; and assault. One more – public violence – was added subsequently. These courts were, predictably enough, once again recruited solely from senators, thereby perpetuating the corruption issues.

Then, in 80 BCE, for reasons that remain enigmatic, Sulla resigned. Julius Caesar said he should never have done this, and accused him of political illiteracy,[6] but Sulla retired to Campania, where he died in 78 BCE. Plutarch gives a lurid account of his last days: feasting, drinking, parties with vulgar entertainers, marriage to a beautiful flirty new wife and death from 'ulcers in the intestines which resulted in the whole flesh being corrupted and turning into worms'.[7]

It would be 'the memory of Sulla's example and methods that proved most enduring',[8] and there were immediate challenges to his system. M. Aemilius Lepidus (Consul, 78 BCE) proposed the restoration of the tribunes' powers, giving back the confiscated lands and recalling the Marian exiles. When he failed he raised an army to march on Rome. He was defeated, but his supporters joined up with M. Perperna and went to join Q. Sertorius, a Marian *Popularis* who had established an alternative Roman government in Spain. Pompey was entrusted with the command against Sertorius, and although it took him six difficult years to emerge victorious, and he benefitted immeasurably from the fact that Perperna murdered Sertorius and usurped his leadership, another Pompeian triumph was on the cards.

While Pompey was in Spain, Italy was facing the slave revolt of the man that Karl Marx described as 'the most splendid fellow in the whole of ancient history'[9]: a Thracian gladiator called Spartacus.

He led a group of desperate men, highly trained in hand-to-hand combat, in a break-out from a gladiatorial school near Capua in 73 BCE, which subsequently attracted many runaway slaves from the *latifundia*. Their early successes against an inept Roman response led the rebels to go on a nationwide rampage. In 72 BCE, shame and fear prompted the Senate to send out both Consuls but, when Spartacus' slaves kept winning, M. Licinius Crassus, an ex-lieutenant of Sulla who had made vast fortunes during Sulla's proscriptions and was probably the richest man in Rome, was appointed to the supreme command.

When Crassus' subordinate Mummius disobeyed orders and was defeated, Crassus restored discipline by 'decimating' the survivors: he took 500 of the greatest cowards, divided them into 50 squads of 10 men each and put to death one man, chosen by lot, from each squad. Meanwhile, Spartacus marched south with the intention of invading Sicily with the help of some pirates from Cilicia, but the pirates took his money and promptly sailed off, leaving him and his army stranded in the toe of Italy. Crassus built a ditch some 65 km long from sea to sea, but Spartacus still managed to get a third of his army across it on a wintry night. However, when they defeated a pursuing force under two of Crassus' subordinates, the slaves became overconfident. They sought a direct confrontation with Crassus, which simply played into his hands. Skirmishing escalated into a full-scale battle; Spartacus killed his own horse, saying that the enemy had plenty of good horses that would be his if he won, then charged straight at Crassus. He never made it. His troops took flight, while he stood his ground and died fighting to the last. There was no 'I'm Spartacus!' moment; 6,000 of his surviving supporters were crucified on the Appian Way.

Crassus never got the official credit he deserved, since Pompey, returning from Spain, mopped up 5,000 fugitives who were escaping to the north. Technically, the man who concluded the war got the triumph, which Pompey celebrated magnificently. Nevertheless, despite the burgeoning animosity between them, he and Crassus agreed to stand for the consulship of 70 BCE. Pompey would be six years too young, had held no magistracies, and was not a senator, but he had been holding pro-consular power for the past seven years, so it was unreasonable to expect him to stand for anything else. The two men were duly elected.

The scandal of the day was the sensational prosecution of C. Verres by M. Tullius Cicero. Verres was an appallingly corrupt governor of Sicily, but the evidence against him was so compelling that in effect the whole Senate, who comprised the jury, were themselves on trial. In the end Verres went into exile before the verdict, and was condemned *in absentia*. The *Praetor* L. Aurelius Cotta then transferred the courts from exclusive senatorial control to that of the Senate, *Equites* and *tribuni aerarii*, a wealthy economic group slightly beneath, but with broadly the same interests as, the *Equites*. Under the Licinio/Pompeian laws, the tribunes were restored to full power, too. The censorship was also revived and sixty-four senators were immediately ejected. So by 70 BCE almost all Sulla's reforms had been repealed or undermined, primarily by Pompey. But Sulla's increase in *Quaestors* to twenty, with still only two Consuls every year, really intensified the race for the highest office. There were too many highly competitive losers.

A new individual was now starting to make his presence felt: Gaius Julius Caesar, who held the *Quaestorship* in 68 BCE. He adopted a consistently *Popularis* stance, partly because he lacked strong connections with the top families and had no great wealth: 'There are many Mariuses in this fellow Caesar,' Sulla had said.[10]

By the 60s BCE another problem had emerged: piracy. This was not a case of the odd swashbuckling, parrot-wearing buccaneer: entire communities were engaged in it, and the pirates had spread their tentacles into Cyprus, the southern slopes of the Taurus Mountains, Crete, the Asia Minor coast, the Peloponnese and even the shores of Italy. But the Romans were partly complicit in this, since the pirates were at the heart of the slave trade. However, when Rome's corn supply came under threat, the Roman government had to act. In 67 BCE Pompey found himself at the head of the campaign with 500 ships, 120,000 infantry, 5,000 cavalry, 24 legates, 2 *Quaestors*, vast financial resources, and a 3-year command whose *imperium* applied throughout the Mediterranean and its coasts, extended 50 miles inland and may have been *maius*, i.e. greater than that of the other governors. Popular confidence in Pompey was so great that on the day of his appointment the price of bread dropped dramatically. And the confidence was justified: within three months the entire campaign was over.

The problems with Sertorius, Spartacus and the pirates had taken Mithridates of Pontus off the Roman radar, which precipitated the Third Mithridatic War in 74 BCE. L. Licinius Lucullus – the Roman politician famous for his luxury, who once spent 50,000 *sestertii* on a banquet at a time when the annual pay of a soldier was 480 – invaded Pontus and defeated Mithridates, although he failed to capture the elusive Pontic king himself. Mithridates took refuge with his son-in-law King Tigranes of Armenia, so Lucullus invaded Armenia, but without the Senate's permission. Once again he failed to catch Mithridates, and, to make things worse his troops mutinied, allowing Mithridates to hit back. As if this wasn't bad enough, the *Equites* were implacably opposed to Lucullus' financial arrangements for the province of Asia, where he had reduced the debt dating back to Sulla's day and fixed the interest rate at 12 per cent; Rome's hard-core ruling elite were annoyed that he had attacked Tigranes without permission; and the *Popularis* faction didn't like him because he was one of the *Optimates*. He was stripped of his command.

The burning question, with the obvious yet highly controversial answer, was who would replace Lucullus. In 66 BCE C. Manilius proposed putting Pompey in command, and even Cicero, whose default position was to disapprove of this type of thing, added his voice to those in favour. What Cicero didn't say was what motivated him above all else – he needed Pompey's support in his bid to become Consul. Still, his involvement lent respectability to Manilius' cause and the bill was passed. Pompey feigned displeasure at the new 'burden', but Roman politicians were not slow to expose this cynical piece of play-acting for what it was.

In essence, Pompey had two things to do: (1) capture/kill Mithridates; (2) make this look difficult. In this respect he was rather thrown when Mithridates immediately sought peace. So he proposed terms that he knew Mithridates could not possibly accept. At an acrimonious meeting Pompey mocked Lucullus as 'a Xerxes in a toga', and Lucullus compared Pompey to a vulture that had caught no prey of its own, but feasted only on other creatures' kills. Once Lucullus had departed, Pompey defeated Mithridates at a place called Dasteira. Mithridates escaped with a concubine and one other companion, and managed to rally a few troops on the Armenian border; Pompey renamed Dasteira 'Nikopolis' (= Victory City);

Tigranes decided that he had been backing a loser, and offered a reward for the capture of Mithridates; the down-and-out king marched to Panticapaeum in the Crimea; Pompey used his fleet to blockade Mithridates, and conquered Pontus; Mithridates hatched a Hannibal-style plan to march up the Danube, and invade Italy over the Alps.

Pompey then turned his attention in the opposite direction, moving through Syria, which he annexed, and, in 63 BCE, down into Judaea, where he received news that Mithridates was dead: facing a rebellion by one of his sons, he had taken poison. However, after fifty years or so of taking daily antidotes, he had pretty well immunized himself. The poison didn't kill him, so a loyal servant duly obliged, and so provided the inspiration behind the famous verses written by the classical scholar and poet A.E. Housman in *A Shropshire Lad*:

> I tell the tale that I heard told.
> Mithridates, he died old.

Pompey proceeded to deploy his skills as the brilliant organizer that he was. His so-called Eastern Settlement laid the foundations for two centuries of Pax Romana in the East by means of a three-faceted arrangement that involved creating a virtually continuous ring of provinces from the southern shore of the Black Sea to Syria/Palestine, founding new cities and organizing and promoting independent client states outside the ring of provinces. Syria was taken away from the Seleucid dynasty, putting an end to one of the greatest kingdoms to have grown out of Alexander the Great's conquests. It is said that Pompey founded about forty cities, which, on the whole, began to flourish, bringing a 70 per cent increase in revenue from the region. The client states were designed to protect the new provinces from threats from the northern tribesmen or from Parthia (east of the Euphrates). These states, many of whose rulers owed their position to Pompey, were nominally independent, and maintained friendly relations with Rome, in an arrangement modelled on that between a high-ranking Roman patron and his clients. Pompey was now in a very powerful position.

There was much political manoeuvring in Rome while Pompey was away. The *Optimates* were jealous of Pompey's success, and fearful that he would 'do a Sulla'; Julius Caesar was doing well, having put on some fantastic games, and become Pontifex Maximus; Crassus, also jealous, was using his gigantic wealth to make loans to *Optimates* and *Populares* alike, and championing the interests of the *Equites*.

In the thick of all this was a colourful patrician called L. Sergius Catilina ('Catiline'). Contemporary sources (the hostile Cicero and the moralistic Sallust) describe him as a perverted, destructive, violent, cunning, greedy, extravagant, overambitious traitor, although they do acknowledge his mental and physical energy, toughness, daring and ability to win friends and influence people. After the elections of 66 BCE, the two Consuls had been unseated for electoral corruption, and new ones chosen instead. Catiline had wanted to stand in this re-election, but he was disqualified, either because he had submitted his nomination too late, or because he was facing an accusation of extortion. Everyone knew he was guilty: Cicero said he would only be acquitted if 'the jury decide it is night time at noon' – and they did. Then, in 63 BCE, Cicero became Consul alongside C. Antonius 'Hybrida', beating Catiline in the process.

Due to his political failures Catiline was badly in debt, and when Crassus withdrew his support he stood again for the consulship of 62 BCE on a platform of 'cancellation of debts'. This was attractive to a wide range of individuals, and, although the indebtedness of the poor was a big issue, many wealthy property owners would also have benefited from Catiline's programme. Things turned nasty in Rome, and, when Catiline was again not elected, he turned to non-constitutional means. There were armed risings in Etruria and terrorism in Rome. On 21 October 63 BCE Cicero exposed Catiline's conspiracy in the Senate, and the *SCU* was passed, yet Catiline stayed in Rome, plotting Cicero's murder and trying to face him down. Cicero was well protected, though, and on 8 November he made his *First Catilinarian Speech* in the Senate, forcing Catiline to quit Rome and join his henchman Manlius. Their co-conspirator Lentulus stayed on in Rome, and on 9 November Cicero's magnificent *Second Catilinarian Speech* was delivered to the people. The key moment in the whole affair came at the end of the month, when the conspirators approached some envoys of the Gallic Allobroges tribe, who chose not to get involved, and passed on the information to Cicero. He now had written proof of the conspiracy. On 3 December the conspirators at Rome were arrested, and Cicero made the *Third Catilinarian* to the people. Two days later the Senate discussed the punishment of the conspirators, with Cicero making his *Fourth Catilinarian* in favour of the death penalty. Cicero oversaw their execution, famously responding to the question of what had happened to them with an elegant use of Latin's perfect tense: 'They have lived.' Catiline himself was hunted down, defeated and killed early in 62 BCE; Cicero was proclaimed 'Father of the Fatherland', but became vulnerable to accusations of having executed Roman citizens without trial.

No sooner had Catiline been dealt with than another scandal broke. P. Clodius Pulcher was in love with Caesar's wife, Pompeia, who, apparently, was amenable to his advances. Her public duties included presiding over the women-only festival of 'the Good Goddess' (*Bona Dea*), which was celebrated in Caesar's house. Every male creature had to be removed from the household, so Clodius took the opportunity to dress up as a woman and take advantage of Caesar's absence (and of his wife). But his voice gave him away. Clodius was indicted for sacrilege, and various other allegations were made against him, one of which was adultery with his own sister, who, under her literary name of Lesbia, was the lover of the poet Catullus. Caesar proclaimed Pompeia's innocence, but still divorced her: 'I considered that my wife ought not to be even suspected'[11], he said. At Clodius' trial, Cicero comprehensively destroyed his alibi, but he was still acquitted (he never forgave Cicero).

At the end of the year Pompey arrived back from the East, disbanded his army, celebrated a stupendous triumph, but then ran into a problem. He had two needs and one want: land for his veterans; ratification of his Eastern settlement; and marriage into the family of the *Optimate* Cato. However, obstruction by the *Optimates* prevented him achieving any of these aims.

Pompey wasn't the only man to be frustrated by the Senate either. Crassus was the spokesman for a syndicate of Equestrian tax farmers. Peace was expensive, and the Romans expected that their Empire should 'happily pay for this continual peace and tranquillity, which benefits her.'[12] Tax collection ('tax farming') was privatized, and the syndicates who carried it out were pretty ruthless. Furthermore, provinces that had difficulty paying their taxes frequently resorted to borrowing money from Equestrian businessmen, who were very often the same people who had the contracts for tax collection. The province was often charged exorbitant rates of interest, with an APR of 48 per cent not unknown. It was also said that the governors needed to make three fortunes out of their provinces: one to pay their debts incurred in getting appointed in the first place; one to bribe their judges when they finished their term; and one for themselves. However, on this occasion Crassus' syndicate had made a bad deal for collecting the taxes of Asia. They wanted to renegotiate it retrospectively. It was an outrageous request, and the *Optimates* blocked it.

Caesar also wanted to have his cake and eat it by holding a triumph for his campaigns in Spain and standing for the consulship of 59 BCE. The rules said that you had to wait outside the city-boundaries for a triumph, but appear in Rome in person to submit your candidacy for election. When the *Optimates* refused to allow him to stand *in absentia*, he gave up the triumph and arrived in Rome. So the *Optimates* allocated him the third-rate post of Commissioner for the Forests and Cattle Drifts of Italy, should he get elected: this was not acceptable for any ex-consul, and certainly not to Caesar.

Caesar, Crassus and Pompey were not especially friendly to one another, but they knew that they could achieve their individual desires if they got together. So they formed an *amicitia* (an informal political deal), later known as The First Triumvirate, which enabled them to dominate Roman politics.

Caesar was elected Consul for 59 BCE along with the *Optimate* L. Calpurnius Bibulus, who vetoed Caesar's bill for Pompey's veterans, and then, in a cynical piece of manipulation of Rome's religious sensibilities, declared a 'sacred period', and went home to take the auspices – for the rest of the year. No legislation could legally be passed during such a period, although Caesar went ahead and legislated anyway. Land was secured for Pompey's veterans; 20,000 allotments of *ager publicus* in Italy were distributed to the urban poor (= 20,000 guaranteed votes for Caesar); Pompey's Eastern Settlement was ratified; Crassus got his tax rebate; and Caesar got Cisalpine Gaul and Illyricum as his *provincia* for five years, along with three legions, plus Transalpine Gaul and another legion when its governor died at a convenient (though not suspicious) moment. Pompey also agreed to a marriage alliance with Caesar's daughter Julia.

Clodius was elected tribune in order to remove Cicero, which he did by proposing that any magistrate who had put Roman citizens to death without trial should be exiled. The spineless Pompey, cowed by Clodius, abandoned Cicero and kept a very low profile.

Caesar's successful military conquests in Gaul now started to make everyone else jealous. Clodius was harassing Pompey (perhaps financed by Crassus), who retaliated by organizing a rival gang under T. Annius Milo and getting Cicero recalled (by a majority of 416 to 1 – Clodius). Yet amid all the stresses the three amigos still needed one another: Crassus wanted a military command to bolster his prestige; Caesar had to complete his conquest of Gaul; and Pompey was not guaranteed the support of the *Optimates* even if he broke away from the others. So before the campaigning season of 56 BCE they thrashed out a deal that gave them total control of Rome: Pompey and Crassus became joint Consuls in 55 BCE; Crassus then got Syria for five years; Pompey got Spain for five years but could stay in Rome; Caesar's *provincia* was extended for five years; and great building projects, including Pompey's theatre and Caesar's Forum, were initiated in Rome. It was all looking good.

Then, Julia, whom Pompey loved dearly, died in childbirth in 54 BCE; Pompey refused another marriage alliance with Caesar in favour of one with the *Optimate* Q. Caecilius Metellus Pius Scipio; the anarchy in Rome became so bad that there were no Consuls in the first half of 53 or in 52 BCE; the mob-violence culminated when Clodius was murdered by Milo on the Appian Way, and the Senate House became his funeral pyre; worst of all, Crassus started an unprovoked war with Parthia and was defeated at Carrhae with the loss of 20,000 dead and 10,000 prisoners. Only 10,000 escaped, and Crassus was not one of them.

A civil war was not yet inevitable, but it was increasingly likely. Caesar's conquests in Gaul, which included his two expeditions to Britain in 55 and 54 BCE, were bringing him up to Pompey's level, but he was occupied with a rebellion led by Vercingetorix. In any case, Pompey didn't want to provoke him unnecessarily. In the crisis of 52 BCE Pompey was made sole consul, and extended his own command over Spain for another five years. His position was very strong: Caesar needed him for his political survival, and the *Optimates* needed him to uphold law and order.

Caesar's political survival became the deal-breaker. Various proposals were made in 50 BCE suggesting that Pompey and Caesar should relinquish their commands, and the Senate eventually agreed to this by a margin of 370 to 22; C. Marcellus (Consul, 50 BCE) spread rumours that Caesar was marching on Rome; Pompey openly committed himself to the *Optimate* cause; Caesar proposed simultaneous disarmament, but threatened civil war; moderate opinion favoured disarmament, but Lentulus (Consul, 49 BCE) was implacably opposed; Pompey's father-in-law Scipio insisted that Caesar should disband his army or be made a public enemy; the tribunes Mark Antony and C. Cassius Longinus vetoed this; Cicero tried reconciliation, but the hard-liners were in no mood to back down; the *SCU* was passed; Caesar's tribunes were 'run out of town' (although this might have been staged); Pompey assumed command of the Republican forces in Italy; and in January 49 BCE Caesar crossed the Rubicon river from Gaul into Italy. The die had been cast.

Civil Wars, Dictatorship and the 'Egyptian Woman'

It was a war that everyone and no one wanted. Legally speaking, Caesar started it, but he would probably have preferred not to fight; Pompey's actions hadn't helped, but he probably felt that the threat of force would have made Caesar back down; the Senate's voting record shows that the majority wanted peace; the hard-liners simply wanted Caesar destroyed whatever the cost; but for all parties, war seemed better than compromise.

The smart money was on a Pompeian victory, but Caesar overran Italy, then, via Spain and Massilia (Marseilles), he moved into Greece, laid siege to Pompey's forces at Dyrrhachium, and inflicted a shattering defeat on them at the Battle of Pharsalus on 9 August 48 BCE. Pompey fled to Alexandria in Egypt, where the young Cleopatra was involved in a power struggle with her brother Ptolemy, only to be stabbed in the back as he stepped ashore. 'Dead men don't bite.'[13]

Caesar reached Alexandria a few days later to be presented with Pompey's signet ring and severed head. He summoned Cleopatra and Ptolemy, with a view to putting Egyptian affairs in order, but, in order to get into the palace unobserved, Cleopatra then performed one of history's sexiest tricks:

> She stretched herself out at full length inside a sleeping bag, and Apollodoros, after tying up the bag, carried it indoors to Caesar.[14]

This stunt captivated the Roman, but he still ended up having to fight a military action that set fire to, and destroyed, the great library at Alexandria. He defeated Ptolemy in March 47 BCE, enjoyed a fortnight's amorous respite with Cleopatra, and then set out for Syria, where he won his famous *veni, vidi, vici* battle over Pharnaces II at Zela. He left Cleopatra with the kingdom of Egypt, and, some say, a son who his mother called Ptolemy Caesar, but who is better known as Caesarion.[15]

Pompeian opposition in Africa was then eradicated by Caesar's victory at Thapsus, and as soon as he returned to Rome in 46 BCE he celebrated a four-day triumph in which Cleopatra's younger sister Arsinoë was paraded. Cleopatra and Caesarion followed Caesar to Rome. On Caesar's orders a golden statue of her was placed in the temple of Venus Genetrix, while she was installed in one of Caesar's villas. But 'the Egyptian woman' was extremely unpopular – the Romans could hardly bring themselves to speak her name.

Still the Pompeian opposition would not lie down, and it took yet another huge defeat at Munda in Spain (45 BCE) to bring the conflict to a close.

Caesar had acquired ever-escalating powers throughout the civil war period, and in 44 BCE he became dictator for life, and his head appeared on Roman coins. Whether or not he ever wanted to be King of Rome is a moot point. Mark Antony offered him the crown, but it is unclear why: was it a way of testing public opinion, or was it a publicity stunt designed to show that Caesar really didn't want it? Whatever the answer, it looks like he had no comprehensive view of the Roman State: Roman citizenship was granted to Transpadane Gaul; overseas colonies were promoted, notably Corinth; the Senate's membership was increased to 900;

traffic problems in Rome were addressed; the courts were given to the Senate and *Equites* in equal numbers; and the astronomer Sosigenes of Alexandria was employed to sort out the calendar, which was in a total mess due to the mismatch of the solar and lunar years. With one important modification, we use the Julian calendar today, and July is still named after Caesar.

The old-school Senators hated Caesar: the perpetuity of his dictatorship cut them to the quick; they detested the subtext behind the erection of a temple to *Clementia Caesaris* ('Caesar's Clemency') because *clementia* was a kingly virtue – Cato the Younger committed suicide rather than receive Caesar's *clementia*; the prospect of Caesar as king and Cleopatra alongside him appalled the Romans; and the fact that Caesar's statue was erected in the temple of Quirinus (the deified Romulus) also rankled. For his part, Caesar seems to have felt that Rome's political institutions would simply wither on the vine, but misjudging this was his undoing. As the *augur* Spurinna had predicted, on 15 March 44 BCE (the 'Ides of March'), he was murdered – not for what he might become, but for what he already was. He never realized that the men who joined him did so for their own benefit, not his.

There was nothing clandestine about the assassination. It was carried out on the steps of Pompey's theatre. The twenty-three conspirators who were actively involved were led by M. Iunius Brutus (to whom Caesar did not say '*et tu Brute?*' but, according to Suetonius,[16] the Greek words '*kai su teknon?*'(= 'You too, my son?') and his co-tyrannicide C. Cassius Longinus. Some were motivated by a belief that the Roman Republican system could be restored. Others had even been pro-Caesar, but were disillusioned because he was not doing what they had expected. Yet they all badly misjudged the true state of the Roman system, and simply precipitated a series of civil wars far worse than the previous ones.

The nominal leader of both the Roman State and the Caesarean faction was Caesar's friend – the dissipated, ambitious and ruthless Mark Antony. But Antony was not the only man with his sights set on power. A rival appeared in the shape of an 18-year old, Gaius Octavius (historians tend to call him 'Octavian'), who at the time of Caesar's murder was completing his education in Greece. Caesar was his mother's uncle, and had named him as his adopted heir in his will, as well as making him the beneficiary to three-quarters of his estate. The appearance of a comet at Julius Caesar's funeral games was widely interpreted as proof that Caesar had been received among the gods, and later the expectation was that his adopted son would be deified as well. The youth raised an army of 3,000 loyal veterans, secured a great deal of funding, and started using the name Gaius Julius Caesar, which he was now entitled to do. This was crucial, and Antony knew it: 'You, boy, owe everything to your name.'[17]

Antony would not hand over Caesar's legacy, but Octavian attached himself to Cicero, who not only recommended him to the Senate, but also managed to get them to declare Antony a public enemy. They ordered the consuls A. Hirtius and C. Vibius Pansa Caetronianus to drive Antony out of Italy, but when the rival forces met in battle near Mutina, it worked out perfectly for Octavian: Antony was defeated, and both the consuls were killed. At this stage Cicero was hoping to use Octavian against Antony to restore the Republic – 'He is a young man to be praised, honoured, and removed'[18] – but the reality would be the other way round. Octavian exploited Cicero's eloquent attacks on Antony in the *Philippic Orations*, and got himself appointed as a senator in 43 BCE. The deaths of Hirtius and Pansa also left Octavian in sole command of the consular armies, and he now demonstrated unequivocally where the real power lay by marching on Rome and demanding to be made Consul. He was only twenty years old – it was a ludicrous request; but it was granted all the same. To make things worse, Octavian promptly struck a deal with Antony, and they had Caesar's assassins proscribed as outlaws. Brutus and Cassius had no choice but to leave Italy.

Cool, calculating and opportunistic, Octavian met up with Antony and M. Aemilius Lepidus (another significant player among the friends of Caesar) near Mutina, where the three men formed the Second Triumvirate. Unlike the First Triumvirate (November 43 BCE), but like their predecessors, they divided the Roman world between them: Antony took Gaul; Lepidus Spain; Octavian Africa, Sicily and Sardinia. Proscriptions followed: some 300 senators and 2,000 *Equites* fell victim to this, and, on Antony's insistence, the man at the top of the list was Cicero.

Octavian, whose popular prestige was further enhanced by the official deification of Julius Caesar (he was now the 'son of a god'),

set off for Greece with Antony against Brutus and Cassius. The
resolution came at Philippi in north-east Greece in 42 BCE. Brutus
routed Octavian's forces and captured his camp (Octavian was
conspicuous by his absence), while Antony did the same to Cassius.
The attrition rate was high, and in the confusion neither side was
aware of what the other had done. Cassius retired to Philippi and,
only able to see his own captured camp, ordered his slave Pindarus
to kill him (though some think that he didn't wait to be asked). A
three-week stand-off ensued until Octavian and Antony started to
experience logistics trouble and realized the need for swift action;
Brutus, on the other hand, tried to delay as long as possible.
However, Brutus' troops grew so restive that he eventually yielded
to pressure from his officers and led his men out. 'Both sides
divined equally that this day and this battle would decide the fate of
Rome completely; and so indeed it did.'[19]

Antony and Octavian prevailed, and in despair Brutus called
upon his friend Straton to kill him. It had been one of the world's
most politically significant battles: Octavian had finally avenged the
murder of Julius Caesar, and there was no longer any question of
civil war in defence of the Republic – any future conflict could only
be about who would rule Rome.

Octavian took over Spain, Sardinia and Africa; undertook to put
down Sextus Pompeius (the son of Pompey), whose piratical
activities were menacing Rome's grain supply; and accepted the job
of settling the veterans. This involved the summary dispossession of
thousands of Italian farmers, but it was worth it to Octavian
because he became the soldiers' patron. The poet Virgil narrowly
avoided losing his estates in all this, and he alludes to it in his first
Eclogue, where the shepherd Meliboeus laments:

> To think of some godless soldier owning my well-farmed fallow,
> A foreigner reaping these crops! To such a pass has civil
> Dissension brought us: for people like these we have sown our
>   fields.[20]

Such grievances were exploited by Antony's wife, Fulvia, and his
brother Lucius Antonius (Consul, 41 BCE), who raised eight legions
and occupied Rome. Octavian managed to dislodge them and drove
them to Perusia, which fell in 41 BCE. He was merciless to the

PoWs, and according to some sources, he chose 300 prisoners of equestrian or senatorial rank, and offered them as human sacrifices on the Ides of March at the altar of the Divine Julius.

While Fulvia was working dutifully on Antony's behalf, her husband was falling for Cleopatra. He was planning an invasion of Parthia, and had summoned her to Tarsus in Asia Minor. She was now in her late twenties, 'the age when a woman's beauty is at its most superb and her mind at its most mature',[21] and she knew how to ensnare Roman men:

> Her own beauty . . . was not of that incomparable kind which instantly captivates the beholder. But the charm of her presence was irresistible, and there was an attraction in her person and her talk, together with a peculiar force of character which . . . laid all who associated with her under its spell.[22]

She arrived fashionably late, sailing up the river Cydnus in an astonishingly opulent barge, reclining beneath a canopy of cloth of gold, dressed as Venus, with her most beautiful waiting-women attired as Nereids and Graces, while heady perfumes wafted to the river-banks.

Antony never stood a chance. He postponed the Parthian expedition and went to Alexandria with Cleopatra. There they indulged in extravagant debauchery until Antony's deteriorating relations with Octavian forced him to return to Italy in 40 BCE, leaving behind his new-born twins Alexander Helios and Cleopatra Selene. The triumviral differences were patched up by the Treaty of Brundisium, which in effect divided east and west between Antony and Octavian, and sidelined Lepidus. The pact was sealed by a marriage alliance: Antony married Octavian's sister, Octavia (Fulvia had recently died). Octavian also divorced his wife Scribonia in order to marry Livia, with whom he lived happily ever after.

With the help of the highly capable M. Agrippa, Octavian defeated and killed Sextus Pompeius in 36 BCE, discharged around 20,000 men from the forty or so legions that he now had at his disposal, and returned to Rome, where he squeezed the maximum psychological advantage out of Antony's absence in the east. While he campaigned against the tribes in Illyricum, cleared the Adriatic of pirates and initiated major public projects in Rome, Antony renewed his liaison with Cleopatra (Ptolemy Philadelphos was born in 36 BCE). However, his Parthian expedition ended in a disastrous reverse, and the 'Donations of Alexandria', where he granted to Cleopatra and her children huge tracts of territory in the east, was an even bigger propaganda gift to Octavian. Even so, not everyone backed Octavian: both Consuls and more than 300 senators left Rome to join Antony early in 32 BCE. Octavian nominated fresh consuls; Antony divorced Octavia; Octavian published Antony's will; Antony crossed to Greece with Cleopatra; Octavian deprived Antony of his remaining powers, secured a declaration of war against Cleopatra, and, as Consul, crossed to Greece for the final showdown.

Octavian had a slight superiority in forces (possibly 600 ships and 80,000 infantry *v.* 500 ships and 70,000 infantry), and an excellent admiral in Agrippa, whereas Cleopatra's presence on Antony's side was disruptive. Quite what happened at the Battle of Actium itself, fought on 2 September 31 BCE, is hard to pinpoint in detail, but the end result was that Cleopatra's squadron escaped, Antony followed in her wake, and the remainder of his forces surrendered. The poet Virgil imagined that the hero Aeneas had the scene prophetically emblazoned on his shield, and presents it, not as a civil war, but as a conflict between virtuous Romans and obscene barbarians:

> On one side Augustus Caesar, high up on the poop, is leading
> The Italians into battle, the Senate and People with him . . .
> On the other side, with barbaric wealth and motley equipment,
> Is Anthony . . .
> Egypt, the powers of the Orient and uttermost Bactra
> Sail with him; also – a shameful thing – his Egyptian wife.[23]

Antony fled with Cleopatra to Egypt, where both committed suicide in 30 BCE; the poet Horace wrote of the mood of celebration that followed Octavian's victory over the Egyptian Queen and her 'squalid pack of diseased half-men':

> Today is the day to drink and dance on. Dance, then,
> Merrily, friends, till the earth shakes.[24]

Octavian spared Antony's children by Cleopatra, but he had his eldest son by Fulvia put to death, and, of course, Caesarion. He annexed Egypt, but, because it was a major supplier of grain to Rome, he took it under his own personal administration, although he fudged the issue in his propaganda: 'I added Egypt to the empire of the Roman people.'[25]

The Final Settlement: Augustus' Principate

Octavian had no military or political rivals; he was the wealthiest citizen in the empire; he controlled all the legions; he was master of the Roman world. The gates of the Temple of Janus were ceremonially closed to signify universal peace; historians of the day sang his praises:

> There is no boon that men can desire of the gods or gods grant to mankind, no conceivable wish or blessing which [Octavian] did not bestow on the Republic, the Roman people, and the world.[26]

Later commentators are not so generous – Ronald Syme described him as 'a chill and mature terrorist' – but what set him apart from the likes of Marius, Sulla, Pompey, Caesar and Antony was a talent for statesmanship that only now began to manifest itself. What mattered above all was to maintain Republican protocol: he was undeniably an autocrat, yet unlike Caesar he never rubbed people's noses in it, and he would give the world 'a large measure of peace and stable government for the next two hundred years'.[27]

Octavian returned to Rome in 29 BCE and celebrated a triple triumph; the Senate voted him a triumphal arch inscribed *re publica conservata* ('The Republic saved'), which would become a leitmotif for his regime; he was Consul every year from 31 to 27 BCE, and the designation Imperator ('general', which gives us the English word 'Emperor') became an official title. He downsized the Senate to around 800 members, although he still needed to find a place for them in his new order. He was always acutely aware of what had happened to Julius Caesar, who had disrespected the Senate, and in any case he would need the Senate's experience and expertise. The big moment came in January 27 BCE when, sensationally, in his own words:

> After I had put an end to the civil wars, having by universal consent acquired control of all affairs, I transferred government from my own authority to the discretion of the Senate and people of Rome.[28]

After howls of protest, heartfelt or otherwise, he agreed to retain control of Spain, Gaul and Syria for ten years (that was where the bulk of the legions were stationed), and also kept control of Rome's foreign policy by assuming the rights of war and peace and treaty-making. At that point he assumed the name 'Augustus', a brilliantly chosen epithet, rather than a title, which had quasi-religious overtones of fruitful increase: *augeo* = 'I increase/enlarge/enrich/embellish' (it is the same word in origin as the English 'wax' as in 'waxing moon'), and *augustus* = 'majestic/august/venerable/worthy of honour.' So it sidestepped the issue of formal power, and the way he presented the total package is most illuminating:

> Henceforth, I exceeded all men in authority (*auctoritas*), but I had no greater power than those who were my colleagues in any given magistracy.[29]

This personal and moral *auctoritas* guaranteed that in all key areas his will would be done.

In addition, Augustus was to be known as *Princeps* ('first citizen'/'first among equals'), an honorary title with sound Republican precedents. Historians conventionally call the Roman Imperial period (for that is what we have now entered) the Principate, rather than the Empire, because of this. In a sense, they too have swallowed Augustus' propaganda. Of course, he was not able to pull the wool over everyone's eyes (if indeed this was what he was trying to do): Tacitus regarded him as a power-crazed hypocrite, deviously concealing his autocratic behaviour under a veneer of republicanism, but at the time there was a willingness to buy into the idea of a restored Republic. Augustus' challenge was to find a permanent solution that would maintain political stability without outraging traditional feeling. And he succeeded. Rome's empire (with or without a capital 'E') would last for more than another 400 years – at least.

14

ROMAN EPIC: VIRGIL'S *AENEID*

> My state must not be lacking in art; the peace that I am
> establishing is in need of art as much as that of Pericles, who
> gloriously crowned his by building the sky-towering Acropolis.
> Caesar Augustus, speaking in H. Broch, *The Death of Virgil*[1]

Augustus' Principate was Rome's 'Golden Age' of literary
creativity. Horace, Ovid, Propertius, Tibullus and Livy all wrote at
that time, but the poet Virgil (Publius Vergilius Maro) stands out
even against this stellar background. Virgil was also at the sharp end
of the political events of his time, and his work not only reflects the
ideas and ideals of the Augustan Age, but had a role to play in
creating them.

Virgil was born near Mantua in 70 BCE. A fourth century CE *Life
of Virgil* tells us that he was tall, dark and rustic-looking, had a
number of health issues, didn't eat or drink much, and was given to
passions for boys. He had a narrow escape during the proscriptions
of the Second Triumvirate, but he eventually became an extremely
rich man, friendly with Augustus himself. He worked by dictating
a large number of improvized lines in the morning, and then
spending the rest of the day refining them. His unfinished
masterpiece the *Aeneid*, started in 30 BCE, acquired celebrity stature
almost from its inception. Augustus pestered Virgil to show it to
him and, when he did read some extracts, one line caused Augustus'
sister Octavia to faint with emotion. By 19 BCE Virgil had allocated
three years to the final polishing of the *Aeneid*, but he fell ill in
Greece, and died at Brundisium that October.

Virgil had asked his friend Lucius Varius to burn the *Aeneid* if anything befell him, but Varius published it at Augustus' request. It acquired 'classic' status soon after his death: the satirist Juvenal bewails the fate of the schoolteacher working in a shed with smoking lamps so that 'every Virgil is grimed with lampblack';[2] schoolboys in Roman Egypt studied him; and the opening lines of the *Aeneid* were frequently scrawled on the walls of Pompeii as graffiti.

The *Aeneid* is written in 12 books of between 705 and 952 lines of hexameter verse. It is based around the legend of the establishment of the Roman race. Aeneas, a Trojan who was also a mythical ancestor of Augustus, escaped when the Greeks sacked Troy, and his destiny was to lead a small group of survivors to Italy and prepare the ground for Rome, ultimately to become the ruler of the world.

'Talent borrows, genius steals', and right at the beginning of the *Aeneid* Virgil acknowledges his influences by 'imitating' the beginnings of Homer's *Iliad* and *Odyssey* with the immortal words *Arma virumque cano*, 'I sing of war and the hero'. This tells us that his poem is both an *Iliad* – a story of war (*arma*)[3] – and an *Odyssey* – the story of a hero/man's (*virum*) adventures: in Homer's Greek, 'man' is the first word of the *Odyssey*, and the man is defined, by both Homer and Virgil, in a relative clause 'who . . .'. But the men are very different: Homer's is trying to survive and get his comrades home; Virgil's is trying to found a city and march his gods into new territory. It is also noticeable that whereas Homer seeks his Muse's inspiration, Virgil confidently starts in the first person: '*I* tell'. Virgil's opening five lines reflect the opening sentence of the *Odyssey*, but Virgil's sentence is seven lines long – just like that of the *Iliad* — and Virgil has further synthesized Homer's two opening sentences by arranging them in a chiasmus (a crosswise ABBA arrangement where the order of the second phrase inverts that of the first).

Additionally the key deities are included too: '*the will of Zeus*' in line five of the *Iliad* is picked up by '*the brooding anger of Juno*' in Virgil's fourth line. So Books 1 to 6 of the *Aeneid* become Virgil's *Odyssey*, whose itinerant hero is defined by the relative clause of line one ('*who*' first from Troy's frontier, displaced by destiny, came to the Lavinian shore), and Books 7 to 12 become his *Iliad*, whose martial hero is defined by the participial phrase of lines 5–7 ('*suffering much in war*' until he could found a city and march his gods into Latium). This kind of literary trickery is going on right through the *Aeneid*.

Homer and the *Aeneid* share the hexameter metre; a distinctive vocabulary; similes; the divine machinery; major incidents such as storms, games, a journey to the Underworld, night raids and duels. But Virgil is not 'ripping Homer off': he is alluding, evoking and challenging, in exactly the same way as contemporary rappers do. His approach is very close in ethos to that of the Hellenistic Greek scholar-poets, whose work is crammed with allusions to pre-existing material: Kallimakhos wrote, 'I sing of nothing that hasn't been sung about before.'[4] Yet Virgil is definitively Roman, and highly original. What at first appears to be straightforward comparisons and likenesses often betray significant differences beneath the surface. So although parallels are set up between, say, Aeneas and Odysseus, they are actually very different: 'wily' Odysseus is a great individualist; *pius* Aeneas (regularly translated 'god-fearing', 'good-hearted' and 'the true') is not – his overriding quality is the quintessentially Roman *pietas*, a sense of duty to your gods, state and family. So although much of the *Aeneid* comes out of Homer, nothing is the same any more: *I* sing; I am Roman; I am Virgil.

The narrative jumps in at the point where, seven years into their wanderings, Aeneas and his Trojans have reached Sicily. However, Juno, whose hatred of Trojans goes back to losing the Judgement of Paris to Aeneas' mother Venus, embroils them in a storm. Aeneas' destiny is both divinely ordained and divinely opposed. Neptune steps in and calms the sea like a respected man of *pietas* calming a mob seething with *furor* (= 'violence/hysteria/madness/frenzy/loss of rational control'). Aeneas himself will have to confront *furor* with *pietas*, but, as his mother testily observes, his *pietas* is not getting him very far. When she challenges Jupiter about this, he gives her a prophecy about the glittering future of the Romans: 'To these I set no bounds, either in time or space; Unlimited power I give them.'[5]

Venus guides the Trojan ships to Carthage in North Africa and conveys Aeneas to the city in a cloud. There he is hospitably received by Queen Dido. Carthage now has many impressive completed infrastructure projects, including a temple of Juno that is adorned with scenes of the Trojans' ordeals, but Dido and her people also acknowledge 'tears for human suffering',[6] even if Dido has already achieved much of what Aeneas will have to do. He respects her greatly for this.

Venus then makes Dido fall in love, and at an opulent banquet she asks Aeneas to tell her about his wanderings. What she gets is an intense eye-witness account of Troy's last night, as Aeneas begins with the Wooden Horse, which is now one of the incidents most commonly associated with the Troy story, but did not play a particularly prominent part in the Greek literary tradition – it only assumes massive importance through Virgil's poetry. The Greeks had pretended it was a votive offering for their safe return, but filled it with their finest warriors and sailed away to the nearby island of Tenedos, as though they had abandoned their campaign. However, they did leave Sinon behind to signal to them with a beacon.

The Trojans assumed that the siege was over, despite the suspicions of the priest Laocoon, who tried to stop them taking the Horse into the city. It was he who told the Trojans to 'beware of Greeks bearing gifts',[7] and he thrust his spear into the Horse to prove that it was hollow. However, Sinon, pretending to be a deserter, persuaded them that it was a *bona fide* offering, and his evidence seemed to be corroborated when two enormous serpents emerged from the sea, made straight for Laocoon and his two small sons, crushed them all in their coils, devoured their flesh with their venomous fangs, and slithered away to Troy's citadel. The Trojans misguidedly interpreted these horrors as punishment for advising against accepting the Wooden Horse, and for spearing the goddess's offering. They joyfully dragged the 'engine of Fate' into their city, although even then it might not have been too late, had anyone listened to the prophetess Cassandra. But no one ever believed her. The Trojans' blissful sleep was shattered by violence and terror. The Greek fleet moved in from Tenedos; Sinon released the warriors; the city gates were flung open; and the Greeks swarmed in.

The fall of Troy, seen from Aeneas' perspective, was not a wonderfully heroic feat, but a tale of brutality, murder, rape and enslavement. Hector's ghost told him to escape, but Aeneas was still thinking like a Homeric hero: he believed death in battle to be a good thing. Yet his life was not his own to throw away. The sheer savagery of the Greek assault was rammed home in the repulsive slaughter of Priam. Aeneas was a helpless bystander as the old king, who was taking refuge at an altar, watched Achilles' son Pyrrhus slaughter his son Polites. Priam cast his spear at Pyrrhus, but his throw was too weak. After taunting him, Pyrrhus dragged him by the hair through a pool of his own son's blood, right up to the altar, and buried his sword in his side: 'His tall body was left lying headless on the shore, and by it the head hacked from his shoulders: a corpse without a name.'[8] Aeneas would have killed Helen if Venus had not intervened, and told him that the fall of Troy was fated. She showed him a supernatural vision of the gods destroying the walls of Troy, and ordered him to collect his family and leave. His old father, Anchises, initially refused to go, and again Aeneas expressed his desire to die at Troy, but when a flame appeared like a halo around his son Ascanius' head without harming him, and a shooting star flashed across the night sky and landed on Mount Ida, he knew he must escape.

His *pietas* then shined through as he carried Anchises on his shoulders, and led Ascanius through the carnage to safety. Sadly his wife Creusa got lost in the confusion, and Aeneas endangered himself yet again by trying to find her, but her ghost re-emphasized that a new fate awaited the Trojans under his leadership, in the shape of a new city in Italy, destined one day to rule the world. Virgil concluded the meeting with a memorable image lifted from Homer, where Odysseus had tried to embrace the ghost of his mother:

> Three times I tried to put my arms round her neck, and three times
> The phantom slipped my hands, my vain embrace: it was like
> Grasping a wisp of wind or the wings of a fleeting dream.[9]

Aeneas finally accepted defeat and headed for the hills.

Dido then learns about Aeneas' years of wandering. The Trojans set sail, landing at Thrace, various Cycladic islands and Crete, where Apollo prophesied that their final goal was Hesperia, from where Dardanus, one of the founders of the Trojan race, originally sprang. They then survived a storm, negotiated the islands of the Harpies, and received a prophecy from the Harpy Celaeno to the effect that they would not be given a city before they had been forced to gnaw round the edges of their tables.[10]

On they went, past Zacynthus, Dulichium, Same, Neritos and Ithaca, and then, in a transparent reference to Augustus' victory over Antony and Cleopatra, they celebrated games at Actium.

From there they headed for Buthrotum in Epirus, where they encountered Hector's ex-wife Andromache, now married to the Trojan prophet Helenus, living in an imitation Troy. Helenus prophesied that the place for their city would be a spot by a river, under some holm-oaks on the shore, where they would find a great white sow with a litter of thirty all-white piglets.

Westwards they went again, near the Ceraunian Rocks, making a brief landfall in southern Italy, and, thanks to Palinurus' expert seamanship, safely avoiding Charybdis. Arriving in Sicily near Etna, they encountered the Cyclopes and rescued Achaemenides, a survivor of Odysseus' encounter with the monster. Again, Virgil lets us see the similarities and differences between Odysseus (full of prowess and ingenuity; very proactive) and Aeneas (full of horror and suffering; often passive). Having put to sea in haste, the voyagers managed to avoid Scylla and Charybdis (again), and then sailed clockwise around Sicily to Drepanum on the west. It is here that Aeneas' father Anchises died. With a brief mention of the storm that drove them to Carthage, Aeneas brings us back to where the narrative started in Book 1.

Although Virgil has used the Medea of the poet Apollonius Rhodius and the Ariadne of Catullus as models, along with various heroines of Greek tragedy, the version of the Dido mythology that he presents in Book 4 is very much his own. So far we have seen that she is beautiful, happy, brave, dynamic and kind. But after Aeneas' story she is overwhelmed with passion and cannot sleep and, as dawn breaks, she talks about it to her sister Anna. However, she does not want to be unfaithful to the memory of her dead husband, Sychaeus, no matter how tempting a prospect Aeneas might be. Anna, though, comes up with a number of persuasive arguments for starting a relationship with him. Her words are persuasive; Dido stops dithering; she is ablaze with passion, compared in a simile to a deer that has been accidentally and unknowingly shot and wounded by a shepherd hunting in the woods; she cannot bear to be without Aeneas; she becomes clingy when she is with him; and yearns frantically when she is not.

All the building work in Carthage grinds to a halt, and during the lull Juno offers Venus a truce and a deal: she will let Aeneas marry Dido, and Carthage will be the dowry. This is a fairly transparent trick to make Carthage all-powerful, but, although Venus sees through it, she still accepts. The next day a hunting party assembles, and Dido finally appears in her full exotic royal splendour, decked out in purple and gold; Aeneas joins her, as radiant and graceful as Apollo. On the mountains they find deer in abundance, and little Ascanius has the time of his life.

Then a storm breaks; the torrential downpour makes Aeneas and Dido take shelter in a cave; and amid thunder and lightning and wailing nymphs – with all the forces of nature and the supernatural imitating the events of a real wedding ceremony – Dido and Aeneas consummate their passion. But what Aeneas regards as enjoyable casual sex, Dido interprets as serious commitment. It is the beginning of a tragedy.

Rumour – personified as a terrifying monster covered with eyes, tongues and ears – now flies through Libya spreading the gossip, the most significant recipient of which is Dido's spurned suitor, Iarbas, the son of Jupiter/Ammon. He furiously taunts his father for allowing him to be scorned by a foreign woman and an eastern adventurer, and his prayers hit home. Jupiter orders Mercury to remind Aeneas about his great mission, and to add the guilt-trip that if Aeneas' own ambition is dead, he has no right to ruin his son's hopes. Mercury responds with alacrity. He swoops down to the coast of Libya, and what he sees is a shocking sight: Aeneas is supervising the building of Carthage, dressed in a cloak that Dido has given him; he should be building Rome wearing a toga. Mercury's message puts Aeneas in a terrible situation: he has to obey (he is Mr *Pius*), but breaking the news to Dido is going to be difficult. He genuinely loves her, but, by trying to soften the blow, he makes the situation far, far worse. Hoping that he will be able to find a good time to tell her, he orders the fleet to prepare to sail.

Aeneas and Dido have both made mistakes that countless ill-starred lovers have made ever since: she mistook sex for commitment; he waited for the perfect time to tell her it was over, but someone else told her first. When Dido hears the inevitable rumours of what is happening she confronts Aeneas before he can get a word in. She tries all manner of emotional manipulation to get him to stay; he remembers Jupiter's warning, suppresses his churning emotions, and responds directly and assertively. Virgil only gives him this one chance to get it right, and where her appeal was to the heart, his is to the head. He acknowledges his debt to her, and says that he can never forget her, but he protests that he never planned to mislead her or to marry her. He tells her about Mercury's orders, and concludes by saying: 'It is not by my own will that I search for Italy'. Modern readers frequently pour scorn on him for this, but he has to choose between *pietas* and passion, and it tears him apart. He certainly has wronged Dido, but he did not deceive her; tragically, she has deceived herself.

Dido clearly does not believe all the stuff about 'oracles' and 'messengers from heaven', and her response is one of unmitigated scorn and rage. When she faints and is carried away by her maids, Aeneas prepares to sail. Dido comes round, sends Anna to ask him at least to stay until the weather is fair, but like an Alpine oak battered by the north winds, Aeneas remains firm.

Dido now prays for death, and her resolve is strengthened by uncanny portents. To keep Anna in the dark about her true intentions, she pretends to have consulted a sorceress, who has advised her to erect a pyre and burn every memorial of Aeneas, in the hope of either winning him back or curing her passion. The completely unsuspecting Anna helps her build it.

During the night Mercury appears to Aeneas in a dream and warns him with the notorious line 'a woman is an unstable and changeable thing' that Dido could be dangerous.[11] He puts the fleet to sea immediately, and as dawn breaks Dido sees the Trojan ships and realizes it is too late. She prays that if Aeneas must reach Italy, that it should be with a curse upon him and all his descendants:

> I pray that we may stand opposed, shore against shore, sea against sea and sword against sword. Let there be war between the nations and between their sons for ever.[12]

These references to hostilities between Dido's and Aeneas' people and his are to Hannibal and the Punic wars.

Dido sends Sychaeus' old nurse Barce to ask Anna to bring everything for the magic rite. She then climbs on to the pyre and draws a sword that Aeneas once gave her. Her final words add up to a statement that just as she has been great in life, so she will be great in death. Then she falls on the sword. There is blood everywhere. Anna rushes to Dido, reproaching her, but also blaming herself; her feelings turn to love and pity; she tries to staunch Dido's wound with her own dress; Dido tries to lift her eyes, but cannot; after three unsuccessful attempts to raise herself up, she falls back with a groan of agony; Juno sends Iris down from Olympus to end her pain; Iris takes a lock of her hair as the Death-god's due, and releases her soul from her body.

As Aeneas and his men sail away from Carthage, watching the flames from Dido's pyre on the horizon, they are unaware of what has transpired. Another storm then forces Aeneas to revisit Sicily, where he visits his father's tomb and celebrates games in his honour. These games are based on the funeral games of Patroclus in the *Iliad*, but they also have a special contemporary interest, primarily in respect of Augustus' Actian Games. The boat race is contested by men who will become ancestors of great Roman families; and in the foot race Nisus deliberately trips Salius so that his dear friend Euryalus can win. Aeneas needs a good deal of tact to deal with the damaged egos, and he also exercises shrewd judgement when he intervenes to prevent the mighty boxing champion Dares being unexpectedly battered to death by the veteran Entellus. Finally, an archery contest ends in a miraculous omen when Acestes' arrow bursts into flames and leaves a trail of fire until it fades into thin air like a shooting star. The games are rounded off with a glittering ceremonial cavalry parade of boys, led by Ascanius, but the event is interrupted when some disaffected Trojan women try to set fire to the fleet. Jupiter saves all but four of the vessels by sending a rain storm, but the incident is such a shattering blow to Aeneas' self-confidence that it requires the appearance of his father's ghost to persuade him to carry on. The death of the helmsman Palinurus, who is lost overboard during the night, affects a neat transition to the next book: Aeneas' journey to the Underworld.

The Trojans land at Cumae in Italy, where Aeneas goes to the temple of Apollo to request that the Trojans should be allowed to settle in the country. The priestess of the temple is the prophetic Sibyl, and the famous Sibylline Books of prophesies were said to have been bought from a Sibyl of Cumae by King Tarquinius Superbus, so when Aeneas vows to build a temple to Apollo where the Sibyl's oracles will be deposited, Virgil is making an obvious reference to the Temple of Apollo on the Palatine hill dedicated by Augustus in memory of Actium, to which he had the Sibylline

Books transferred. Once again, the historical perspective is deliberately distorted: we are in two different periods at once.

Aeneas asks the Sibyl if he can go down to the Underworld (the entrance is close by) and visit the ghost of Anchises. She grants his wish, instructs him to find a Golden Bough, which will act as his 'ticket' to the Underworld, and then behaves like a high-quality tourist guide as Aeneas undergoes all the traditional experiences of the trip. He goes past various personified abstractions such as Grief, Death, Perverted Pleasures, War and Discord, and then sees various mythical monsters – Centaurs, the Hydra of Lerna, the Chimaera, Gorgons and so on. Next he comes across the first of four groups of variously categorized ghosts that each contains a significant person from his past. This group comprises shades of the unburied, pathetically begging to be allowed to cross the River Styx. In rather cinematic fashion, Virgil moves from the wider scene to a close focus on the helmsman, Palinurus, whose body is still being tossed around in the sea. He learns that he will have a headland named after him.

Aeneas crosses the Styx in the boat of Charon, who is beautifully characterized as a filthy, unkempt jobsworth, and the Sibyl adeptly administers soporific drugs to the Underworld's guard-dog, Cerberus. They then reach the souls of the prematurely dead, which include, in the Vales of Mourning, a number of Greek heroines who are victims of unhappy love. Dido is here, too, and with their previous roles reversed Aeneas pleads and she remains unmoved. He reiterates that it was not of his own free will that he left Carthage, but in accordance with heaven's commands; only now does he realize that his going had brought such terrible agony to her. However, she will not even look at him, and finally vanishes into a shadowy wood to join her first husband, Sychaeus, who reciprocates her love. Aeneas weeps tears of compassion, even though he feels neither guilt nor remorse. His *pietas* meant that he had no alternative but to follow his destiny, but Virgil still forces him to confront his past face to face.

Beyond the Vales of Mourning are the great warriors. Virgil 'zooms in' on Deiphobus, the Trojan who had married Helen after the death of Paris, but who was horrifically mutilated during the fall of Troy, bringing back all the horrors and hopelessness of that terrible night. Once again Aeneas has to come to terms with his past before he can move on.

Aeneas and the Sibyl then reach a fork in the road: to the left is Tartarus, whose inhabitants have all been condemned for extreme wickedness and are receiving their traditional Greek mythological punishments. Aeneas is not allowed to go there, so he and his guide turn right, deposit the Golden Bough at the palace of Dis and enter the homes of the blessed. Everywhere on their journey so far has been grey, dingy and eerily quiet, but now they enter an area of light, colour, sound and fragrance. Aeneas finds Anchises there, conducting a survey of his future descendants. An emotional reunion follows in which Virgil uses *precisely* the same three lines that described Aeneas' attempt to embrace his mother's ghost in Book 2.

Aeneas catches sight of a multitude of souls who are awaiting reincarnation. In the light of his own unhappy experiences, he is sceptical and amazed that they should have 'this terrible longing for the light'.[13] Anchises responds by expounding the doctrine of the transmigration of souls in a style that owes much to the Roman philosophical writer Lucretius, although the subject matter is a curious mash-up of the Stoic doctrine of the 'world spirit' (*anima mundi*) with the Platonic/Orphic teaching of rebirth. The souls in question are those of eminent Romans, allowing Aeneas a vivid insight into Rome's glorious future, which for Virgil's audience, of course, was a celebration of Rome's glorious past.

The 'procession' of souls is not organized chronologically, but, covering a period that would stretch from about 1053 to 753 BCE if viewed 'historically', it starts with the immediate 'future' with Aeneas' last child, Silvius, and moves via four more kings of Alba Longa (Procas, Capys, Numitor and Silvius Aeneas) down to Romulus. From the traditional founder of Rome we move, via a quick mention of Julius Caesar, to Emperor Augustus:

> And here, here is the man, the promised one you know of –
> Caesar Augustus, son of a god, destined to rule
> Where Saturn ruled of old in Latium, and there
> Bring back the age of gold.[14]

Then Anchises goes back via several Roman kings, to the Brutus who overthrew the last Roman king Tarquinius Superbus, but whose name also recalls the Brutus who assassinated Julius Caesar. A quick mention of some old Republican-era heroes leads us to recent Roman history with Caesar (again) and Pompey. Anchises finally surveys the military successes of more distant times, finishing up with Q. Fabius Maximus Cunctator, who fought Hannibal to a standstill in Italy.

The climax of the whole passage comes when Anchises contrasts Rome's imperial greatness with Greek cultural genius:

> Let others fashion from bronze more lifelike, breathing images –
> For so they shall – and evoke living faces from marble;
> Others excel as orators, others track with their instruments
> The planets circling in the heavens and predict when stars will
>   appear
> But, Romans, never forget that government is your medium!
> Be this your art: – to practice men in the habit of peace,
> Generosity to the conquered, and firmness against aggressors.[15]

Anchises' survey concludes in a minor key when Aeneas asks about the soul of Marcellus, Augustus' nephew and heir, who had in fact died in 23 BCE. Anchises tells his son not to probe into the sorrows of his kin, and laments Marcellus' destiny. The *Life of Virgil* tells us that when he recited these lines to Augustus and his family, Marcellus' mother Octavia passed out.[16]

Aeneas returns to the land of the living, rejoins his comrades and coasts along to the harbour of Caieta. From there the Trojans skirt the uncanny island of Circe, and reach the mouth of the River Tiber. Aeneas' *Odyssey* is over; his *Iliad* is about to begin.

In a new evocation to the Muse Erato, Virgil speaks of a 'greater work' that he is now embarking on. This directly echoes the Sibyl's prophecies of war, battles and princes driven to their deaths, not, incidentally by Fate – this ultimately is a needless, pointless conflict – but by their pride of spirit. Initially, though, all goes well. The 'prophecy of the tables' is fulfilled when the famished Trojans have to eat 'open sandwiches' and Ascanius quips: 'Look! We are eating our tables too!' Their travels are at an end. The next day an embassy is sent to the local King Latinus. He is the son of Faunus, god of agriculture and cattle, and he rules an austere community of farmer/soldiers, very much modelled on the way in which the Romans saw their early society. Straight away Latinus betroths his daughter Lavinia to Aeneas, in accordance with an oracle:

> Do not seek to join your daughter in marriage to a Latin . . .
> Strangers will come to be your sons-in-law, and by their blood raise
> our name to the stars. The descendants of that stock will see the
> whole world turning under their feet and guided by their will.[17]

However, the happy situation is shattered by Juno, who enlists the
Fury Allecto to breathe raging anger into Latinus' wife Queen
Amata – who desperately wants Lavinia to marry the handsome
Rutulian warrior Turnus – and then into Turnus himself. Allecto
inflames a group of local peasants when Ascanius shoots a stag; they
demand revenge; Juno opens the Gates of War; ploughshares are
turned into swords; and war begins.

Virgil provides a catalogue of the Italian contingents that rally
against Aeneas. They are led by Mezentius from Etruria, a cruel
scorner of the gods, and include his son Lausus, a beautiful and
much more sympathetic character; Messapus; Clausus, ancestor of
the Claudii; Halaesus, one of Agamemnon's ex-soldiers, and an
enemy of all things Trojan; Turnus, the fairest and tallest of them all,
wearing a triple-plumed helmet with a Chimaera breathing fire
from it; and Camilla, the fleet-footed, battle-hardened warrior-
maiden of the Volsci. The list allows Virgil to emphasize the
martial spirit of the Italians, for, although they are Aeneas' enemies,
they are also the people from whom the Romans derive their
language and institutions: real Romans were far more Italian than
Trojan.

The river-god Tiber comes to Aeneas in his sleep, prophesies the
fulfilment of the prodigy of the white sow, and tells him to head
upstream and seek out the Arcadian King Evander, who is
constantly at war with the Latins. Aeneas finds the sow, sails up the
Tiber and arrives at Pallanteum (later known as the Palatine, one of
the Seven Hills of Rome), where he finds Evander. The king takes
Aeneas round his city: it might be unimposing, but it does occupy
the future site of Rome. Meanwhile, Venus uses her sexy allure to
get her husband Vulcan to make divine weaponry for Aeneas. He
goes to his forge under Mount Etna, and addresses the Cyclopes:
'Give me your attention. We have arms to make for a man, a mortal
warrior of high spirit.'[18] The emphasis on 'man' is striking: Vulcan
doesn't normally work for mortals.

As the Cyclopes warm to their task, Evander promises to assist

Aeneas and advises him that the Etruscans, led by Tarchon, have revolted from the oppression of Mezentius:

> Why, he would even have live men bound to dead bodies,
> Clamping them hand to hand and face to face – a horrible
> Method of torture – so that they died a lingering death
> Infected with putrefaction in that most vile embrace.[19]

Finally, Evander tells Aeneas that he will send his son Pallas with him. Aeneas and Pallas head off in a clatter of hooves, and just before they get to the Etruscan camp Venus appears and presents Aeneas with his fabulous armour: a helmet that pours forth flame, a death-dealing sword, a gleaming cuirass, greaves fashioned from gold and electrum, a spear, and a wonderful shield on which are depicted scenes of the story of Italy and the triumphs of the Romans.

Aeneas' shield takes its inspiration from that of Achilles in the *Iliad,* but its context and imagery are very different: Achilles *needs* new armour, but Aeneas does not; when Achilles dons his armour, he goes out to fight for his own glory, whereas when Aeneas dons his, he puts on the future of his people; the scenes on Achilles' shield are very generalized, those on Aeneas' illustrate specific historical moments, such as the she-wolf suckling Romulus and Remus, the 'Rape of the Sabine Women', the attack of the Gauls on Rome in 390 BCE, Catiline in the Underworld, and, in the centre, the Battle of Actium. These scenes also illustrate significant Roman virtues – faithfulness, worshipping the gods, courage in adversity and the consequences of not adhering to this code.

While all this is happening Juno sends Iris to advise Turnus and his Rutulians to assault the Trojan camp. The Trojans decline open battle, but when Turnus shifts his attention to the Trojan fleet, the goddess Cybele, whose sacred grove had provided the wood for the ships, intervenes, prompting Jupiter to transform the vessels into sea-nymphs. Frustrated and furious, Turnus delivers a speech in which he casts himself in the role of a second Menelaus (both have had their brides 'stolen'), and practically summarizes the *Iliad*: he has no need of Vulcan's armour like Achilles wore, no thousand ships, no Trojan Horse. His Italians are a different prospect to Homer's Achaeans.

During the night the two young men, Nisus and Euryalus (who we met in the foot-race at Anchises' funeral games) try to establish contact with Aeneas. Although Nisus is older and more sensible, he makes the tragic mistake of allowing the impetuous Euryalus to accompany him. Worse, the plan evolves beyond just getting a message through to Aeneas into an ill-conceived scheme to ambush the Italians and bring back lots of booty. Initially all goes well, as Nisus and Euryalus make the first killings of the war, but, as they are heading back, a stolen helmet that Euryalus is wearing catches the moonlight and alerts a passing cavalry patrol. Euryalus is apprehended and, when Nisus tries to rescue him executed by his captors. Nisus hurls himself into the midst of the group, drives his sword into its leader's mouth, but he is cut down.

Virgil's narrative then turns back to the siege of the Trojan camp. Turnus destroys a fortified tower and then nine Trojans in quick succession. His brother-in-law Numanus Remulus delivers a harangue that is 'both fit and unfit to repeat': we Italians, he says, are hardy sons of toil, brought up as hunters, farmers and warriors well into old age; you Trojans, with your clothes dyed yellow and purple, delight in dancing and idleness – you are Phrygian women, not Phrygian men![20]

Because real Romans are descended from these Trojans, such a slur cannot go unchallenged. So Ascanius shoots Numanus in the head with a Jupiter-guided arrow. Turnus manages to fight his way into the Trojan camp, but, as his victim-count moves well into double figures, he omits to open the gates to allow in his army. He gets isolated and is forced to swim across the Tiber in full armour to escape.

Back on Mount Olympus, Jupiter has summoned a council of the gods. His jealous pro-Italian wife Juno and unruly pro-Trojan daughter Venus are bickering 'like a pair of rhetorically trained fishwives'.[21] Utterly exasperated, the king of the gods declares that from now on he will remain neutral: 'the Fates will find their way'.

While the Trojans have been fending off Turnus, Aeneas has successfully secured the support of King Tarchon, and together they sail back to the Trojan camp. We get a catalogue of the different Etruscan contingents, including the remarkable Cupavo, who commands the great ship *Centaur*, which itself becomes a centaur, threatening the waves with a massive rock before reverting to ship shape; Ocnus, the founder of Virgil's home town of Mantua; and Aulestes whose ship *Triton* seems to merge into the sea-monster that gives it its name. As Aeneas steers his vessel through the night, the nymphs who used to be his ships appear, and their spokes-woman Cymodocea urges him to hurry back and fight.

Dawn breaks; Aeneas signals his return; the Trojans, like a flock of cranes flying before the storm winds, hurl their spears; and Turnus and the Rutulians see Aeneas with magical fire pouring from his helmet and shield. Turnus is far from overawed, though. He encourages his men to attack, and in one of Virgil's incomplete lines, he shouts: 'Fortune favours the bold!'[22] Aeneas conducts an orderly disembarkation, but Tarchon crashes his ship and writes it off on a shoal. Turnus takes the opportunity to engage.

Now is the time for Aeneas' first *aristeia*. He slaughters a series of strange or exciting 'B-list' adversaries, but with the arrival of the 'A-list' Italians – Clausus, Halaesus and Messapus – the fighting evens out. Pallas, too, has his *aristeia*, eradicating a dozen enemies in a variety of brutal ways. Among them were the identical twins Thymber (decapitated) and Larides (hand chopped off), and Halaesus, to whom it had been foretold that he would die by the arms of Evander – which Pallas is wearing.

The Italian Lausus restores the equilibrium, but, though he struggles to confront Pallas, Fate forbids it: both are destined to die at the hands of greater foes. For Pallas this is Turnus, whose goddess sister Juturna tells him to take Lausus' place. The mighty Rutulian relishes the prospect: 'Pallas is mine and mine alone. I wish his father were here to see it.'[23] Turnus bears down on Pallas; the warriors exchange spear throws; Pallas grazes Turnus; but Pallas' shield, for all its layers of iron, bronze and bull's hide, cannot withstand the impact of Turnus' spear, which penetrates his breastplate and then his breast. Pallas dies as he removes the spear, and the gloating Turnus strips Pallas' heavy, ornamented sword-belt from him. Virgil intervenes in the narrative to emphasize that Turnus will come bitterly to regret doing this.

Aeneas' response to the death of Pallas is a mixture of mad anger (*furor*) and *pietas*: this was the young man's first battle, and Aeneas has failed in his duty of care. He engages in a second *aristeia*, but this time it is an orgy of ruthless, indiscriminate vengeance: he captures eight men so that he can (and will) sacrifice them at Pallas' funeral; he kills Magus as he begs for mercy; chops down a priest of Apollo and Diana; he hacks off the shield-arm of Anxur; when he slays Tarquitus he declares that his body will remain unburied; he is compared with Aegaeon, the fire-breathing, hundred-handed, mythical adversary of Jupiter; he spears Lucagas in the groin, and then dispatches his brother Liger with the words: 'Die now. A brother's place is with his brother'. His onslaught lifts the siege.

The carnage makes Juno suffer a failure of nerve. She creates a phantom Aeneas, which runs away when Turnus attacks it. Turnus pursues it on to an Etruscan ship, Juno breaks the mooring ropes, the ship floats out to sea, the phantom disappears, and Turnus is left to make a despairing speech as he drifts back to his home town of Ardea. His place in the battle is taken by Mezentius. For this impious warrior his right hand and spear are his god, but his missile glances off Aeneas' shield and kills one of the other Trojans; when *pius* Aeneas hurls his spear, he hits Mezentius in the groin. As the Trojan moves in for the kill, Lausus intervenes to save his father, and although a protective hail of Italian spears allows Mezentius to retreat, Aeneas buries his sword in Lausus' chest. This seems to shock Aeneas, particularly when he recalls his love for his own father, and he is moved by an uneasy admiration for his victim. When Mezentius hears that Lausus has died, he mounts his horse Rhaebus and seeks combat, despite being so badly wounded as to stand no chance. He rides round Aeneas, showering him with missiles, until Aeneas drives his spear through the horse's temples. When Rhaebus falls on top of Mezentius and pins him to the ground, the warrior deliberately offers his throat to the sword, and Aeneas obliges.

The Trojans now have possession of the battlefield. They erect a trophy, begin the funeral procession of Pallas, and agree to a twelve-day truce with the Italians. Rumour makes its way to Evander's palace with the news of his son's death. Both sides perform the due funeral rites, with the bereaved women and children cursing the war that had brought them ruin, and the betrothal of Turnus that had caused it.

The idea of resolving the war by a duel between Turnus and Aeneas had been gathering momentum since the Italians sought the truce, and now Drances, the Italian who led that embassy, but who is no friend of Turnus, tries to make it happen. Latinus, who never wanted the war in the first place, is more conciliatory: we have land, he says, that we could give the Trojans; or we could help them to rebuild their fleet; we should send 100 envoys

> holding out the branches of peace in their hands and bearing gifts, talents of gold and ivory, and the throne and robe which are the emblems of our royal power.[24]

But this would be tantamount to surrender, and it gives Drances, who is a typical politician, his opportunity. His argument is essentially: yes, things are bad; we all know what really needs to be done, but no one is saying it openly; the real problem is the proposed marriage of Lavinia to Aeneas, which is why Turnus started the war – so Turnus himself must force the issue in single combat with Aeneas. Turnus responds angrily: he is a soldier; he distrusts politicians; he thinks the war can still be won; but if a duel must be fought, so be it: 'Does Aeneas challenge me alone? I accept and welcome his challenge.'[25] However, the Trojans have started advancing again. The duel will have to wait.

As Turnus arms himself, Camilla arrives. This lovely, impulsive, warrior-maiden agrees to take command of the Latin cavalry while Turnus prepares an ambush against the main Trojan force. Surrounded by her beautiful companions, who are compared with the original Amazons, Camilla kills a dozen warriors in fewer than eighty lines. However, unaware that she is being shadowed by the sinister religious fanatic Arruns, and 'burning with all a woman's passion for spoil and plunder', she tries to track down the glamorous ex-priest Chloreus. She doesn't even hear the arrival of Arruns' spear. The nymph Opis, Diana's sentinel, then shoots Arruns, but Camilla's death results in a full-scale Italian retreat. Those inside the city shut the gates on their own men, and the area outside becomes a killing field. Turnus (in a frenzy – another *furor* moment') foolishly abandons his ambush, allowing Aeneas to return unscathed, and, as night draws in, both sides encamp on the plain.

Turnus, who is distraught with love, then sends a message to Aeneas that he wants to confront him one-on-one. Turnus equips himself with a sword that Vulcan tempered in the River Styx, and furiously prepares to bring down the 'effeminate Phrygian'. He is like a bull pawing the ground, whereas Aeneas' preparations are calm, considered and quietly confident. The Trojans and Latins gather to watch. Virgil, though, makes us wait, by shifting focus back to the divine level. Turnus' sister Juturna was made immortal by Jupiter in recompense for raping her, and Juno, who is not usually friendly to one of her husband's erotic conquests, tells her that Turnus is in mortal danger, and asks her either to snatch Turnus from death or to stir up a war and destroy the treaty.

Back in Italy, Aeneas prays to the Sun, Jupiter, Juno (somewhat pointedly), Mars and all the other gods, and asks them to witness this statement: if Turnus wins, the Trojans will withdraw to the city of Evander; if Aeneas wins he will not seek royal power for himself, and both Italians and Trojans shall move forward into an everlasting treaty, undefeated and equal before the law. As the two combatants move into public view the Rutulians are dismayed – Turnus seems boy-like in comparison to Aeneas. But again Virgil sells us a dummy, making Juturna disguise herself as Camers to harangue the Rutulians and persuade them that they should all be fighting, not just Turnus. She sends an omen; Tolumnius the augur interprets it, and then throws a spear at the Trojans that kills one of the nine sons of Gylippos and Tyrrhena; the surviving eight brothers want revenge; and this leads to more slaughter by spear, sword and setting fire to one warrior's beard.

Aeneas tries to remind his allies about the treaty, but he is hit mid-speech by an arrow, and has to leave the field for treatment. Turnus charges forward, accounting for another thirteen victims. Aeneas is desperate to get back to the battle, and tries to extract the arrowhead himself. When the healer Iapyx is unable to cure his wound, Venus picks some dittany in Crete and secretly tinctures the water with it. Aeneas recovers miraculously. He kisses Ascanius and tells him to remember him and his 'Uncle Hector', before entering the fray. This time, however, Aeneas does not kill anyone at first: his focus is solely on Turnus.

The disguised Juturna then knocks Turnus' driver out of his chariot and takes his place and his physical appearance. As Aeneas tries to follow the chariot, the plumes of his helmet are sheared off by Messapus' spear. Only after this does he rush into the battle, full of *furor*. He and Turnus both kill many more men, and Turnus hangs the severed heads of Diores and Amycus on his chariot. Everything is evenly poised.

At this juncture, Venus gives her son the idea of attacking the Latins' city, and, when Queen Amata sees the enemy approaching, she assumes that Turnus has been killed and hangs herself. In her grief, Lavinia tears her golden hair and rosy cheeks, while Latinus rends his clothes and dirties his hair with handfuls of dust. Turnus, who by this time is running out of energy, hears the wailing coming from the city, and confesses that he has known for some time that his charioteer is actually Juturna. He wants to fight, and is prepared to die, so he leaps from the chariot and rushes towards the city like a boulder crashing down from a mountain. He appeals for an end to the fighting so that the duel can take place between himself and Aeneas. The armies part and leave a space between them.

The two great adversaries start by throwing their spears, then fight with swords and shields, clashing like bulls fighting for mastery of the herd. Jupiter lifts up a set of scales to see who will live and die, but Virgil does not tell us the outcome. Turnus strikes a blow at Aeneas; a great shout arises from both sides; but then they see Turnus' sword lying in fragments on the sand – in his excitement he has grabbed an ordinary man-made weapon, not the Vulcan-made one that he had been using so effectively before. He runs, and Aeneas gives chase; Turnus keeps having to retrace his steps to avoid a great marsh, the walls of the city and the Trojans; Aeneas cannot press home his advantage because his wounded leg hampers his pursuit; Turnus calls for his divine sword; Aeneas threatens death to anyone who gives it to him; in lines based on Achilles' pursuit of Hector in the *Iliad*, they run five times in a circle; it is a crazy race (*ludicra*) and would be funny in any other context. Then the initiative swings back Turnus' way. Aeneas runs to where his spear landed when he first hurled it at Turnus, but it has stuck in the root of a wild olive tree sacred to Faunus. While Aeneas struggles to free it, Juturna hands Turnus his magic sword, and with it the advantage. But Venus frees the spear for her son, and the two warriors stand with their spirits and weapons restored, breathing heavily.

A divine interlude of almost 100 lines now occurs, building the tension, but also resolving one of the key issues of the poem. Jupiter forbids Juno to go on harassing the Trojans. She agrees, but she wants this to be the end of Troy, and will be reconciled with the Trojans only if the Italians become the dominant partners in the alliance from which the Roman people will spring; they must not change their language or native dress; and when the two people unite they must be called 'Latins' or 'Italians', not 'Trojans'. Jupiter accepts.

As Aeneas and Turnus confront each other for the last time, Jupiter sends down a Dira, a Fury-like demon that assumes the form of a small owl that sits on tombstones at night. It repeatedly flies screeching into Turnus' face. He is overwhelmed with fear, and Juturna realizes what it means and backs off, lamenting the fact that Jupiter has granted her immortality, when what she really wants is to die with her brother. Aeneas moves in on Turnus, taunting him as he does so; Turnus sees a huge boundary-stone, put there, ironically, 'to keep these fields free from strife' (a dozen of today's strongest men could not lift it). We expect Turnus to heave it at Aeneas, but it falls short; he is in the middle of what seems like a bad dream, unable to run, weak and voiceless; his wits are scrambled; he is on his own. Aeneas simply bides his time, and, when he does strike, his spear roars louder than a stone hurled by siege artillery or a thunderbolt, and lodges in Turnus' thigh. The wound forces him to his knees like a suppliant. He admits that he was wrong; foregoes his claim to Lavinia, and pleads for his life in a way that recalls Anchises' words in Book 6: 'war down' the proud, but spare the conquered.

Aeneas hesitates, running his eyes over Turnus as he speaks. The longer this goes on, the more indecisive Aeneas becomes. But then he catches sight of the sword-belt that Turnus captured from Pallas; memories of Pallas and Evander flood back; the passions those memories arouse rise higher; driven by his *pietas* towards Pallas and Evander, and by terrible *furor*, Aeneas cries, 'It is Pallas who exacts the penalty in your guilty blood', and plunges his sword into Turnus' breast. There the *Aeneid* ends.

Did *furor* win in the end, or *pietas*? The emotional and moral effects of the ending are highly ambiguous. What Aeneas does is entirely believable, particularly to an audience that had known almost 100 years of civil war. Modern readers are frequently disgusted at Turnus' death, but the really unsettling thing is that it is very hard to say, hand on heart, that if we had gone through what Aeneas had we might not have done the same in that split second. More prosaically, the death of Turnus was necessary for the plot. Although they are not dramatized in the *Aeneid*, the subsequent events that led to the eventual foundation of Rome some 400 years later have been prophesied by Jupiter in Book 1. On Aeneas' death, Ascanius will take over and rule the settlement at Lavinium, and then transfer the seat of power to Alba Longa. Here a series of kings will rule for 300 years until Romulus founds the city of Rome. These Romans, Jupiter said, would not be constricted by time or space, and would wield unlimited power. For Aeneas, it is mission accomplished.

15

ROMAN SOCIAL LIFE

Rome stands built upon the ancient ways of life and upon her men.

Ennius

Free Romans

As Virgil makes clear in the *Aeneid*, the enormous, mighty, cosmopolitan city of Rome grew out of a small farming village on the banks of the Tiber. The people who initially made Rome so powerful were highly conservative, with a great respect for the traditions of their ancestors, which they called the *mos maiorum*, an ethos that is eloquently expressed by Horace, whose father told him:

> I will have achieved my aim if I can train you in the ways of the worthy folk of the days of old, and keep your name and life unspoiled.[1]

The preservation of the *mos maiorum* was important to the stability, cohesiveness and continuity of Roman society. Because Rome was originally an agricultural community that often had to defend itself, the qualities of successful farmers and soldiers became transformed into virtues, most notably *gravitas* (a sense of responsibility end earnestness), *frugalitas* (frugality of taste) and *pietas* (a sense of duty towards family, state and gods). Soldiering, too, was laudable because it represented patriotism. Recall Horace's famous line: *dulce et decorum est pro patria mori*[2] It is sweet and honourable to die for your fatherland. Even when the rustic village had metamorphosed into an imperial metropolis, these gritty values remained at the heart of the Roman self-image.

Obviously the reality did not always match the ideal: there were plenty of frivolous, lazy, scrounging Romans, and nowadays the word 'Roman' is more likely to be associated with orgies, mad emperors and crowds baying for blood in an amphitheatre. Nevertheless, throughout their history, the Romans had a clearly defined notion of how they were expected to behave, and a classic example of this is the legendary Horatius Cocles, a farmer-soldier who, in 508 BCE, single-handedly repelled the attacking Etruscans from the one bridge over the River Tiber while the other Romans chopped it down. He saved Rome because he was tough, persistent and, above all, had the *pietas* to put his own life on the line. His courage and *pietas* were rewarded with glory (a statue was erected in his honour) and farmland (as much as he could plough in one day), and it is interesting to contrast him with the Greek heroes Achilles, who put himself before the communal safety of his comrades, and Odysseus, who prevailed because he was quick-witted.

The Romans lived in an extremely class-conscious society, in which the older and nobler your family, the higher you stood on the social ladder. A Roman's status was determined by the possession (or lack) of wealth, freedom and Roman citizenship, and the division between those who had Roman citizenship and those who did not was fundamental. Until 212 CE three groups of men (not women) qualified for Roman citizenship:

1. Free-born men whose parents were from a Roman citizen background;
2. Freedmen: men freed from slavery. Ex-slaves became citizens and could vote, and, although they could not stand for high office, become a Senator or be one of the *Equites*, their sons could;
3. Individuals or communities who were granted citizenship by the Roman government, e.g. ex-soldiers from the provinces received Roman citizenship on retirement.

In the early Republic citizenship conferred a number of public and private rights. In the public arena citizens could vote on legislation and at elections, and hold office as magistrates. This brought an obligation to pay taxes, serve in the legions and be subject to the magistrates. In private, the right of *conubium* recognized the validity of a marriage, the bequests in a will and the right to hold inherited property; *commercium* conferred the right to buy land and to get a fair price for what was sold; and *provocatio* granted the right of appeal to an Assembly against the act of a Roman magistrate. The statement, 'I am a Roman citizen,' was a crucial one, and an especially famous example of someone asserting this was Saint Paul:

> And as they bound him with thongs, Paul said unto the centurion that stood by, Is it lawful for you to scourge a man that is Roman, and uncondenmed? When the centurion heard that, he went and told the chief captain, saying, Take heed what thou doest; for this man is a Roman. Then the chief captain came, and said unto him. Tell me, art thou a Roman? He said, Yea.[3]

However, not everyone was as fortunate as Paul. Cicero described how Gaius Verres, a corrupt governor of Sicily in the 70s BCE committed heinous atrocities against Gavius of Consa, a Roman citizen. Gavius was:

> dragged into the middle of the forum, stripped, tied, and whipped. The poor man shouted out that he was a Roman citizen, a resident of Consa, that he had served in the army. [Verres ignored this and] the whole time, while he [Gavius] suffered, while the whip cracked, no groan, no cry of any kind was heard from the tortured man except 'I am a Roman citizen.'[4]

Eventually Verres crucified him.

Citizens' rights were held to be so important that in 90 BCE the Italians went to war with Rome to win them. Full Roman citizenship was ultimately extended to all free people in Italy, and the process of granting citizenship to the inhabitants of the Empire outside Italy continued – for instance, in 49 BCE Julius Caesar gave the franchise to Transalpine Gaul, a Gallic legion and several provincial towns. Roman citizenship was ultimately granted to all free people (women included) within the borders of the Empire by Caracalla in 212 CE under the *constitutio Antoniniana* (Antonine constitution). This can be seen either as a liberal move to eradicate the distinctions between Roman citizens and non-citizens within the Empire or as a cynical ploy to increase the numbers liable to taxes on citizens by around 300 per cent. Any free person born in Britain, Spain, Greece, Egypt or Syria could therefore assert 'I am a Roman citizen', although by that time the most important privileges of citizenship only applied to the higher of the two citizen classes: the *honestiores* (Senators, *Equites*, army officers, etc.) and the *humiliores* (everyone else). In law the *honestiores* were subject to less severe punishments – rarely death, and never crucifixion, being thrown to the beasts or forced labour in the mines – which again emphasizes how extremely class-conscious was Roman society.

One possible safety-net for Rome's poor population was the patron–client relationship. The fundamental unit of Roman society was the *familia*, at whose head was the *paterfamilias*. Although it gives us our word 'family', *familia* included dependants and property as well as blood relatives – 'household' is a better translation. The *paterfamilias* had responsibility for the welfare of his wife, children, relatives by blood or adoption, freedmen and slaves, and they owed total obedience to him. A similar situation applied at State level, since the Romans regarded membership of the State (the *res publica*, 'public matter') as analogous to membership of a *familia*. The Senators (not called *patres*, 'fathers', entirely by coincidence) were expected to look after the welfare of those inferior to them, in return for respect. In practice, of course, the arrangement did not always work like this, but it led to a crucial paternalistic relationship at the heart of Roman society: that between *cliens* ('client') and *patronus* ('patron').

The way the system was intended to work is outlined in the *Leges Regiae* ('Royal Laws') attributed to Romulus. He allowed every plebeian to choose any patrician that he wanted as his patron. It was the duty of the patricians to explain the laws to their clients; to do everything for them that fathers do for their sons with regard to money; to go to court on their behalf when they were wronged; and to defend them against anyone who brought charges against them. As time went on, some plebeian families also rose to a position where they might become patrons, but in the early days patrons tended to come from the Senatorial class, and they expected their clients to work on behalf of their political careers, vote for them and to appear with them as retainers in public. The more clients you had, the greater your status.

The entire patron/client system was, in theory, a mutually beneficial arrangement, but as time went on there was a shift in the way it operated. Manumitted slaves automatically became *clientes* of their ex-masters, and because they tended not to be native Romans, they had a different take on the relationship. Furthermore, in the Imperial period, when opportunities for political campaigning were severely curtailed, both parties needed to find new ways of maintaining the relationship. As a consequence of the *salutatio* ('morning salute'), which publicly acknowledged the patron's superiority, the role of *cliens* frequently came to be that of a cringing, sycophantic parasite. Clients would turn up at a patron's house in the morning wearing togas (it was considered indecent to dress in anything else) and queue in order of their social status before greeting their patron as *dominus* ('master'). The client might be hoping for distributed food (*sportula*), gifts, cash, dinner invitations or even inheritances. In the first century CE writers such as Seneca and Martial were very disparaging about both the degeneration of the *clientes* and the corresponding arrogance of the patrons.

There was even a hierarchy of patrons: Martial indicates that if you went to see your patron, there was a chance that he might not be there because he was visiting *his* patron. Most frustrating, particularly if your patron lived on the other side of Rome. Yet, as Seneca tells us in his *Essay About the Brevity of Life*, even if your patron was at home, there was no guarantee of a successful outcome. He might be still in bed, ignore you or rush off on a pretence of urgent business after keeping you waiting for ages. He might not even be able to remember your name,[5] and the poet Juvenal adds that even a 'successful' meeting might not be worth all the degradation, if all you got was a bimonthly invitation to a dinner with appalling wine and ghastly food.[6]

Rome's emperors tended to treat the urban population of Rome as their own *clientes*. Under the Republic this often volatile and dangerous group of people had frequently been manipulated by ambitious politicians, but when Augustus finally established himself as *Princeps*, he remained acutely aware of the practical aspects of keeping the plebs docile. No one could outbid him:

> To every man of the common people of Rome I paid 300 *sestertii* in accordance with my father's will; and in my own name I gave 400 *sestertii* from the spoils of war in my 5th consulship . . . These gratuities of mine reached never fewer than 250,000 persons . . . I gave 60 *denarii* to each of the common people then in receipt of the corn-dole, namely slightly over 200,000 persons.[7]

The 200,000 people sufficiently poor to qualify for the corn dole is not the same as the number of those 'out of work and claiming benefit', because they would need to supplement this with income from a variety of jobs. But the 'conventional wisdom' of the upper classes towards them is illuminated by Cicero, who said that the 'vulgar' livelihoods are those of hired workmen who are paid for manual labour rather than for artistic skill; those buying from wholesale merchants to retail immediately; mechanics; and trades that cater for sensual pleasures, such as fishmongers, butchers, cooks, perfumers and dancers. On the other hand, professions requiring a high degree of intelligence, or from which significant benefit to society is derived – medicine, architecture, teaching, etc. – are proper for those whose social position they become. But, of all the occupations by which gain is secured, none is better than agriculture.[8]

The Roman plebs often appear as a rather faceless mass ignored by Roman writers: the vast majority of our literary sources do not come from the 'man-or-woman-in-the-street'. That cliché, 'woman-in-the-street', is more relevant to Rome than it is to Athens. In comparison to their Athenian counterparts, Roman women enjoyed relative freedom both inside and outside the home, and the history of Rome resonates with women who left their mark in a way that those of Athens could never do. The emphasis of many ancient historians, and the salacious interests of some of the poets, can leave a distorted picture of intrigue, immorality and high-level political chicanery, but even so they provide fascinating insights. If we are aware of who is being referred to, what stratum of society she belonged to, what her age and marital status was, and what the context and purpose of the source were, we can get a long way into the everyday workings of Roman society.

Roman law said that women had *infirmitas sexus* ('the weakness of their sex') and *levitas animi* ('light-mindedness'). In childhood a woman was under the authority (*manus*) of the *paterfamilias*, who had absolute power, extending (theoretically) to taking her life. Because there was a choice between types of marriage, he also decided whether his daughter would ultimately live under the *manus* of her husband after she got married or remain under his. There were three forms of marriage in which the woman was subject to the *manus* of her husband: *confarreatio* (formal marriage); *coemptio* (marriage consisting of a mutual 'mock sale' by which the wife was released from her own family); and *usus* (cohabitation for one year). Quite how much authority the husband had over his wife in these types of marriage is debatable: Cato tells us that husbands had the right to kill their wives for adultery or drinking (because drinking leads to adultery), but Dionysius of Halicarnassus states that the husband had at least to confer with the woman's relatives first. The marriage without the *manus* of the husband (*sine manu*) is well attested also. The advantage is that the property of the woman's family does not transfer to the husband's, and it was a common form of marriage in the Republic, although it was a cause of instability because it was easy for the woman to return to her family.

Roman marriages were often political in nature, designed to cement links between influential families: Julius Caesar married off his daughter Julia to Pompey; Octavian married off his sister Octavia to Mark Antony; and in legend Aeneas loved Dido, but ultimately made a dynastic marriage with Lavinia. This is nothing new in the ancient world, although in Rome we do hear of women initiating the marriage, as Valeria did when she won over the dictator Sulla.

According to the definition of Herrenius Modestinus, Roman marriage was 'a joining together of a man and a woman, and a partnership (for life) in all areas of life, a sharing in divine and human law'.[9] It usually took place when the girl was around fourteen years of age, and would be preceded by a formal betrothal and usually accompanied by a dowry, which was transferred to the husband for the duration of the marriage. Although childbirth was dangerous and infant mortality high, the man essentially took a wife for the procreation of children, and in early Rome he had the right to decide whether or not a pregnancy should continue and whether or not to keep any children that were born. Under the Principate, although there was still some disapproval, contraception and abortion were practised by women who were unwilling to bear children. A doctor in Trajan's reign advised that it was better to prevent conception taking place and only to resort to abortion to prevent later danger in childbirth if the uterus is too small, has swellings or cracks at the entrance, or some such difficulty.[10] He goes on to give a number of methods of contraception using herbs and medicines. In about 200 CE abortion was criminalized, although exposure was not outlawed until 374 CE.

Divorce was relatively easy and by the first century BCE could be initiated by either party through the withdrawal of *affectio maritalis* (the reciprocal attitude of regarding one another as husband and wife), but, if the woman was still in the *manus* of her father, it was also possible for him to dissolve the marriage. The dowry was a major concern and, unless the woman was divorced for immoral conduct, it would be returned to her family. Julius Caesar divorced Pompeia after the Bona Dea scandal; Pompey divorced Mucia Tertia who had been unfaithful to him during his absence from Rome in the 60s BCE; yet we hear very little of divorce on the ground of an adulterous *husband*, largely due to the double standard that saw relationships with slaves and/or prostitutes as healthy and acceptable, or at least preferable to those with other men's wives:

> The sight of a famous aristocrat leaving a brothel drew
> a famous remark from Cato: 'Keep up the good work!' he said.
> 'Whenever a young man's veins are swollen by accursed lust
> he's right to go down to that sort of place instead of grinding
> other men's wives.[11]

An adulterous husband is only punished if he consorts with another man's *wife*. Getting caught in the act could involve extremely painful and humiliating retribution if the wronged husband was able to overpower his rival – Catullus speaks of the adulterer having a horse-radish (considerably bigger than the English variety) or a mullet shoved up his backside.[12]

Childlessness might also be a reason for the dissolution of a marriage. An inscription called the *Laudatio Turiae* shows that Turia 'did the right thing' and offered her husband a divorce on these grounds, although he rejected the idea. The children of divorced parents remained with their father.

Widows were encouraged to remarry yet also to remain faithful to the memory of their dead husband in accordance with the very Roman ideal of the *univira* (= a woman that has only had one husband). This serves to illustrate the considerable, and often conflicting, demands that were made on Roman women. The ancient sources are full of *exempla* (role models) whose behaviour reinforces an ideal of virtue, with a great stress on chastity, although these particular women tend to be mythical, upper-class and either heroines or villains, so the tales don't tell us what life was really like. The tombstone of Amymone indicates that the qualities admired in a Roman *matrona* and *materfamilias* included being beautiful, a maker of wool, dutiful, respectable, a good housewife, chaste and a stay-at-home,[13] although this too should perhaps be treated with caution because funerary monuments tend to idealize the deceased.

The growth of Rome's empire, the influx of wealth and slaves that went with it, marriages *sine manu*, and the repeal of various austerity laws, were all instrumental in giving new independence and assertiveness to some Roman women. Certain women also came to be better educated under Greek influence, and artistic and literary accomplishments could enhance a woman's reputation: Pompey's cultured wife Cornelia was praised for her lyre-playing, geometry and philosophy. Occasionally, however, it went too far for Roman taste, as in the case of Sempronia, who, says Sallust, was well educated in Greek and Latin literature, but had greater skill in lyre-playing and dancing than any respectable woman really needed. Seemliness and chastity were not her greatest assets, yet he acknowledges that she could write poetry, crack jokes and converse with decorum, tenderness or wantonness, and that she was truly 'a woman of ready wit and considerable charm'.[14] It was women like this that Roman poets often wrote about: Catullus' Lesbia, Tibullus' Delia, and Ovid's Corinna are all well-educated, intelligent, independent, high-maintenance girlfriends.

Unlike Athenian women, Roman women spent a large amount of time in public. They were permitted to attend the circus, theatre and amphitheatre, subject to certain rules (e.g. in the theatre they had to sit behind the men, though this was not the case in the circus), and could accompany their husbands to dinner parties. In fact, even Rome's first Emperor could not control the women of his own household, despite his high-profile public concern with morality, married life and families. His daughter Julia was married to his stepson Tiberius, who spent a lot of his time away from Rome, and things went badly awry. She was thirty-eight, 'a time of life approaching old age',[15] but obviously didn't regard herself as an old maid (she had her grey hairs removed by a slave girl), and she became the leader of a smart, extravagant, pleasure-loving set. But in 2 BCE Augustus banished her:

> She had been accessible to scores of paramours; in nocturnal revels she had roamed about the city; the very forum and the rostrum, from which her father had proposed a law against adultery, had been chosen by the daughter for her debaucheries; she had daily resorted to the statue of Marsyas, and, laying aside the role of adulteress, there sold her favours.[16]

Despite the trends towards greater emancipation of women, certain ingrained male attitudes remained pretty unreconstructed. In a proposal of 21 CE that makes Roman military wives sound like modern footballers' 'Wags', Caecina Severus argued that Romans going abroad as governors should not be allowed to take their wives along, on the grounds that a company of women makes a Roman march more like a barbarian invasion. Women might be weak and not up to the physical exertion, but they are ferocious, meddlesome and soon have the centurions under their thumb.[17] His proposal was defeated, however, on the grounds that 'if a woman does wrong, it is her husband's fault'.

Children and Education

Like other members of the *familia*, children were totally under the control of the *paterfamilias*. The *Leges Regiae* gave the father the power to imprison his son, scourge him, put him in chains, keep him at work in the fields or put him to death.[18]

In Rome's early days, education placed great emphasis on the *mos maiorum*, the family and one's seniors. A child's initial upbringing was entrusted to the mother until, at the age of seven, a boy came under his father's supervision. An upper-class *paterfamilias* would teach his son reading, writing, PE, how to use weapons and, using the legends of Rome and its heroes, moral and social conduct, plus a knowledge of Roman law as enshrined in the Twelve Tables. The boy would accompany his father as he went about his business, and learn the art of public speaking by listening to the speeches of the great orators.

The importance of role models was paramount. At sixteen the boy assumed the *toga virilis* (gown of manhood) and might well be placed under the charge of an older person of distinction to be educated in public affairs. Such a period was called *tirocinium fori*. The youth would then do a similar apprenticeship as an aide to a military officer.

The values inculcated in the young Roman emphasized patriotism and the greater good of the community. Luxury and softness initially had no place in an education programme that was less about developing the individual than about preparing the citizen for practical life. However, in the third and second centuries BCE Greek culture began to impinge on Roman life and some Romans started to adopt elements of Greek educational practice. A system of schools developed, although some upper-class students were educated at home by a private tutor, usually a Greek slave or freedman, in which case their education was bilingual in Greek and Latin. In fact, the vast majority of teachers were Greek. From the ages of seven to eleven, both boys and girls might go to a primary school where they were chaperoned by a *paedagogus*, a slave who might act as a personal tutor, and who accompanied them to, at and from their lessons, which were taught by a *Litterator* or *Ludi Magister*. The curriculum would be centred on learning to read, write and do basic arithmetic.

From age twelve upwards, the children – now more boys than girls (who would be getting married at around fourteen) – attended a secondary school under the tutelage of a *Grammaticus*. They studied grammar, literature and general subjects such as history and philosophy. Both Greek and Latin authors were studied, often with quite detailed analysis of the original language.

The student's tertiary education mainly revolved around the study of rhetoric conducted by a *Rhetor*. If the boys (hardly any girls by this stage) wanted an advanced education, they might go abroad to a Greek 'university town' such as Athens or Rhodes. The ultimate goal of this educational track was facility in rhetoric, although there was also a strong emphasis on morality.

Not everyone approved of this system, however, and by the early second century BCE there were two clearly discernible trends in Roman education: the traditional one espoused by conservatives such as M. Porcius Cato, who was hostile to pretty much all things Greek; and a Greek-influenced one embraced by the likes of the 'Scipionic Circle' and epitomized by the education of Scipio Aemilianus, the son of Aemilius Paullus, who was surrounded by Greek teachers, scholars, rhetoricians, sculptors, painters, overseers of horses and hounds, and instructors in hunting (Terence's *The Brothers* may be a topical reflection of the issues of the day).

Strongly developed skills in public persuasion were a ticket to high office, authority within the Senate and influence with the plebs. So suspicious of this art were the traditionalists that in 161 BCE teachers of rhetoric were banned from living in Rome, and an edict passed in 92 BCE outlined the conservatives' specific objections to rhetoricians: they were undermining the *mos maiorum*. Nevertheless, they remained in demand. The *Rhetores* were a close approximation of the Greek Sophists, and there were certain fixed conventions or rules for orators, which were assimilated by their students through various preparatory exercises. Then the pupils had to compose imaginary speeches and deliver them to their fellow students. An important part of this exercise (*declamatio*) was using the appropriate facial gestures and hand movements.

There were two different kinds of *declamatio*. One, called *suasoria*, was rather like an undergraduate essay assignment, since it involved producing a speech justifying some historical or fictional course of action: 'Should Sulla have resigned his dictatorship?', 'Should Cato have committed suicide?', etc. The second type was the *controversia*, which involved arguing for or against particular legal cases, such as: Suppose that the law states that if a woman has been raped she can choose either to have the rapist condemned to death or to marry him without giving him any dowry. A man rapes two women on the same night. One asks for him to be put to death, the other chooses to marry him. Defend either proposal.

In a culture that was predominantly oral, there was considerable relevance in cultivating an art that would be useful in the law courts and politics, where aspiring young Romans often sought to make their mark. However, with the demise of the Republic it became far too dangerous for wannabe politicians to speak their minds, so the art of *declamatio* metamorphosed into a rather artificial exercise practised for its own sake. Its themes became totally improbable, and the whole thing became a triumph of style over content. In first century CE Petronius opened his *Satyricon* with a tirade against the 'ludicrous amalgamation of honeyed words and delicate phrases that fit ill with the bloody subject-matter';[19] and the Younger Pliny summarized the decline beautifully:

> Has the news reached you? Valerius Licinianus has taken up teaching rhetoric in Sicily. What a fall. What a drop. Only yesterday he was a senator and an orator – now an exile and a *rhetor*. At his first lecture he came in dressed in a Greek cloak and announced that he would dilate on this theme: 'how the mighty are fallen'.[20]

Slaves

A Roman would be unlikely to include slaves in a chapter on Roman society, since slaves were not regarded as a social group. They were property. But they were nevertheless an integral part of Rome's social fabric. Rome was a slave-owning society for its entire history – so was everywhere else at the time – and the institution went unquestioned, even if a few intellectuals began to explore the morality of the actual treatment of slaves. Yet it is extremely difficult to generalize about things like the lifestyle, position, treatment, opportunities and life-expectancy of slaves, since this was entirely dependent on issues such as: where they came from; how they had been sourced (captured in war, kidnapped by pirates, born into slavery?); how well educated they were; whom they belonged to; what tasks they carried out; and so on.

Although the Romans always took for granted the existence of slaves, they also lived in perpetual fear of them, neatly expressed in the proverbial phrase *tot servi quot hostes* (= 'as many enemies as you have slaves'). In some ways their fear was entirely justified, and it certainly dictated legislation and public attitudes. In 135 BCE some slaves on a large farm in Sicily started a revolt that went on for nearly four years and ultimately involved more than 70,000 slaves before the Roman army crushed it; another revolt occurred in Sicily in 104–101 BCE; and the most famous revolt was that of Spartacus

(73–71 BCE). The memory of Spartacus' rebellion may well be behind the story of the Senate rejecting a proposal to distinguish slaves from freedmen by their dress, on the grounds that it would be extremely dangerous if the slaves became aware of their numbers.[21]

The Romans had a number of sources of supply for slaves, including: anyone captured in war; people seized by pirates or kidnappers; unsuccessful rebellious provincials; people enslaved for debt (prior to 326 BCE); criminals convicted of capital crimes; exposed children 'rescued' into slavery; children sold by families who could no longer feed them; and the offspring of slaves. Like any other form of property, you could buy them, give them to someone, inherit them, and acquire them by sequestration (i.e. as part of a debt from someone else's property), but you could also breed them. From the mid-second century BCE the island of Delos became the greatest slave-market yet known, allegedly capable of both admitting and sending away 10,000 slaves on the same day.[22] From sources like this slaves were then sold in the Forum at Rome.

It was common to stereotype the tasks of a slave by nationality: Gauls or Spaniards would make good herdsmen; Greeks would make good doctors; and so on. In a large household a slave might do a specialized job, perhaps as a shorthand writer (*notarius*), clerk or accountant. An ex-slave of Augustus' time left more than 4,000 slaves in his legacy, and the fictional Trimalchio, a nouveau-riche ex-slave with taste inversely proportional to his staggering wealth, also owned a vast number of slaves, including one boy with a carefully grown mop of hair on which he would wipe his hands. In a reasonably affluent home there might be a specialist tutor or a nurse, plus any number of litter-bearers, cooks, gardeners, hair-dressers, laundrywomen and the like. In a smaller household there might be just one or two slaves whose duties would be spread more widely. Many of the slave characters in Roman comedy are of this type, helping their masters in the fields, doing odd jobs and generally enjoying a reasonably affable relationship with them. They might also receive a *peculium*, a grant of property (usually a business), which the slave was permitted to manage (but not own) and which might in time provide the financial wherewithal for buying his freedom.

Domestic service was infinitely preferable to work on a farm, in a mine or factory, or as a public slave. City-owned slaves worked on things like construction projects, while other slaves were used by factory owners or large landowners, for whom they would literally slave away at one dreary lifelong job. Among the most unfortunate were those purchased to serve as gladiators or prostitutes.

Varro gives advice on the purchase of slaves; reads like a visit to a cattle market, and the similarity is not just fortuitous. A reputable slave dealer, in a process that, in terms of attitudes and prices, resembles a second-hand car dealership would certify that the slave was in good health, not a runaway (i.e. someone else's property), and was not guilty of any crime. A second-century CE papyrus document from Roman Egypt shows us how Julius Germanus took possession of a female slave, about twenty-five years old, from Agathos Daemon: she was non-returnable (except if she was epileptic), cost a whopping 1,200 *dr.* and came with a warranty.[23]

Many family slaves were also born in the household. The Roman term for such a slave was *verna*, and, while these tended to experience better conditions, the master, too, might benefit from the fact that they would be able to speak (and probably read) Latin, and would (hopefully) be attached to his family, work better and not revolt. Cicero's friend Atticus had a household consisting entirely of *vernae*.

If you did not want to invest your capital in buying slaves, you could rent them. A rental agreement made in 186 CE by the slave-owner Glaukios shows just how dismal the plight of a rental slave could be – rental customers tended to be less concerned about the welfare of the property they had hired, and in this case the slave was allowed eight days holiday a year, and if her master needed her during the night to bake bread, he could summon her without anything being deducted from the rental fee.[24]

There are a number of works, such as the Elder Cato's *On Agriculture*, which give slave-owners the hard-nosed advice to sell aged or unhealthy slaves in the way that you would offload old work oxen or blemished sheep. Varro's *De Re Rustica* also contains interesting material on the management of slaves, advocating the use of slaves who are neither cowed nor high-spirited, not controlling them with whips if they can achieve the same result with words, avoiding having too many slaves of the same nationality, and granting overseers a bit of property of their own, as well as mates from among their fellow slaves to bear them children.[25] Columella, who wrote a treatise that provides guidance to owners of fairly large agricultural estates, recommends being pretty circumspect about what types of slave you should appoint as overseers: it is not a good idea, he says, to appoint a physically attractive overseer, or one who has been 'engaged in the voluptuous occupations of the city'.[26] This lazy and sleepy-headed class of slaves, he says, are accustomed to idling, the circus, the theatres, gambling, taverns and bawdy houses, and carry that ethos into their farming, to the detriment of their master.

Columella's comments about lazy, sleepy-headed slaves should not deflect us from the stark fact that slaves were still chattels with hardly any rights. The master could inflict punishment or even kill the slave without sanction, as well as to use him or her sexually (as a favourable alternative to adultery). Even if the slave was to perform this 'service' unwillingly, the man's wife might still be jealous of the slave who had aroused her husband's interest, as is a suspicious wife in Juvenal's *Satire* 6. Her husband has ignored her in bed, so she has most of her household punished:

> The wool-maid's had it, cosmeticians are stripped and flogged,
> The litter-bearer's accused of coming late. One victim
> Has rods broken over his back, another bears bloody stripes
> From the whip, a third is lashed with a cat-o'-nine-tails:
> Some women pay their floggers an annual salary.[27]

Worse forms of sadism are also well documented, notably in the person of Vedius Pollio, who used to throw slaves into ponds of lamprey eels so that he could enjoy watching them being eaten alive. So, not surprisingly, some slaves tried to run away. Some masters would brand their slaves, or make them wear identification collars giving specific instructions about how to return the slave, and professional slave-hunters made a living by tracking down fugitives, whose crime was interesting: as the property of their masters, they had technically stolen themselves.

There were times when slaves were driven to murdering their master, but Roman slave-owners had zero tolerance for such a crime. In these cases the entire household of the slaves would be executed. In 61 CE a slave murdered the Prefect of the City of

Rome, so all 400 of his household slaves were sentenced to death. On this occasion the Roman populace tried to get the Senate to show leniency, but C. Cassius stated the case for execution – 'you will not restrain such a motley rabble except by fear'[28]. The punishment was carried out.

Despite this undeniably harsh treatment of the slave population, there is also solid evidence for more liberal attitudes. Masters generally had a vested interest in being good to their slaves, since it benefitted them financially, but there is also widespread proof of genuine affection: Cicero for one was on very friendly terms with his slave Tiro, eventually manumitting him (to the heartfelt approval of his brother), and the slaves in the comedies of Plautus and Terence often have warm relationships with their masters. Indeed, with a good master in an affluent household, a slave might be materially better off than a poor free person – clothed, fed, housed, provided with all the basic needs and possibly allowed to have a concubine. As a Stoic, Seneca the Younger believed that all men were equal insofar as they were all citizens of the universe, and also that an angry and cruel slave-owner damaged himself by becoming dominated by negative emotions. The Stoics did not advocate the abolition of slavery (nobody did, and Seneca owned a lot of slaves), but they did recommend humane treatment.

A certain amount of protective legislation came in during the Imperial era, including under Claudius a prohibition on the abandonment of sick slaves, with Hadrian imposing restrictions on taking a slaves' evidence while under torture, forbidding masters to kill their slaves, and defining more closely which slaves could be sold to a pimp, a gladiator trainer or sent to fight wild beasts in the amphitheatre. The late Roman Empire is often popularly portrayed as an age of decline and depravity, but it was a period when some genuinely humane legislation was passed, and certain liberal attitudes emerged, particularly a feeling that slaves' lowly status was not valid under natural law because, according to the law of nature, all men are equal.[29]

The ultimate goal for any slave, of course, was freedom. The process of becoming a freedman or freedwoman (*libertus/liberta* in relation to your ex-master; *libertinus/libertina* in relation to the state) was called 'manumission', literally 'releasing from *manus* (the hand of authority)'. This could take a number of forms:

in the master's will; at a special hearing before a magistrate (the *vindicta*: this was initially the rod with which a slave was touched in the ceremony, and then came to mean the ceremony itself); by letter; making a special announcement among witnesses (*inter amicos*); and, since in a slave economy every human being has their price, buying your freedom from your savings. The motives of the master might vary: pure cynicism (liberating a slave who was ill or weak and so shirking any duty of care, or trying to defraud creditors); financial (benefitting from the income generated); a desire to gain social status by increasing the number of *clientes*; sheer practicality (it gave other slaves a powerful incentive to work); or basic *humanitas* ('humanity'/'kindness').

The Roman willingness to liberate slaves was fairly liberal in comparison with many other ancient societies, especially since the ex-slave usually became a citizen. As the Roman Republic expanded, slaves were initially of Italian, and then of Greek, Semitic and Asiatic origins, and frequently had as good an education as their masters, if not better. As many of them became freedmen, the ethnic and cultural make-up of the Roman citizen population shifted. The concern about the effects of this is illustrated by a measure to restrict all freedmen to the four urban tribes (which had less political influence than the older 'rustic' ones) in around 220 BCE, and by a series of measures implemented by Augustus aimed at making it extremely difficult for slaves to be freed, and still more difficult for them to attain full independence.[30] However, if Augustus' intention was to maintain the 'purity of the Roman race', the satirist Juvenal, writing a century or so later, would undoubtedly have said he had failed:

> I cannot, citizens, stomach
> A Greek-struck Rome. Yet what fraction of these sweepings
> Derives, in fact, from Greece? For years now Syrian
> Orontes has poured its sewerage into our native Tiber –
> Its lingo and manners, its flutes, its outlandish harps
> With their transverse strings, its native tambourines,
> And the whores who hang out round the race-course.[31]

Some (vague) estimates have 90 per cent of the population of Rome being of slave origin in Juvenal's day. Whether this is accurate or not, the Romans of the Principate were a more ethnically diverse people than those of the Republic. In between Augustus and Juvenal, Emperor Claudius had employed talented eastern freedmen such as Pallas (finance), Narcissus (secretary of state) and Callistus (petitions) as ministers and political advisers. However, Vespasian, Trajan and their successors reversed the trend, and recruited their State-Secretaries from the Equestrian Order, for which freedmen were ineligible. Neither could freedmen be members of the Senatorial Order, hold the highest Roman and municipal magistracies and priesthoods, or serve in the legions.

Freedmen were obliged to give *obsequium et officium* ('service and duty') to their ex-masters. This entailed services (*onera*) for a certain number of days each year, and, although it was not supposed to be so excessive as to prevent the ex-slave making a living, neglect of the duty was punishable by beating, exile, forced labour and so on. However, in return the patron was bound to do all he could to assist the freedman's welfare, and the relationship was generally regarded as a win–win situation.

Sons born to a freedman after manumission suffered none of the restrictions that their parents did, although they sometimes had to contend with social discrimination. They were always identifiable by their servile *cognomen* – Marcus Tullius Cicero's freedman Tiro came to be called Marcus Tullius Tiro – and on certain formal occasions they had to wear their 'cap of liberty'. That said, many of them were highly aspirational in a way perfectly exemplified by the poet Horace, the son of a freedman, who became friends with Maecenas and Augustus, even if he did have to face a certain degree of prejudice:

> I revert now to myself – only a freedman's son,
> run down by everyone as only a freedman's son,
> now because I'm a friend of yours, Maecenas.[32]

The stigma of slavery might become fainter in the second generation, but it never went away entirely, even for one of Rome's greatest poets.

16

ROMAN RELAXATION, RECREATION AND RELIGION

Writers who have passed on to us the ancient customs of Rome say that our ancestors washed only their arms and legs every day, since these parts of the body were covered with dirt from farm work. The rest of the body was washed only once a week. Of course, someone will at this point, say, 'Sure, but they were very smelly men.' And what do you think they smelled of? Of the army, of farm work, and of manliness!

Seneca the Younger, *Letters* 86.1.11[1]

The Roman Baths

The Romans had not always been addicted to the baths: Hannibal's nemesis Scipio Africanus bathed in rather muddy water, and didn't do it every day. Yet by the fourth century CE there were almost 1,000 public bath buildings (*thermae*) in Rome alone, and almost every small town in the Empire had at least one communal bath suite. These functioned not unlike twenty-first-century gyms or health spas, and often had areas for ball games, jogging, working out, swimming, sun-bathing and massage, as well as the baths proper, which were all about getting sweaty in the nude.

Baths varied in size from domestic bath suites providing the bare essentials of what scholars call the *calidarium* (a hot room), *tepidarium* (warm room) and *frigidarium* (cold room) to enormous complexes like the Baths of Caracalla in Rome, where you might find a *laconicum* ('Spartan bath' – a dry-heat sweat room), a *destrictorium* (where oil and perspiration were removed with *strigils* – scrapers), snack bars, libraries, meeting halls, gardens, fountains and possibly prostitution (although there is some dispute about this at Pompeii, where the decoration of the Suburban Baths included some rather athletic erotic scenes). Essentially the *thermae* offered a holistic approach to well-being and acted as social centres. On the whole, the entrance fees were low, and many people visited the baths on a daily basis.

The Forum *Thermae* at Pompeii are an excellent example of a Roman public bath suite. They date to *c.*80 BCE, and, although they are relatively small, they survive in very good condition. There are separate sections for men and women, which was normal. The men's section gave the option of three entrances from different streets, and your first port of call would be the *apodyterium* (changing room), a rectangular, barrel-vaulted chamber with seating on three sides that was lit by a glazed window. The walls were adorned with a figured frieze in stucco relief, and the window was decorated with an Oceanus head and Tritons. Guide books often tell us that there was a rigid sequence of events for Roman bathing – cold to warm to hot (or vice versa; the guide books disagree) then a cold plunge – but there is no evidence for this, and the layout of the buildings is determined more by economic use of energy than anything else. The forum's *apodyterium* gave access to the *frigidarium*, the *tepidarium,* the *palaestra* (open-air exercise area) and, down a corridor, to the *praefurnium* (the 'heating plant'). This was located so that the hot rooms are closest to it, and then the warm rooms, thus making efficient use of the heat it generated. Its hot-water tanks were fed from a well that was equipped with a machine for hoisting water, as well as a large reservoir across the street.

The *frigidarium* was a circular room with a conical ceiling and four semi-domed niches painted with shrubs and trees, and was almost entirely filled by a circular sea-blue plunge pool. The barrel-vaulted *tepidarium* has similar dimensions to the *apodyterium*. It was warmed by braziers, rather than being equipped with a state-of-the-art under-floor heating system (*hypocaust*), where hot-air flues beneath a hollow pavement were supported on small pillars of tile (*suspensurae*). The room provided niches for storing clothes, separated from one another by terracotta Telamons (figures rather like Atlas, who hold up the entablature above them). A glazed window with a bronze frame provided the light, and the ceiling was elaborately decorated in stucco relief.

The *calidarium* was the largest room, barrel vaulted, with an apsidal, semi-domed end. It was lit by three windows in the southern end of the vault and a circular window in the semi-dome. The floor was raised on *suspensurae* and paved with black and white mosaic; the walls were covered with *tegulae mammatae* ('breasted-tiles': flat, rectangular tiles with small breast-like protuberances near the four corners of one side), which created a space between themselves and the walls that acted as a flue. The hot air would rise from hypocaust system, warm the walls and escape through vents at the top. Other bath suites used square flues set into the wall to create the same result. The vault was stuccoed in a rib pattern, the semi-dome with figured reliefs.

In the apse was a fine marble *labrum* (wash-basin); its bronze lettered inscription records that it was installed at the cost of 5,420 *sestertii* in 3/4 CE, while at the opposite end of the room there was a marble-lined hot-water pool fed from the *praefurnium* next door. The small porticoed *palaestra* had a masonry bench running along the back wall, and a deep barrel-vaulted *exedra*, which looks like a suitable venue for intimate conversation.

The women's section looks like a later addition, since it is a completely independent building that encroaches on the surrounding pavements. As a woman you would get similar, but smaller, facilities to those of the men, but no *palaestra*. From an entrance lobby provided with benches you went down a short corridor to the *apodyterium*, where the *frigidarium* was simply a small square basin in an alcove. But both the *tepidarium* and *calidarium* were raised on *suspensurae*, and had hollow walls.

Bread and Circuses

The poet Juvenal famously wrote:

> The public has long since cast off its cares; the people that once bestowed commands, consulships, legions and all else, now meddles no more and longs eagerly for just two things: bread and Circuses.[2]

Although he was attacking the general political apathy of his day, rather than ranting against the games or the grain handouts, he wasn't the first to express the idea. More than 100 years before, the Republican Varro had complained about the heads of families abandoning the sickle and the plough in favour of the theatre and the Circus.[3]

What these complaints don't do, however, is prove that the Roman *plebs* sat in the Circus day in, day out, scrounging off the State: the number of public entertainment events, the size of the buildings, and the level of the corn dole, all show that this could not have been the reality. The corn doles provided generously for a single person, but not enough for a family, and they were designed so as not to divert people too much from their normal occupations. Neither was the corn dole free until 58 BCE, when Publius Clodius made it so. Taken literally, the 'Circuses' part of Juvenal's comment implies chariot-racing, but he is really talking about public entertainments in general. Giving to receive was part of Roman politicians' stock-in-trade, and they promoted spectacular games and entertainments from the first century BCE to the end of the fourth century CE, and whereas corn doles were directed at the *plebs,* games and shows brought the entire community together: all classes attended.

According to legend, Rome's founder Romulus introduced the first games (probably) in the eighth century BCE. Then, in 364 BCE, a plague struck Rome, and the Romans vowed to hold theatrical festivals in honour of the gods. In the course of the next century, the Roman entertainment industry expanded dramatically, partly influenced by contact with the Greeks, and partly because games were pledged to the gods in times of war – during the war with Hannibal, for instance, the Romans instituted the *Ludi Plebeii* (Plebeian Games) in honour of Jupiter, which featured chariot-racing. The process was given impetus by Rome's imperial success, as their burgeoning power also generated a desire for display that partly manifested itself in the foundation of new festivals.

Animal hunts and fights between animals (*venationes*) were first seen by the Romans in 186 BCE, when lions and panthers fought, but many Senators initially disapproved of this, and the import of wild animals from Africa was prohibited. The ban was soon lifted, though.

The English word 'virtue' comes from the Latin *virtus* (= 'manliness'). Gladiatorial combat was the ultimate expression of that ideal, and the historian Livy tells us the date of the first of these contests: 264 BCE, at the funeral of Decimus Junius Pero. So gladiatorial contests were not originally part of the public games (*ludi*); at first they normally took place in the Forum, and were held in honour of influential dead Romans. The fulfilment of the instructions about Pero's funeral that the deceased left in his will was an important duty of his heirs, and was known as the *munus*. So the term for a gladiatorial contest was *munus* (plural: *munera*), as opposed to the games (*ludi*), which were dedicated to a deity and organized by representatives of the state. The idea of shedding human blood beside a dead man's grave is very old, and actually occurs in most ancient Mediterranean cultures. This religious origin of the *munera* was never forgotten in Rome. Fourth-century BCE frescoes from Paestum, south of Naples, depict funeral games, including a duel between two warriors with a referee beside them, implying that they were participating in contests in honour of the dead, very like the *munera* of Rome. It is usually assumed that the Naples area (Campania) was where gladiatorial fights originated.

One obvious question is: 'How did it all get out of hand in a way that even struck the Romans?' When Livy talked about the origins of the Roman theatrical festivals he concluded that by his day (he lived from 59 BCE to 17 CE) things had reached a point where 'opulent kingdoms could hardly support their mad extravagance'.[4] The answer is that it was a gradual process. As Rome expanded in the Mediterranean, vast wealth flooded into Rome at a time when only a few leading families held all the major public offices. The rivalries between these families were intense, and the Senate vainly tried to control extravagance by passing new laws: the *lex Fannia* of 161 BCE limited expenditure on a banquet to 25 *sestertii*; by 81 BCE the sum had risen to 300; and a generation later L. Licinius Lucullus spent 50,000 on one. Meanwhile, at the opposite end of the social scale, Rome's urban *plebs* lobbied for cheap grain, and were often supported by politicians, either out of a genuine desire to solve social problems, or because they saw it as a way of acquiring influence over potential voters. Or both.

The career of Julius Caesar is a perfect example of this. He was a shrewd investor of money for political gain, but was also a big fan of gladiatorial combat. He actually maintained a gladiatorial school of his own, and the fights he staged in honour of his late father put everything of the kind seen before into the shade, prompting his opponents to pass a law limiting the number of pairs of gladiators that any one person might engage at 320, and so giving Caesar the publicity he craved. Once he had established his dominance at Rome, the festivities he presented in 46 BCE went further still: every citizen received generous allocations of grain and oil, 400 *sestertii*, plus Caesar paid them all a year's rent. His public shows included a gladiatorial contest, stage-plays, chariot-races, athletic competitions, a mock naval battle on an artificial lake, five consecutive days of wild-beast hunts, and culminated with a battle between two armies of 500 infantry, 20 elephants and 30 cavalry. Suetonius tells us that such huge numbers of visitors flocked to these shows that the pressure of the crowd crushed people to death.[5]

Caesar had raised the bar very high, but this was as nothing compared with Augustus, who boasted of eight gladiatorial spectacles featuring some 10,000 men, 27 state games, and 26 wild-beast hunts in which some 3,500 beasts were killed. A novelty occurred when Emperor Gaius (Caligula) transgressed all social norms by performing as a gladiator, charioteer and dancer, singing along with the actors at the theatre, and supposedly having an affair with the actor Mnester. However, chariot-racing was his real passion. He had a favourite horse called Incitatus, and he instructed his troops to enforce absolute silence on the day before the races. Incitatus was endorsed with a marble stable, an ivory stall, purple blankets, a jewelled collar, a house, furniture and slaves, and was made a Senator.[6]

As with Gaius, the picture we have of Emperor Nero comes from hostile sources, all of which concur that he was trained in singing and in playing the lyre. During his debut in Rome he surrounded himself with a claque of 5,000 supporters who showered him with adulation, and he allegedly sang an epic on the *Fall of Troy* during the Great Fire at Rome in 64 CE. This story of Nero 'fiddling while Rome burned' is most likely bogus, but there is reliable evidence for his persecution of the Christians, and although *damnatio ad bestias* (condemnation to being killed by wild beasts) was a pretty standard sentence for any criminal, not just Christians, Nero devised such sadistic methods of execution (torn apart by dogs, or nailed to crosses, or set on fire and burned alive to provide light at night[7]), that even the most hard-nosed Romans felt sympathy for the victims.

Constantine the Great made Christianity a State-tolerated religion under the Edict of Milan in 313 CE, and this enabled bishops openly to campaign against theatrical performances, chiefly on the grounds that they presented lewd and pornographic material, which were a temptation to sin. In 314 CE the Council of Arles excommunicated actors. Constantine also banned criminals being sentenced to gladiatorial training, but there were still gladiators; in fact Pope Damasius engaged a whole troop as his bodyguard in 367 CE. However, the end of the gladiatorial contests was not far off: the emperor Honorius formally abolished them in 404 CE.

On the other hand, chariot-racing and *venationes* continued to be very popular even under the Christian emperors. The official intolerance of pagan cults under Theodosius did not really affect them, and chariot-racing flourished through to Byzantine times. It wasn't until the crusaders captured Constantinople in 1204 CE that the great age of chariot-racing came to an end.

So, what happened at these events? Gladiatorial schools were commercial enterprises, run by a *lanista*, who hired out fighters. Some gladiators were condemned criminals, others were volunteers, but all were trained to a high level of fitness and received a well-balanced diet and proper medical attention. Success enhanced a gladiator's market value, and the Romans were great keepers of statistics, be this on the programmes of the games, graffiti or tombstones: 'To the spirits. Asiaticus, first fighter, released after 53 combats.'[8]

We also have the remains of nearly 200 amphitheatres. These should never be confused with theatres (tourist guides often wrongly use 'amphitheatre' when they mean 'a big theatre'). An amphitheatre is an oval, or occasionally circular, arena surrounded by rising tiers of seats, and the earliest surviving example is at Pompeii, built after 80 BCE. A Pompeiian wall painting shows this amphitheatre, and what might be the great riot of 59 CE between the Pompeians and the Nucerians, which led to it being closed for ten years on Nero's orders. It is unusual in having external stairways rather than the internal stairs that were common later on, and the painting suggests that its exterior was covered in stucco. We can also see the large awning that provided shade for the spectators.

The Colosseum at Rome (also known as the Flavian Amphitheatre) was built in less than ten years by the Flavian emperors and opened in 80 CE. Its enormous structure was designed to accommodate some 50,000 spectators, and its structural success stems from superb foundations combined with judicious selection of materials: the main load-bearing skeleton is dressed stone masonry – travertine for the external facade, tufa on the inside – and the vaults and upper internal walls are of concrete; timber seating was used to reduce the stress on the unsupported outer wall. The orders decorating the outer facade are 'applied', i.e. purely decorative: Doric on the lower level, Ionic, Corinthian and then Composite (an Ionic/Corinthian hybrid) on the top, which is the normal way of stacking up the orders. The whole edifice depends on a very Roman combination of concrete, arches and vaults, which is then clothed in Greek architectural form.

The arena floor had a sandy surface (*harena* = 'sand', giving the English 'arena'), and in many amphitheatres it stood on wooden staging above a complex underground substructure called the *hypogeum*. The *hypogeum* contained storerooms, dressing rooms, and passages into the arena for the gladiators, wild beasts and ancillary staff, as well as lifts to bring the participants up into the arena. A few amphitheatres had large basins of water dug into the arena, which could be covered for normal performances, but then used for special events such as hunting crocodiles and hippopotamuses, or for titillating mythological tableaux featuring bathing nymphs. However, these basins were far too small to stage naval battles (*naumachiae*), and the often stated cliché that the whole arena could be flooded to stage naval battles is wrong: these were not staged in the amphitheatres, but on artificial or natural lakes. The largest of these events was held by in 52 CE by Claudius on Lake Fucino, where 19,000 condemned prisoners manned the ships. These men hailed Claudius with the words, '*Ave Caesar; morituri te salutamus!*' ('Hail Caesar, we who are about to die salute you!'),[9] but there is no evidence that these famous words were ever shouted by gladiators in the amphitheatre.

Health and safety was also a prime concern – at least for the spectators. Gladiators, wild animals, prisoners and criminals are potentially dangerous, so they were strictly managed and only given access to weapons once they were in the arena itself. Crowd trouble at the *munera* seems to have been relatively rare and, apart from the Pompeii riot, we hear little about hooliganism of the kind familiar from modern football. Fans of the Circus and the theatre seem to have been far more violent than those of the amphitheatre.

Gladiatorial combat is unique in that the surrender of the loser is not the end of the event. That person's ultimate fate was decided by the *editor*, although he usually followed the audience's desires: they would either wave the hems of their togas and shout *missum* or *mitte* ('release him!'), or turn their thumbs (*pollice verso* – up or down? We don't know for certain, although most commentators think up = death) and scream *iugula!* ('kill him!'). The defeated gladiator would then kneel, with his arms clasped behind his back, or embrace the legs of his conqueror, and 'take the iron' (*ferrum recipere*). As he died, the audience yelled *habet!* ('he has it!'), and his body was taken away on a covered stretcher to the mortuary, where his throat was cut to make sure that the bout had not been rigged. Gladiators were never dragged out of the arena by a hook, as many writers assert – that was the fate of criminals.

To the victor the spoils: a palm branch and a cash prize, even if he was a slave. Successful gladiators could live well on the proceeds of their celebrity, and we know that such prospects tempted volunteers. The winner would take a lap of honour, waving the palm branch. The ultimate aspiration was to win the wooden sword (*rudis*), a symbol of no longer being under the obligation to fight again. We also have evidence for female gladiators: a marble relief now at the British Museum in London commemorates the *missio* (discharge) of two women fighters, 'Amazon' and 'Achillia', who won their freedom through giving consistently outstanding performances.

Gladiators were expensive, so the question arises as to how many duels actually ended in a fatality, particularly as the promoters were under considerable pressure to turn their thumbs. We have evidence that in the first century CE you had about an 11 per cent chance of death at the start of the fight, going up to 25 per cent if you lost, but that the death rate rose in the second and third centuries: at the start of your fight you had a 33 per cent chance of dying, rising to 50 per cent if you lost. On the positive side, though, it seems that a normal gladiator didn't fight too often; we even hear complaints that they were wasting the best years of their lives because so few contests were held. It stands to reason that most gladiators were killed at the start of their careers: (a) you got better with experience, and (b) once you got famous your supporters wouldn't dispatch you if you suffered an unexpected defeat. This helps to explain the fact that some gladiators boast 100 victories on their tombstones, monuments which suggest that gladiators lived to an average age of 27.

Despite one or two dissenting voices – the Stoic philosopher Epictetus[10] deplored the fact that respectable citizens enjoyed discussing incidents in the arena – it seems that the amphitheatre was popular across all social classes, and we certainly know that Roman women found gladiators very attractive: Juvenal tells us about the upper-class lady Eppia lusting after one particular fighter:

> There was a huge wart on the middle of his nose which was rubbed by his helmet, and a bitter matter dripped continually from one eye. But he was a gladiator . . . She preferred this to her children and her country . . . What these women love is the sword. [11]

The *venationes* (hunts) originated during the Punic Wars, when the Romans took elephants and other exotic animals as war-booty, and by the Imperial period they had become a regular feature of the *munera*. Being inferior to gladiators in prestige, the huntsmen and animal fighters (*venatores*) – who were recruited from among prisoners of war, slaves, condemned criminals and volunteers – featured on the morning agenda. Some *venatores* hunted deer, ostriches and wild asses, while others fought on foot with lions, tigers, leopards and bears. They had to fight a continuous series of animals, despite injury or exhaustion, until the audience thought they had done enough, but, in contrast to modern bull-fighting, the animal itself was sometimes granted the *missio* – some lions killed a whole series of *venatores* during their 'careers'.

Executions were regularly carried out in the context of the *venationes*. *Noxii*, prisoners condemned *ad gladium* (to the sword) or *ad bestias* (to the wild beasts) were allocated to *editores*, who dreamed up various ways of killing them, often in the form of grotesquely horrific dramatic productions of a mythological character. The *noxii* never had a chance. They were, for instance, exposed to the big cats naked (apart from a loincloth), unarmed, bound and carrying placards that listed their crimes. Christians were 'thrown to the lions', although other beasts were also used, and the reality was more complex and often even more gruesome.

Usually the Christian had been denounced by an informer after a disaster caused by divine anger – drought, famine, plague, etc. Christians were held responsible because of their 'impious' attitudes and practices, and because they rejected the Roman traditions for appeasing the wrath of the gods. If the Christians were prepared to honour the gods, they would be released, although many refused the offer. The martyrdoms of SS Perpetua and Felicitas show us how an execution took place in three clearly defined stages:

1. Preparation and exhibition of the prisoners, including dressing them in the robes of a priest of Saturn or a priestess of Ceres, and flogging;
2. Exposure to the beasts of the men, and then the women;
3. Survivors exposed to more beasts, or killed by a gladiator.

The crowd's responses seem to have varied between hostility towards the martyrs, compassion, boredom and blood lust.

On a different sector of the moral compass, chariot-races attracted would-be exponents by offering fabulous amounts of prize money, and valuable gifts in kind, at far less risk. We hear of purses of between 30,000 and 50,000 *sestertii* at a time when a highly educated tutor was earning 100,000 *sestertii* per annum at best,[12] and there were charioteers with more than a thousand victories to their credit. A Circus usually comprised a flat elongated racecourse, rounded at one end and open or square at the other, with the central axis (*spina*) marked by monuments. The largest track was the fourth century CE Circus Maximus, 610 m long and 198 m wide, which could hold 250,000 spectators who were quite tribalistic. The names of the different factions reflected the colours of the clothing worn by the charioteers – Reds, Blues, Greens and Whites – and, although the drivers always regarded money as more important than loyalty to any one faction, the spectators never changed sides. As with football team supporters today, once they had decided which colour to support, they were fanatical.

Roman emperors invested enormous sums of money on *ludi* and *munera* because it helped to keep the populace out of politics. M. Cornelius Fronto, tutor of Marcus Aurelius, described the cosy relationship between him and his people like this:

> The emperor did not neglect even actors and the other performers of
> the stage, the circus, or the amphitheatre, knowing as he did that the
> Roman people are held fast by two things above all, the corn-dole
> and the shows.[13]

The 'corn-dole and the shows', like the stereotypically luxurious
baths, banquets, and orgies, are central to the modern popular
perception of Imperial Rome as a culture devoted to luxury and
pleasure, and doomed by its decadence. But the reality is more
nuanced, and we have to remember the traditional and religious
basis of some of these activities, which were also indicators of a very
prosperous society, albeit not of a politically dynamic one. 'Bread
and Circuses' were one way in which the Emperors tried to
maintain the support of all sections of society: they were important
elements in social control, just like alcohol and reality TV are in
2010.

Roman Religion(s)
The history and nature of the Roman games show that the Romans
didn't really make the clear-cut religious/secular distinctions that
we often do. Our word 'temple' comes from the Latin *templum*,
probably derived from the Greek *temenos*, a sacred enclosure.
However, *templum* did not refer primarily to what we call a temple-
building, but to the circuit of the heavens or 'a space marked out',
particularly a ritually defined space, set aside through sacred words
or gestures for the purpose of taking auspices. A priest called an
augur would mark out a portion of the sky and then watch it
('con*templ*ate' it) for omens, which often meant observing the flight
of birds or monitoring their eating habits. Romans seldom
undertook a major project without taking the auspices, and would
call it off if their interpretation indicated divine displeasure.
However, the process could be cynically manipulated, as happened
when L. Calpurnius Bibulus invalidated all of Julius Caesar's
legislation by retiring to his house 'to take the auspices' in 59 BCE.
Yet it did not always pay to be too sceptical, as Claudius Pulcher
found out to his cost: he took the auspices and discovered that the
sacred chickens would not eat, so he threw them into the sea,
saying: 'If they won't eat, let them drink'. He then engaged the
enemy in a naval battle and, of course, he lost.[14]

The *templum* on the ground had to allow you to mark out the semicircular *templum* of the sky. This 'ritualization of space' is characteristically Roman: whereas most Greek temples face east towards the dawn, most Roman temples simply face away from natural obstacles, to give a good view. The essential elements of a proper *templum* were: an open viewing space called the *area*; some sort of boundary wall; an altar for making sacrifices; and, optionally, an *aedes* (= 'house', what we call a temple) to house the objects dedicated to the god, including the cult image, if there was one. Many official activities had to take place in a *templum*, most notably meetings of the Senate – the Curia (Senate House), and the Rostra (speaker's platform) were *templa*. Again this shows how closely religious life was integrated into politics.

The appearance and arrangement of early Roman temples owed a great deal to Etruscan prototypes, and their primary characteristics may be summed up as:

- axiality: the *aedes* was often placed at the far end of a rectangular area, centred on an axis running from the sanctuary entrance;
- elevation: the building was placed on a relatively high podium;
- frontality: the temple was usually approached by a flight of steps, and could only be entered from the front.

Yet, there is also a Greek influence at work, because the Etrusco-Italic structure appears to be wearing Greek dress: the architectural ornament (columns, entablature, detailing, etc.) is derived from the Greek tradition.

A very fine example of a Roman temple is the Maison Carrée at Nîmes: we can date it accurately (16 BCE); its external preservation is excellent; and its style seems to be purely Roman. It is a fairly small (about 13.4 × 26.2 m) pseudoperipteral-hexastyle Corinthian temple (which means it has sham colonnades at the sides and six leafy columns at the front), built out of good quality local limestone. It stands on a stepped podium, at the top of which there is a deep prostyle porch (i.e. one with columns at the front) with three open bays on each side. The columns have richly carved capitals with an elegant egg-and-dart motif on the top. The arrangement is equivalent to that of a temple with 6 × 11 columns, but eight of the columns on each side, and the six at the back are engaged (set into the wall). The architrave is in three bands, separated by bead-and-reel motifs, and crowned by egg-and-dart. The frieze provides a good example of the floral 'Roman scroll' motif, except on the facade, which carried an inscription in bronze letters that read:

C. CAESARI. AVGVSTI. F. COS. L. CAESARI. AVGVSTI. F.
COS. DESIGNATO.
PRINCIPIBVS. IVVENTVTIS.

This is a reference to Gaius and Lucius Caesar, the Emperor Augustus' grandsons. The pediment has a much steeper pitch than a Greek temple, and, as is usual in a Corinthian temple, has no sculpture. The temple faced the Forum, and the podium is reached by fifteen steps. Under the podium were rooms for the sanctuary's archives and the treasure.

The Maison Carrée has survived so well because of almost continuous use since Antiquity; so has what is perhaps the most influential building in Western architecture: the Pantheon in Rome. When it was built, you would have approached via a colonnaded forecourt that was much lower than the modern pavement level, and the porch would have stood on a five-stepped platform. This would have accentuated the key elements of preparation, tension and release that make entering the building such an incredible experience: you initially think it is large, but otherwise quite ordinary.

The porch, on the north side of the building, is 105 Roman feet wide, and on it stand eight monolithic unfluted Corinthian columns, 5 Roman feet wide, made originally from grey Egyptian granite, with a slight *entasis* in their shafts, and white marble bases and capitals. The front row of columns is connected to the main building by four more pairs of reddish Egyptian granite columns. The outer columns carry a normal entablature surmounted by a very steep pediment that may have been adorned with an imperial eagle. The level of the horizontal cornice of the columned porch lies between those of the lower and middle cornices of the circular wall behind it (the wall of 'the rotunda'). The roof of the porch was supported by some 200 tonnes of bronze framework.

Between the columned porch and the rotunda is a solid structure ('the block') that acts as a transition to the interior. It is as wide as the porch and as high as the wall that it joins at the back. It has a large arched opening that leads to the door to the temple, with semi-domed niches on either side, which probably carried statues of Augustus and M. Agrippa. The uppermost cornice of the rotunda runs along the top of the block, and the cornice below that is also carried across it, until it meets the gabled roof of the columned porch: this cornice serves as the lower limit of another pediment, which is slightly less steep than the one of the porch and stands at a higher level. The entire entablature of the columned porch is carried on marble pilasters that stop at the rotunda wall. Between these pilasters was some elaborate marble veneering. The lowest cornice of the rotunda also terminates when it meets the block.

The rotunda exterior was, for most of its circumference, probably veneered, stuccoed or done in a combination of the two. It was crowned by a cornice of which the terracotta and stone elements were stuccoed, and divided by two similar lower cornices into three bands, of which the lowest is the tallest. Above the crowning cornice lies a flattish dome, the lower portion of which comprises a series of large steps that were once clad with gilt-bronze tiles. Overall, the exterior detailing of the rotunda and the portico, and the way they interrelate, looks a bit of a mess.

However, it is not really the exterior that matters, since the approach through the porch sets you up for a jaw-dropping surprise. On walking through the door you find yourself in an enormous cylindrical space crowned by a hemispherical dome. The internal height (43.2 m) is equal to the diameter. Cornices divide the internal walls into two zones, of which the lower is the taller. Corinthian columns and pilasters at ground level carry an entablature, which is broken at the entrance and at the niche directly opposite it. Above the entablature comes a smooth band of blue-white marble underneath a repeating pattern of pilasters and blind windows, ornamented with veneered circles and rectangles. Above this is another cornice, and above that springs the truly amazing dome. There is not one person who does not stop and look skywards to that dome when they first walk in. It is faced with concrete, and features deep coffering that may originally have been gilded, in five diminishing layers of twenty-eight compartments. At the top is the *oculus* (central circular hole), about 8.8 m across, lined with a ring of bronze, which provides the only natural light source apart from the door. And a wondrous light it is: in sunny conditions an ellipse of light gradually tracks across the interior.

The construction of the dome was a formidable engineering enterprise, and it is still the largest concrete dome in the world. The architect's success depends on a number of factors: the enormous strength of the mortar; the corresponding strength of the foundations; and the clever use of aggregates of different weights and strengths for the concrete of different parts of the building – the Pantheon gets lighter as it gets higher, thereby taking the stress off the rest of the structure. Numerous cavities throughout the body of the rotunda reduce the weight of the masonry: the main wall is in fact eight huge piers joined by curtain walls. Except at the entrance and the niche opposite it, which are crowned with arches, it looks as if the upper wall rests directly on the entablature supported by the Corinthian columns, but all the piers are connected by huge relieving arches (not visible) that displace the pressure away from the columns, and on to the piers. Smaller arches focus the pressure from the space between the main arches and the entablature directly on to the columns. The brilliant use of the arch (with its spin-offs the vault and the dome) and of concrete were the Romans' great contributions to world architecture, and nowhere were they more effectively combined, structurally or aesthetically, than in the Pantheon.

When you finally bring your eyes downwards, you are standing on a floor paved in squares, and circles within squares, of coloured granite, marble and porphyry.

The cosmic symbolism of the basic design is obvious enough: the dome = the vault of the heavens. Beyond that there is great dispute. Should we try to fit the images of fifteen of the major deities into the apse and niches, or the seven deities of the celestial pantheon (Mercury, Mars, Venus, Jupiter, the Moon, the Sun and Saturn)? Why does the building face north? What is the significance, if any, of the twenty-eight coffers in each ring of the dome? What is not in doubt, however, is the date. It has an inscription that reads:

M. AGRIPPA. L .F . COS. TERTIVM. FECIT
(Marcus Agrippa, son of Lucius, three times consul, made this)

M. Agrippa had dedicated a sanctuary on the site in *c.*25 BCE, but it had been burned twice, and it was replaced by Hadrian with the new Pantheon, although he kept the original inscription. Brick stamps from the rotunda allow us to date it to between 118 and 128 CE. It is Hadrian's building.

The religion that these temples were part of can seem very alien to us now. Among the many different religions operating throughout the Roman Empire the citizens of Rome regarded 'the State Religion' as definitively their own. It was extremely traditional, and, since its principal function was to keep the State safe and prosperous, the Romans could usually feel that it *worked*. So they were very keen to maintain it. Priests were state officials; temples were state-funded; individuals could be both magistrates and priests (e.g. Julius Caesar was Consul and Pontifex Maximus) because both had a duty to promote the welfare of the State, and in that context there existed a reciprocal relationship where the State protected the religion and the religion protected the State.[15]

Roman religion held that all the important processes in the world were divinely activated, and that different gods oversaw particular functions and spheres of activity. Romans saw the working of a divine spirit (*numen*) where we tend to see the working of science or nature. The historian Polybius summed up the attitude very well:

> Those things of which it is impossible to ascertain the causes may
> reasonably be attributed to a god or to Fortune, if no cause can easily
> be discovered.[16]

Early cults show how farmers deified agricultural operations: Pomona (Fruit), Consus (the Storer of Grain), Robigus (Blight) and so on were extremely important divinities and, because the Romans were polytheists, new ones were introduced as need arose: for example, an economic slump in the early fifth century BCE called for the institution of the cult of Mercury, for success in business transactions. Natural objects were also venerated: the Elder Pliny wrote that trees were the temples of spirits. In his day, simple farming communities would still dedicate an outstanding tree to a god. Urban settlements also had patron deities, such as Vulcan at Ostia, Minerva at Falerii and Juno at Veii.

These forces were not naturally sympathetic to humans; they were neutral. However, their effects might be very harmful: hail and crop disease are not deliberately malevolent, but they can ruin a farmer's livelihood. So Roman religion tried to propitiate these forces and keep them favourable; and since doing so could ensure the success and prosperity of both the individual and the community, it was essential for all citizens to maintain the *Pax Deorum* (= 'Peace with the Gods'). This entailed performing the right actions at the right times for the right outcomes; it was a set of formal observances more concerned with the correct procedure of worship than with inner morality: 'Jupiter is called best and greatest, not because he makes us just or sober or wise but healthy and rich and prosperous.'[17] Yet this does not mean that there was no link between morality and Roman religion. Maintaining the *Pax Deorum* was a constant process in which two Latin concepts were crucial: *pietas* (the sense of duty to family, state and gods that was Aeneas' great quality), and *cultus* ('cultivation'). In practice *cultus deorum*, the cultivation of the gods, meant acknowledging them through the methodical performance of traditional, unchanging, precise ritual – because that had been successful in the past. The *pius* person always does this scrupulously, and so morality and ethics are a function of *pietas*.

Just as the State took responsibility, on behalf of the community, for keeping good relations with the gods, the *paterfamilias* assumed responsibility, on behalf of the *familia*, for doing the same. There were a number of vital household divinities including Vesta, the spirit of fire or of the hearth; the Lares, spirits of the farmland or of dead ancestors; the Penates, the spirits of the store cupboard (*penus*), who worshipped together with the Lares; Genius, the procreative power that ensured the continuance of the family; and Janus, the two-faced spirit of the door. The door was the focus of great 'specialization' in respect of the gods: Janus Patulcius was in charge of opening the door, Janus Clusivius of closing it; Limentinus looked after the threshold (*limen*); Cardea was the divinity of the hinges (*cardes*), and you might hang a *tintinabulum* (a winged phallus with the hind legs of a lion, and with bells on) by the door to ward off evil. Likewise, lands had to be protected: boundary stones (*termini*) were venerated every year at the Terminalia festival; the land within the boundaries was fertilized at the Ambarvalia; and the spirits of the land (the Lares again) had to be placated at the Compitalia.

There were similar observances concerning crucial stages in the propagation of the family, and so we get rites of passage at birth, puberty, marriage and death. But even then the ritual did not cease: there were family ceremonies such as the Lemuria, in which the *di manes* (= ghosts of the dead), were placated and expelled, and the Parentalia, at which the graves of the deceased were decorated with flowers.

Prayers would usually be accompanied by an offering to suit the importance of the occasion. Our word 'sacrifice' comes from Latin, *sacrificium* (= 'making something holy'). This usually happened in one of two ways: food offerings, comprising salt meal, fruit, honey, milk or wine; or animal sacrifice. Male animals were offered to gods, and female ones to goddesses, with colour, size and age also relevant – black for deities of the Underworld, white for Juno or Jupiter, etc. Professionals were available if desired – e.g. a *cultarius* to make the kill; a flute player to drown out ill-omened sounds – but were not strictly essential. The animal was decorated and led (willingly or not at all) to the altar; everything and everyone had to be ritually clean; the participants covered their heads with their togas; they sprinkled flour on the victim, and on the knife; the prayers were said; one of the attendants (the *popa*) shouted, 'Am I to strike?', and then stunned the animal with a hammer blow; the *cultarius* would turn the animal's head first to the sky and then down to the earth, and cut its throat; the entrails would be examined and, if they were good, they would be burnt on the altar and the lean meat eaten. Precision was absolutely crucial and if any slip-ups were made the entire procedure had to be repeated. The deity had to be addressed with all the correct titles, and often with an escape clause, such as, 'Jupiter Optimus Maximus or by whatever other name you wish to be addressed', and if the right divinity had been invoked with the correct formula, it would be thought unreasonable and ungod-like for the request not to be granted. Alternatively, the support of the gods could be invoked by means of a vow, where the deity only received the offering if the prayer was answered.

Other ways of interacting with the gods could be by divination, the art of interpreting signs contained in natural phenomena such as thunder and lightning; *auspicium* (augury, from the Latin *avis* = bird;

specio = 'I look'), analysing bird behaviour which was interpreted by an *augur*; or *extispicium,* checking out the entrails of sacrificial animals, interpreted by a *haruspex.* This was not about trying to guess the future, but about testing the potential of a given plan by canvassing the gods' opinions: it simply sought a 'yes'/'no' answer.

The State also took responsibility for renewing the community's relationship with gods on a regular basis through various festivals. Again, the correct performance of the ritual is what the gods wanted most. *Feriae* was the name for the Roman festival day (even though it is a plural word), and *feriae* fell into two main types: *feriae privatae* observed by individuals and families (such as birthdays or periods of mourning), and *feriae publicae.* There were three types of public festival: *feriae stativae* (annual, fixed-date events); *feriae conceptivae* (annual, but not on a fixed date); and *feriae imperativae* (one-off events). Roman citizens were not obliged to attend these festivals, however, because the State shouldered that responsibility.

Since religion was a function of the State, priesthoods were occupied by politicians. In the Republic, the Pontifex Maximus was the State priest, the *paterfamilias* of the community, while his advisers formed the major 'Colleges' (*collegia*) of priests, the *pontifices* and the *augures.* By the end of the Republic there were sixteen *pontifices*, who held office for life, controlled the religious calendar, and arranged the holy days and, until Caesar's reforms of the calendar, the intercalary months inserted into the calendar to bring the solar and lunar years into synch. The Vestal Virgins were part of the College of Pontiffs. There were six of them, generally from patrician families, who served for thirty years, administering the cult of Vesta, goddess of the hearth fire. They were not allowed to marry while in service, and unchastity could be punished by being buried alive. Also part of the College of Pontiffs were the fifteen *flamines*, who looked after the cults of individual gods. The three major *flamines* were attached to the cult of Jupiter (the *flamen Dialis*), Mars (the *flamen Martialis)* and Quirinus[18] (the *flamen Quirinalis).*

The college of *augures* consisted of sixteen official diviners who interpreted whether the gods approved or disapproved of various proposed actions. Other colleges and groups included the fifteen 'Men for Conducting Sacrifices', who kept and consulted the Sibylline Books; the twelve *Fratres Arvales* (who performed ancient agricultural ceremonies); the Luperci (who presided over a festival that culminated in young men rushing around the Palatine Hill in loin-cloths, flagellating anyone in their way with strips of goatskin, particularly young girls who hoped to become fertile because of this); and the twenty Fetiales who handled the declaration of war, which they did by hurling a spear on to a piece of land in front of the Temple of Bellona, which was regarded as enemy territory for the purpose of the ritual.

As polytheists, the Romans were generally open-minded about other religions, and indeed absorbed many foreign beliefs (the process is called syncretism) without ever losing the core values that they adhered to. Bacchus, Cybele (Magna Mater), Isis, Mithras and ultimately even deified emperors rubbed shoulders with the traditional deities without much friction. All of these cults embraced people of all races and social classes. Judaism, however, did not. Yet, as a racially exclusive religion, Judaism did not seek to convert gentiles either: Jews did not involve themselves in the religious life of those around them, and they hoped that no one would interfere with theirs. On the whole, this was the case: Philo reminded the Emperor Gaius that Augustus did not force the Jews to violate their ancestral traditions or abandon their places for prayer meetings, and nor did he forbid them to gather to receive instruction in the laws.[19] However, the problem the Romans had with monotheism was down to the fact that they believed that the well-being of the State was dependent on meticulous worship of the State gods. Many people attributed the horrors of the civil wars at the end of the Republic to neglect of religious observance: Horace told his audience 'You neglected the gods, and they heaped many grievous calamities on Italy.'[20] So the refusal of the Jews to worship any god but their own was seen as threatening. Augustus' successor Tiberius suppressed Egyptian cults and Judaism, and forced those who embraced such 'superstitions' to burn their holy objects; young Jews were sent to do military service in provinces with harsher climates; and he banished their compatriots from Rome under threat of slavery. However, he was not exclusively anti-Jewish: he also expelled astrologers.

Christianity posed different challenges to the Roman authorities. It attracted adherents because the Saviour promised them a happy life after death, because 'God is Love' and the Olympians weren't, because Jesus was seen to have fulfilled the scriptures, and because it preached equality between men, women, children, rich and poor. Since they had a sacred mission to spread the 'good news', the Christians went out to evangelize in a way that the Jews did not. In its early days Christianity had much in common with the cults of Cybele, Bacchus, Isis and Mithras, in that they all offered the revelation of mysteries, redemption, resurrection and life after death, but Christian teaching was seen as particularly subversive because it threatened social revolution, especially with its emphasis on, and appeal to, the lower classes: tenets like 'the meek shall inherit the earth' are very frightening to a slave-owning society; the Eucharist, taking the body and blood of Christ, was equated with cannibalism; and Christians insulted the State because they rejected pagan worship.

The third-century CE Christian writer Minucius Felix gives a fascinating catalogue of the accusations that people like himself – the 'dregs of society' – had to face: credulous women who had fallen prey because of the natural weakness of their sex; wicked conspirators who gathered for secret nocturnal assemblies and inhuman dinners; adherents to a religion of lust, in which they called one another brothers and sisters so that normal sexual intercourse became incest by the use of the sacred name. Tales circulated about initiations in which infants were wrapped in bread dough that the initiate had to strike, thereby unwittingly killing the child, after which they would lick up the blood and tear its limbs apart. There were rumours of drunken, incestuous orgies. Their secrecy proved their wickedness:

> [You] Christians abstain from innocent pleasures. You don't watch the public spectacles, you don't take part in the processions, you absent yourselves from the public banquets, you shrink away from sacred games, sacrificial meat, and altar libations. That's how frightened you are of the gods whose existence you deny![21]

Christ was crucified in the reign of Tiberius, but by Claudius' time, when people who believed that 'Chrestus' (as he is designated in Tacitus' text) was the Messiah were still thought of as Jews, Roman officials were becoming worried about the unrest that the new belief was causing, so 'Jews' causing disturbances at the instigation of Chrestus were expelled from Rome. Claudius' successor Nero came to have a terrible reputation as a persecutor of Christians, using them as a scapegoat for the Great Fire of 64 CE, yet, despite more widespread persecutions under Domitian, Marcus Aurelius, Decius, Diocletian, Galerius and others, Christianity survived to become the dominant religion of the Empire. When Constantine converted to Christianity, won the Battle of the Milvian Bridge on 28 October 312 CE, and ultimately secured control of the Roman Empire, Christianity's future was guaranteed: Christians were granted freedom of worship, and from that moment they worked tirelessly to eradicate the pagan cults, which Theodosius achieved officially in 391 CE.

17

THE ROMAN CITY

We think of Rome, imperial, imperious, imperative . . . What was
their civilization? Vast, I allow: but vile. Cloacae: sewers. The Jews
in the wilderness and on the mountaintop said: *It is meet to be
here. Let us build an altar to Jehovah*. The Roman, like the
Englishman who follows in his footsteps, brought to every new
shore on which he set his foot . . . only his cloacal obsession. He
gazed about him in his toga and he said: *It is meet to be here. Let
us construct a watercloset.*

James Joyce, *Ulysses*, Episode 7, Aeolus,
'The Grandeur that was Rome'

A Natural Disaster in the South of Italy
In 79 CE an enormous eruption of Mount Vesuvius in Campania in
southern Italy both destroyed and preserved the towns of Pompeii
and Herculaneum, along with a number of other settlements and
some seaside villas owned by affluent Romans. The circumstances
of their preservation, and the sheer extent of the archaeological sites,
provide us with invaluable information about social, economic,
religious and political life in both the public and private arenas, and
across every stratum of society.

The towns had originally been settled by people who spoke
Oscan, an Italian language not dissimilar to Latin. They then came
under the influence of Greeks who had settled in the area in the
eighth century BCE. This Greek influence was superseded by
the Etruscans in the seventh century, until their sea power was
destroyed by Hieron I of Syracuse in 474 BCE. This second period

of Greek hegemony was terminated by the Samnites, a warlike Italic tribe who conquered Campania around the end of the fifth century BCE. Pompeii gets its first mention in the histories when, in 310 BCE, it became embroiled in the wars between Rome and the Samnites, at the end of which Campania became a part of the Roman confederation, and the cities became 'allies' of Rome.

Pompeii sided with the Italians in the Social War and was besieged by Sulla in 89 BCE. After the war, Pompeii received Roman citizenship, but a colony of Roman veterans was established there to keep an eye on it. Latin replaced Oscan as the official language, and the city soon became fully Romanized. There was a riot in the amphitheatre in 59 CE, where the inter-town rivalry with Nuceria escalated from abuse to stone-throwing and the wielding of weapons. A fresco depicting the event was found in the house of Actius Anicetius, and graffiti proudly boasts, 'Campanians, in our victory you perished with the Nucerians',[1] but the Pompeians were banned by the Roman authorities from holding any such events for ten years, and the local magistrates were removed from office.[2]

Herculaneum, which had far fewer inhabitants than its noisy neighbour, was built on a seaside promontory between two streams that flowed down the western base of Mount Vesuvius just 7 km from the volcano's peak. Tradition connected Herculaneum with Herakles, hinting at Greek origins, and it followed a similar history to Pompeii, becoming a Roman *municipium* in 89 BCE, when it was defeated in the Social War.

In 62 CE a violent earthquake 'largely demolished the populous Campanian town of Pompeii',[3] and 'part of the town of Herculaneum [was] in ruins'.[4] But such seismic activity was not abnormal and, amid a booming economy, repair, redecoration and restructuring was in progress. It has been estimated that Pompeii supported between 6,400 and 20,000 inhabitants at the time of its destruction.

We have an incredibly vivid eye-witness account from letters written by the Younger Pliny, whose uncle, Pliny the Elder, commanded the naval base at Misenum. Traditionally it was IX Kal. Septembris, i.e. 24 August 79 CE, although there is now some doubt about this: Pliny's text could possibly read 30 October, 1 November or 23 November (Roman months and numerals are easy to mistranscribe if you are a medieval monk). Many victims were wearing heavy woollen garments; and quantities of autumnal fruits have been found, along with a coin of Emperor Titus, which bears the legend 'with Tribunician power for the 9th time, acclaimed Imperator for the 15th time [this honour could not have been granted before September], Consul for the 7th time [dating the coin to 79 CE], Father of his Country'.[5] But if the date remains unclear the sequence of events is not.

The eruption of Vesuvius caught everybody unprepared: no one realized that Vesuvius was still active. Seneca had recently written a treatise on earthquakes, but did not connect them with volcanic activity, and no one interpreted the earth tremors as a harbinger of things to come. Pliny's uncle was actually relaxing after a bath and lunch, and when he saw the eruption column he reacted with curiosity rather than fear.

In the late morning a minor explosion of steam (the 'phreo-magmatic opening phase') occurred. Then around noon an enormous column of hot gas and pumice erupted from the volcano, rising to a height of 15–30 km in a shape that Pliny said resembled an umbrella pine tree. Volcanologists now call this phase of explosive volcanic eruptions the 'Plinian phase' after the way Pliny described it.[6] For the next seventeen hours or so fragments of ash, pumice and rock were carried on a south-easterly wind. These fell on Pompeii at about 15 cm per hour, and Pliny speaks of hot, thick ash, pumice and stones charred and cracked by the flames, and of broad sheets of fire and leaping flames blazing at several points on the mountain. The courtyard giving access to his room was filling with debris, and if he had stayed there any longer he would never have got out. People tied pillows over their heads to protect themselves from falling objects, and throughout the night buildings were 'shaking with violent shocks, and seemed to be swaying to and fro as if they were torn from their foundations'.

By around daybreak Pompeii was covered to a depth of more than 3 m. A total of 394 victims of the ash-fall deposit have been recovered from the pumice layers, 88 per cent of them in collapsed buildings. Herculaneum received relatively little pumice (20 cm or so) at this stage, although Pliny says that the darkness was blacker and denser than any ordinary night. Tsunamis now struck the coast, sucking the sea back from the shore and marooning sea creatures on dry sand, before rushing in again.

At this stage the panic-stricken crowds who fled into the open had a greater chance of survival than those sheltering indoors. But this changed at around 5 a.m. as the eruption began its 'Peléan phase':[7] the column began to collapse, and the first of six pyroclastic density currents (PDCs), ground-hugging avalanches of hot ash, pumice, rock fragments and volcanic gas, hurtled down the sides of Mount Vesuvius at speeds of 100 kph or more, killing almost everyone in their path:

> A dense black cloud was coming up behind us, spreading over the earth like a flood . . . Darkness fell, not the dark of a moonless or cloudy night, but as if the lamp had been put out in a closed room.[8]

Herculaneum was overwhelmed to a depth of 3 m by searing hot ash. Although less than a dozen casualties were found in the town itself, more than 300 victims were found in the arcades by the sea: a woman swept off a terrace 20 m above; a soldier knocked face down, still clutching at the sand; a small horse; a lady wearing gold jewellery; a seven-month old baby in the arms of a fourteen-year-old girl; and a boat tossed keel-up on the beach, its helmsman grasping an oar. An hour or so later a second PDC hit Herculaneum, depositing another 1.5 m of ash, demolishing walls, dislodging columns, sweeping away statues, and extending the coastline by about 400 m. The town was buried by 15–18 m of what used to be thought was boiling mud, but which was in fact ignimbrite – gas trapped in the deposit of pyroclastic flows escapes, while the ash and other fragments become welded together and form a solid, hard rock. In places the heat of the material, up to 400 °C, carbonized the wooden frameworks of houses and furniture, pieces of cloth and loaves of bread, yet elsewhere it left rope, eggs and fishing nets intact, and some wax tablets perfectly legible.

The third PDC reached the Herculaneum gate of Pompeii at about 6.30 a.m. An hour later, the fourth overwhelmed the interior of the town, killing many of the surviving residents by asphyxiation, thermal shock or physical trauma; 650 of their remains have been discovered. About half of these victims were indoors at the time, and the majority were in groups rather than on their own. The negative spaces in the volcanic material left by their decomposed bodies can be filled with plaster to reveal their final moments, and these casts leave one of the most moving records of the inhabitants. Once seen, Pompeii and Herculaneum can never be regarded as 'merely' archaeological sites: there is a group with the family silver; a slave impeded by iron shackles; a pregnant late-teenage girl and her elderly, arthritic parents or grandparents; a guard-dog chained to the entrance of its owner's house; 18 people in the lavatory of the great gymnasium; and a rich lady taking refuge in the gladiatorial barracks, who is often said to have been conducting a sordid affair with a hunky gladiator: most likely she simply ended up there (with another seventeen people and a dog) in her vain attempt to escape.

Pliny's asthmatic uncle collapsed and died amid the dense fumes. Guide books repeat the mantra that Pompeii is a 'city frozen in time', which gives us a 'snapshot of Roman everyday life'. It is not. It is a city frozen in unmitigated terror and panic.

Two more PDCs hit Pompeii in quick succession, smashing the upper floors of the houses, killing any survivors and depositing a further 60–180 cm of debris. The subsequent volcanic activity eventually left Pompeii buried some 6–7 m deep.

Precisely how many people died is hard to tell, although current estimates lean towards approximately 2,000 at Pompeii. Interestingly, there are proportionately fewer young males, who may have abandoned the women, children and elderly to their fate. However, since the destruction also encompassed the rural areas, they may have died in the countryside or at sea. The new emperor, Titus, was certainly prompted to make disaster relief a priority and created a fund for rebuilding the stricken cities, but, although the region as a whole recovered reasonably quickly, the cities were neither rebuilt nor reoccupied. The remains are riddled with tunnels dug by Roman looters: 'House tunnelled', says a piece of graffiti on the doors of one grand house that had been comprehensively ransacked; but bodies with a hoe and a pick found in the House of Menander suggest that this was a perilous undertaking.

Knowledge of Pompeii, Herculaneum and other sites in the region was not entirely lost, since they appear on the Peutinger Table, a twelfth-century CE medieval copy of a fourth-century CE Roman road map. In 1592 Domenico Fontana came across the ruins of Pompeii whilst digging a canal, but no one followed this through very seriously. Herculaneum was really discovered first, when a peasant accidentally sank a well-shaft into the ancient theatre in 1709, and was systematically excavated throughout the nineteenth century, attracting the Grand Tourists of the day. The first formal work at Pompeii started in 1748 under Roque Joaquin de Alcubierre, and then in 1763 the discovery of an inscription reading REI PUBLICAE POMPEIANORUM conclusively identified the site. In the nineteenth century Giuseppe Fiorelli, a proper archaeologist rather than a treasure hunter, took control. He divided Pompeii into nine regions; numbered the rectangular *insulae* (blocks, literally 'islands') of each region; and gave each door on the street a number. So every house is now identified by three numerals – the House of the Vettii (VI.15.1 = region VI, insula 15, door 1); the House of the Chaste Lovers (IX.12.6); the fullery of Stephanus (I.6.7), and so on.

Intensive excavation was resumed after the Second World War under Amedeo Maiuri, who uncovered significant areas of Pompeii, although the publication of his work was sketchy in the extreme. Since the 1960s the progress has been much more circumspect, with the focus now primarily on conservation, restoration and studying the evidence already uncovered. The archaeological areas of Pompeii, Herculaneum and Torre Annunziata now have UNESCO World Heritage status.

The Urban Environment
Inside Herculaneum's modest city walls were at least three *decumani* (east–west streets), intersected by five perpendicular *cardines* (north–south streets), which led down to the harbour area. The grid of lava-paved streets divided the town into *insulae* containing residential, public and religious buildings. Pompeii is more irregularly shaped and its 3 km of walls have seven gates and enclose an area of some 66 ha. Most of the city adheres to a grid-plan concept, with the main Via Stabiana running south-east to north-west, intersected by the Via dell'Abbondanza and the Via di Nola. The wider streets can accommodate two-way traffic, while others may have operated one-way systems (as evidenced by the wear and tear around the corner kerb-stones). Traffic calming was enforced by steps, bollards, cul-de-sacs or inconvenient fountains, and the Forum seems to have been pedestrianized. Most streets have quite high-raised pavements and lava kerb-stones, with the

pavement surfaced with brick chips and mortar. Holes were drilled into the edges of the pavement, possibly to secure sun-blinds or tether animals, and some pavements have inlaid designs: *HAVE* ('Welcome'), it says outside the House of the Faun (VI.12.2).

The road surface is convex, facilitating the run-off of water, and large stepping stones are placed to allow vehicles drawn by pairs of animals to pass over them with the beasts and wheels on either side, resulting in a road surface scarred with ruts carved by the traffic. The stepping stones allow pedestrians to cross without getting wet or filthy, since the street might well have been awash with a disgusting mixture of rotting food waste, human and animal excrement, and, if we believe Suetonius, human body parts.[9] However, the high kerb-stones channelled rainwater through the streets and, because Pompeii is on a sloping site, heavy downpours would effectively sluice out the garbage, which may account for the surprisingly sporadic provision of drainage.

Pompeii's Via dell'Abbondanza seems to evoke a very 'in your face' street environment: penthouses above the shops; balconies and galleries projecting from the facades; loggias gracing the upper stories; doors adorned with bronze studs; and inscriptions that constantly talk to you – there are election 'posters' painted on the walls and graffiti that ranges from scurrilous smut to quotations from Virgil, the results of gladiatorial combats, accusations, children's ABCs, erotic encounters, shopkeepers' accounts, situations vacant, workmen's advertisements, lists of market days and the birth of mules. Pompeii's archaeology is very noisy. Yet the many vineyards, fruit trees and gardens now suggest that the land use was less intensive, and the population smaller, than had once been thought.

Outside the gates, access to the city of the living is via the city of the dead. Funerary practices change from inhumations during the fourth to second centuries BCE, to cremations after the Romans founded the colony at Pompeii, and the largest funerary monument is that of Pompeii's most celebrated woman, Eumachia, a priestess who was honoured by the city's guild of fullers and was buried just by the Nuceria Gate. Elsewhere a warrior's tomb reflected Rome's mighty imperial conquests, but was defaced by a woman – 'Atimetus got me pregnant'[10]; the tomb of a highly respected freedman called C. Munatius Faustus was nevertheless overshadowed by that of his wife Naevoleia Tyche, who inherited his business and erected a much grander monument, complete with a résumé of his achievements.

Inside the walls, Pompeii's main public buildings are grouped mainly in three areas: the Forum; the Amphitheatre and *Palaestra*; and the Triangular Forum. The latter is the site of a sixth-century BCE Doric temple, originally of Hercules, which is the oldest in the city. To the east of this the Great Theatre, the Little Palaestra and the Small Covered Theatre were built during the Hellenistic era, with the temple of Zeus Meilichius and the Temple of Isis situated close by. A large square *quadriporticus* (piazza) lies behind the stage building of the Great Theatre and was ultimately converted into a gladiatorial school.

There were three complexes of public baths in Pompeii: the Stabian Baths, whose female section was the only part in fully working order in 79 CE; the state-of-the-art but as yet incomplete Central Baths; and the fully functioning Forum Baths. There were also a number of private bath-suites, such as those on the estate of Julia Felix, which advertised themselves as 'an elegant bath-suite for prestige clients', or the Suburban Baths, of which the terrace provided delightful views over the sea, and the changing room featured a series of explicit erotic paintings.

These baths provided an essential area of social intercourse, but the heart of any Roman town's commercial, political, administrative, social and religious life was the Forum. At Rome itself the Forum was the focus for civic pride, and the orator Cicero often used it to push the patriotic buttons of his listeners. Pompeii's Forum was a large rectangular piazza surrounded by a two-storey colonnaded portico, which also integrated a temple, a basilica and various ancillary buildings. The dominating building, framed by two triumphal arches and with Vesuvius glowering behind it, was the temple dedicated to the Capitoline triad of Jupiter, Juno and Minerva. This typically axial, elevated, frontal temple stood on a high podium, approached up a flight of steps, and had a deep porch with six columns. Moving clockwise we come to the *Macellum* (meat and fish market), a large rectangular courtyard with a central *tholos* (circular building), beneath which large quantities of fish bones were found. Next along was a large unroofed square courtyard with an apse at one end and recesses on two other sides containing niches for statues, which is conventionally called the Sanctuary of the Public Lares (guardian deities), but may in fact be an imperial cult building.

Immediately to the south come two structures with associations to prominent Pompeian women: the 'Temple of Vespasian', perhaps erected by the priestess Mamia, which may really be dedicated to the Genius of Augustus, the colony or Pompeii; and the Eumachia Building, the biggest edifice in the Forum, which an inscription tells us the affluent Eumachia dedicated to Concord and to *Pietas*. It may have functioned as the headquarters of the fuller's guild, a huge fullery, a place to store and sell cloth or a meeting place for the Augustales. At the south-east corner of the Forum is the *Comitium*, where the municipal elections were probably held, and along the south side are three large halls that are usually said to be the offices of magistrates and town councillors.

The basilica opens on to the south-west corner of the Forum. As a building type, this represents one of the most influential innovations in Roman architecture, in that it ultimately provided the blueprint for the ground plan of the typical Christian church. However, Pompeii's basilica was not a religious structure, but one used for social and commercial interaction, and for hearing lawsuits. The local who scrawled, 'C. Pumpidius Dipilus was here . . . 3 October 78 [BCE]'[11] gives us an inkling as to its date, as do the brick stamps, which suggest construction in *c*.100 BCE.

It measures 54 × 24 m. The external sides and the rear are built of stucco-coated rubble masonry enhanced with tufa piers and door posts. The main facade is built from tufa blocks and is accessed via entrances that could be closed by wooden shutters. Four steps lead up through four Ionic columns into a central space articulated into a long nave with a surrounding corridor with a further twenty-eight substantial stucco-clad brick columns with tufa capitals. The side walls, the lower levels of which are covered in plaster worked in relief to simulate stone blocks, then painted to complete the effect, feature engaged Ionic columns carrying a Corinthian order above them. At the far end of the building is the tribunal, a raised platform with six Corinthian columns across its front, perhaps used for trials and auctions. The rooms on either side and underneath may have been used as premises – where Pompeii's magistrates conducted their business.

At the back of the Basilica was the temple of Venus Pompeiana, who had been the patroness of the city since the founding of the Roman colony in 80 BCE. Across from the basilica to the north was the Corinthian Temple of Apollo, enclosed by a portico of forty-eight columns. In a recess in the outer wall of the temple precinct was the Table of Official Weights and Measures, while just down from there was the *Horreum,* a storehouse for agricultural produce. The Forum area was very much the hub of Pompeii's life, and a series of wall paintings from the estate of Julia Felix gives a fine impression of the vibrancy of what went on there: a down-and-out with his dog gets a handout from a well-dressed lady; kids play among the columns; women shop for shoes and haggle for fabrics; and a schoolboy gets a thrashing. The basilica walls contain a wonderful selection of graffiti that proves that the goings-on there were not always particularly legalistic: 'Suavis wishes to drink jars full of wine, please, he really does'; 'My life, my delight, let us play this game for a while: this bed be a field and I your steed'; 'O Chios, I hope your piles reopen and burn even more than they did before'; and 'I admire you, o wall, for not having collapsed under the weight of the tedious scribblings of so many writers'.[12]

Outside Pompeii's Forum one significant industry – noisy, messy and hideously smelly – was the fulleries (*fullonicae*), where newly woven woollen material was finished or old material washed. In the *fullonica* of Stephanus (I.6.7) the cloth was examined for blemishes before being stiffened by soaking in (male) human or animal urine collected in portable urinals situated outside the shop and on street corners, which came to be known as *vespasiani* after the Emperor Vespasian introduced a tax on them. A wall painting showing children trampling cloth in vats, like the five small ones in Stephanus' establishment, suggests that child labour was used for unpleasant jobs such as this. The cloth was then washed in a mixture of water and a degreasing agent called 'fuller's earth'. Next, after being stretched and beaten, the material was washed in three large vats at the back of the *fullonica.* The finished cloth could be hung to dry, and there were dedicated rooms for combing, brushing and clipping it. Whites were laid over hemispherical wooden cages on the roof and bleached by burning sulphur underneath them. Finally the fabrics were flattened using a large press. There was also a large vat that functioned as part of the laundry service. Money in a bag found with a body inside the *fullonica* of Stephanus totalled 1,089.5 *sestertii*, a considerable sum, though it is impossible to tell if this was from the shop or belonged to a fugitive who happened to end up there.

Equally smelly and lucrative was the production of *garum*, a fish sauce for which Pompeii was famous. Roman cuisine was based around it, and there was even a kosher variety. It is made by mixing the innards of different types of fish with salt water and allowing them to ferment in the sun for anything up to three months. What results is a clear liquid, *liquamen*, which was distributed in vessels known as *urcei*, plus a sediment known as *allec* and a brine called *muria*. A character called Scaurus got rich on the proceeds of this, selling *liquaminis flos* ('flower of liquamen'), *liquaminis flos optimus* ('best flower of liquamen'), *liquaminis floris flos* ('flower of flower of liquamen') and a special mackerel version of it to clients as far away as Gaul.

There were more than thirty bakeries in Pompeii, one of which was the Bakery of the Chaste Lovers (at IX.12.6-8) on the Via dell'Abbondanza. Entering through a vestibule with access to upstairs rooms, a visitor would see four flour mills at the back of the main room. These consisted of a lower, conical part (*meta*) set into a round masonry base, with a wooden stake inserted vertically into the top of it as a pivot. A biconical hollowed upper stone (*catillus*) sat on top of the *meta*, and grain was poured into the top of the *catillus*, which was then rotated using wooden handles. The flour dropped into a lead-faced trough at the bottom. The muscle power was provided by slaves or, in this establishment, horses, mules, donkeys or hinnies, which were stabled on the premises. The dough was prepared in stone bowls or on a wooden table. When they were ready for baking, they were passed through a hatch to the oven area. Roman ovens were big – one in Herculaneum fitted eighty-one loaves – and not unlike the pizza ovens used in Italy today: the fire is lit inside the oven, and the bread is baked next to it. A long-handled spade is used to put the bread in and take it out, and the smoke is drawn up a flue along the front of the oven and out through a chimney.

Pompeii's streets were also teeming with bars, taverns and what guide books call *thermopolia* ('hot food shops'), but which Romans usually called *popinae*. These have a masonry counter right on the pavement with large jars (*dolia*) embedded in it and display racks behind, and are often attractively decorated with paintings or coloured fragments of marble. Though the *popinae* may have sold wine and hot food to a population on the hoof, the *dolia* are porous and awkward to clean, so they must also have served dry foods such as nuts, dried fruits, beans and chick peas. Restaurants and inns vary from upmarket places with gardens, to sleazy dens, and our sources portray the *popina, caupona* (bar that doesn't serve hot food), *hospitium* (guest house) and *stabulum* (tavern for travellers with animals) as sordid centres of drunkenness, gambling, violence and sex: a graffito outside one bar triumphantly announces 'I shagged the landlady'.

The boundaries between inn-keeping and prostitution were somewhat blurred and, although the identification of brothels has become an issue of scholarly contention, the *lupanar* ('brothel', derived from *lupa* = 'she-wolf', and hence 'prostitute') at VII.12.18 was undoubtedly used for sex. The ground floor has five rooms and a latrine opening off a short corridor decorated with a menu board showing various couples performing explicit and rather vigorous sexual activities, one couple studying a tablet (looking at porn?) and an image of a bizarre double-phallused Priapus. Whether or not there were male prostitutes is uncertain, although the graffiti refers to anal sex, and, though we find out the girls' names, there is no way of telling whether these are real or 'professional' monikers. Each room has a stone bed, hopefully covered with cushions when in use, and there is much earthily illuminating graffiti: 'Phoebus the perfumer fucks the best'; 'Arphocras had a good screw with Drauca [for a] *denarius*' (quite expensive – you could get the same in a bar for one-eighth of the price); and so on.[13]

Roman prices and earnings fluctuated according to local conditions, and it is difficult to create exact equivalents, but the estimated average daily spend for a family in Pompeii was 6–7 *sestertii*. The lowest denomination coin was the copper *as-* 4 *asses* = 1 bronze *sesterius*; 4 *sestertii* = 1 silver *denarius*; and 25 *denarii* = 1 gold *aureus*.

We have invaluable information about domestic living arrangements from the hundreds of single family homes (*domi*, sing. *domus*) buried by the eruption, along with a detailed description written by the architect Vitruvius, which together illuminate the arrangement and functions of the various rooms. Interestingly, the divisions Vitruvius indicates within the house are made on the criteria of 'common' (entrance acceptable without an invitation, and visible from the street if the door is open) and 'exclusive' (by invitation only, and often not visible).

The general arrangement is firmly axial, allowing a view from the front door right through to the garden, and also comprising a front (Italian) part assembled round an *atrium*, and a rear (Hellenistic) part around a *peristylium*, a garden surrounded by colonnades with rooms of various sizes opening off it in the manner of the men's rooms of a Greek house. It is significant that the names of the front rooms of a Roman house are Italian (*vestibulum, fauces, atrium, ala, tablinum, cubiculum*), while those of the back are Greek (*peristylium, triclinium, oecus, exedra*) (see Table 17.1, below).

Table 17.1 Rooms in a Roman house

Vestibulum	A hallway between the entrance of the house and the street
Fauces	'throat/jaws': a narrow entrance passageway
Atrium	Central courtyard, for reception of visitors and domestic work
Impluvium	Central basin for collection of rainwater (*pluvia*), with a cistern underneath
Cubiculum	'Chamber'
Ala	Small room or alcove on either side of the *vestibulum*
Tablinum	Open room between the atrium and the peristyle used as a reception room and office
Triclinium	Dining room that had space for three dining couches
Peristylium/Peristyle	Colonnades surrounding a building or a courtyard
Exedra	Hall for entertaining guests
Oecus	Hall or 'salon' for entertainment
Hortus	Garden

Roman houses face inwards and tend to be mainly built on one floor, or with a few rooms on the upper floor constructed on an *ad hoc* basis. They are easily accessible to the street, but well insulated from it. The facades are fairly plain, windows are small and infrequent, and only the large double doors adorned with bronze studs, knockers, handles and decorative frames distinguish the entrances of the great houses from the surrounding self-contained commercial establishments, which do not connect with the house and may have been rented out. There might be a small enclosed space called the *vestibulum* leading from the street to the door, and security was clearly a major concern, as is indicated by the existence of elaborate locks and the famous *CAVE CANEM* ('Beware of the dog') mosaic from the House of the Tragic Poet (VI.8.3), which shows a large chained beast baring its teeth to unwelcome visitors.[14]

Through the door, the *fauces* (= 'jaws'/'throat') led directly into a large open-plan courtyard living area centred on the *atrium*, which was also the abode of the household deities and the ancestral images. This lofty, cool and often elaborately decorated space was lit through a large central opening (*compluvium*). Some 'tetrastyle' *atria* had four columns supporting the beams at the corners of the *compluvium*, but the non-columned 'Tuscan' type was the most fashionable at Pompeii and Herculaneum. Beneath the opening was a pool (*impluvium*) to catch rainwater from the roof, to be drained off into an underground cistern. This was particularly important prior to the provision of 'mains' water supply via the aqueduct system. Around the *atrium* were the *cubicula* (sing. *cubiculum*, conventionally translated 'bedroom', but more multi-functional than that), which were part of the private 'exclusive' areas of the house.

The core of the house's functionality was the *tablinum*, located on the central axis and open to the *atrium*, although a fixture in the aptly named 'House of the Wooden Partition' in Herculaneum shows clearly that it could be screened off if necessary. This was crucial to the hierarchical nature of Roman society, since here the *patronus* would receive his *clientes* and conduct business. To either side of it, also open to the *atrium*, were the *alae* ('wings', sing. *ala*), open-fronted rooms, where funeral masks were sometimes displayed, and beyond it, still in 'open plan', a courtyard surrounded by a colonnade called the *peristylium*. Elite Roman dwellings tended to use the *peristylium* as a garden, particularly once they could secure permanent running water. Roman gardens might be formal, informal or kitchen, and were exploited for a combination of pleasure and profit. Often adorned with wall paintings, they boasted pools, fountains and irrigation channels, and could contain peach, apple, pear or apricot trees, shrubs, flowers, vegetables and vines.

Social mores meant that the dining room (*triclinium*), which could come in a summer or winter variety, was especially elaborate, since that was where you could display your affluence and generosity, as you might also do in an *exedra* or an *oecus*.

The interiors of *domus* houses were often decorated with wall paintings and mosaics, which served a further purpose as expressions of wealth, status or aspiration. Vitruvius viewed changing fashions in wall-painting as a barometer of Rome's moral decline, and nowadays his scheme has been distilled into four basic styles linked to specific historical periods, though, as Mary Beard, rightly observes, 'the fixation of some modern archaeologists with the Four Styles is much too rigid[15]': trying to identify any given style in a Roman house is often very tricky, and several styles of decoration might well appear in the same house. This decoration was normally designed in three horizontal zones. The painters prepared the wall by applying several coats of increasingly refined lime plaster. Then, starting at the top, the paint was applied.

The pigment does not 'sink in' to the plaster, as is sometimes said; rather, lime is drawn to the surface, reacts with carbon dioxide in the air and forms a crystalline layer that 'seals' the pigments and makes the finish both durable and lustrous. Guide lines would be drawn or incised on the plaster, and the artist would work while the plaster was still damp ('true fresco' technique), adding any ornaments or figures by either: pressing on the plaster to bring more moisture to the surface; applying the colours in a specially prepared solution of lime-water once the plaster had set (the 'fresco secco' technique); or binding the colours with an organic medium to 'glue' them to the surface ('tempera' technique).

The Pompeian palette is very distinctive: white was derived from calcium carbonate, calcareous clay and remains of fossils known as *Attiorum*, after the Atii, who had a shop in Pompeii; black was made by burning ivory, pine resin, needles or bark; Pompeian blue (or Alexandrian frit) was manufactured in Egypt and was very expensive; various reds came from *rubrica* (red ochre based on ferrous oxides and haematite), cinnabar (*minimum*, mercury sulphide), which gave bright vivid hues, and the calcification of yellow ochre; Vitruvius said that for yellows *sil atticum* was superior to the other yellow ochres used; green came from celadonite, glauconite or malachite; and violet or *purpurissum* was extracted from murex shells, and was also used for cosmetics.

The First 'Incrustation' Style[16] (*c.*150–80 BCE) uses moulded plaster and painting to imitate rectangular stone blocks or marble facings.

The Second 'Architectural' Style[17] (*c.*80–14 CE) deploys *trompe l'oeil* architecture to 'open up' the wall surface and create an illusion of depth based on three planes: the actual wall surface; the colonnade 'in front'; and the open-air world 'beyond' the wall. Colonnades rise from podiums and support architraves that appear 'in front' of the wall, while 'openings' provide views of architecture receding into the distance. Shadows are projected from the light source of the room itself, and the artists show a decent knowledge of linear perspective, using several vanishing points along the vertical axis. Sometimes there are three symmetrically placed doorways as in theatrical scene-painting.

In the Third 'Ornate' Style[18] (*c.*14–62 CE) the perspective disappears as the architectural framework becomes less realistic and more ornamental. Delicate candelabra, very slender columns and twining foliage become fashionable, and the podium becomes just a flat, decorative dado, while the upper zone's architecture becomes independent of the middle zone. The wall is articulated into symmetrical zones and panels, and colour is very important in defining the layout, with, say, a black dado, red central zone and yellow upper zone, or the central zone featuring alternating black and red panels. Framed landscapes, still lifes, theatrical, mythological and genre scenes regularly decorate the central zone, and free-floating figures appear in the subsidiary panels.

The Fourth 'Intricate' Style[19] appears after the earthquake of 62 CE and accounts for about 80 per cent of what survives at Pompeii and Herculaneum. It is a kind of mash-up of both the Second and Third Styles, making it quite tricky to pin down. Solid-looking but fantastic ornamental architecture 'opens up' the wall again in the upper zone, but there is often no connection between that and the central zone, which sports subsidiary panels of fantasy architecture, as well as flat, ornamental panels depicting mythological scenes, still lifes, landscapes, 'floating' figures and 'theatre sets' with mythological 'actors'.

Mosaic floors were popular with those who could afford them:

signinum, cement with a pattern of white tesserae, complemented the First Style, with ceilings possibly continuing the imitation-masonry theme; *lithostraton,* rectangular tesserae scattered with irregular pieces of bright stone, went with the Second, the ceilings of which often imitated coffering and panelling in stucco; all-over geometric black and white floors came on trend thereafter, although the commonest form of flooring in 79 CE was *opus sectile,* made from cut marble segments of a variety of colours; Third Style ceilings often placed figures and ornaments in stuccoed or painted panels; and the Fourth Style ceilings tend to be richer and integrate the painting and stucco-work more tightly.

The most luxurious Campanian houses were built under Hellenistic influence between *c.*200 and 80 BCE. One, the palatial House of the Faun (VI.12.2) in Pompeii, named after the statue of a dancing faun that adorned its *impluvium,* occupies an entire city block (3,000 square metres). Insulated from the street by shops, its internal walls were decorated with out of date, but exceptionally high quality, First Style painting. It sported two *atria* (one Tuscan, one Tetrastyle), four *triclinia,* two peristyle gardens and an *exedra* where the stunning 'Alexander mosaic' was found. This enormous virtuoso work used well over a million tesserae to produce (probably) a copy of a lost Hellenistic painting. Achieving incredible three-dimensional effects, the unknown artist shows Alexander the Great hurtling into the thick of the fray to defeat the Persian forces of Darius III, who is about to flee amidst the chaos. As Darius' charioteer manoeuvres his horses out of Alexander's way, the king's chariot tramples one of its own side. A wonderfully foreshortened horse occupies the centre of the scene; a fallen Persian soldier looks at his own reflection in a shield; faces are full of intense emotions; gestures are eloquently expressive; this is a real *tour de force* of dramatic narrative art.

The unknown owners of the house were clearly connoisseurs of fine mosaics, and owned other first-rate pieces: Bacchus as a child riding on a lion and drinking from an oversized cup; a cat seizing a quail; ducks sitting among a still-life of fish, seafood and birds; and so on. Somewhat unusually, the house had dedicated service quarters featuring a kitchen, a domestic shrine, a bath with a latrine, a stable and various rooms decorated in the Third Style. Skeletons discovered here included a woman wearing heavy gold jewellery, although the normal occupants would have been more like the slave Martha – who scrawled, 'This is Martha's banqueting room, as she craps in this banqueting room' on the latrine wall of the House of the Centenary (IX.8.6), misspelling *triclinium* (= 'banqueting room') as *trichilinium* in the process.

Fewer houses were erected after 80 BCE, and these tended to be less imposing, although more elaborately decorated. The House of the Vettii (VI.15.1) offers interesting insights into the attitudes and tastes of its prosperous merchant owners, which might be indicative of 'new money'. The entrance features a painting of Priapus, symbolizing good luck and prosperity, studiously weighing his enormous phallus against a bag of money on a set of scales. The *atrium*, where two iron-clad bronze chests were displayed, had no *tablinum*, but opened directly on to a nice peristyle, where a fountain/statue of Priapus 'ejaculated' water from his erect penis. Many of the rooms were decorated in the newest Fourth Style, with mythological scenes such as Pentheus being torn limb from limb by frenzied bacchants, Dirce dragged to her death by a raging bull, and Hercules strangling the snakes that Hera sent to destroy him; and a large *triclinium* has some quite charming friezes of cupids engaged in various activities, including making garlands and perfumes, racing chariots, working metal, and buying and selling wine.

Only a pretty wealthy Roman could afford a *domus*, but an extremely wealthy individual might also be able to afford the luxury of at least one other property in the country. Wealthy landowners, who generally lived in the city, possessed large agricultural estates, which would have a large complex called a *villa* that provided accommodation for the landowner, his family, the overseer, the workers and often even livestock, as well as the necessary storage and work rooms. Such establishments were not necessarily purely commercial, since the rich felt the need for relaxation in the country or at seaside resorts, and owning such a residence pandered to the ideal of the citizen-farmer, even though no noble Roman had got his hands dirty on the land since the third century BCE.

As if to symbolize architecturally that country life was the antithesis of urban life, the *villa* was a *domus* turned inside out, open to the surrounding landscape, with the *atrium* set back as a private living room and the peristyle at the front. This was the layout of the Villa of the Mysteries, situated a short walk from Pompeii's Herculaneum Gate. Built early in the second century BCE, and remodelled after the earthquake of 62 CE, it has sixty rooms and covers 0.56 *ha*. It included an industrial section featuring a wine press, although we do not know how much land its owner farmed. Entering from the east, you would find yourself in a peristyle of sixteen Doric columns, surrounded by several *cubicula*, an apsidal room (a *lararium*/reception room/bath suite), a Tuscan *atrium*, a tetrastyle *atrium* that gave access to a small bathing complex and a kitchen yard with a couple of ovens. The rooms around the Tuscan *atrium*, which at some stage was walled off from the *tablinum*, had Second Style wall paintings. There was a *cryptoporticus* (semi-subterranean vaulted corridor) running under the main floor to the north, west and south, which provided a shady place to walk, and along the edge of the platform on which the house rested were two terraces planted with hanging gardens, arranged symmetrically around an *exedra*, all providing glorious vistas over the Bay of Naples. The rest of the western wing was occupied by suites of *cubicula* offering all manner of views and lighting, but the *pièce de résistance* is the wonderful painting located in a room at the south-western corner that shows scenes relating to Dionysos, and which gives the *villa* its name.

It is one of the finest, and most enigmatic, examples of ancient painting that survives. The work of a Campanian artist of the first century BCE, it comprises a frieze of life-size figures against a red architectural background that covers all four walls. The focal image shows Dionysos reclining in the lap of Ariadne, amid various overlapping scenes: a naked boy reads a scroll; a woman with a tray turns to look at us; a woman with two attendants sits with her back to us; an old satyr plays the lyre; a 'female Pan' suckles a goat; a woman recoils from the activity on the end wall; a Silenus and two satyrs drink and display a theatrical mask; a kneeling woman prepares to unveil a phallus; a semi-naked winged female demon in high boots flagellates a young woman who buries her head in a companion's lap; a naked woman dances on tiptoe with castanets; a winged cupid holds up a mirror to a woman who is having her hair braided; and a mantled woman sits looking on. The artistic quality of the work is sensational, full of swirling draperies, fine expressive portraits and convincing anatomy. But quite what it actually portrays is open to discussion: are the scenes sequential or simultaneous? Where do they start? Does it show the transition of girlhood to womanhood? Is it a woman's initiation into a Dionysiac mystery cult (the default position, which has given the *villa* its name)? Nobody knows; the Villa of the Mysteries remains just that.

Ordinary Romans did not live in *domi* or *villae*. Farming families frequently owned or rented small plots of land and lived in small huts, while urban dwellers often inhabited one- or two-roomed *tabernae*. Open to the street, except for folding shutters, these functioned as shops and workrooms as well as residences. There was sometimes a back room or a mezzanine that offered a modicum of privacy, and some dwellings were of the 'flats over the shop' type, with stairs or ladders leading to an upper living space. These structures could rise to three storeys, constructed from *opus craticium* (a wooden frame filled with rubble and plaster), even though, as Vitruvius said, 'they are like torches ready for kindling'.[20]

The introduction of concrete (*opus caementicum*) allowed builders to produce more solid apartment blocks called *insulae* ('islands'), the walls of which were commonly built as a concrete core held in place by a facing of which the surface pattern was achieved with bricks or stones set into the concrete: the fishnet pattern of *opus reticulatum* was more pleasing to the eye, but liable to crack, whereas the old-fashioned, more irregular *opus incertum* was less aesthetic, but stronger. If fired bricks replaced the stones of *opus reticulatum,* it was called *opus latericium,* and a concrete core faced with alternating rows of rectangular blocks and courses of brick or tile, was known as *opus vittatum mixtum.*

Insula dwelling became the norm, and the fourth-century CE *Curiosum Urbis Romae Regionum* XIV indicates that Rome contained 46,602 *insulae* and just 1,797 private houses. At Rome's port of Ostia, the *insulae* feature plain facades of brick-faced concrete, sometimes relieved by balconies above ground-floor level and large windows. They seldom exceeded five storeys, probably to comply with building regulations. The House of Diana was quite representative, with *tabernae* along the street frontage, two of which had back rooms. An interior courtyard, accessed via two entrance corridors, was surrounded at ground level by a corridor and several suites of rooms. The courtyard served to provide light and air, and contained a water cistern. One of the rooms in the block was converted into a stable, while a latrine and a porter's lodge served the whole complex. On the second storey were various apartments, facing either the street or the courtyard.

No town could survive without an effective water supply, and the Romans saw themselves as world leaders in this. The engineer Frontinus, who wrote *On the Aqueducts of Rome*, put it beautifully: 'Compare the idle pyramids of the Egyptians . . . when we have all these important structures, carrying so much water!'[21] Drinking water at Pompeii and Herculaneum came from wells and the *impluvia* installed in the houses, but, once an aqueduct system was constructed throughout Campania around 27 BCE, some wealthier households acquired piped 'mains' water, generating a whole new style of garden design involving elaborate water features. Given that the average Roman (in Rome) used about 285 litres of water per day, getting water into and out of any city demanded immense structures and considerable planning and surveying expertise. Vitruvius tells us that water conduits should have a fall of not less than 1 in 200, and that the channels should be arched over to protect the water from the sun. A reservoir should be located where the channels come to the city walls, with pipes to distribute the water. If there are hills between the city and the fountain head, he recommends that underground tunnels be dug and air shafts installed; and advocates avoiding pressurized systems if possible. Earthenware pipes represented a cost-effective option (so long as a build-up of air did not burst them), especially as anyone could repair a fault, and interestingly Vitruvius knew that water from lead pipes is said to be harmful, which gives the lie to the facile 'lead pipes caused the downfall of the Roman Empire' cliché: Vitruvius was writing more than four centuries before the fall of Rome in the West.[22] This aqueduct engineering could be spectacular. Brilliantly combining practicality and aesthetics, the Augustan aqueduct that brought water 56 km to the provincial town of Nemausus (Nîmes) and included the magnificent Pont du Gard, 48.75 m high and 270 m long.

Using systems like this the Aqua Marcia at Rome could deliver around 1.1 million litres an hour, and there were severe penalties for tampering with this fundamental aspect of Roman life:

Whoever shall . . . intentionally pierce, break, or countenance or attempt to pierce or break, the channels, conduits, arches, pipes, tubes, reservoirs, or basins of the public waters which are brought into the City . . . shall be condemned to pay a fine of 100,000 *sestertii* to the Roman people; [and repair] what he has damaged.[23]

At Pompeii the water flowed into the *Castellum Aquae* ('Water Castle') at the highest point of the city, from where a system of water towers and fountains distributed it throughout the town. The water towers had a lead tank at the top, which regulated the hydraulic pressure, and lead pipes ran under the pavements to the public fountains, which dispensed continually flowing water into large stone troughs and to nearby houses. The earthquake of 62 CE badly damaged Pompeii's water supply, and a major overhaul of the entire system was still under way when Vesuvius erupted. The priority had clearly been to restore the public fountains, since many grand houses had lost their connections, and quite a few private bath suites had fallen into disuse. Water kept the Roman city alive, and the expert provision of this vital commodity to even the most unassuming provincial town represents what Vitruvius dubbed 'the most remarkable achievement anywhere in the world.'[24]

18

THE END OF ROME

It's like the Roman Empire. Wasn't everybody running around just
covered in syphilis? And then it was destroyed by the volcano.
                    Joan Collins, interviewed for *Playboy* (31 [1981] no. 4)

Those looking for a single cause for the downfall of Rome will be
disappointed. Indeed, it can be argued that the Roman Empire in
the East did not fall until Mehmet the Conqueror sacked
Constantinople in 1453 CE. Like the rise of Rome, it's fall was a
gradual and complex process: environmental issues, disease, moral
decadence, lead pipes, dysgenic breeding, war, manpower shortages
and 'race-suicide' have all been cited, as have army discipline,
dynastic problems, taxation, Christianity, overcentralization of
power, inept foreign policy and weak frontier defence. But we can
be certain that there was no volcano, and syphilis had not yet
reached Europe. Many of these factors had already been in existence
when Augustus became Rome's first emperor in 27 BCE: dynastic
in-fighting, civil wars, barbarian threats, religious conflicts,
inflation, the overinfluential role of the army in politics, and so on
were endemic problems throughout Rome's history, and a
devastatingly severe plague in the mid-third century CE caused a
horrendous death-toll. Yet Rome did not fall.

In 293 CE the emperor Diocletian, the most vicious persecutor of
the Christians, established the 'tetrarchy' (= four people sharing
power), a *collegium* of emperors comprising two older Augusti as
the decision makers and two younger Caesars as executives. Each
man controlled soldiers and had a specific sphere of operation –
Maximian, Italy and Africa; Constantius, Gaul and Britain;

Galerius, the Danube region; and Diocletian, the East – and had his own residence in the part of the empire that he ruled (Milan, Trier, Sirmium and Nicomedia respectively). Rome itself was no longer the effective capital of the Empire.

Bad health caused Diocletian to abdicate on 1 May 305 CE, and chaos ensued the following year when Constantius died at York and the armies of Britain and Gaul proclaimed his son Constantine as Augustus. Maxentius, son of Maximian, had himself proclaimed Augustus in Rome, and ultimately there were seven people all laying claim to that title: Maximian, Galerius, Constantine, Maxentius, Maximinus Daia, Licinius and Domitius Alexander. The deaths of Maximian, Alexander and Galerius followed, the latter from gluttony:

> The whole of his hulking body, thanks to over-eating, had been transformed . . . into a huge lump of flabby fat, which then decomposed and presented those who came near with a revolting and horrifying sight.[1]

This left Constantine and Maxentius in the West, and Licinius and Maximinus Daia in the East. Constantine invaded Italy and fought with Maxentius. During the campaign Constantine had a vision of a lighted cross in the sky and declared himself a Christian. After his comprehensive victory at the Battle of the Milvian Bridge near Rome, he struck a deal with Licinius, and they garnered the support of the Eastern Christians by guaranteeing them freedom of worship under the Edict of Milan of 313 CE. When Maximinus Daia fell ill and died in the same year, Constantine and Licinius remained as the two leaders of the Empire.

It was a recipe for unrest: Constantine took the offensive in 316 CE; Diocletian died; a truce followed, under which Constantine and Licinius designated three potential Caesars from their infant sons (two of Constantine's, one from Licinius), but there was still a huge gulf between the two: Constantine was pro-Christian; Licinius reintroduced persecutions; and in 324 CE war broke out again. Licinius was defeated and executed, along with his son; Constantine's son Constantius was named Caesar, along with his elder brothers Crispus and Constantine the Younger. At this point Constantine founded Constantinople as the 'New Rome' on the site of Byzantium in 324 CE. It became the administrative capital of the empire.

When Constantine died on 22 May 337 CE, his sons divided the Empire among themselves and eradicated all other family members: Constantine II took the West; Constantius II the East; and Constans I got Italy, Africa, and Illyricum. In 340 CE Constantine II attacked Constans I, but got killed in the process, after which peace then broke out between him and Constantius II, until a mutiny occurred in 350 CE in which Constans was killed in Lugdunum (Lyons) by a British-born usurper called Magnentius. Magnentius defeated Constantius II in the titanic Battle of Mursa (351 CE), but eventually committed suicide. Constantius II's administration was dominated by informers, spies and meddling bureaucrats. He named his cousins as Caesars: Gallus (cruel, incompetent and ultimately got rid of) in the East; and Julian (so dangerously successful that he was proclaimed Augustus in 361 CE, in spite of Constantius II's opposition) in Gaul. However, Constantius II's death in November 361 CE averted the inevitable civil war. Julian was in sole control.

Julian had studied rhetoric and philosophy at Ephesus and Athens, and had clandestinely apostatized ('gone back to being a pagan') some ten years before, so when he became Emperor he proclaimed his paganism, argued with Christian intellectuals, banned Christians from teaching, began rebuilding the temple at Jerusalem and restored many pagan shrines. The Christians regarded him as the Antichrist. Julian was intent on military glory against the Persians in the Mesopotamia region, but he was defeated near Ctesiphon and subsequently died in a skirmish in 363 CE in which he was shot by an arrow, possibly fired by an anti-pagan Christian soldier rather than an anti-Roman Persian. His successor Jovian was a moderate Christian: he restored religious tolerance, negotiated an unfavourable peace with the Persian king Shapur II and died early in February 364 CE from asphyxiation by fumes from a charcoal stove.

Valentinian I was now chosen as emperor. A moderate Catholic Christian who generally tolerated heretics and pagans, he governed the West and delegated the East to his brother Valens. This marks the definitive moment when the Roman Empire was split into East and West. Valentinian I successfully fought the Alemanni,

Sarmatians and Quadi, while in Britain his general, Count Theodosius the Elder, put down the 'barbarian conspiracy' of Picts, Scots, Attacotti (Irish?), Saxons and Franks who had overrun Hadrian's Wall, killed the Count of the Saxon Shore and overwhelmed Fullofaudes, Duke of Britain. Domestically Valentinian I embarked on a reign of terror, executing senators for magic or sex crimes.

Meanwhile Valens had survived an attempted usurpation by Procopius (365–6 CE). But Valens was an extremist subscriber to Arianism, a heresy which held that the Son or Word was a creature created before time, and therefore that the Father and the Son were totally unalike. This ran contrary to the council of Nicaea of 325 CE, which had affirmed that the Son was 'of the same substance' as the Father. The result was that the East descended into religious turmoil. Elsewhere the Ostrogoths and the Greutingi were being displaced by the Huns and appeared on the Danube frontiers in 375 CE, and the following year Valens allowed them to enter Thrace. But things went horribly wrong: the Goths raped and pillaged, and Valens got killed in the disastrous Battle of Adrianople on 9 August 378 CE.

Valentinian I became so angry with a deputation of insolent barbarians on 17 November 375 CE that he died of a stroke. His teenage son Gratian took over the West, although the army at Aquincum also promoted Gratian's four-year-old half-brother, Valentinian II, who received Illyricum under Gratian's guardianship. In 379 CE Gratian proclaimed Theodosius I (the Great), son of the recently executed Count Theodosius the Elder, as Augustus of the Eastern empire. It was no longer possible to expel the Goths, so Gratian and Theodosius I agreed to allow them into the Empire, and Gratian also admitted the Salian Franks. The barbarian takeover of the Roman Empire was well under way.

On 27 February 380 CE Theodosius I decreed that the faith professed by Pope Damasius and by Peter, Bishop of Alexandria, was the true Catholic faith, and deposed the Arian Bishop of Constantinople. Gratian also deprived the pagan priests and the Vestal Virgins of their privileges, thereby adding a number of disgruntled pagans to his opponents, and in 383 CE the army of Gaul and Britain elected its leader, Magnus Maximus, who appears in Welsh legend in *The Mabinogion* and *The Dream of Macsen Wledig* as Emperor. He conquered Gaul; Gratian was killed; Valentinian II, who was now in Milan, expelled Maximus from Italy; but in the end Valentinian II was defeated and put to death by Theodosius I at Aquileia in 388 CE.

Theodosius I now ruled both West and East, and paganism's days were numbered: possibly influenced by Ambrose, Bishop of Milan, he issued an edict outlawing all forms of pagan worship. A short-lived pagan revival was nipped in the bud when the Christian-but-pagan-sympathetic Eugenius was proclaimed as Emperor, but then crushed at the Battle of the River Frigidus on 6 September 394 CE.

Theodosius the Great wanted to install his sons as rulers – Honorius in the West and Arcadius in the East – but he died unexpectedly early in 395 CE. His armies had contained a barbarian majority, and the half-Vandal Stilicho, who had married Theodosius I's niece Serena, now ruled as regent on behalf of Honorius. Stilicho temporarily checked the seaborne invasions into Britain in 396–8 CE, as Britannia herself tells us in a poem by Claudian:

> Stilicho gave me aid when I was at the mercy of neighbouring tribes, when the Scots raised all Hibernia against me, and the sea foamed with hostile oars. Thanks to his care, I need not fear the weapons of the Scots or tremble at the Pict, or keep watch along my shores for the Saxon who would come whatever wind might blow.[2]

However, the Eastern leaders rejected Stilicho, and any plans he might have had to intervene in the affairs of Constantinople were stymied by having to deal with Alaric the Visigoth, Radagaisus the Ostrogoth and the great invasion of 31 December 407 CE. The Huns had driven the Vandals, Suebi, Alani, Burgundians and Alemanni across the Rhine into Gaul. Stilicho had intended to reunite the Empire by installing Theodosius II as Emperor in Constantinople, but found himself the victim of a *coup d'état*. Meanwhile Alaric moved on Rome itself, layed siege to it three times, and finally took it on 24 August 410 CE.

The effects of the barbarian invasions are vividly illustrated by the ramifications in Britain. Stilicho had to withdraw troops from there, and the incursion of the Vandals, Suebi, Alani and Burgundians severed Britain's communications with Rome. The remaining British forces elected a Briton called Constantine III, who felt that the threat of invasion from the continent would best be met by a pre-emptive strike, crossed the Channel in 407 CE and achieved some successes. Unfortunately, his British general Gerontius rebelled, the barbarians got the upper hand and he had to surrender to Honorius, who executed him. In 410 CE the remaining Britons appealed to Honorius, but there was nothing he could do. It is not entirely clear whether the Britons actively sought independence from Rome in the end or simply slipped out of the Roman orbit, but the severance from Rome brought with it barbarism.

Honorius was succeeded by his son Valentinian III in 423 CE, and he ruled the western Empire until 455 CE, during which time the barbarians gradually consolidated their position in the West. The second half of the fifth century CE saw Attila the Hun invading Gaul and Italy, and, following Valentinian III's death in 455 CE, the western emperors became mere puppets of various German chiefs. Emperor Majorian's attempt to fight back ultimately ended in his defeat and assassination, and in 476 CE Attila's follower Odoacer deposed the last emperor, Romulus Augustulus (who ironically bore the name of Rome's founder and its first emperor, albeit in the diminutive 'Little Augustus'). It was the end of the Roman Empire in the West, but by then it is unlikely that many people cared.

In the first book of Virgil's *Aeneid*, Jupiter had prophesied the future of the Roman race: 'For the empire of these people I impose neither limits of space nor time: I have given them power without end.'[3] Odoacer's coronation might seem to belie that prophetic vision, yet as T.S. Eliot very pertinently wrote:

> We are all, so far as we inherit the civilization of Europe, still citizens of the Roman Empire, and time has not yet proved Virgil wrong'.[4]

Rome's history, in a sense, is our present; the foundations of modern Western civilization lie there; the saying goes that all roads lead to Rome, but it might be better to say that they lead *from* Rome.

RECOMMENDED READING

Allison, P.M., *Pompeian Households: An Analysis of the Material Culture*, Los Angeles, CA: Cotsen Institute of Archaeology, Monograph 42, 2004.

Baldock, M., *Greek Tragedy: An Introduction*, Bristol: Bristol Classical Press, 1989.

Beacham, R.C., *The Roman Theatre and its Audience*, London: Routledge, 1991.

Beard, M. *Pompeii: The Life of a Roman Town*, London: Profile, 2008.

Beard, M., North, J., and Price, S., *Religions of Rome*, Cambridge: Cambridge University Press, 1998.

Berry, J., *The Complete Pompeii*, London and New York: Thames & Hudson, 2007.

Boardman, J., Griffin, J., and Murray, O. (eds), *The Oxford History of the Classical World*, Oxford: Oxford University Press, 1986.

Bryce, T., *The Trojans and Their Neighbours*, London: Routledge, 2006.

Burkert, W., *Greek Religion: Archaic and Classical*, trans. J. Raffan, Oxford: Blackwell, 1985.

Buxton, R.G.A., *The Complete World of Greek Mythology*, London: Thames & Hudson, 2004.

Camps, W.A., *An Introduction to Virgil's Aeneid*, Oxford: Oxford University Press, 1969.

Cartledge, P. (ed.), *Cambridge Illustrated History of Ancient Greece*, Cambridge: Cambridge University Press, 1998.

— *The Spartans: An Epic History*, London: Channel 4 Books, 2002.

Castleden, R., *The Mycenaeans*, London: Routledge, 2005.

Chadwick, J., *The Decipherment of Linear* B, Cambridge: Cambridge University Press, 1958.

Davidson, J.N., *The Greeks and Greek Love: A Radical Appraisal of Homosexuality in Ancient Greece*, London: Weidenfeld & Nicolson, 2007.

Dover, K.J., *Aristophanic Comedy*, Berkeley and Los Angeles, CA: University of California Press, 1972.

— *Greek Homosexuality*, London: Duckworth, 1979.

Easterling, P.E., and Muir, J.V. (eds), *Greek Religion and Society*, Cambridge: Cambridge University Press, 1985.

Forrest, W.G., *A History of Sparta, 950–192 BC*, New York: W.W. Norton & Co., 1969.

Foster, J., and Lehoux, D., 'The Delphic Oracle and the ethylene-intoxication hypothesis', *Clinical Toxicology* 2007, 45(1), 85–9.

Fowler, R. (ed.), *The Cambridge Companion to Homer*, Cambridge: Cambridge University Press, 2004.

Goldsworthy, A., *The Fall of the West: The Death of the Roman Superpower*, London: Weidenfeld & Nicolson, 2009.

Gransden, K.W., and Harrison, S.J. (eds), *Virgil: The Aeneid*, 2nd edn., Cambridge: Cambridge University Press, 2004.

Griffin, J., *Homer: The Odyssey*, Cambridge: Cambridge University Press, 1987.

Hall, E., *The Return of Ulysses: A Cultural History of Homer's Odyssey*, London and New York: I.B. Tauris, 2008.

Harrison, S. (ed.), *A Companion to Latin Literature*, Oxford: Blackwell, 2005.

Henderson, J., *The Maculate Muse: Obscene Language in Attic Comedy*, 2nd edn, Oxford: Oxford University Press, 1991

Hornblower, S. and Spawforth, A.J., *The Oxford Classical Dictionary*, 3rd edn, revised, Oxford: Oxford University Press, 2003.

Hunter, R.L., *The New Comedy of Greece and Rome*, Cambridge: Cambridge University Press, 1985.

Jahemski, W., *The Gardens of Pompeii: Herculaneum and the Villas Destroyed by Vesuvius*, 2 vols, New York: Aristide D. Caratzas vol. I 1979, vol. 2, 1993.

Jenkins, I., Kerslake, I., and Hubbard, D., *The Parthenon Sculptures in the British Museum*, London: British Museum, 2007.

Joint Association of Classical Teachers, *The World of Athens: An*

Introduction to Classical Athenian Culture, 2nd edn, Cambridge: Cambridge University Press, 2008.

Jones, P., and Sidwell, K. (eds), *The World of Rome: An Introduction to Roman Culture*, Cambridge: Cambridge University Press, 1997.

Kershaw, S., *A Brief Guide to the Greek Myths*, London: Robinson, 2007.

Lane Fox, R., *The Classical World: An Epic History of Greece and Rome*, London: Penguin, 2007.

Latacz, J., *Troy and Homer: Towards a Solution of an Old Mystery*, trans. K. Windle and R. Ireland, Oxford: Oxford University Press, 2004.

Luongo, G., Perrotta, A., Scarpati, C., De Carolis, E., Patricelli G., and Ciarallo, A., 'Impact of the AD 79 explosive eruption on Pompeii: II. Causes of death of the inhabitants inferred by stratigraphic analysis and a real distribution of the human casualties', *Journal of Volcanology and Geothermal Research* 126, 2003, 169–200.

McLeish, K., *Roman Comedy*, Basingstoke: Macmillan, 1976.

Marshall, C.W., *The Stagecraft and Performance of Roman Comedy*, Cambridge: Cambridge University Press, 2006.

Ministry of Culture of the Russian Federation Pushkin State Museum of Fine Arts, *The Treasure of Troy: Heinrich Schliemann's Excavations*, Milan: Leonardo Arte SRL, 1996.

Pollitt, J.J., *Art and Experience in Classical Greece*, Cambridge: Cambridge University Press, 1972.

Potter, D.S. (ed.), *A Companion to the Roman Empire*, Oxford: Blackwell, 2006.

Potter, D.S., and Mattingly, D.J. (eds), *Life, Death and Entertainment in the Roman Empire*, Ann Arbor, MI: University of Michigan Press, 1998.

Rabinowitz, N.S., *Greek Tragedy*, Oxford: Blackwell, 2008.

Riddle, J.M., *Conception and Abortion from the Ancient World to the Renaissance*, London: Harvard University Press, 1992.

Ross, D.O., *Virgil's Aeneid: A Reader's Guide*, Oxford: Blackwell, 2007.

Rousseau, P. (ed.), *A Companion to Late Antiquity*, Oxford: Wiley-Blackwell, 2009.

Scheid, J., *An Introduction to Roman Religion*, Edinburgh: Edinburgh University Press, 2003.

Schein, S.L., *The Mortal Hero: An Introduction to Homer's Iliad*, Berkeley and Los Angeles, CA: University of California Press, 1984.

Schofield, L., *The Mycenaeans*, London: British Museum Press, 2007.

Schreiber, T., *Athenian Vase Construction: A Potter's Analysis*, Malibu: J. Paul Getty Museum, 1999.

Taplin, O., *Greek Tragedy in Action*, London: Methuen, 1978.

Toner, J., *Leisure and Ancient Rome*, Cambridge: Polity Press, 1995.

Veyne, P., *Bread and Circuses: Historical Sociology and Political Pluralism*, London: Allen Lane, 1990.

Wallace-Hadrill, A., *Houses and Society in Pompeii and Herculaneum*, Princeton, NJ: Princeton University Press, 1994.

Wardle, K.A., and Wardle, D., *Cities of Legend: The Mycenaean World*, London: Bristol Classical, 1997.

Warren, P., *Aegean Civilisations*, 2nd edn, Oxford: Phaidon, 1989.

Welch, K., *The Roman Amphitheatre from its Origins to the Colosseum*, Cambridge: Cambridge University Press, 2007.

Wickham, C., *The Inheritance of Rome: A History of Europe from 400 to 1000*, London: Penguin, 2010.

Wood, M., *In Search of the Trojan War*, updated edn., Berkeley and Los Angeles, CA: University of California Press, 1996.

Woodford, S., *The Art of Greece and Rome*, Cambridge: Cambridge University Press, 1982.

Woolf, G., (ed.), *Cambridge Illustrated History of the Roman World*, Cambridge: Cambridge University Press, 1998.

NOTES

Introduction

1. G.W.E. Russell, *Collections and Recollections*, ch.1, London: Smith, Elder & Co., 1898.
2. From Edgar Allan Poe's 1845 revision of his poem 'To Helen'. First published as 'To_ _ _' in *Union Magazine*, November 1948, published as 'To Helen' in New York Daily Tribune, 10 October 1849

Chapter 1

1. Homer, *Odyssey* 19.172–9, trans. E.V. Rieu, *Homer: The Odyssey*, Harmondsworth: Penguin, 1946.
2. Even though 'no trace of it remained' in his day: Pliny, *N.H.* 35.29.85.
3. Quoted by D. Powell, *The Villa Ariadne*, London: Hodder & Stoughton, 1973, 22. Despite his frustration, Evans employed both Christian and Muslim workers, 'so that the work at Knossos might be an earnest of the future co-operation of the two creeds . . . the experiment proved very successful' (ibid., 260).
4. A.J. Evans, *The Palace of Minos at Knossos*, vols i-iv, with index volume, London: Macmillan, 1921–36.
5. Powell, *The Villa Ariadne*, 30.
6. The Admonitions of IPW-WER 3, Papyrus of Leiden.
7. Sir (pseud.: B. Eckstein-Diener) Galahad, *Im Palast des Minos*, Munchen: Albert Langen, 1913.
8. The Atlantis theory can no longer withstand serious analysis: see S.P. Kershaw, *A Brief Guide to the Greek Myths*, London: Robinson, 2007, 424 ff.

Chapter 2

1. *AP* IX.101, trans. E. Morgan, in P. Jay (ed.) *The Greek Anthology and Other Ancient Epigrams*, Harmondsworth: Penguin, 1973.
2. Graves I–V were excavated by Schliemann; VI by P. Stamatakes.
3. Telegram dated 28 November 1876 to King George of Greece: H. Schliemann, *Mycenae: A Narrative of Researches and Discoveries at Mycenae and Tiryns*, New York: Charles Scribner's Sons, Bell & Howell Co, 1880, 380–1. See also D.A. Traill, *Schliemann of Troy: Treasure and Deceit*, Penguin: London, 1995, 162; S.P.M. Harrington, W.M. Calder III, D.A. Traill, K. Demakopoulou, and K.D.S. Lapatin. 'Behind the Mask of Agamemnon', *Archaeology* (July/August 1999), 52.
4. Schliemann telegram to a Greek newspaper: Tr. W.M. Calder III and D.A. Traill, eds., *Myth, Scandal, and History: The Heinrich Schliemann Controversy and a First Edition of the Mycenaean Diary*, Detroit: Wayne State University Press, 1986, 234.
5. Homer, *Iliad* 11.632 ff., trans. R. Lattimore, *The Iliad of Homer*, Chicago, IL: University of Chicago Press, 1951.
6. Despite its evocative name, it is not a treasury and had nothing to do with the mythical Atreus.

7. Corbelling is a technique in which each course of blocks slightly overlaps the one below in order to reduce the span still to be roofed.

8. A stone consisting of naturally cemented together pebbles, cobblestones and other sediments.

9. See below, p. 168 f.

10. Pausanias 2.16.4. He was immensely impressed with the walls, which he regarded as no less marvellous than the Egyptian pyramids (9.36.3).

11. Trans. R. Castleden, *The Mycenaeans*, London: Routledge, 2005, 108.

12. Tn 316.

13. Homer, *Iliad* 10.263 ff.

14. Ibid., 7.219–23, although Aias' shield also incorporates a boss, which tower shields did not have.

15. See above, pp. 14–16.

16. Henry Miller, *The Colossus of Maroussi*, New York: New Directions, 1941, 86.

Chapter 3

1. Homer, *Odyssey* 20.232–5. Ganymede's abduction is sometimes said to have been perpetrated by Zeus himself, by an eagle on his behalf, or by Zeus in the form of an eagle, but Minos, Tantalos and Eos (Dawn) are also mentioned. Ganymede usually pours nectar into Zeus' cup, rather than wine.

2. *Don Juan*, Canto IV, stanza 101.

3. T. Moore, *Life of Lord Byron: With his Letters and Journals*, Vol. 5, new edn., London: John Murray, 1854, 70.

4. Report of 4 August 1872, in Schliemanm, H., *Troy and its Remains*, London: John Murray, 1875, p. 211.

5. C.W. Blegen, *Troy and the Trojans*, London: Thames & Hudson, 1963, 20.

6. C.3000–2100 BCE on other scholars' datings.

7. Or *c.*3000–2500 BCE.

8. Or *c.*2500–2300 BCE.

9. See above, p. 23 f.

10. Or *c.*2300–2100 BCE; or 2300–2200 BCE.

11. See above, p. 18.

12. Or *c.*2100–1700 BCE. Together Troy IV and V comprise what Korfmann calls the 'Anatolian-Trojan' culture.

13. Or *c.*1700–1250 BCE.

14. There is a move to recategorize Troy VIIa as 'Late Troy VI and Troy VIi, formerly Troy VIIa', because of the cultural continuity between these levels. However, Dörpfeld's original designation is generally kept to avoid confusion.

15. Some writers have seen the myth of the Trojan Horse as a metaphor for this earthquake, in that the horse was sacred to Poseidon, the Greek god of earthquakes. This seems an unconvincing rationalization: Poseidon *built* Troy's walls, and he backed the Trojans in the war.

16. Or *c.*1250–1000 BCE.

17. Trans. F. Stark, quoted in J. Latacz, *Troy and Homer: Towards the Solution of an Old Mystery*, Oxford: Oxford University Press, 2004, 106–7.

18. Trans. P.H.J. Houwink ten Cate, 'Sidelights on the Ahhiyawa Question from Hittite Vassal and Royal Correspondence,' *Jaarbericht Ex Oriente Lux* 28, 1983–4, 40.

19. Trans. O.R. Gurney, in J. Garstang and O.R. Gurney, *The Geography of the Hittite Empire*, London: British Institute of Archaeology in Ankara, 1959, 111–14.

20. M.I. Finley, J.L. Caskey, G.S. Kirk and D.L. Page, 'The Trojan War', *Journal of Hellenic Studies* 84, 1964, 1–20.

21. 'Peter Jones reviews *The Trojan War: A New History* by Barry Strauss (Hutchinson)', *Sunday Telegraph*, 25 February 2007.

22. Euripides, *Trojan Women*, 1319 ff., trans. P. Vellacott, in *Euripides, Three Plays: Alcestis; Hippolytus; Iphigenia in Tauris*, Harmondsworth: Penguin, rev. edn, 1974.

Chapter 4

1. Trans. M. McCarthy, in S. Weil and R. Bespaloff, *War and the Iliad*, New York: New York Review of Books Classics, 2005.
2. Homer, *Iliad* 12.310 ff., trans. R. Lattimore, in *The Iliad of Homer*, Chicago, IL: University of Chicago Press, 1951.
3. Ibid., 3.38 ff.
4. Ibid., 6.466 ff.
5. Ibid., 9.604 f.
6. Ibid., 15.661 ff.
7. Ibid., 16.83 ff.
8. Ibid., 18.98 ff.
9. Ibid., 22.104 ff.
10. Ibid., 22.317 ff.
11. Ibid., 24.503 ff.
12. Ibid., 24.518 ff.
13. J. Redfield, *Nature and Culture in the Iliad: The Tragedy of Hector*, Chicago, IL: University of Chicago Press, 1975.
14. Homer, *Odyssey* 2.104 f., trans. R. Lattimore, in *The Odyssey of Homer*, New York: Harper, 1999.
15. Lyrics from 'Moon River' by Henry Mancini.
16. Homer, *Odyssey* 1.119 ff., trans. E.V. Rieu, in *Homer: The Odyssey*, Harmondsworth: Penguin, 1946.
17. Homer, *Odyssey* 4.556 f. , trans. Lattimore.
18. Homer, *Odyssey* 4.605 ff., trans. D.M. Gaunt, in *Surge and Thunder: Critical Readings in Homer's Odyssey*, Oxford: Oxford University Press, 1971, 106.
19. Homer, *Odyssey* 6.119 ff., trans. Lattimore.
20. Ibid., 9.466 f.
21. Homer, *Odyssey* 9.19 ff., trans. Gaunt.
22. Homer, *Iliad* 9. 105 ff., trans. E.V. Rieu, in *Homer: The Illiad*, Harmondsworth: Penguin, 1950.
23. Ibid., 9.252 f.
24. Homer, *Iliad* 9.387 ff., trans. R. Lattimore.
25. Ibid., 9.504 f.
26. Ibid., 9.534 f.
27. Ibid., 11.114 f., exactly echoing Polyphemus' hopes: cf. 9.534 f.
28. Ibid., 11.205 ff.
29. Ibid., 11.410 f. In Aeschylus' *Agamemnon* it is Clytemnestra who takes the lead role in the murder, with Aegisthus a rather cringing weakling. See below, p. 173.
30. Ibid., 18.96 ff.
31. Ibid., 18.281 ff.
32. Ibid., 22.41.
33. Ibid., 22.470 ff.
34. John Keats, *On First Looking into Chapman's Homer*, 1816.
35. Published privately – the first public edition, published posthumously, was 1775.
36. Trans. T.E. Kennedy and P. Sherrard, in C.P. Cavafy, *Collected Poems,* The Hogarth Press, 1984.
37. Recorded by Joyce's pupil Georges Borach in his journal on 1 August 1917. See R. Ellman, *James Joyce*, Oxford: Oxford University Press, rev. edn, 1983, 429–30.
38. T.S. Eliot, 'Ulysses, Order, and Myth', *Dial* 75.5, November 1923, 480.

39. Rupert Brooke, *Fragment* 2, 1915, published in *Collected Poems of Rupert Brooke with a Memoir*, London: Sidgwick and Jackson, 1918.
40. P. Shaw-Stewart, 'Achilles in the Trench', 1916, Found after his death, written in his copy of A.E. Houseman's *A Shropshire Lad*, now in Eton College library.
41. J. Buchan, *Memory Hold-the-door*, London: Hodder & Stoughton, 1940.

Chapter 5

1. Aristotle, *Politics* 1327b, trans. T.A. Sinclair, in *Aristotle: The Politics*, Harmondsworth: Penguin, 1962.
2. Thucydides, I.142.
3. Greek *agora* = 'market'.
4. *Elegies,* 53 ff., trans. J.B. Bury and R. Meiggs, *A History of Greece to the Death of Alexander the Great,* 4th rev. edn, London: Macmillan, 1975, 113.
5. Aristotle, *Athenaion Politeia,* 5.
6. Plutarch, *Solon* 24, trans. I. Scott-Kilvert in *The Rise and Fall of Athens: Nine Greek Lives*, Harmondsworth: Penguin, 1960.
7. Aristotle, *Athenaion Politeia* 8.1. The previous system had been simply by *hairesis* (direct election).
8. Herodotus, 1.59.
9. Ibid., 1.61.
10. Ibid., 5.66; cf. Aristotle, *Athenaion Politeia.* 20.1: 'he attached the people to his following, by proposing to give political power to the masses'.
11. Herodotus, 5.105
12. Plutarch, *Moralia,* 347C.
13. Herodotus, 7.141. The actual authenticity of this *post eventum* oracle is highly questionable.
14. Ibid., 7.226
15. Aeschylus, *The Persians,* 408 ff, trans. P. Vellacott, in *Aeschylus: Prometheus Bound, The Suppliants, Seven Against Thebes, The Persians*, Harmondsworth: Penguin, 1961.
16. Thucydides, 1.98.
17. It is important not to confuse the 'First Peloponnesian War' of 461–446 BCE with *The* Peloponnesian War of 431–404 BCE.
18. Thucydides, 2.65, trans. R. Warner, in *Thucydides: History of the Peloponnesian War*, Harmondsworth: Penguin, 1972.
19. Ibid., 2.41
20. Aristotle, *Rhetoric* 1407a.
21. Thucydides, 1.76, trans Warner, *Thucydides.*
22. Ibid., 1.99. Cf. Plutarch *Kimon* 11.
23. Ibid., 1.23.
24. Ibid.
25. Aristophanes, *The Acharnians,* 514 ff., trans. A.H. Sommerstein, in *Aristophanes: The Acharnians, The Clouds, Lysistrata*, Harmondsworth: Penguin, 1973.
26. Thucydides, 4.38, trans. Warner, *Thucydides.*
27. Ibid., 5.101
28. Xenophon, 1.1.23.
29. Plato, *Phaedo,* 118a 16 f.

Chapter 6

1. Aristotle, *Politics* 1275a1 ff., trans. T.A. Sinclair.
2. *IG* I² 374.
3. Thucydides, 7.63.
4. Tod, *GHI* II, no. 100. As a metic, Emporion would work the land, not own it.
5. Pseudo-Xenophon, *Constitution of the Athenians* 1.10 ff., trans. K. Hughes, M. Thorpe,

and M. Thorpe, in *The Old Oligarch*, rev. edn, London: London Association of Classical Teachers, 1986.

6. Pseudo-Aristotle, *Oikonomika* 1.5.1, 1344a22.

7. R. Meiggs and D. Lewis, *A Selection of Greek Historical Inscriptions: To the End of the Fifth Century BC*, Oxford: Oxford University Press, 1969, no. 79a.

8. *Oikonomikos* 9.5, tr. R. Bradley in *The Science of Good Husbandry, or, The Oeconomics of Xenophon: Shewing the Method of Ruling and Ordering a Family, and of Managing a Farm to the Best Advantage*, London: T. Corbet, 1727.

9. Lysias, 24.6, tr. W.R.M. Lamb, *Lysias with an English translation*, London, 1930.

10. Demosthenes, *Against Aphobos* 9, trans. from J. Ferguson and K. Chisholm (eds), *Social and Political Life in the Great Age of Athens*, London: Ward Lock Educational, 1978.

11. Xenophon, *Memorabilia* 2.5. 2.

12. Plato, *Laws* 776c–777d, trans. T.J. Saunders, in *Plato: The Laws*, Harmondsworth: Penguin, 1970.

13. IG², 2 1 no. 1559, 26 ff. The way the ex-slave's name is presented indicates he now has *metoikos* status. 'Defeating' your master is the technical term for saying you have secured your freedom and paid back the loan.

14. Euripides, *Iphigeneia in Aulis* 1400.

15. Aristotle, *Politics* 1252a 31ff., trans. T.A. Sinclair.

16. Ibid., 1255b4 ff.

17. Ibid., 1, 1253b13 By 'the art of getting wealth' he means the supply of food and other necessities, which he says is necessary and honourable, rather than moneymaking per se, which is unnatural.

18. Ibid., 1252a34 ff., 1259a37 ff.

19. Xenophon, *Memorabilia* 2.7.4, trans. from Ferguson and Chisholm, *Social and Political Life*.

20. Plutarch, *Alkibiades* 8.3 ff., trans. I. Scott-Kilvert, in *The Rise and Fall of Athens: Nine Greek Lives*, Harmondworth: Penguin, 1960.

21. Toronto 635, from near Athens, *ARV* 1031,51.

22. Xenophon, *Memorabilia* 2, 2, 4–5, trans. from Ferguson and Chisholm, *Social and Political Life*.

23. Plutarch, *Perikles* 24, trans. Scott-Kilvert, in *The Rise and Fall of Athens*.

24. Alexis in Athenaeus 13, 568a-d.

25. Demosthenes, *Against Neaira*, 122.

26. Homer, *Odyssey* 8.336 ff., trans. E.V. Rieu, in *Homer: The Odyssey*, Harmondsworth: Penguin, 1946.

27. Aristophanes, *Wealth*, 168.

28. Aristophanes, *The Clouds*, 1079 ff., trans. A.H. Sommerstein, in *Aristophanes: The Acharnians, The Clouds, Lysistrata*, Harmondsworth: Penguin, 1973.

29. Lysias, *Against Simon* 6.

30. Aristophanes, *Lysistrata* 15 ff., trans. from Ferguson and Chisholm, *Social and Political Life*.

31. Lysias 1.6, trans. S.P. Pomeroy, in *Goddesses, Whores, Wives and Slaves: Women in Classical Antiquity*, New York, 1975. Lysias' client's trust was misplaced; she had an affair with a neighbour, and the speaker killed him.

32. Plato, *Protagoras* 325d, trans. W.K.C. Guthrie, *Plato: Protagoras and Meno*, Harmondsworth: Penguin, 1956.

33. Aiskhines, *Against Timarkhos* 9, trans. from Ferguson and Chisholm, *Social and Political Life*.

34. Aristotle, *Politics* 1339a.

35. Plato, *Protagoras* 319a, tr. W.K.C. Guthrie, *op. cit.*

36. Ibid., 319a.

37. Xenophon, *On Hunting* 13.1.

38. Plato, *Protagoras* 320c.

39. Ibid., *fr.* 2.
40. Ibid., *fr.* 1.
41. Quoted by Thucydides, 2.45. Aspasia's reputation certainly stands in entertaining contrast to the views attributed here to Perikles.
42. Euripides, *Trojan Women* 648 f.
43. Xenophon, *Memorabilia* 2.7.12, trans. from Ferguson and Chisholm, *Social and Political Life*.
44. Aristophanes, *Ekklesiazousai* 214 ff., trans. D. Barrett, in *Aristophanes: The Knights, Peace, Wealth, The Birds, The Assemblywomen*, Harmondsworth: Penguin, 1978.
45. Aristotle, *Politics*, 1300a, trans. T.J. Sinclair, in *Aristotle: The Politics*, Harmondsworth: Penguin, 1962.

Chapter 7

1. According to Plutarch, *Apophthegmata Lakonika*, 225c.11, this was what Leonidas said to Xerxes before the Battle of Thermopylai.
2. Thucydides, 1.10, trans. R. Warner, in *Thucydides: History of the Peloponnesian War*, Harmondsworth: Penguin, 1972.
3. Tyrtaios, fr. 5 Diehl = frs. 6–7 West.
4. Plutarch, *Lykourgos* 9.
5. Xenophon, *Constitution of the Lakedaimonians* 7, trans. R.J.A. Talbert, in *Plutarch on Sparta*, Harmondsworth: Penguin, 1988.
6. Plutarch, *Lykourgos* 16, trans. Talbert, in *Plutarch on Sparta*.
7. Ibid.
8. Xenophon, *Constitution of the Lakedaimonians* 2, trans. Talbert, in *Plutarch on Sparta*.
9. Ibid.
10. Ibid., 3.
11. Plutarch, *Lykourgos* 15, tr, R.J.A. Talbert, *op. cit.*
12. Ibid., 22.
13. Ibid., 14.
14. Aristophanes, *Lysistrata*, 79 ff., trans. A.H. Sommerstein, in *Aristophanes: The Acharnians, The Clouds, Lysistrata*, Harmondsworth: Penguin, 1973.
15. Plutarch, *Lykourgos* 14, tr, R.J.A. Talbert, *op. cit.*
16. Ibid., 15.
17. Ibid.
18. Aristotle, *Politics* 1269b22, trans. T.A. Sinclair, in *Aristotle: The Politics*, Harmondsworth: Penguin, 1962.
19. Euripides, *Andromache* 595–600, trans. P. Vellacott, in *Euripides: Orestes and Other Plays*, Harmondsworth: Penguin, 1972.
20. Tyrtaios, fr. 5 Diehl = frs. 6-7 West.
21. Plutarch, *Lykourgos* 28.
22. Xenophon, *Hellenika*, 3.3.11, M.M. Austin and P. Vidal-Naquet, *Economic and Social History of Ancient Greece: An Introduction*, London: Batsford, 1986.
23. Aristotle, *Politics* 1285b.
24. Described in Plutarch, *Lykourgos* 26.
25. Tyrtaios, fr. 4 West, trans. M.L. West, Greek Lyric Poetry, Oxford: Oxford University Press, 1994.
26. Xenophon, *Constitution of the Lakedaimonians* 14.
27. Plutarch, *Agesilaos* 2.
28. Reinhold, Meyer, *Classica Americana: The Greek and Roman Heritage in the United States*, Detroit: Wayne State University Press, 1984, 233.
29. Letter to John Scollay, 30 December, 1780, in H.A. Cushing (ed.), *The Writings of Samuel Adams*, New York: G. P. Putnam's Sons, 1904–8, Vol. 4, 238.

30. *Travels in Greece, Palestine, Egypt and Barbary*, translated from the French by F. Shoberl, New York: Van Winckel & Wiley, 1814, 106.

31. M. Proust, *À la recherche du temps perdu*, Vol. 7, *Le Temps Retrouvé*, Abbeville: F. Paillart, 1927, Vol. I, Ch. 2, 154.

32. K. Petter, Preface to O.W. von Vacro, Spata, der Leberskampf einer nordischen Herrenschicht, 2nd edn, Kempten: Arbeitsheft der Adolf-Hitler Schulen, 1942, 1.

33. T. Hill, *The Hidden*, London: Faber & Faber, 2009, 194.

Chapter 8

1. Herondas *Mimiamboi* 4.1 ff. , trans. W. Headlam and A.D. Knox, in *Herodas: The Mimes and Fragments*, Cambridge: Cambridge University Press, 1922.

2. Xenophanes *fr.* 15, trans. P. Jones, *Vote for Caesar*, London: Orion, 2008.

3. Plutarch, *Non posse*, 1105b, tr. W. Burkert, *Ancient Mystery Cults*, Cambridge, Massachusetts, and London: Harvard University Press, 1987, p. 23.

4. Quoted by both the *Artemii Passio* 35 (Philostorg. *Hist. Eccl.* 7. p. 77) and Georgius Cedrenus, *Hist. Comp.* I p. 532, Bekker.

5. Plutarch, *Moralia* 438B, trans. F.C. Babbitt, *Plutarch, Moralia*, Vol. V, Loeb Classical Library, 1936.

6. Lucian, *Bis acc.* 1. *Promantis* can be either masculine or feminine: he uses the feminine here.

7. J. Foster and D. Lehoux, 'The Delphic Oracle and the ethylene-intoxication hypothesis', *Clinical Toxicology,* 2007, 45(1), 85–9.

8. Fontenrose H.23.

9. *Mor.* 404a = Fontenrose H.63.

10. Philo, *Sac.* 116

11. *Pythian Ode* 8.85 f.

12. Thucydides, 1.6.

13. Euripides, *Autolykos, fr.* 282, trans. from J. Ferguson and K. Chisholm (eds), *Social and Political Life in the Great Age of Athens,* London: Ward Lock Educational, 1978.

Chapter 9

1. O. Taplin, *Greek Tragedy in Action,* London: Methuen, 1978, 23.

2. Aristotle, *Poetics* 1449b224 ff., trans. T.S. Dorsch, in *Classical Literary Criticism-Aristotle: On the Art of Poetry; Horace: On the Art of Poetry; Longinus: On the Sublime*, Harmondsworth: Penguin, 1965.

3. Aeschylus, *Agamemnon*, 177.

4. Willy Russell, *Educating Rita*, Act 1, Scene v.

5. Archilochus *Fr.* 120 West = Athenaeus, *Deipnosophistai* 628a–b, trans. M.L. West, *Greek Lyric Poetry*, Oxford and New York: Clarendon, 1994.

6. Pindar *Fr.* 75, 1 ff. = Dion. Hal. *De comp. verb.* 22, trans. W.H. Race, in *Pindar: Nemean Odes; Isthmian Odes; Fragments. Edited and Translated by William H. Race*, Loeb Classical Library, Cambridge, MA:Harvard University Press, 1997. Bromios and Eriboas (= 'Loud Roarer' and 'Loud Shouter') are cult names of Dionysos; 'highest of fathers and Kadmeian women' is a reference to Zeus and Semele, Dionysos' parents.

7. J. Gould, 'Tragedy and Collective Experience', in M.S. Silk (ed.), *Tragedy and the Tragic: Greek Theatre and Beyond*, Oxford: Clarendon Press, 1996.

8. K. Reinhardt, *Sophocles*, 3rd edn, trans. H. and D. Harvey, 3rd edn, Oxford: Blackwell, 1979, p. 86.

9. The basis of iambic metre is a short syllable followed by a long one. Although not in trimeters, Shakespeare's blank verse is iambic:

   Once more unto the breach, dear friends, once more
   Or close the wall up with our English dead!

10. A trochee is the opposite of an iambus, i.e. a long syllable followed by a short one. Henry Wadsworth Longfellow's *Song of Hiawatha* uses trochees:
    Listen to this simple story,
    To this Song of Hiawatha!

11. The anapaest is two short syllables followed by a long one. Clement Clark Moore's *A Visit From Saint Nicholas* is written in anapaests:
    But I heard him exclaim, 'ere he drove out of sight,
    'Happy Christmas to all, and to all a good-night!'

12. IG II² 2318, 17 ff. The *didaskalos* is the 'director', who is often also the author.

13. Aristotle, *Poetics* 1449a16.

14. Athenaeus, *Deipnosophistae* VIII 347e.

15. Ulick O'Connor, *Oliver St John Gogarty: A Poet and His Times*, London: Cape, 1964.

16. Aeschylus, *Agamemnon* 1564. Cf. Aeschylus, *Khoephoroi* 313. The maxim had been common since the time of Hesiod.

17. Aeschylus, *Agamemnon* 218 ff., trans. R. Fagles, *Aeschylus: The Oresteia*, Harmondsworth: Penguin, rev. edn, 1979.

18. Ibid., 258 ff.

19. Ibid., 455 ff.

20. Ibid., 823 f.

21. Ibid., 910 ff.

22. Ibid., 940.

23. Ibid., 1231 f.

24. Ibid., 1318 f.

25. Ibid., 1372 f.

26. S. Goldhill, *Aeschylus: The Oresteia*, Cambridge: Cambridge University Press, 1992, 39.

27. Aeschylus, *Agamemnon*, 1410 ff., trans. Fagles, *Aeschylus: The Oresteia*.

28. Ibid., 1558 f.

29. Ibid., 1659 ff.

30. Ibid., 1672. Again she uses a *kratos*-word here.

31. Aeschylus, *Agamemon* 382 f., 525 f., 813, 1432.

32. Dio Chrysostom *Or.* 52.15.

33. Homer, *Odyssey* 11.271ff., trans. R.D. Dawe, in *The Odyssey*, Lewes, 1994. NB there is no blinding in the *Odyssey* version, and his mother/wife is called Jocasta (*Iokaste* in Greek) in Sophocles' play.

34. Asklepiades *FGrH* 12 F 7a, trans. L. Edmunds.

35. Sophocles, *Oedipus the King*, 7 f., trans. R. Fagles, *Sophocles: The Three Theban Plays, Antigone, Oedipus the King, Oedipus at Colonus*, Harmondsworth: Penguin, 1982.

36. Sophocles, *Oedipus the King* 59 ff., tr. M. Baldock, *Greek Tragedy, an Introduction*, Bristol, 1989, 55.

37. Sophocles, *Oedipus the King* 136.

38. *Poetics* 1453a7 ff.

39. Sophocles, *Oedipus the King,* 219 f., trans. Baldock, *Greek Tragedy*.

40. Sophocles, *Oedipus the King* 328 f., tr. R. Fagles, *op. cit.*

41. *Ibid.* 353; 362.

42. Sophocles, *Oedipus the King* 391 ff., tr. M. Baldock, *op. cit.*, 56.

43. Sophocles, *Oedipus the King* 412 ff., tr. S. Kershaw.

44. Ibid., 622 f.

45. Sophocles, *Oedipus the King* 715 ff.

46. Sophocles, *Oedipus the King* 791 ff. tr. R. Fagles, *op. cit.*

47. Sophocles, *Oedipus the King* 897 ff., tr. C. A. Trypanis, *Sophocles: Three Theban Plays*, Warminster, 1986.

48. Sophocles, *Oedipus the King* 971 f., tr. R. Fagles, *op. cit.*

49. Ibid., 977 ff.
50. Ibid., 1076 ff.
51. Aristotle, *Poetics* 1452a32 f., trans. S. Kershaw.
52. Sophocles, *Oedipus the King*, 1169 f., trans. R. Fagles, *Sophocles: The Three Theban Plays*.
53. Ibid., 1229 f.
54. Ibid., 1329 ff.
55. Ibid., 1530.
56. Ibid., 1455 ff.
57. Aristotle, *Poetics* 1460b33 ff. Cf. Aristophanes, *The Frogs* 959, where Euripides says: 'I wrote about familiar things, things the audience knew about, and could take me up on if necessary.'
58. J.P.A. Gould, 'Euripides', in S. Hornblower and A. Spawforth (eds), *The Oxford Classical Dictionary*, 3rd edn, revised, Oxford: Oxford University Press 2003.
59. Euripides, *Medea* 36 ff., trans. P. Vellacott, in *Medea and Other Plays by Euripides*, Harmondsworth: Penguin, 1963.
60. Gould, 'Euripides'.
61. Euripides, *Medea* 146 ff., trans. Vellacott, in *Medea and Other Plays*.
62. Ibid., 244 ff.
63. Aristophanes, *Lysistrata* 368 f., trans. S. Kershaw.
64. Euripides, *Medea* 407 ff., trans. Vellacott, in *Medea and Other Plays*.
65. Ibid., 540 f.
66. Ibid., 641 f.
67. Ibid., 1029 ff.
68. Aristotle, *Poetics* 1457a37 ff.
69. Sophocles *fr*. 1190, trans. I.C. Storey and A. Allan in *A Guide to Ancient Greek Drama*, Malden, MA, and Oxford: Blackwell, 2005, 157.
70. Muzeo Nazionale, Naples 3240; Beazley *ARV*² 1336.1. It dates from the end of the fifth century BCE.
71. F. Lissarrague, 'Why Satyrs are Good to Represent', in J.J. Winkler and F.I. Zeitlin (eds), *Nothing to do with Dionysos? Athenian Drama in its Social Context*, Princeton, NJ: Princeton University Press, 1990, 228 ff.
72. Horace, *Ars Poetica* 231–3, trans. T.S. Dorsch, in *Classical Literary Criticism: Aristotle: On the Art of Poetry; Horace: On the Art of Poetry; Longinus: On the Sublime*, Harmondsworth: Penguin, 1965.
73. Sophocles, *Trackers* 142ff., trans. E. Dugdale, in *Greek Theatre in Context*, Cambridge: Cambridge University Press, 2008, p. 89. There is a double-entendre here: his 'manly courage' manifests itself in sexual exploits with nymphs, not in combat.
74. *Homeric Hymn to Hermes*, 77 ff., trans. J. Cashford, in *The Homeric Hymns*, London: Penguin, 2003.
75. *Fragment of a Greek Tragedy*, first published in the *Bromsgrovian*, 8 June 1883.

Chapter 10

1. See T. Schreiber, *Athenian Vase Construction: A Potter's Analysis*, Malibu: J. Paul Getty Museum, 1999. It is, apparently, relatively easy to forge ancient Greek vases.
2. British Museum 1971.11-1.1.
3. Florence, 4209, from Chiusi, *ABV* 71.1. It is so-called after the man who assembled it out of the hundreds of fragments in which it was found.
4. Paris, Cabinet des Médailles 222, from Vulci. *ABV* 152, 25.
5. Vatican Museums 344, from Vulci. *ABV* 144, 7.540-30 BCE.
6. Munich, Antikensammlingen 2301, from Vulci. *ABV* 255, 4.
7. Munich, Antikensammlingen 2307, from Vulci. *ARV* 26, 1. *c*.510–500 BCE.
8. Arezzo, Museo Civico 1465. ARV 15, 6. 510–500 BCE.
9. London, British Museum GR 1848.8-4.1 (Vases E 468), from Cerveteri. 500–480 BCE.

10. Naples, Museo Nazionale 2422, from Nola. *ARV* 189, 74. 1st quarter fifth century BCE.
11. Plutarch, *Perikles* 13.
12. Pausanias 1.24.5, trans. J.G. Frazer, *Pausanias' Description of Greece*, London, 1898.
13. Ibid., 1.22.7.

Chapter 11
1. Aristotle, *Poetics* 1448a29 ff.
2. Ibid., 1449a10 ff. As a measure of the difficulty posed by dealing with Ancient Greek, there is dispute as to whether the word *exarkhonton*, here translated as 'leaders', should be rendered 'preludes'.
3. Aristophanes, *The Acharnians* 241–78.
4. Paris, Louvre E 620.
5. See A.W. Pickard-Cambridge, *Dithyramb, Tragedy and Comedy*, Oxford: Clarendon Press, 1927, fig. 18.
6. Attributed to the Gela Painter, *c*.480 BCE. British Museum, 1842.7-28.787 (B509).
7. Malibu, J. Paul Getty Museum, 82.AE.83, the product of an illicit excavation in central northern Italy, now repatriated.
8. Archilichos, *frs.* 41, 42, 43. trans. West.
9. Hipponax, *fr.* 84. trans. West.
10. Aristotle, *Poetics* 1449a38ff.
11. Ibid., 1449a32 ff.
12. Aristophanes, *The Frogs* 98ff., trans. D. Barrett, in *Aristophanes: The Wasps, The Poet and the Women, The Frogs*, Harmondsworth: Penguin, 1964.
13. Ibid., 207.
14. Ibid., 404 f.
15. Aristophanes, *The Frogs* 470 ff., tr. D. Barrett, *op. cit.*
16. Ibid., 479.
17. Ibid., 1043 ff., .
18. Ibid., 1169.
19. Ibid., 123 ff.
20. Ibid., 1285 ff. The lines that make sense come from Aeschylus' *Agamemnon* and *Sphinx*.
21. Ibid., 1308.
22. Aristophanes, *The Frogs* 1331 ff., trans. A.H. Sommerstein, in *The Comedies of Aristophanes, Vol. 9, Frogs*, London: Aris & Philips Ltd, corrected impression, 1999.
23. Aristophanes, *The Frogs* 1403. The line comes from the lost play *Glaukos Potnieus* (Aeschylus *fr.* 38).24. Aristophanes, *The Frogs* 1468 ff. tr. D. Barrett, *op. cit.*
24. ???????????
25. We know the names of 64 writers of Greek New Comedy, of whom the most important were Diphilus, Philemon and Menander.
26. Theophrastus *The Characters* 4, trans. P. Vellacott, in *Theophrastus, The Characters; Menander, Plays and Fragments,* 2nd edn, Harmondsworth: Penguin, 1973.
27. Syrian, In *Hermog* Ii.23 Rabe, trans. S. Kershaw. Aristophanes of Byzantium (*c*.257–180) should not be confused with Aristophanes the comic poet.
28. Menander, *Dyskolos* 63, trans. P. Vellacott, in *Theophrastus, The Characters.*
29. Ibid., 183 f.
30. Ibid., 743 ff.
31. Ibid., 842ff. Three talents is a substantial sum of money: normal dowries from the generation before Menander was writing did not usually exceed one talent.
32. Ibid., 965 ff.

Chapter 12
1. Galen, *Opera* 1.14.631ff.

2. Clement of Alexandria, *The Instructor*, 3.11.77.
3. Horace, *Epistles* 2.1.175f., trans. N. Rudd, *Horace: Satires and Epistles; Persius: Satires*, rev. edn, Harmondsworth: Penguin, 1979.
4. E. Segal, *Roman Laughter*, Oxford: Oxford University Press, 1987, 7.
5. Plautus, *The Swaggering Soldier*, 42 ff., trans. E.F. Watling, in *Plautus: The Pot of Gold and Other Plays*, Harmondsworth: Penguin, 1965.
6. Ibid., 150 ff.
7. Terence, *The Brothers* 643.
8. Aristotle, *E.N.* 112.a.10ff.
9. Theophrastus, *The Characters* 10.
10. M. Freeland, *The Goldwyn Touch*, London: Harrap, 1986.

Chapter 13
1. Nikos Kazantzakis, *The Last Temptation*, trans. P.A. Bien, London: Faber & Faber, 1961.
2. Cicero, *Pro Sestio*, 45, 96, trans. J.A. Shelton, in *As The Romans Did: A Source Book in Roman History*, New York and Oxford: Oxford University Press, 1988, 229. He is, of course, suggesting that the *Populares* are malevolent, shameless, insane and bedevilled by family problems.
3. Sallust, *B.J.* 35.
4. Cicero, *Pro C. Rabirio Perduellionis Reo* 20.
5. Plutarch, *Sulla* 31.
6. Suetonius, *Julius Caesar* 77.
7. Plutarch, *Sulla* 35–8.
8. P.A. Brunt, *Social Conflicts in the Roman Republic*, London: Chatto & Windus, 1971, 111.
9. Karl Marx, in a letter to Engels: Karl Marx/Friedrich Engels, *Werke*, Berlin, 1955 ff., 30, 160.
10. Suetonius, *Caesar* 1.
11. Ibid., 10.
12. Cicero, *Letters to His Brother Quintus* 1.1.11.
13. The words of Theodotos, one of Ptolemy's advisers: Plutarch, *Pompey* 77.
14. Plutarch, *Caesar* 49, trans. R. Warner, *The Fall of the Roman Republic: Six Lives by Plutarch*, rev. edn, Harmondsworth: Penguin, 1972.
15. Born 23 June 47: clearly Caesar's paternity is doubtful.
16. Plutarch, *Caesar* 82
17. Antony, quoted by Cicero, *Philippics* 13.11.24.
18. Cicero, *Letters to his Friends*, 11.20 (24 May 43 BCE).
19. Appian, *Civil Wars*. 4.127, trans. H. White, in *Appian's Roman History, Vol. IV*, London and New York: William Heinemann, 1913.
20. Virgil, *Eclogues* 1.70 ff., trans. C. Day Lewis, in *The Eclogues, Georgics and Aeneid of Virgil*, Oxford: Oxford University Press, 1966.
21. Plutarch, *Antony* 25, trans. I. Scott-Kilvert, in *Plutarch, Makers of Rome: Nine Lives by Plutarch*, Harmondsworth: Penguin, 1965.
22. Ibid., 27.
23. Virgil, *Aeneid* 8.678 ff., trans. Day Lewis, in *The Eclogues*.
24. Horace, *Odes* 1137.1 ff., trans. J. Michie, in *The Odes of Horace*, Harmondsworth: Penguin, 1964.
25. Augustus, *Res Gestae* 27, trans. S. Kershaw.
26. Velleius Paterculus, 2.89, trans. A. Lentin, in K. Chisholm and J. Ferguson (eds), *Rome: The Augustan Age*, Oxford: 1981.
27. H.H. Scullard, *From the Gracchi to Nero: A History of Rome from 133 BC to AD 68*, 5th edn, London and New York: Methuen, 1982, 208.
28. Augustus, *Res Gestae* 34, trans. Lentin, in Chisholm and Ferguson, *Rome: The Augustan Age*.
29. Ibid.

Chapter 14

1. Routledge, 1946.
2. Juvenal, *Satires* 7.227. See R. Cavenaile, *Corpus Papyrorum Latinorum* (1958), 7 ff.
3. Virgil, *Aeneid* 1.1. The usual rendering of *arma* as 'arms' is misleading: the Latin word has much stronger emotional connotations than the English – 'war' or 'fighting' is much better.
4. *Amartyron ouden aeido*: Fragment 442.
5. Virgil, *Aeneid* 1.278 f., trans. C. Day Lewis, *The Eclogues, Georgics and Aeneid of Virgil*, Oxford: Oxford University Press, 1966.
6. *Sunt lacrimae rerum*, ibid., 1.462.
7. He actually says, 'I am afraid of Greeks, particularly when they are bringing gifts'. Ibid., 2.49.
8. Virgil, *Aeneid* 2. 557 f., trans. Jackson Knight, *Virgil: The Aeneid*, Harmondsworth: Penguin, rev. edn. 1958. It could be that Virgil is alluding to the death of Pompey the Great, who was murdered and decapitated after the Battle of Pharsalus 49 BCE as he landed in Egypt.
9. Virgil, *Aeneid* 2.792 ff., tr. C. Day Lewis, *op. cit.* Cf. Homer *Odyssey* 11.206 ff. Virgil will use it again at 6.700 ff.
10. Virgil, *Aeneid* 3.255 ff. trans. D. West, *Virgil: The Aeneid*, Harmondsworth: Penguin, rev. edn., 2003.
11. Virgil, *Aeneid* 4.569 f.
12. Virgil, *Aeneid* 4.628 f., tr. D. West, *op. cit.*
13. Ibid, 6.721.
14. Virgil, *Aeneid* 6.791 ff., tr. C. Day Lewis, *op. cit.*
15. Ibid., 6.847 ff.
16. 32.
17. Virgil, *Aeneid* 7.96 ff., trans. West.
18. Virgil, *Aeneid* 8.440 f., tr. W.F. Jackson Knight, *op. cit.*
19. Virgil, *Aeneid* 8.485 ff., tr. C. Day Lewis, *op. cit.*
20. Ibid., 8.614 ff.
21. D. West, *op cit.*, xxxii.
22. Virgil, *Aeneid* 10.284.
23. Virgil, *Aeneid* 10.442 f., tr. D. West, *op. cit.*
24. Ibid. 11.330 ff.
25. Virgil, *Aeneid* 11.442, tr. W.F. Jackson Knight.

Chapter 15

1. Horace, *Satires* 1.4.115 ff., trans. N. Rudd, in *Horace: Satires and Epistles; Persius: Satires*, Harmondsworth: Penguin, rev. edn, 1979.
2. Horace, *Odes* 3.2.13, trans. S. Kershaw.
3. *Acts* 22.25–27.
4. Cicero, *In Verrem* 2.5.169, trans. J.A. Shelton, in *As The Romans Did: A Source Book in Roman History*, New York and Oxford: Oxford University Press, 1988, 287.
5. See Seneca the Younger, *On the Brevity of Human Life* 14.4.
6. Juvenal, *Satires* 5. 12 ff.
7. Augustus, *Res Gestae* 15, trans. A. Lentin, in K. Chisholm and J. Ferguson (eds), *Rome: The Augustan Age*, Oxford: Oxford University Press 1981.
8. See Cicero, *De Officiis* 1. 150–1.
9. Herrenius Modestinus, *Digest* 23.2.1
10. Soranus, *Gynaecologica* 1.60.
11. Horace, *Satires* 1.2.31ff., trans. Rudd, in *Horace: Satires and Epistles, Persius: Satires*.
12. Catullus, 15.17ff. Juvenal speaks of similar humiliation in *Satire* 10.314 ff.
13. Dessau, 8402.
14. Sallust, *Bellum Catilinae* 25
15. Macrobius, *Saturnalia* 115

16. Seneca, *On Benefits* 6.32.1, trans. J.W. Basore, in *Seneca: Moral Essays*, London and New York, 1935.
17. Tacitus, *Annals* 3.33
18. Dionysius of Halicarnassus 2.9
19. Petronios, *Satyricon* 1 ff.
20. Pliny, *Letters* 4.11, trans. R. Barrow, *Greek and Roman Education*, Basingstoke and London, 1976, p. 84.
21. Seneca, *On Clemency* 1.24.
22. Strabo, 14.5.2. NB: he says that Delos 'could' (*dynamene*) do this, not that it actually did.
23. *P.Oxy* 95. The monthly food allowance for a young apprentice at this time was 5 *dr.*
24. *P.Wisc.* 16.5.
25. Varro, *On Landed Estates* 1.17.1. The children become the property of the master.
26. Columella, *On Agriculture* 1.6–9.
27. Juvenal, *Satires* 6.476 ff. , trans. P. Green, *Juvenal: The Sixteen Satires*, Harmondsworth: Penguin, rev. edn, 1974.
28. Tacitus, *Annals* 14.42 f.
29. *The Digest of Laws* 50.17.32 (Ulpian).
30. Suetonius, *Augustus* 40.3.
31. Juvenal, *Satire* 3.63ff., trans. Green, *Juvenal: The Sixteen Satires.*
32. Horace, *Satires* 1.6.45 ff., trans. Rudd, in *Horace: Satires and Epistles; Persius: Satires.*

Chapter 16
1. Trans. J.A. Shelton, *As The Romans Did: A Source Book in Roman History*, New York and Oxford: Oxford University Press, 1988, p. 312.
2. Juvenal, *Satire* 10.80 f., trans. A. Bell, in E. Köhne, 'Bread and Circuses: The Politics of Entertainment', in E. Köhne, C. Ewiglebe and R. Jackson (eds), *The Power of Spectacle in Ancient Rome: Gladiators and Caesars*, London: British Museum, 2000, 8.
3. Varro, *De Re Rustica*, 37 BCE.
4. Livy, 7.213., trans. B.O. Foster, *Livy: History of Rome, Books V–VII*, Cambridge, MA, and London, 1924.
5. Suetonius, *Caesar* 39
6. Suetonius, *Caligula* 56.
7. Tacitus, *Annals* 15.44. Note the absence of lions in his account.
8. *CIL* 12.5837.
9. Suetonius, *Claudius* 21, 6.
10. *Encheiridion* 33, 2.
11. *Satire* 6.110 ff., trans. M. Jenks, in A. Futrell, *The Roman Games: A Sourcebook*, Oxford 2006, and A. Bell in C. Ewigleben, 'What These Women Love is the Sword', in Köhne et al., *The Power of Spectacle in Ancient Rome*, 125 ff. There is also a sexual double-entendre in 'sword'.
12. *CIL* VI 10047; Suetonius, *De grammaticis et rhetoribus* 17.2
13. *Correspondence* 2, p. 216, trans. A. Bell,. 139.
14. Suetonius, *Tiberius*, 2.2.
15. For the principal State gods and goddesses, see Table 8.1 on p. 149.
16. Polybius, 36.17.
17. Cicero, *On the Nature of the Gods* 3.87.
18. Quirinus is the deified Romulus.
19. Philo, *The Embassy to Gaius* 155 ff.
20. Horace, *Odes* 3.6.6 f., trans. J. Michie, *The Odes of Horace*, Harmondsworth: Penguin, 1964.
21. Minucius Felix, *Octavius* 12.5, trans. Shelton, *As The Romans Did*, 418.

Chapter 17

1. *CIL* IV 1293.
2. Tacitus, *Annals* 14.17 for the riot; *CIL* IV 3340.143 and 3340.144 for the removal of the magistrates.
3. Tacitus, *Annals* 15.22.
4. Seneca, *Natural Questions* 6.1.2. Seneca was writing shortly after the event, and says it took place on 5 February 63 CE. There is still some dispute about who is correct.
5. TR P VIIII IMP XV COS VII PP. The August date is, however, supported by finds of leaves of deciduous trees, herbs that would have finished flowering by autumn and broad beans, which ripen in late summer. Autumnal fruits like pomegranates were also often picked early and preserved.
6. Pliny, *Letters* 6.16; 6.20. The letters are written to the historian Tacitus.
7. So called after a famous and devastating eruption of Mount Pelée on Martinique in 1902.
8. Pliny, *Letters* 6.12, trans. B. Radice, in *The Letters of the Younger Pliny*, Harmondsworth: Penguin, 1963.
9. Suetonius, *Vespasian* 5.
10. *CIL* IV.10231.
11. *CIL* IV.1842.
12. *CIL* IV.1819; CIL IV.1781; *CIL* IV. 1820; *CIL* IV.1904.
13. *CIL* IV 2184; 2193.
14. *CIL* X.877. Mosaic dogs guard other entrances, e.g. those of Paquis Proculus (I.7.1) and the House of Caecilius Iucundus (V.1.26), and one was painted on the wall of Trimalchio's house in Petronius' *Satyricon*, also with *CAVE CANEM*.
15. M. Beard, *Pompeii: The Life of a Roman Town*, London: Profile, 2008, p. 117.
16. Described by Vitruvius, *de Architectura*, 7.5.1. See R. Ling, *Roman Painting*, Cambridge: Cambridge University Press, 1991, 12 ff.
17. Vitruvius, *de Architectura*, 7.5.2. See Ling, *Roman Painting*, 23 ff. (Good illustration at http://www.skenographia.cch.kcl.ac.uk/oplontis/analysis.html.)
18. Vitruvius, *de Architectura*, 7.5.3. See Ling, *Roman Painting*, 52 ff.
19. Vitruvius had died by 62 CE. See Ling, *Roman Painting*, 71 ff.
20. Vitruvius, *de Architectura*, 2.8.20.
21. Frontinus, *On the Aqueducts of Rome* 1.16, trans. C.E. Bennett, *The Stratagems and the Aqueducts of Rome*, London: William Heinemann, 1925.
22. Vitruvius, *de Architectura*, 8, 6, 1–10.
23. Frontinus, *On the Aqueducts of Rome* 1.16. The law was passed in 9 BCE. The penalty is astronomical.
24. Pliny the Elder, *N.H.* 36.121 f. Cf. Strabo 5.3.8.

Chapter 18

1. Eusebius, *Historia Ecclestiastica* 8.16.3 ff., trans. D. Miller, 'How the Mighty Fall: The Fate of Roman Emperors', *Minerva* 20.1 (2009), 52.
2. Claudian, *De Consulatu Stilichonis*, 2.250 ff., r. H.H. Scullard, *Roman Britain: Outpost of the Empire,* London: Thames & Hudson, 1979, 175.
3. Virgil, *Aeneid* I. 278 f., trans. S. Kershaw.
4. T.S. Eliot, 'Virgil and the Christian World', in *On Poetry and Poets*, London, 1959, 135.

INDEX